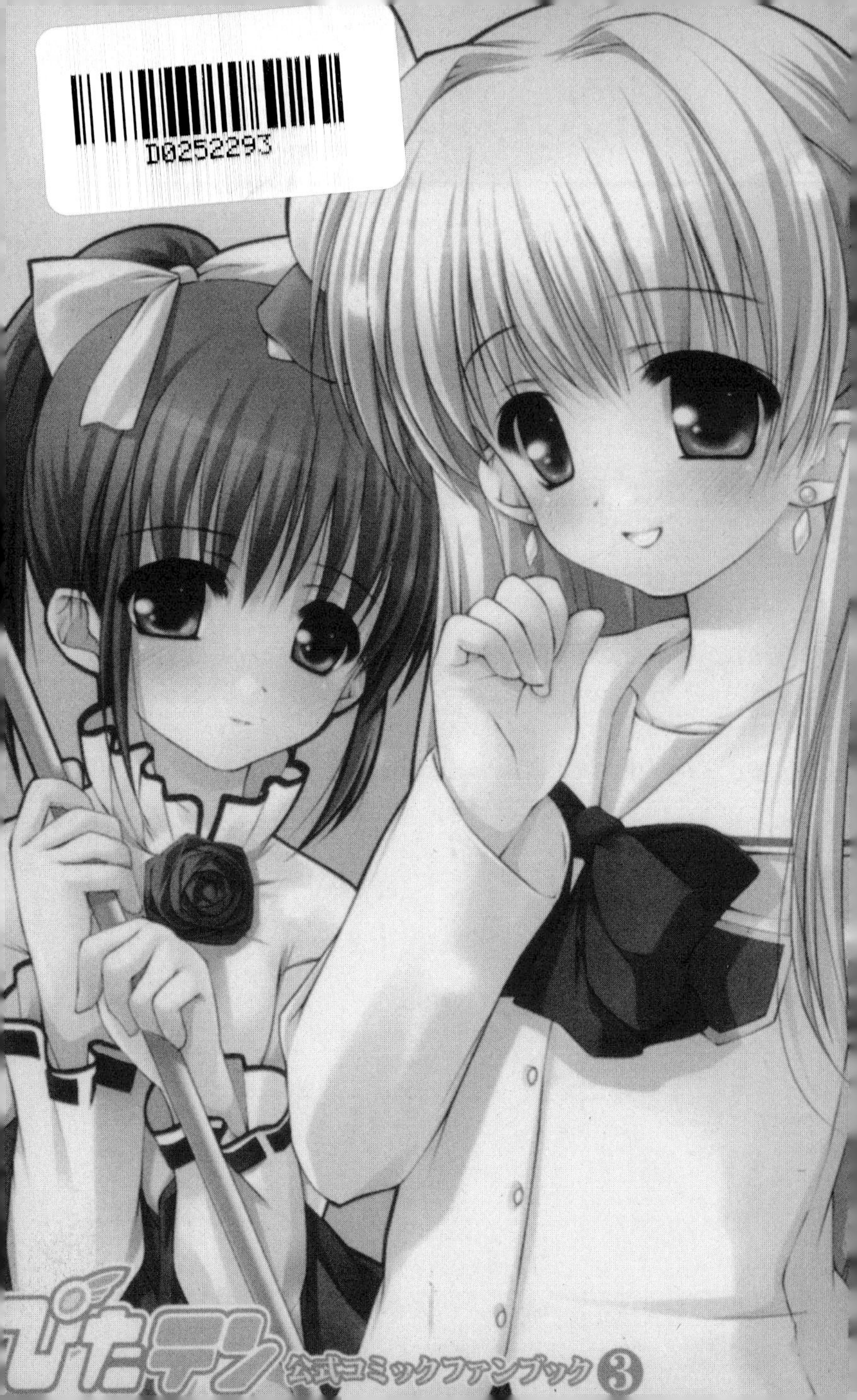

ぴたテン
公式コミックファンブック③

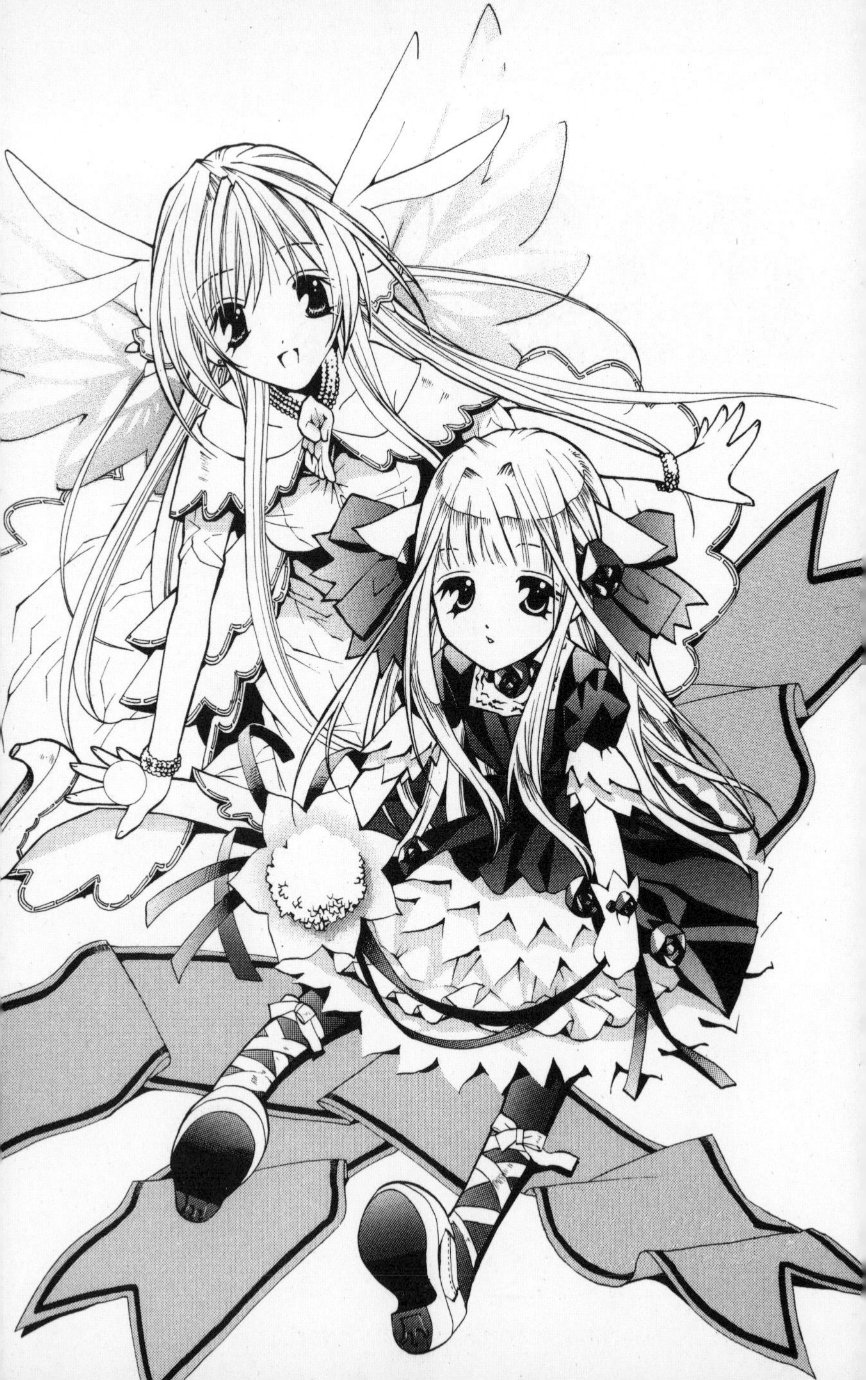

PITA-TEN
Official Fan Book

Volume 3
by
Koge-Donbo

HAMBURG // LONDON // LOS ANGELES // TOKYO

Pita-Ten Official Fan Book Vol. 3
Created by Koge-Donbo

Translation - Nan Rymer
English Adaptation - Adam Arnold
Copy Editor - Hope Donovan
Retouch and Lettering - Jihye "Sophia" Hong
Production Artist - Bowen Park
Cover Design - Al-Insan Lashley

Editor - Paul Morrissey
Digital Imaging Manager - Chris Buford
Production Manager - Elisabeth Brizzi
Managing Editor - Lindsey Johnston
VP of Production - Ron Klamert
Editor-In-Chief - Rob Tokar
Publisher - Mike Kiley
President and C.O.O. - John Parker
C.E.O. and Chief Creative Officer - Stuart Levy

A  Manga

TOKYOPOP Inc.
5900 Wilshire Blvd. Suite 2000
Los Angeles, CA 90036

E-mail: info@TOKYOPOP.com
Come visit us online at www.TOKYOPOP.com

© 2002 Koge-Donbo All rights reserved. No portion of this book may be
Authors: Koge-Donbo, Asuka Izumi, Hiroshi Ueda, o-ji, reproduced or transmitted in any form or by any means
Kouduki Hadime, Konata Hyura, Kodomo Usagi, Eiki Sibusawa, without written permission from the copyright holders.
Umi Sugimoto, Masaya Takamura, Muca Tonami, Miya Hazuki, This manga is a work of fiction. Any resemblance to
Mari Matsuzawa, Mook, Kyuten Yuminaga, Kaori Yosikawa actual events or locales or persons, living or dead, is
All Rights Reserved. First published in 2002 by entirely coincidental.
Media Works Inc., Tokyo, Japan.
English translation rights arranged with Media Works Inc.
English text copyright © 2006 TOKYOPOP Inc.

ISBN: 1-59816-108-3

First TOKYOPOP printing: July 2006
10 9 8 7 6 5 4 3 2 1
Printed in the USA

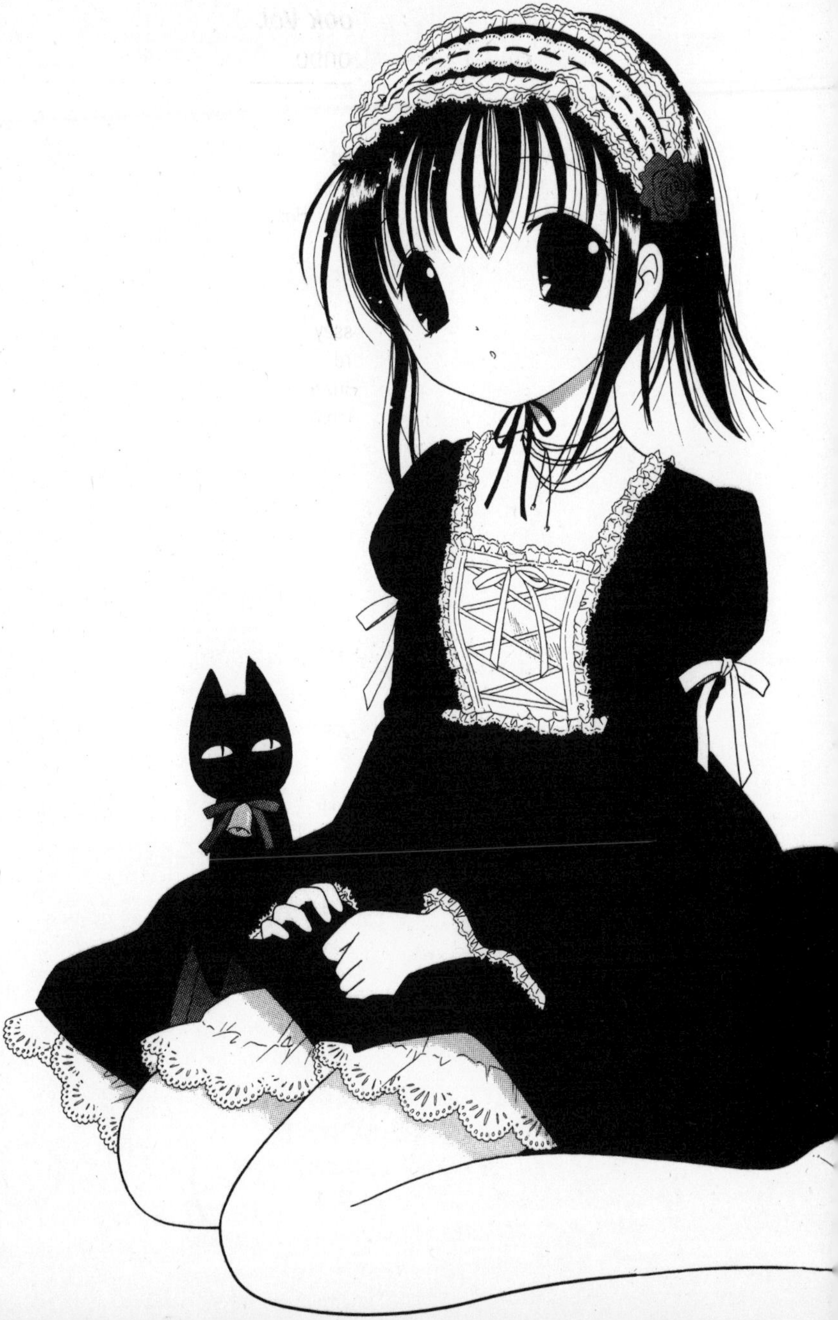

Table of Contents

Cover Illustration: Koge-Donbo
Inside Illustration: o-ji

公式コミックファンブック **③**

PITA-TEN

Official Fan Book

3

PITA-TEN OFFICIAL COMIC FAN-BOOK 3

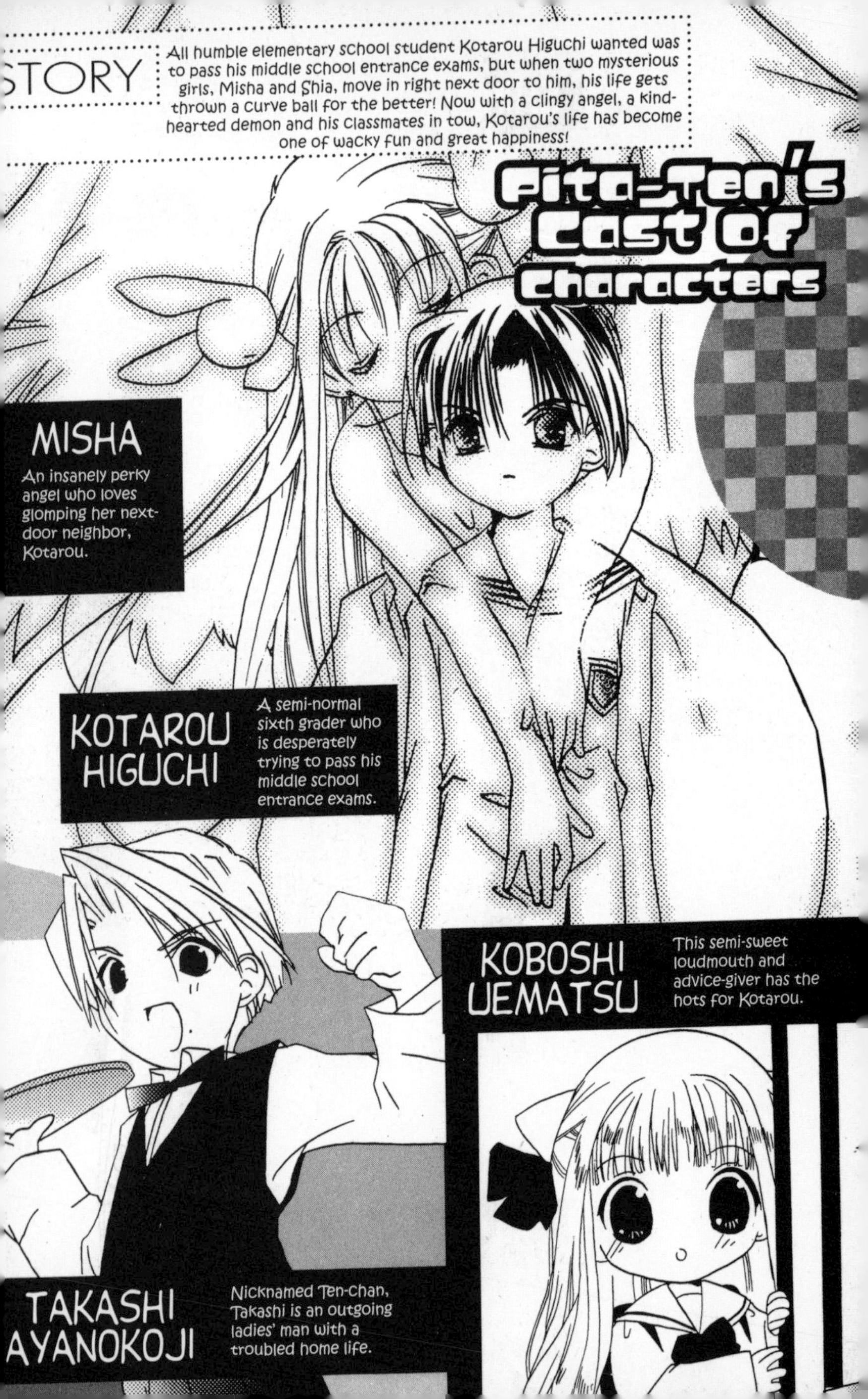
STORY
All humble elementary school student Kotarou Higuchi wanted was to pass his middle school entrance exams, but when two mysterious girls, Misha and Shia, move in right next door to him, his life gets thrown a curve ball for the better! Now with a clingy angel, a kind-hearted demon and his classmates in tow, Kotarou's life has become one of wacky fun and great happiness!
Pita-Ten's Cast of Characters
MISHA
An insanely perky angel who loves glomping her next-door neighbor, Kotarou.
KOTAROU HIGUCHI
A semi-normal sixth grader who is desperately trying to pass his middle school entrance exams.
KOBOSHI UEMATSU
This semi-sweet loudmouth and advice-giver has the hots for Kotarou.
TAKASHI AYANOKOJI
Nicknamed Ten-chan, Takashi is an outgoing ladies' man with a troubled home life.

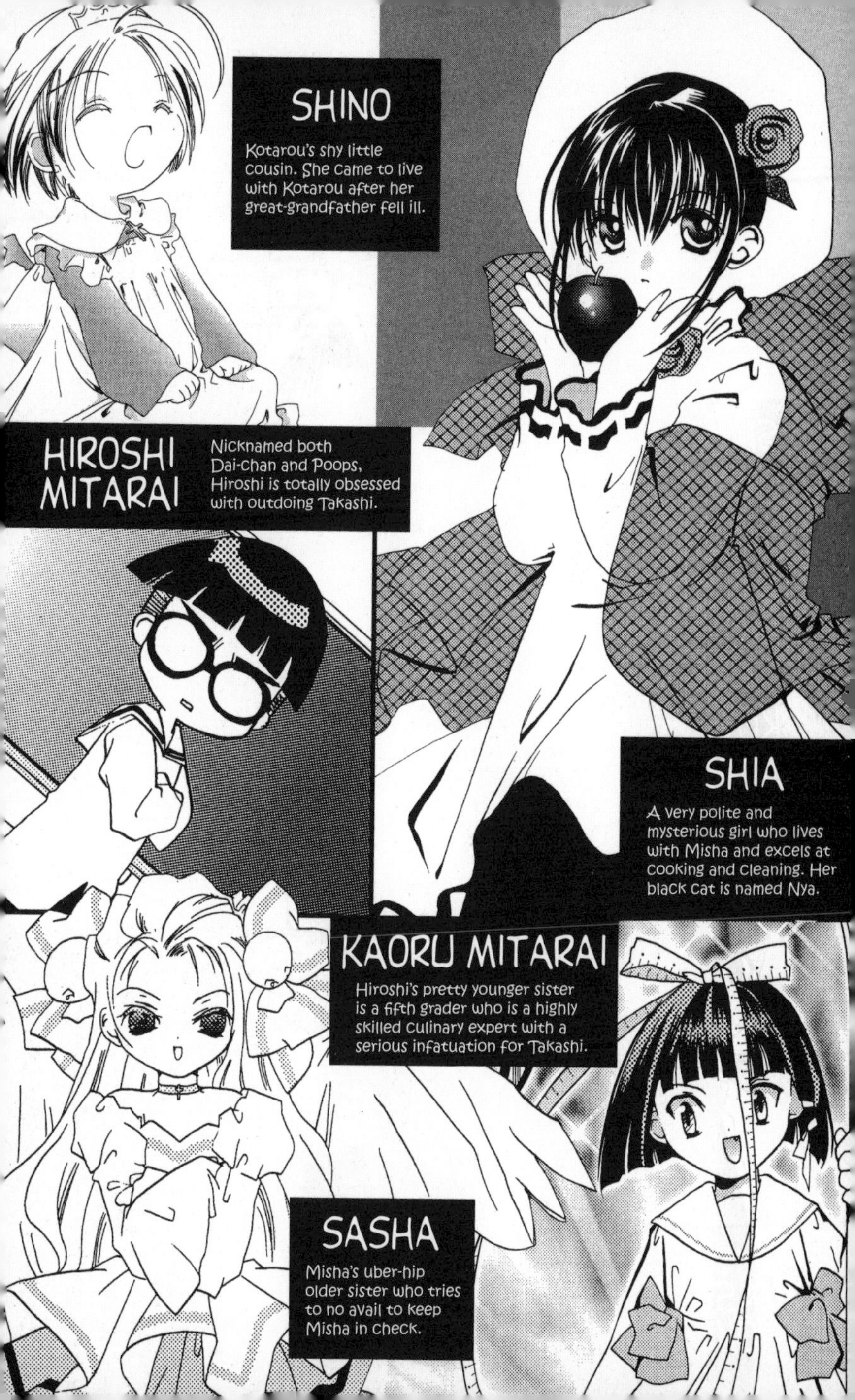
SHINO
Kotarou's shy little cousin. She came to live with Kotarou after her great-grandfather fell ill.
HIROSHI MITARAI
Nicknamed both Dai-chan and Poops, Hiroshi is totally obsessed with outdoing Takashi.
SHIA
A very polite and mysterious girl who lives with Misha and excels at cooking and cleaning. Her black cat is named Nya.
KAORU MITARAI
Hiroshi's pretty younger sister is a fifth grader who is a highly skilled culinary expert with a serious infatuation for Takashi.
SASHA
Misha's uber-hip older sister who tries to no avail to keep Misha in check.

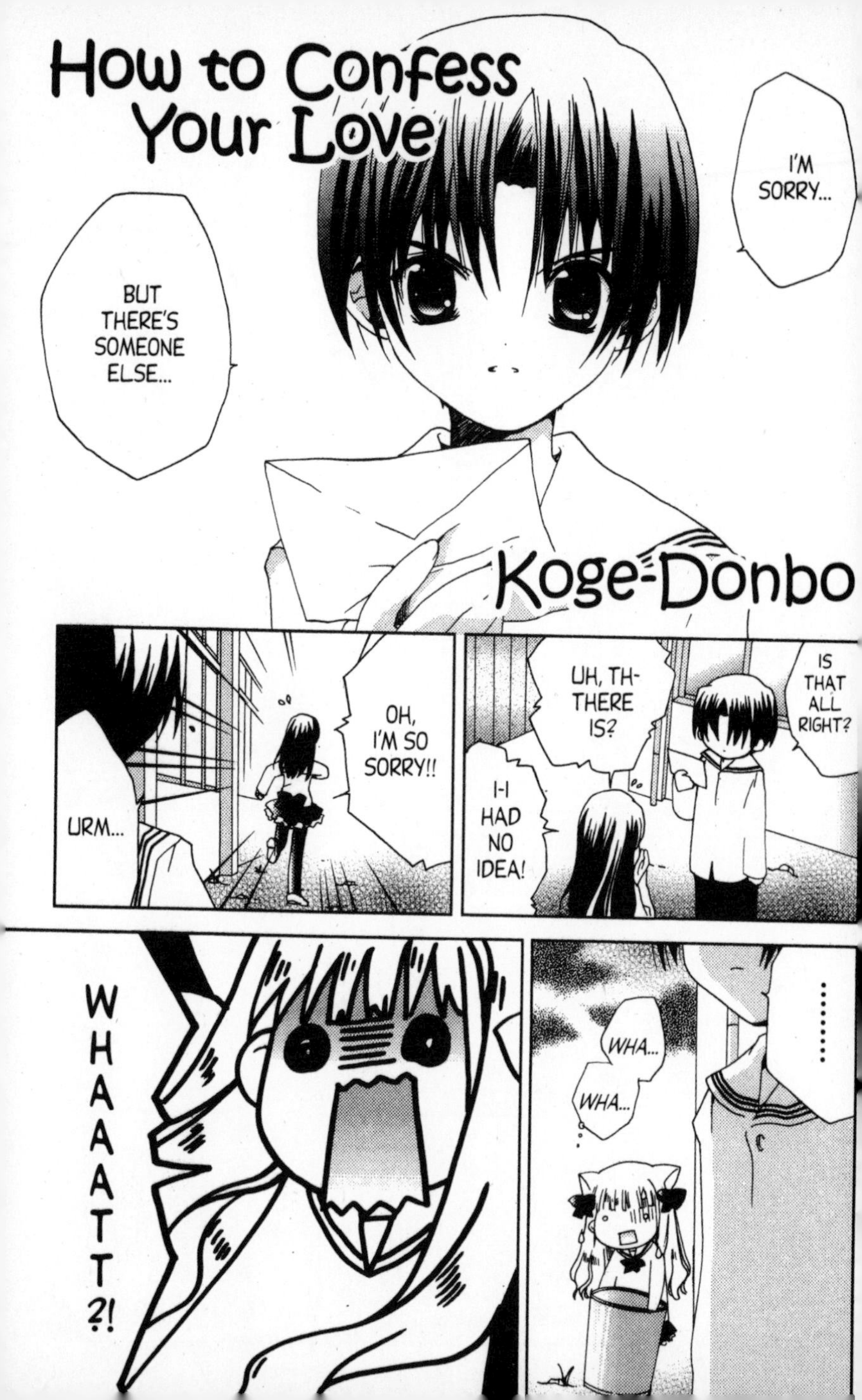
How to Confess Your Love
I'M SORRY...
BUT THERE'S SOMEONE ELSE...
Koge-Donbo
IS THAT ALL RIGHT?
UH, TH-THERE IS?
I-I HAD NO IDEA!
OH, I'M SO SORRY!!
URM...
....
WHA...
WHA...
WHAAAATTT?!

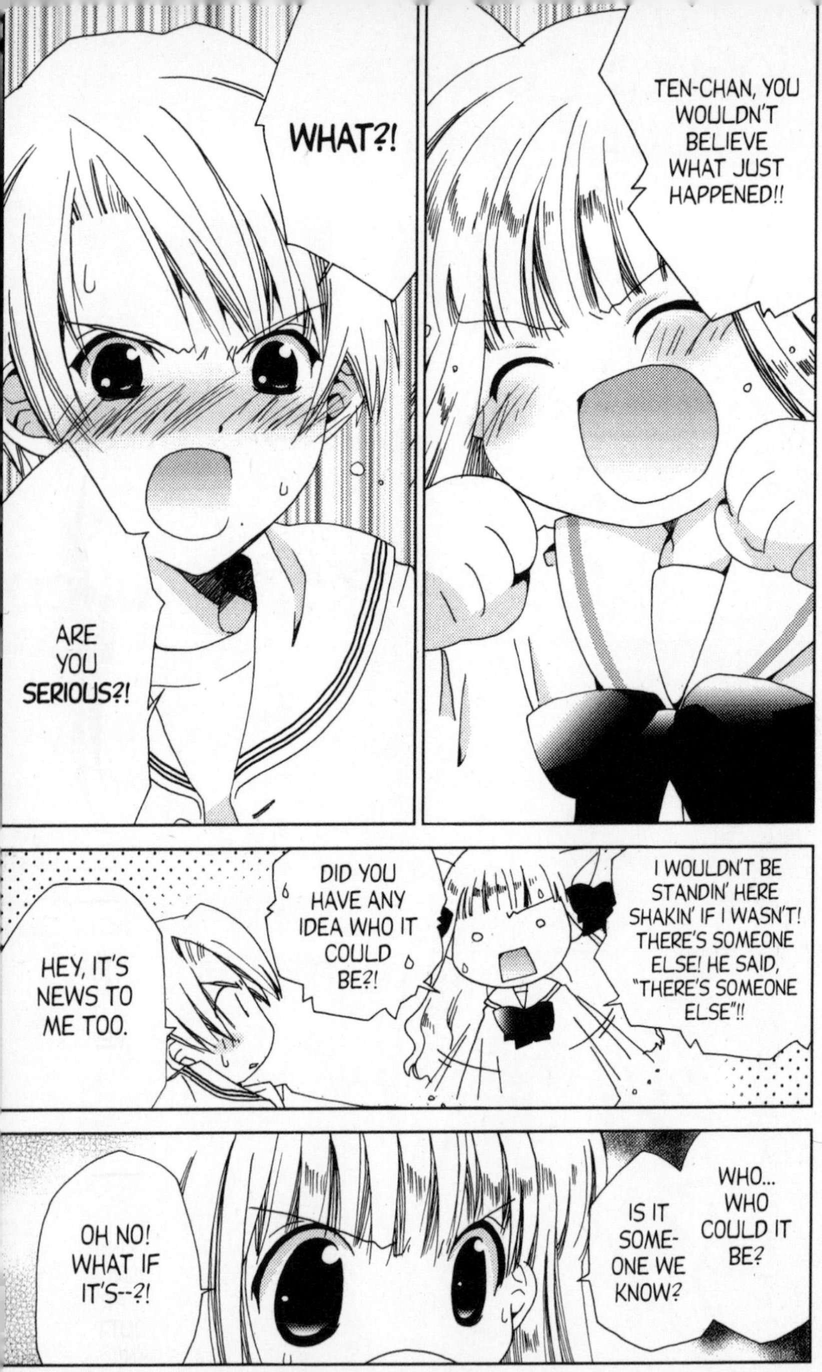
TEN-CHAN, YOU WOULDN'T BELIEVE WHAT JUST HAPPENED!!
WHAT?!
ARE YOU SERIOUS?!
I WOULDN'T BE STANDIN' HERE SHAKIN' IF I WASN'T! THERE'S SOMEONE ELSE! HE SAID, "THERE'S SOMEONE ELSE"!!
DID YOU HAVE ANY IDEA WHO IT COULD BE?!
HEY, IT'S NEWS TO ME TOO.
WHO... WHO COULD IT BE?
IS IT SOME-ONE WE KNOW?
OH NO! WHAT IF IT'S--?!

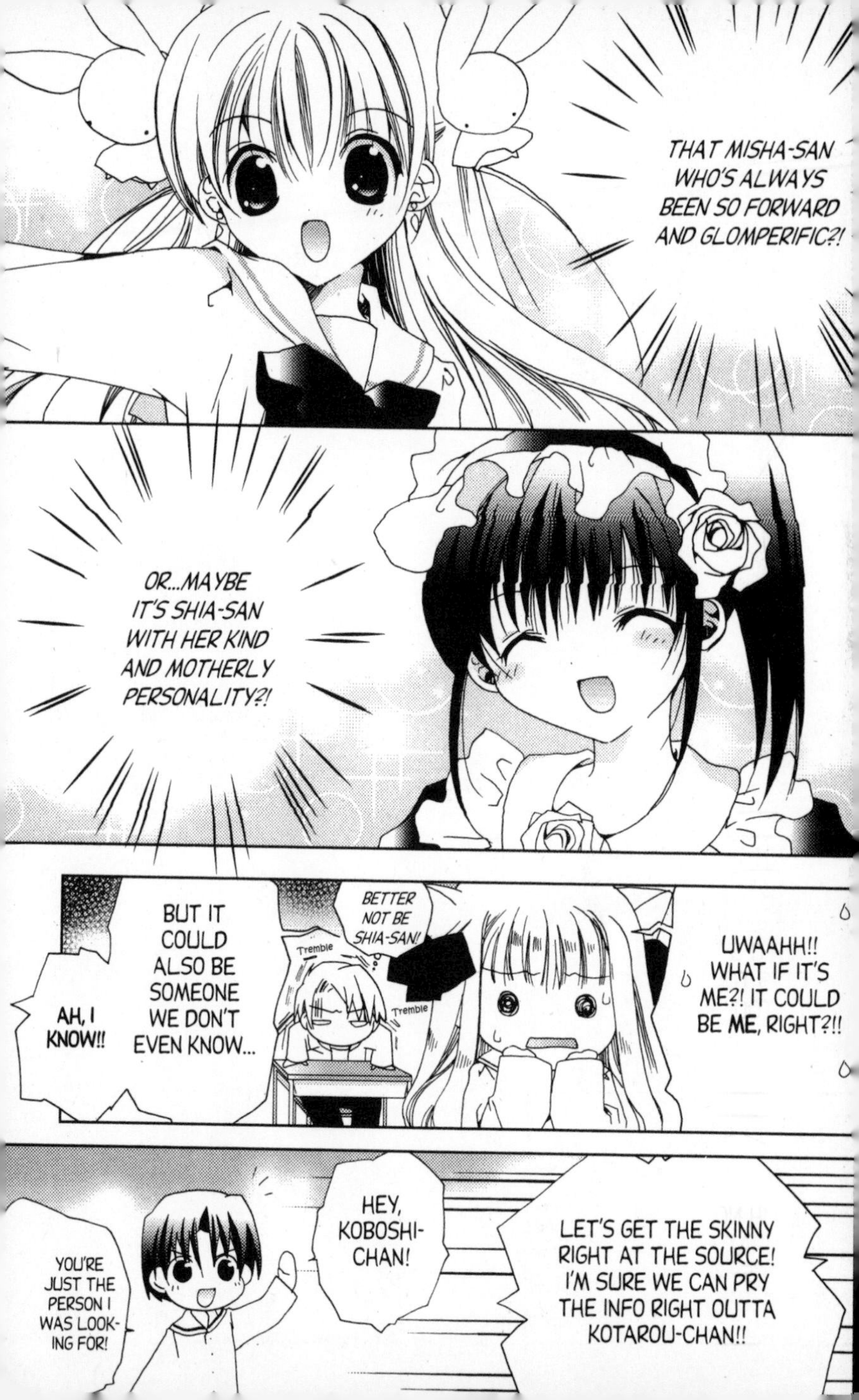
THAT MISHA-SAN WHO'S ALWAYS BEEN SO FORWARD AND GLOMPERIFIC?!
OR...MAYBE IT'S SHIA-SAN WITH HER KIND AND MOTHERLY PERSONALITY?!
UWAAHH!! WHAT IF IT'S ME?! IT COULD BE ME, RIGHT?!!
BETTER NOT BE SHIA-SAN!
Tremble
Tremble
BUT IT COULD ALSO BE SOMEONE WE DON'T EVEN KNOW...
AH, I KNOW!!
LET'S GET THE SKINNY RIGHT AT THE SOURCE! I'M SURE WE CAN PRY THE INFO RIGHT OUTTA KOTAROU-CHAN!!
HEY, KOBOSHI-CHAN!
YOU'RE JUST THE PERSON I WAS LOOKING FOR!

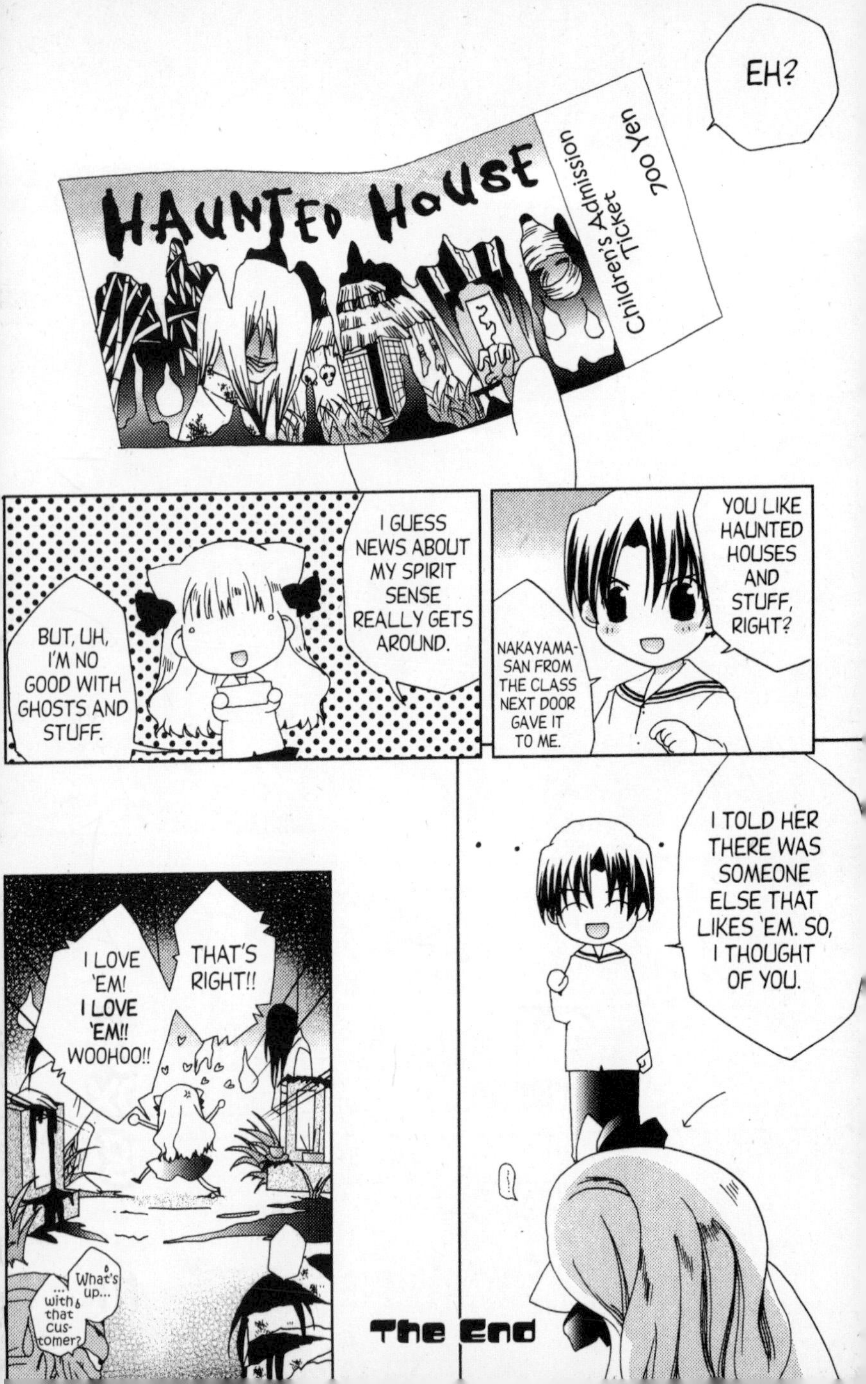
EH?
HAUNTED HOUSE
Children's Admission Ticket
700 Yen
YOU LIKE HAUNTED HOUSES AND STUFF, RIGHT?
NAKAYAMA-SAN FROM THE CLASS NEXT DOOR GAVE IT TO ME.
I GUESS NEWS ABOUT MY SPIRIT SENSE REALLY GETS AROUND.
BUT, UH, I'M NO GOOD WITH GHOSTS AND STUFF.
...
I TOLD HER THERE WAS SOMEONE ELSE THAT LIKES 'EM. SO, I THOUGHT OF YOU.
THAT'S RIGHT!!
I LOVE 'EM! I LOVE 'EM!! WOOHOO!!
What's up...
...with that customer?
The End

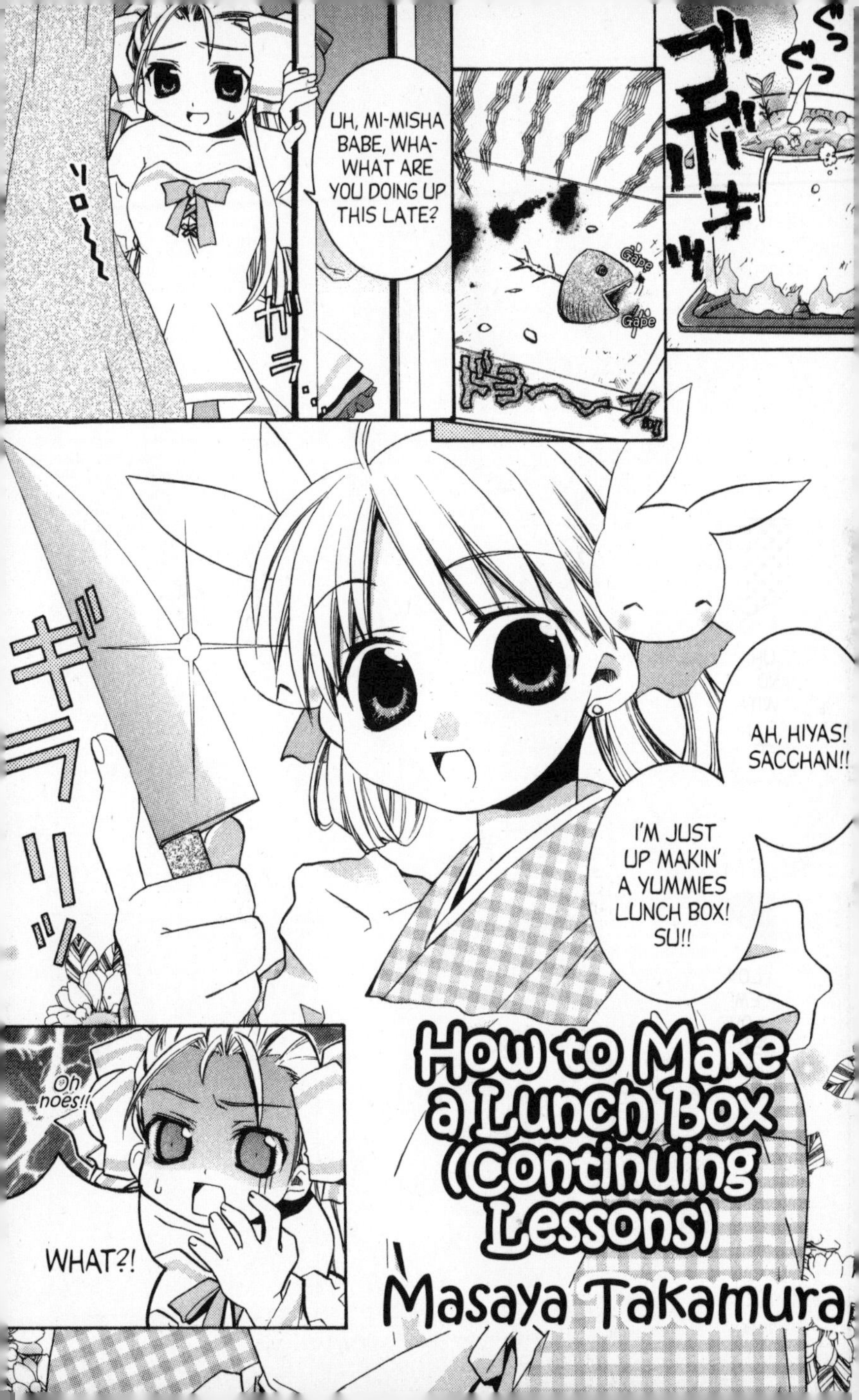
ぐつぐつ
Gape
Gape
UH, MI-MISHA BABE, WHA-WHAT ARE YOU DOING UP THIS LATE?
ソロ〜〜
AH, HIYAS! SACCHAN!!
I'M JUST UP MAKIN' A YUMMIES LUNCH BOX! SU!!
ギラリッ
How to Make a Lunch Box (Continuing Lessons)
Masaya Takamura
Oh noes!!
WHAT?!

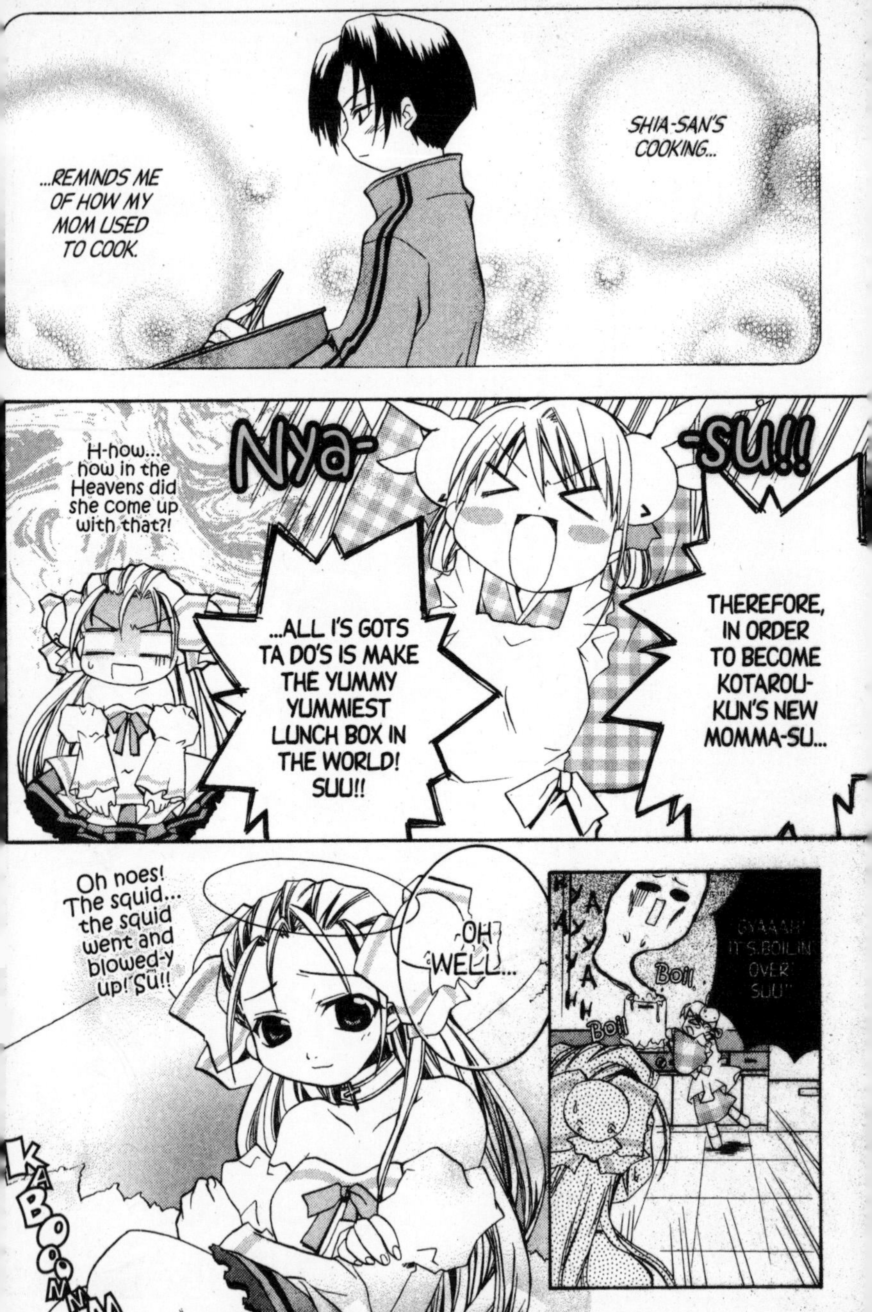
SHIA-SAN'S COOKING...
...REMINDS ME OF HOW MY MOM USED TO COOK.
THEREFORE, IN ORDER TO BECOME KOTAROU-KUN'S NEW MOMMA-SU...
...ALL I'S GOTS TA DO'S IS MAKE THE YUMMY YUMMIEST LUNCH BOX IN THE WORLD! SUU!!
Nya- -su!!
H-how... how in the Heavens did she come up with that?!
GYAAAH! IT'S BOILIN' OVER! SUU!!
Boil
Boil
OH WELL...
Oh noes! The squid... the squid went and blowed-y up! Su!!
KABOOOONNM

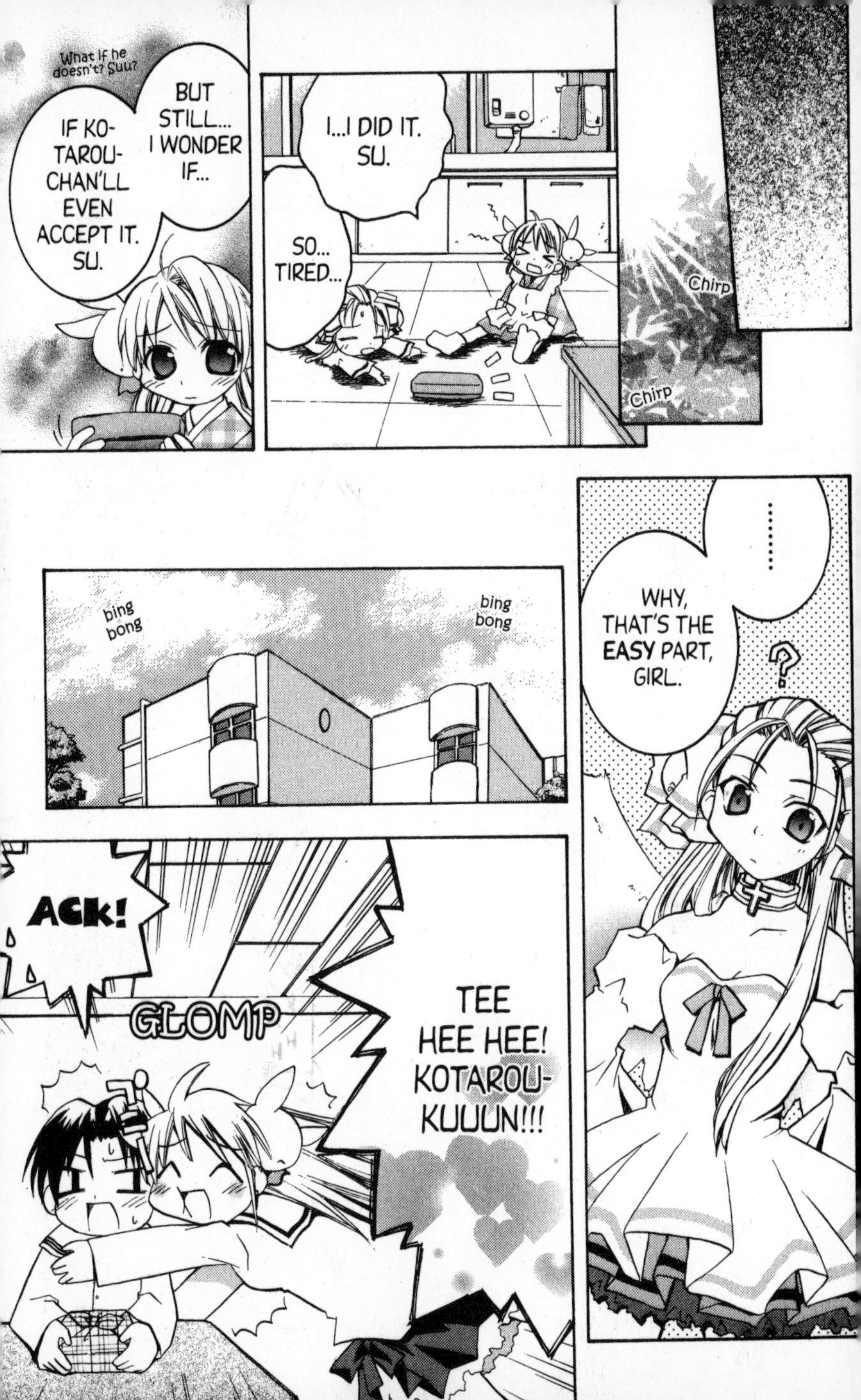
Chirp
Chirp
I...I DID IT. SU.
SO... TIRED...
BUT STILL... I WONDER IF...
IF KO-TAROU-CHAN'LL EVEN ACCEPT IT. SU.
What if he doesn't? Suu?
......
WHY, THAT'S THE **EASY** PART, GIRL.
?
bing bong
bing bong
TEE HEE HEE! KOTAROU-KUUUN!!!
GLOMP
ACK!

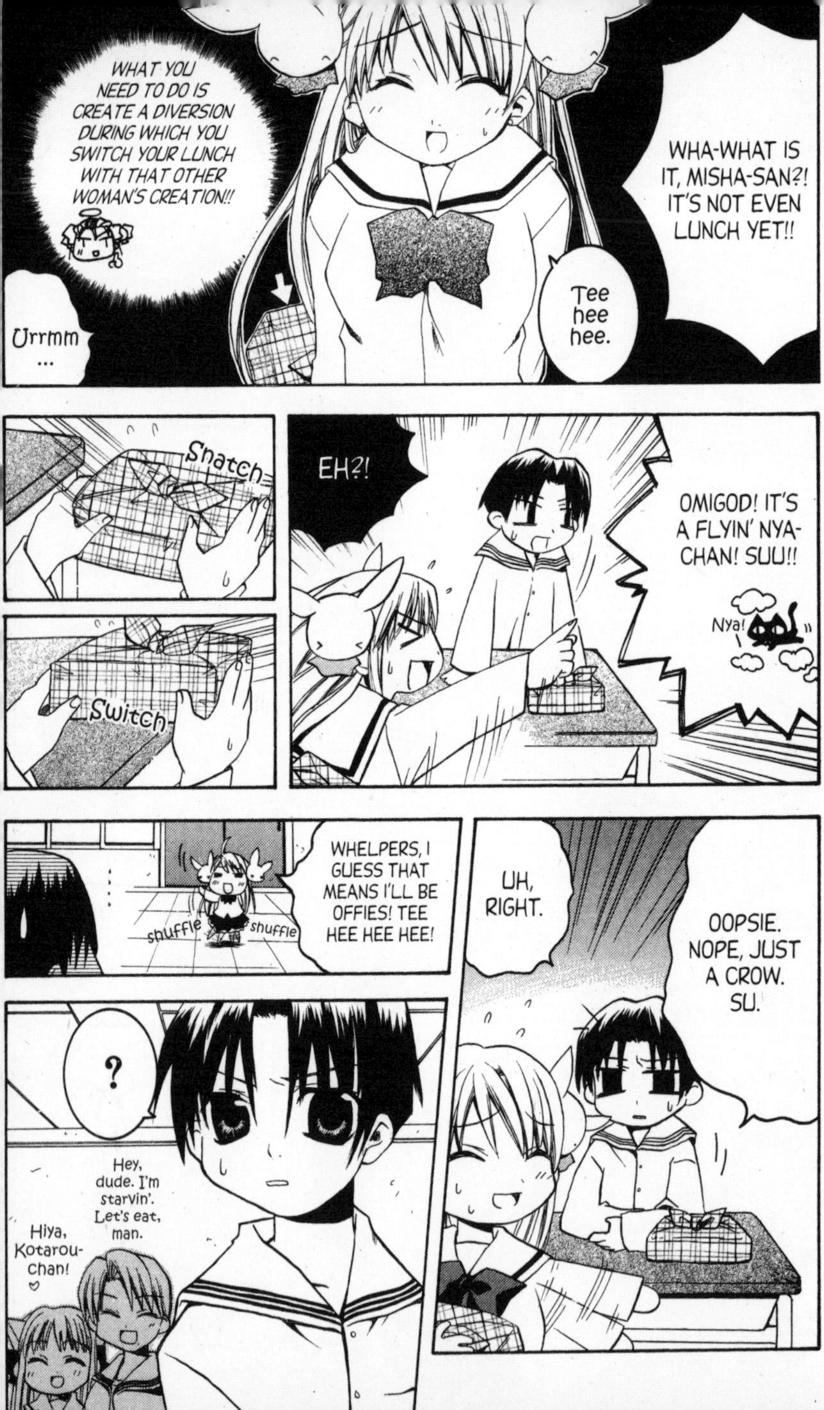
WHA-WHAT IS IT, MISHA-SAN?! IT'S NOT EVEN LUNCH YET!!
Tee hee hee.
WHAT YOU NEED TO DO IS CREATE A DIVERSION DURING WHICH YOU SWITCH YOUR LUNCH WITH THAT OTHER WOMAN'S CREATION!!
Urrmm ...
OMIGOD! IT'S A FLYIN' NYA-CHAN! SUU!!
Nya!
EH?!
Snatch
Switch
OOPSIE. NOPE, JUST A CROW. SU.
UH, RIGHT.
WHELPERS, I GUESS THAT MEANS I'LL BE OFFIES! TEE HEE HEE HEE!
shuffle shuffle
?
Hey, dude. I'm starvin'. Let's eat, man.
Hiya, Kotarou-chan! ♡

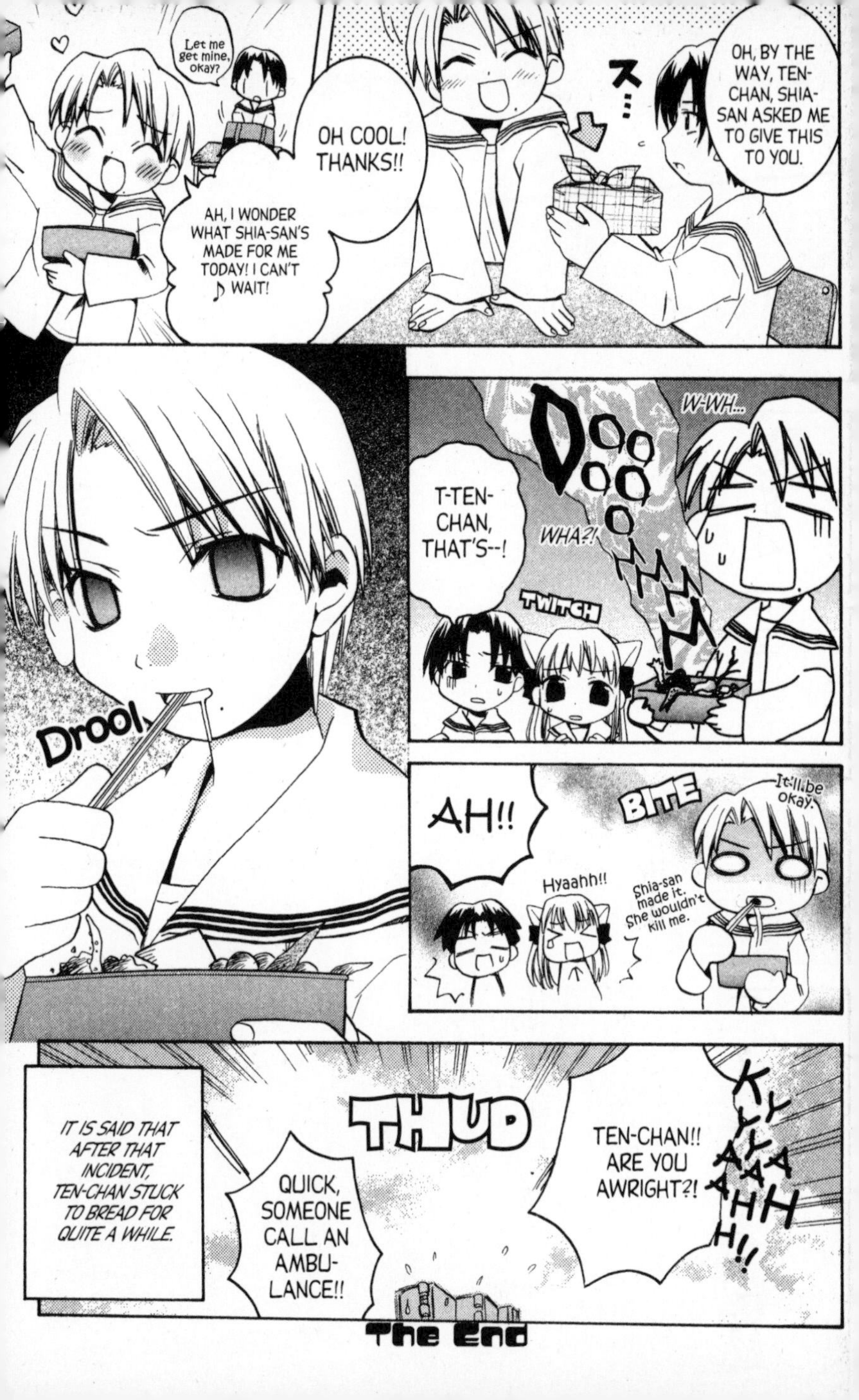
OH, BY THE WAY, TEN-CHAN, SHIA-SAN ASKED ME TO GIVE THIS TO YOU.
ス…
OH COOL! THANKS!!
AH, I WONDER WHAT SHIA-SAN'S MADE FOR ME TODAY! I CAN'T WAIT! ♪
Let me get mine, okay?
W-WH...
DOOOOOOMMMM
WHA?!
T-TEN-CHAN, THAT'S--!
TWITCH
It'll be okay.
BITE
Shia-san made it. She wouldn't kill me.
AH!!
Hyaahh!!
Drool
KYAAAAAHHH!!
TEN-CHAN!! ARE YOU AWRIGHT?!
THUD
QUICK, SOMEONE CALL AN AMBULANCE!!
IT IS SAID THAT AFTER THAT INCIDENT, TEN-CHAN STUCK TO BREAD FOR QUITE A WHILE.
The End

Masaya Takamura

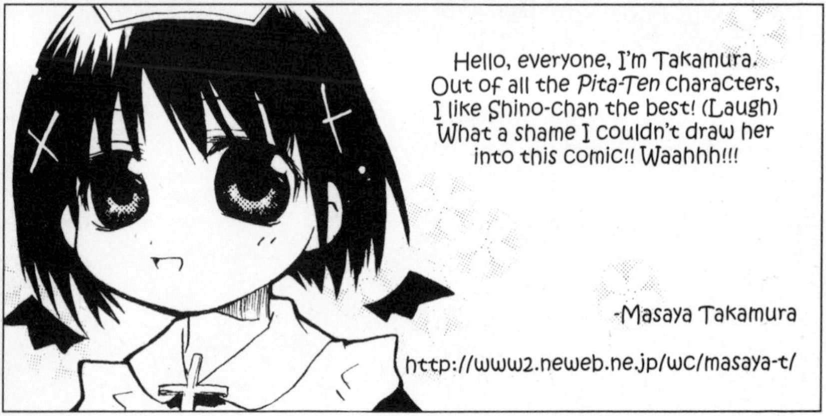
Hello, everyone, I'm Takamura. Out of all the *Pita-Ten* characters, I like Shino-chan the best! (Laugh) What a shame I couldn't draw her into this comic!! Waahhh!!!
-Masaya Takamura
http://www2.neweb.ne.jp/wc/masaya-t/

Writer's Talk

Kodomo Usagi

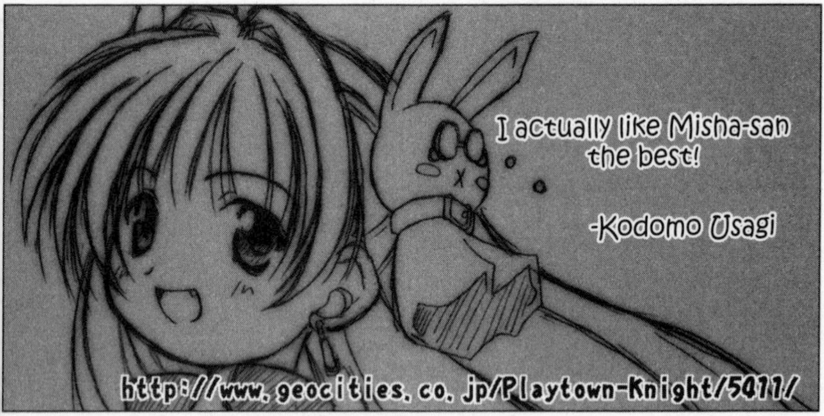
I actually like Misha-san the best!
-Kodomo Usagi
http://www.geocities.co.jp/Playtown-Knight/5011/

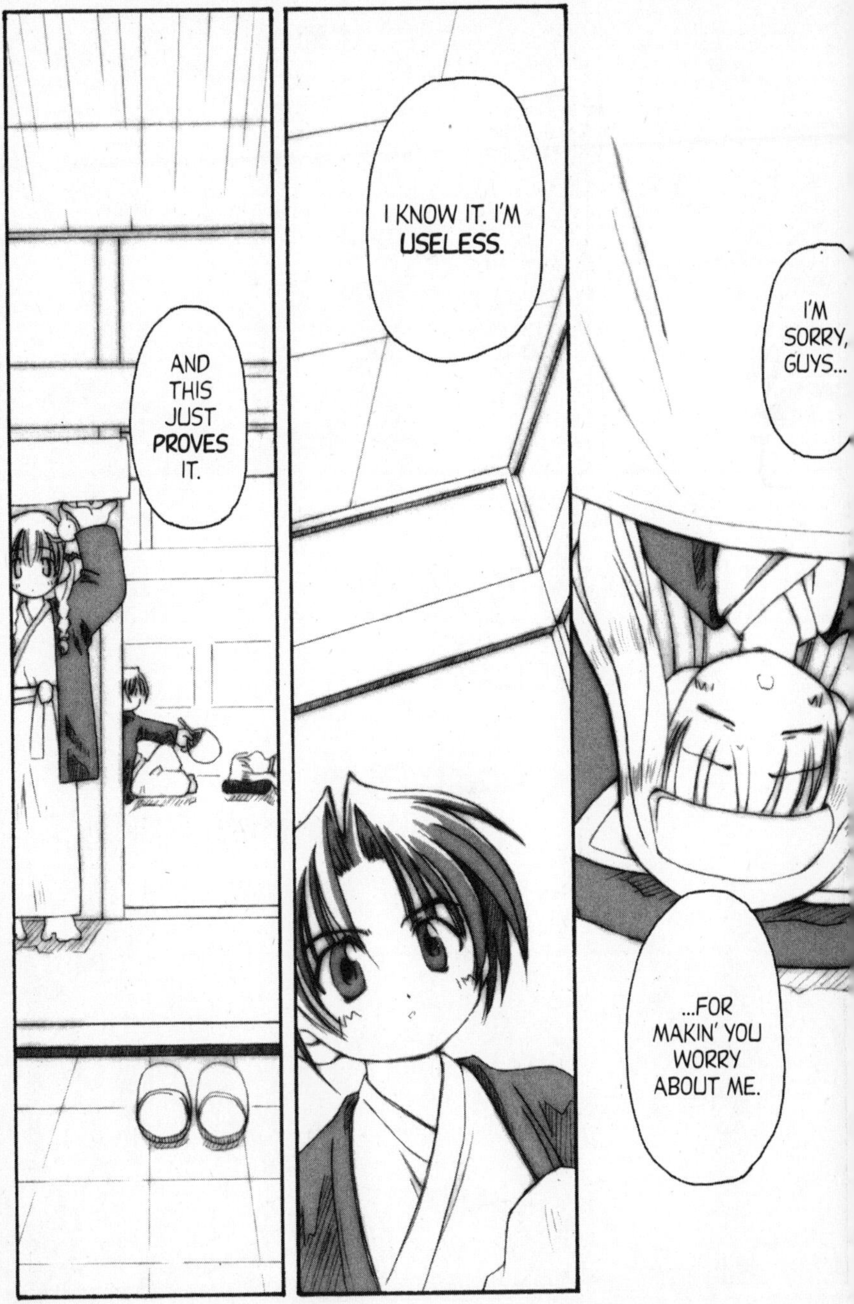
I'M SORRY, GUYS...
...FOR MAKIN' YOU WORRY ABOUT ME.
I KNOW IT. I'M USELESS.
AND THIS JUST PROVES IT.

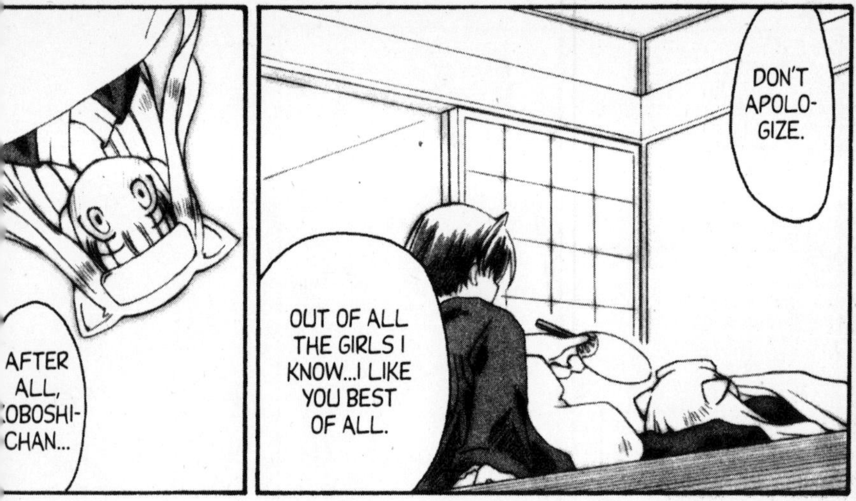
DON'T APOLOGIZE.
OUT OF ALL THE GIRLS I KNOW...I LIKE YOU BEST OF ALL.
AFTER ALL, OBOSHI-CHAN...

...YOU'RE THE ONLY ONE WITH CAT EARS.

How to Grow Cat Ears

Kodomo Usagi

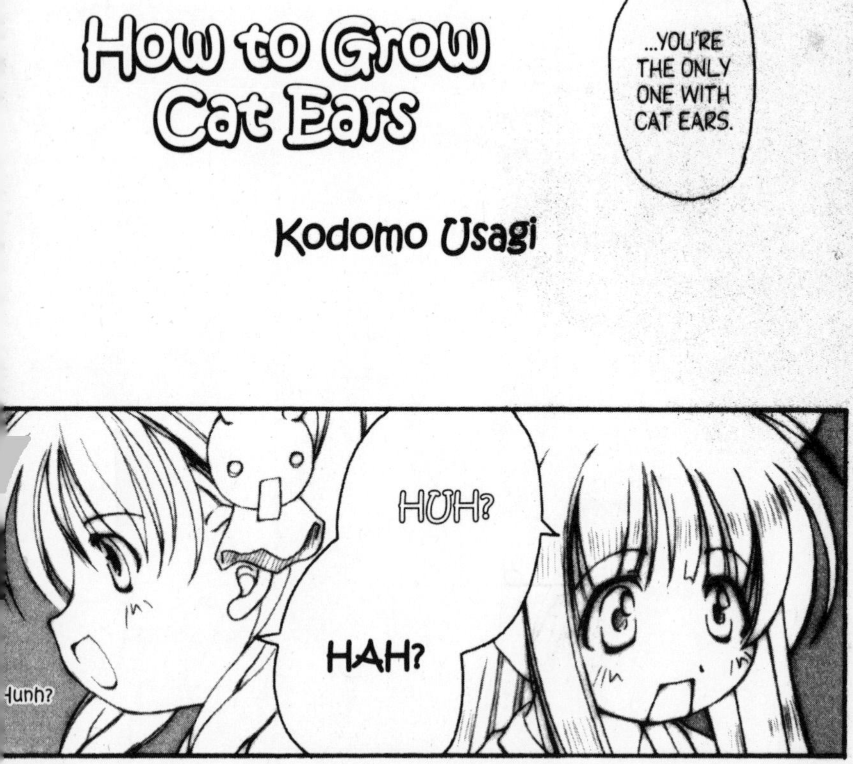
HUH?
HAH?
Hunh?

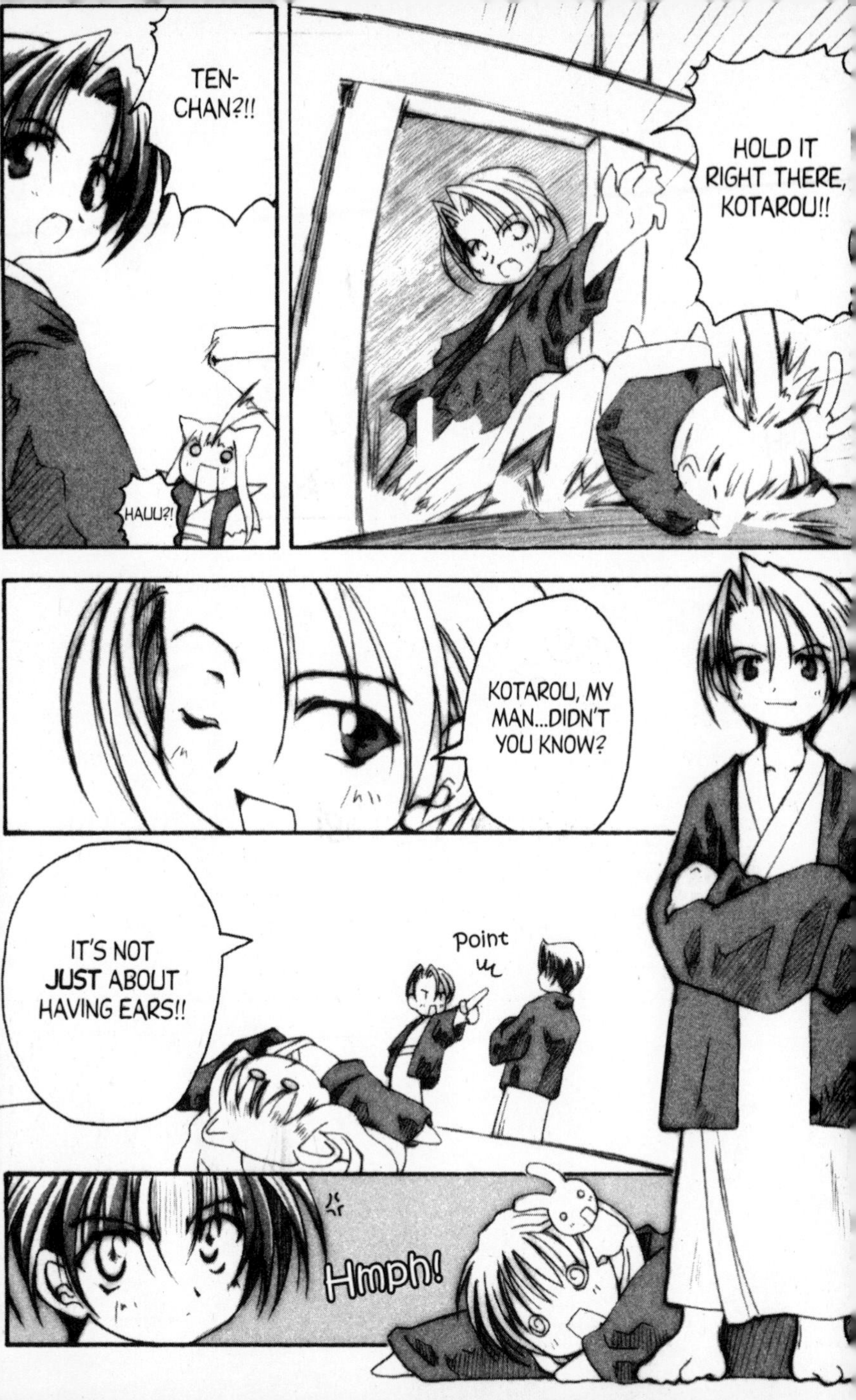
HOLD IT RIGHT THERE, KOTAROU!!
TEN-CHAN?!!
HAUU?!
KOTAROU, MY MAN...DIDN'T YOU KNOW?
IT'S NOT JUST ABOUT HAVING EARS!!
Point
Hmph!

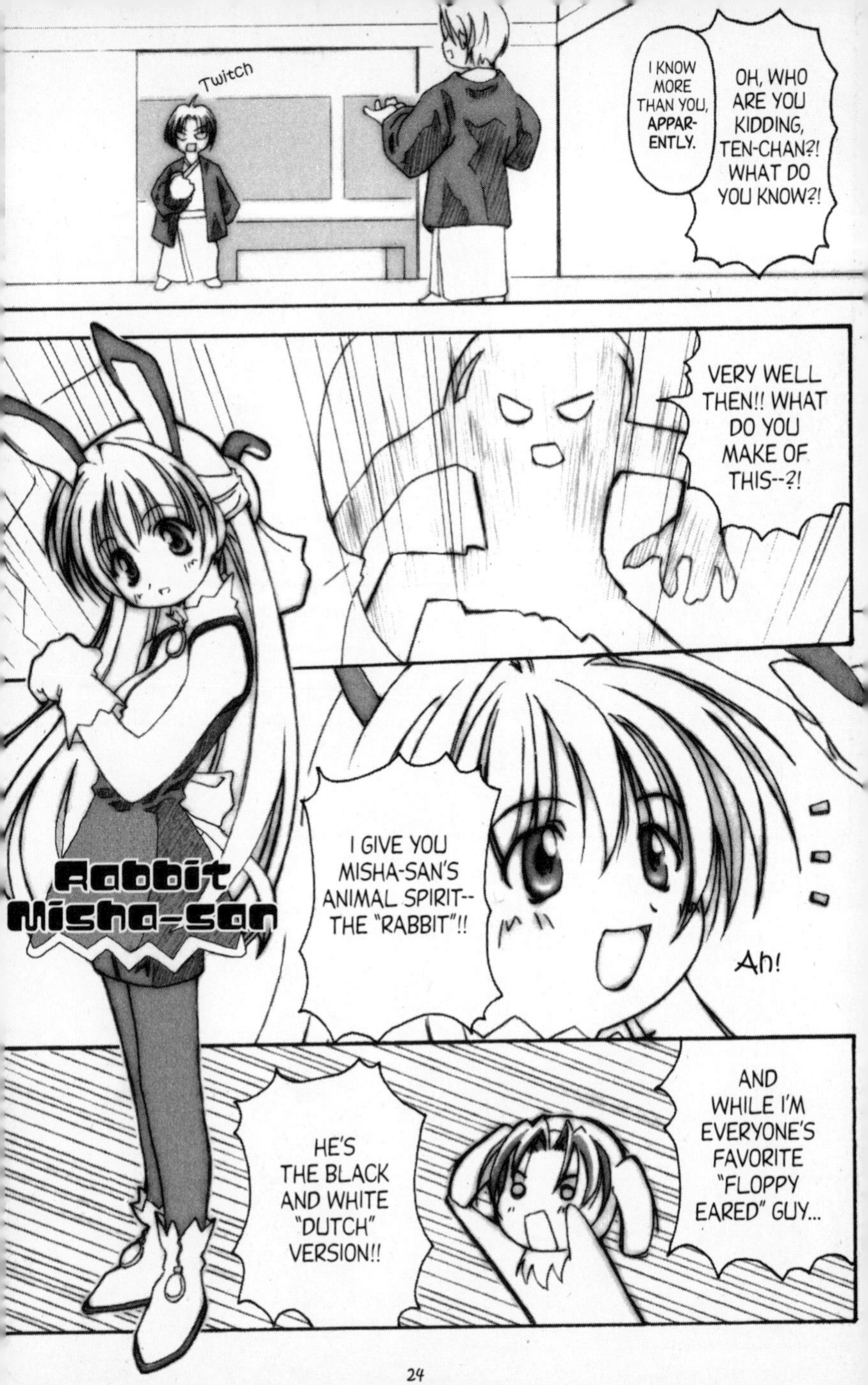
OH, WHO ARE YOU KIDDING, TEN-CHAN?! WHAT DO YOU KNOW?!
I KNOW MORE THAN YOU, APPARENTLY.
Twitch
VERY WELL THEN!! WHAT DO YOU MAKE OF THIS--?!
Ah!
...
I GIVE YOU MISHA-SAN'S ANIMAL SPIRIT-- THE "RABBIT"!!
AND WHILE I'M EVERYONE'S FAVORITE "FLOPPY EARED" GUY...
HE'S THE BLACK AND WHITE "DUTCH" VERSION!!
Rabbit Misha-san

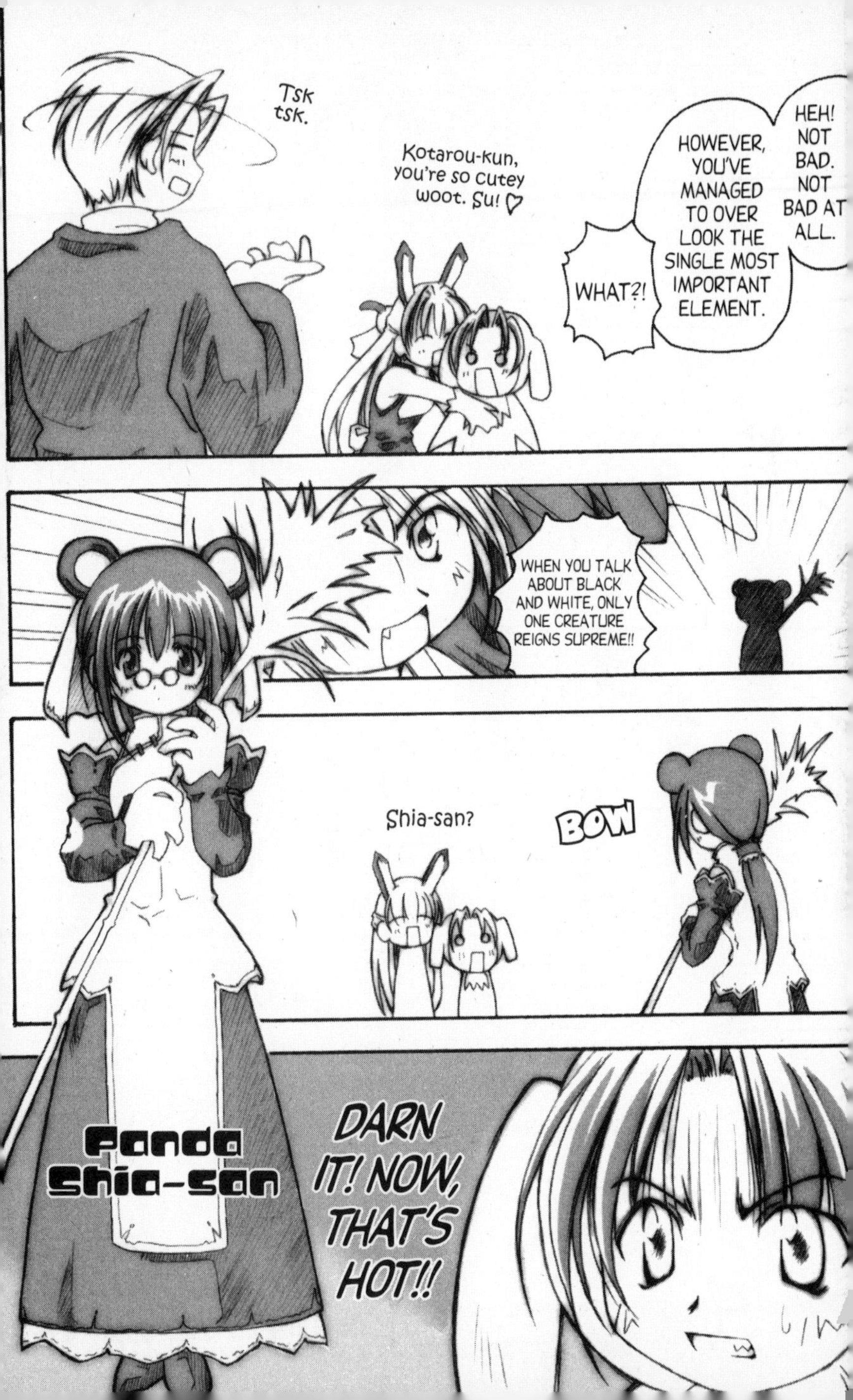
HEH! NOT BAD. NOT BAD AT ALL.
HOWEVER, YOU'VE MANAGED TO OVER LOOK THE SINGLE MOST IMPORTANT ELEMENT.
WHAT?!
Kotarou-kun, you're so cutey woot. Su! ♡
Tsk tsk.
WHEN YOU TALK ABOUT BLACK AND WHITE, ONLY ONE CREATURE REIGNS SUPREME!!
BOW
Shia-san?
DARN IT! NOW, THAT'S HOT!!
Panda Shia-san

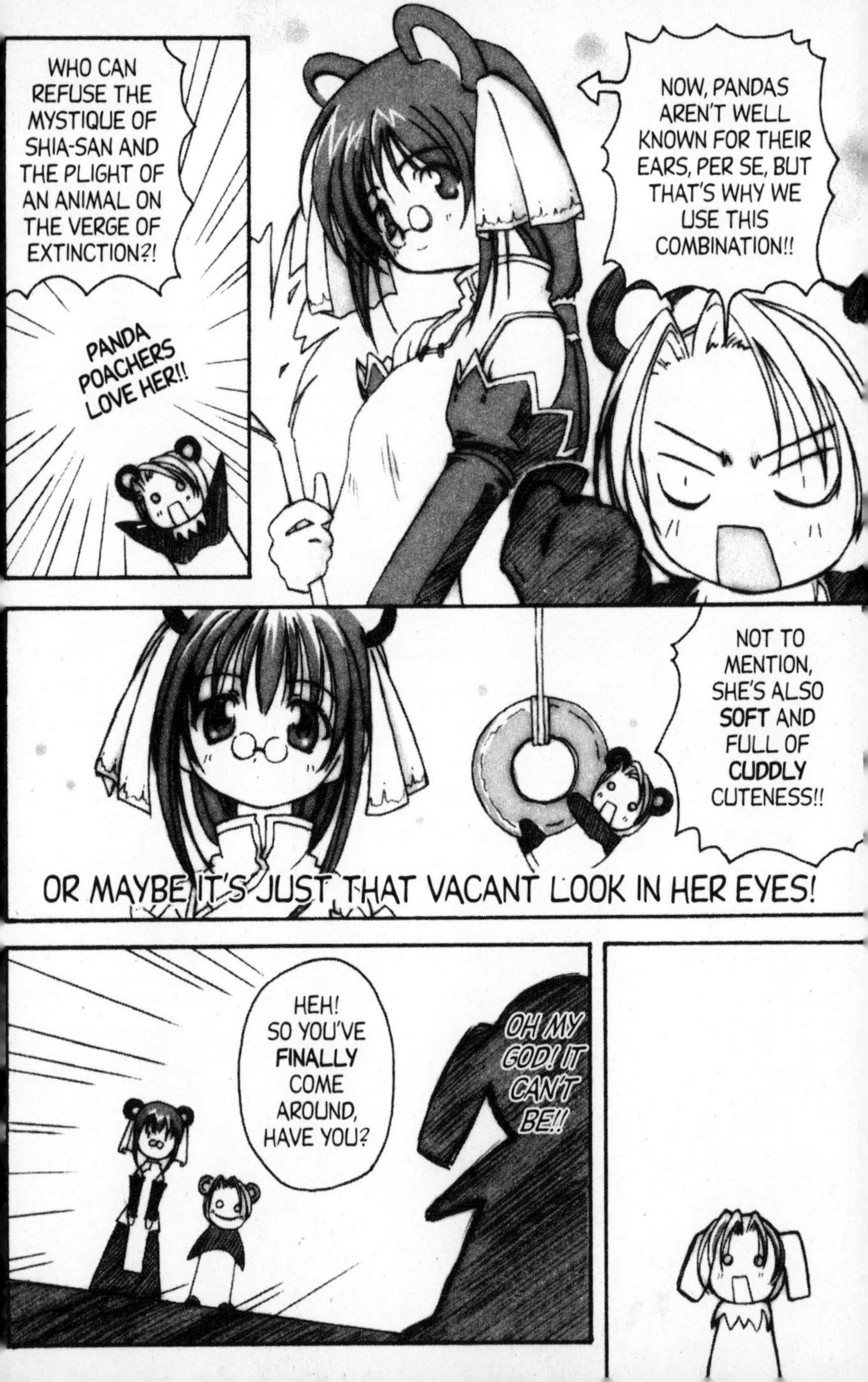
NOW, PANDAS AREN'T WELL KNOWN FOR THEIR EARS, PER SE, BUT THAT'S WHY WE USE THIS COMBINATION!!
WHO CAN REFUSE THE MYSTIQUE OF SHIA-SAN AND THE PLIGHT OF AN ANIMAL ON THE VERGE OF EXTINCTION?!
PANDA POACHERS LOVE HER!!
NOT TO MENTION, SHE'S ALSO SOFT AND FULL OF CUDDLY CUTENESS!!
OR MAYBE IT'S JUST THAT VACANT LOOK IN HER EYES!
OH MY GOD! IT CAN'T BE!!
HEH! SO YOU'VE FINALLY COME AROUND, HAVE YOU?

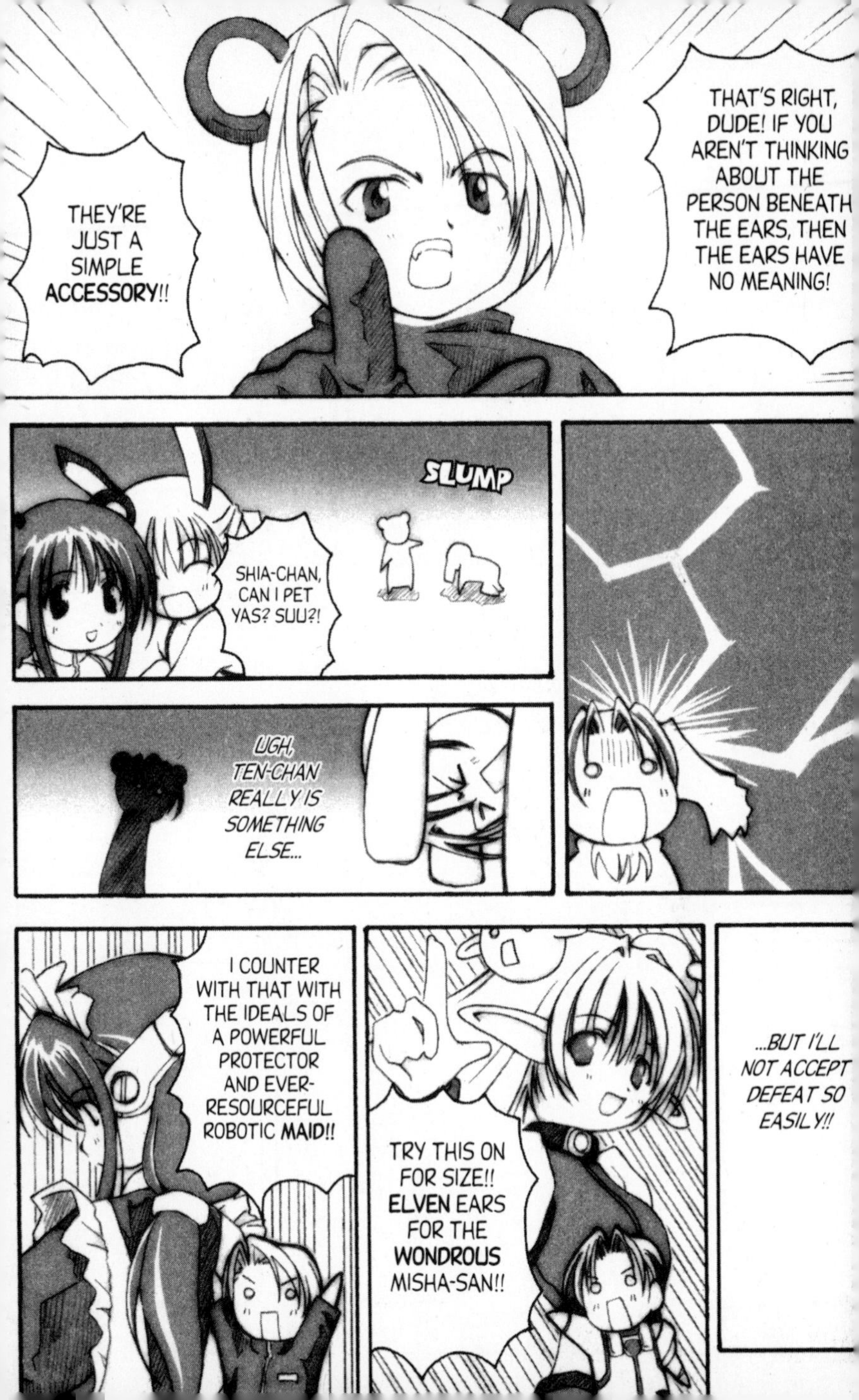
THAT'S RIGHT, DUDE! IF YOU AREN'T THINKING ABOUT THE PERSON BENEATH THE EARS, THEN THE EARS HAVE NO MEANING!
THEY'RE JUST A SIMPLE ACCESSORY!!
SLUMP
SHIA-CHAN, CAN I PET YAS? SUU?!
UGH, TEN-CHAN REALLY IS SOMETHING ELSE...
...BUT I'LL NOT ACCEPT DEFEAT SO EASILY!!
TRY THIS ON FOR SIZE!! ELVEN EARS FOR THE WONDROUS MISHA-SAN!!
I COUNTER WITH THAT WITH THE IDEALS OF A POWERFUL PROTECTOR AND EVER-RESOURCEFUL ROBOTIC MAID!!

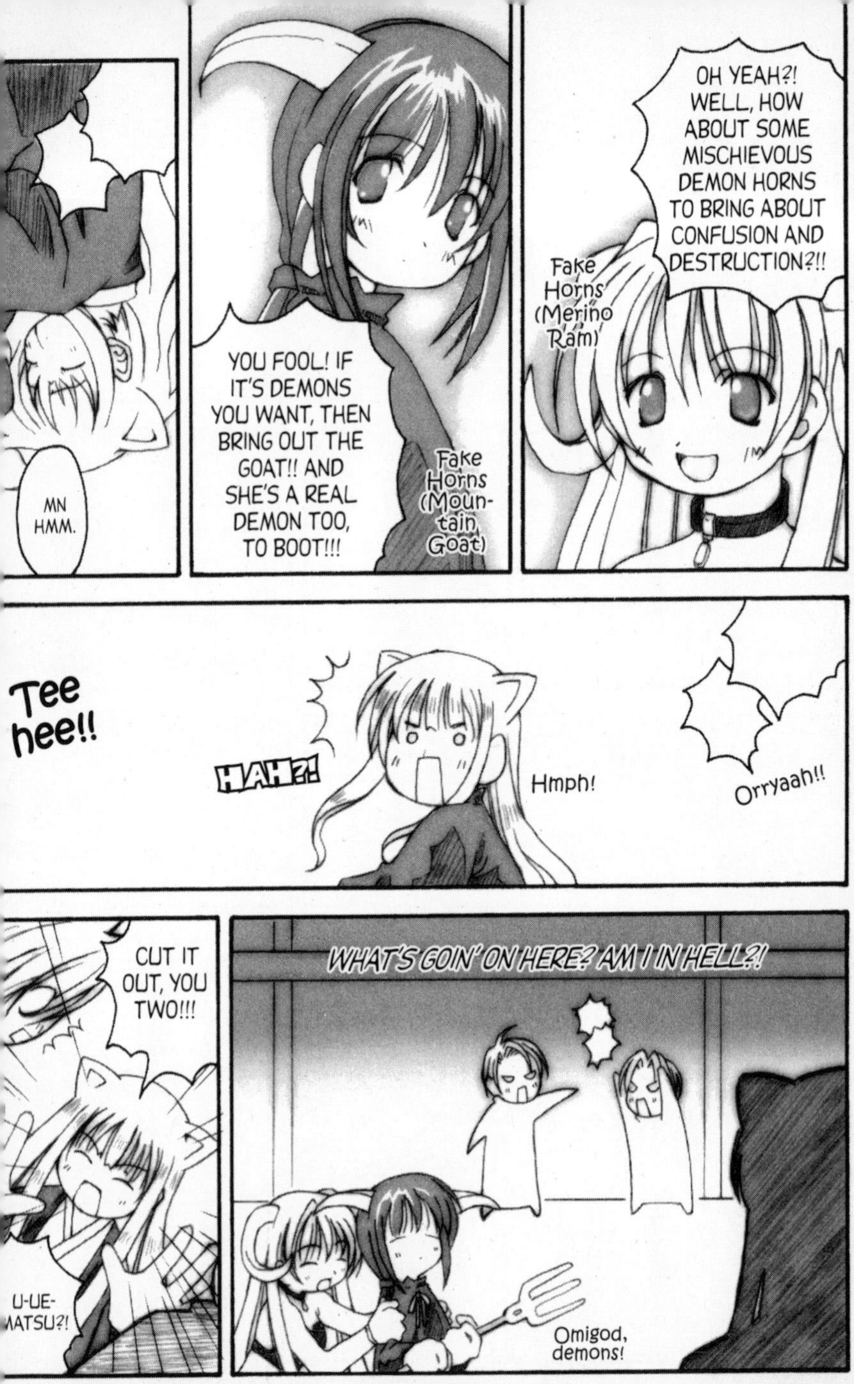
OH YEAH?! WELL, HOW ABOUT SOME MISCHIEVOUS DEMON HORNS TO BRING ABOUT CONFUSION AND DESTRUCTION?!!
Fake Horns (Merino Ram)
YOU FOOL! IF IT'S DEMONS YOU WANT, THEN BRING OUT THE GOAT!! AND SHE'S A REAL DEMON TOO, TO BOOT!!!
Fake Horns (Mountain Goat)
MN HMM.
Orryaah!!
Hmph!
HAH?!
Tee hee!!
WHAT'S GOIN' ON HERE? AM I IN HELL?!
Omigod, demons!
CUT IT OUT, YOU TWO!!!
U-UE-MATSU?!

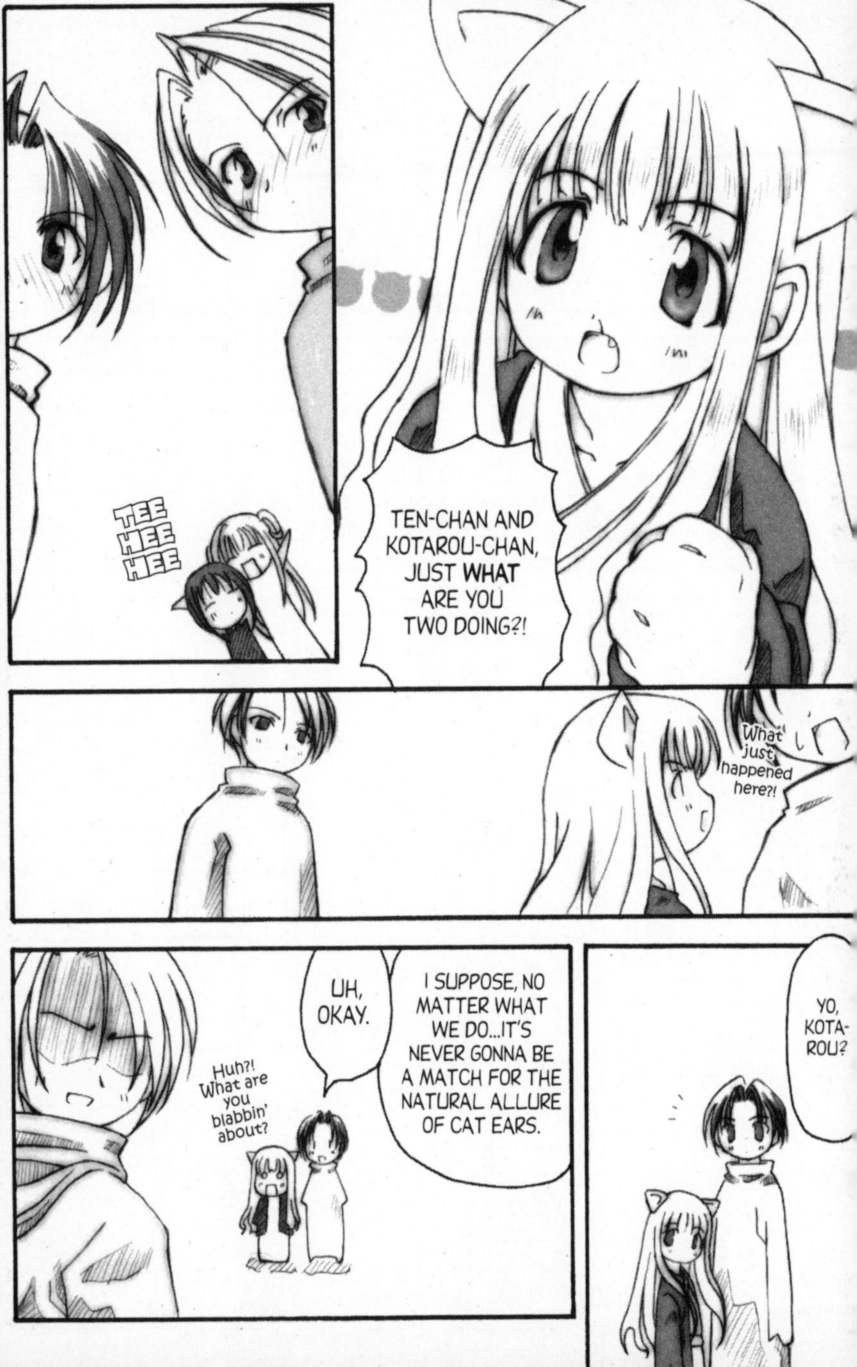
TEN-CHAN AND KOTAROU-CHAN, JUST WHAT ARE YOU TWO DOING?!
TEE HEE HEE
What just happened here?!
YO, KOTA-ROU?
I SUPPOSE, NO MATTER WHAT WE DO...IT'S NEVER GONNA BE A MATCH FOR THE NATURAL ALLURE OF CAT EARS.
UH, OKAY.
Huh?! What are you blabbin' about?

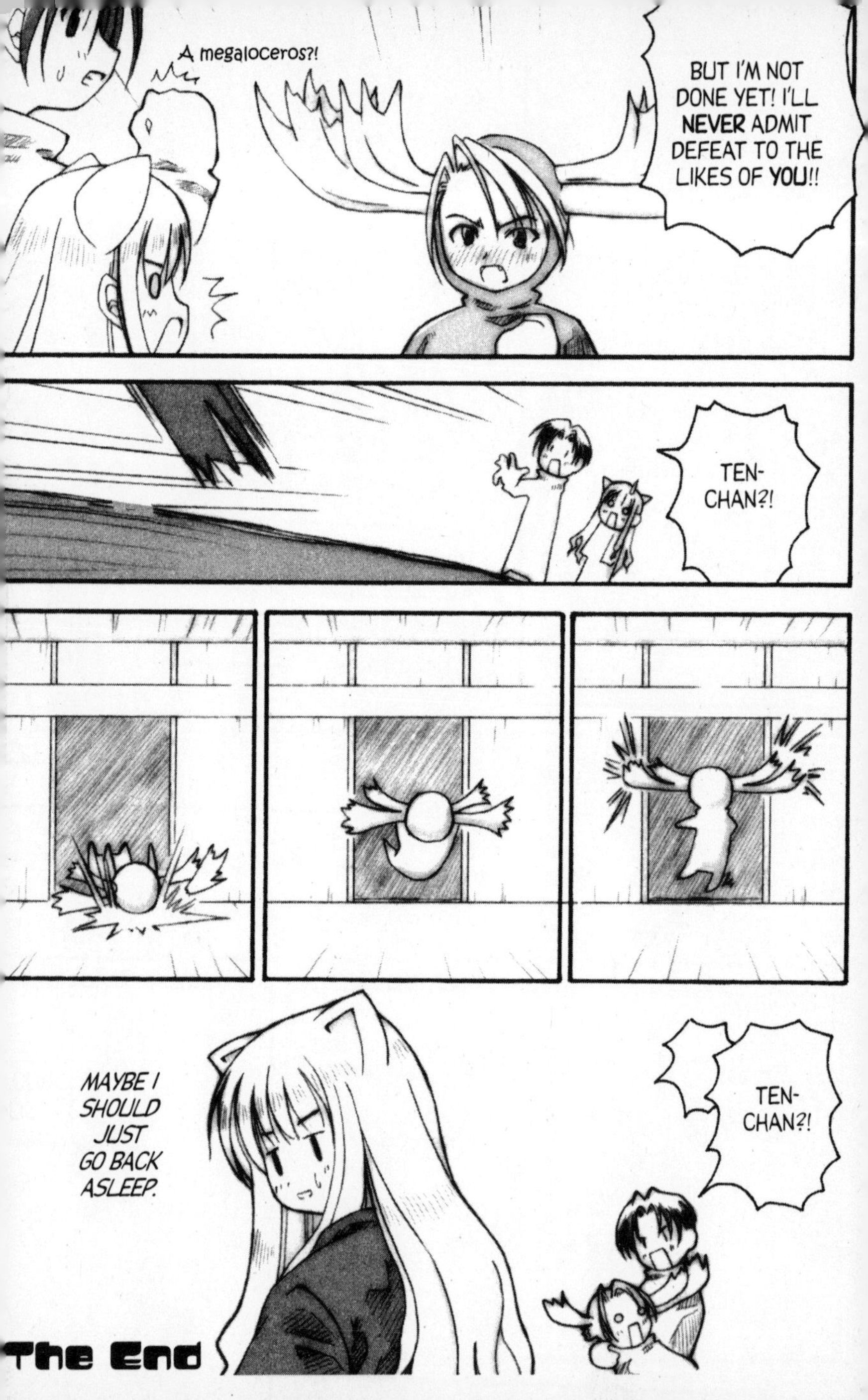
BUT I'M NOT DONE YET! I'LL NEVER ADMIT DEFEAT TO THE LIKES OF YOU!!
A megaloceros?!
TEN-CHAN?!
TEN-CHAN?!
MAYBE I SHOULD JUST GO BACK ASLEEP.
The End

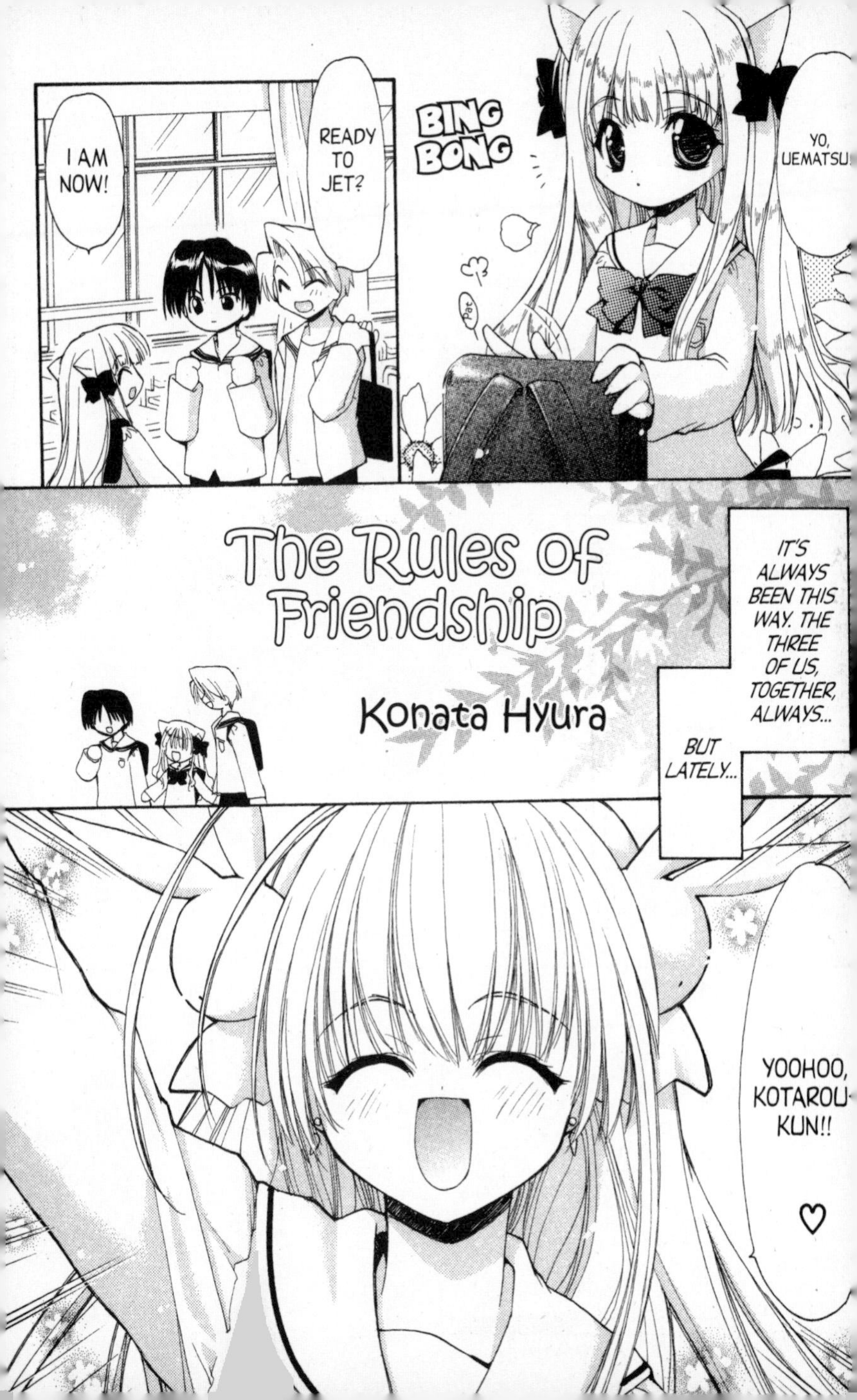
YO, UEMATSU!
BING BONG
Pat
READY TO JET?
I AM NOW!
IT'S ALWAYS BEEN THIS WAY. THE THREE OF US, TOGETHER, ALWAYS...
BUT LATELY...
The Rules of Friendship
Konata Hyura
YOOHOO, KOTAROU-KUN!! ♡

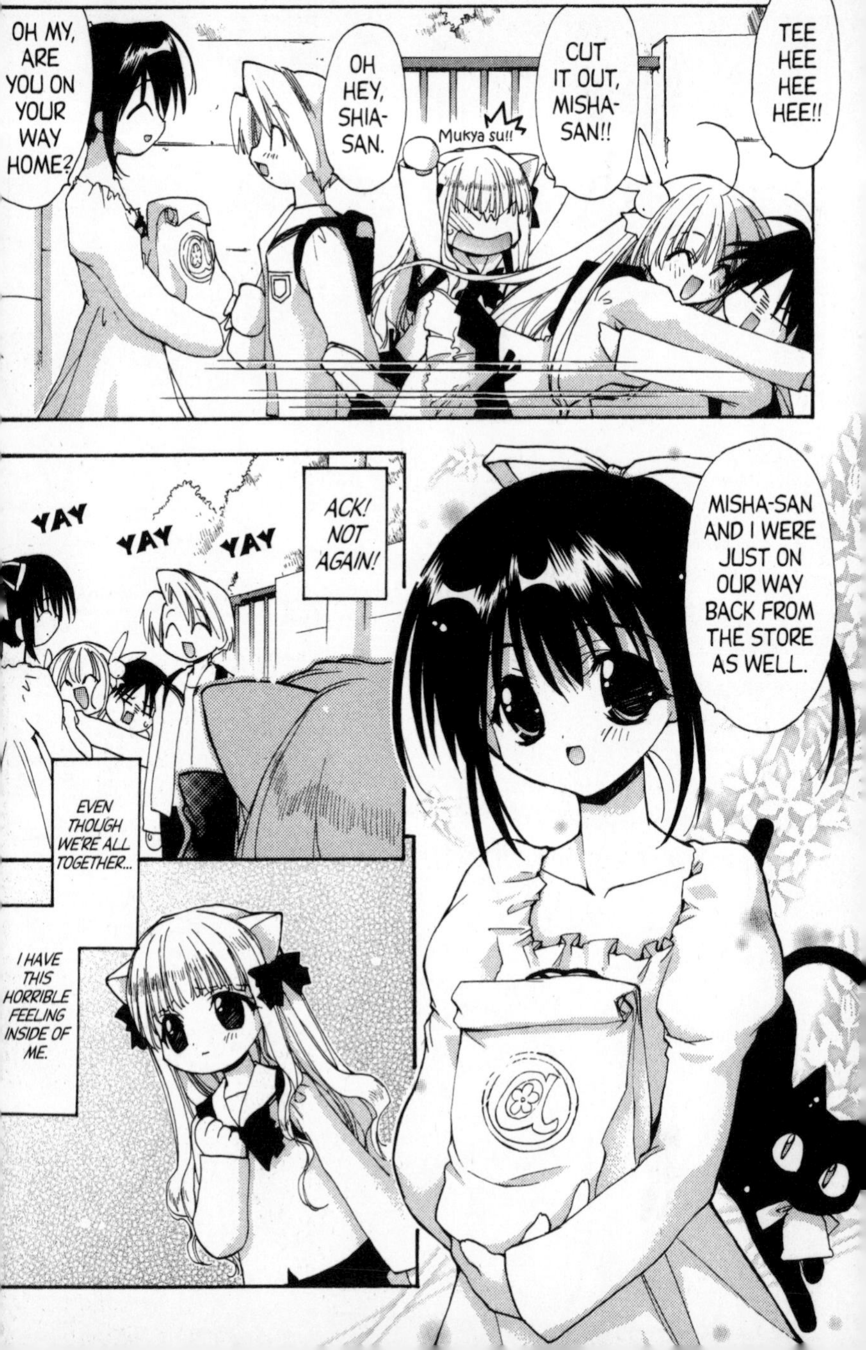
TEE HEE HEE HEE!!
CUT IT OUT, MISHA-SAN!!
Mukya su!!
OH HEY, SHIA-SAN.
OH MY, ARE YOU ON YOUR WAY HOME?
MISHA-SAN AND I WERE JUST ON OUR WAY BACK FROM THE STORE AS WELL.
ACK! NOT AGAIN!
YAY
YAY
YAY
EVEN THOUGH WE'RE ALL TOGETHER...
I HAVE THIS HORRIBLE FEELING INSIDE OF ME.

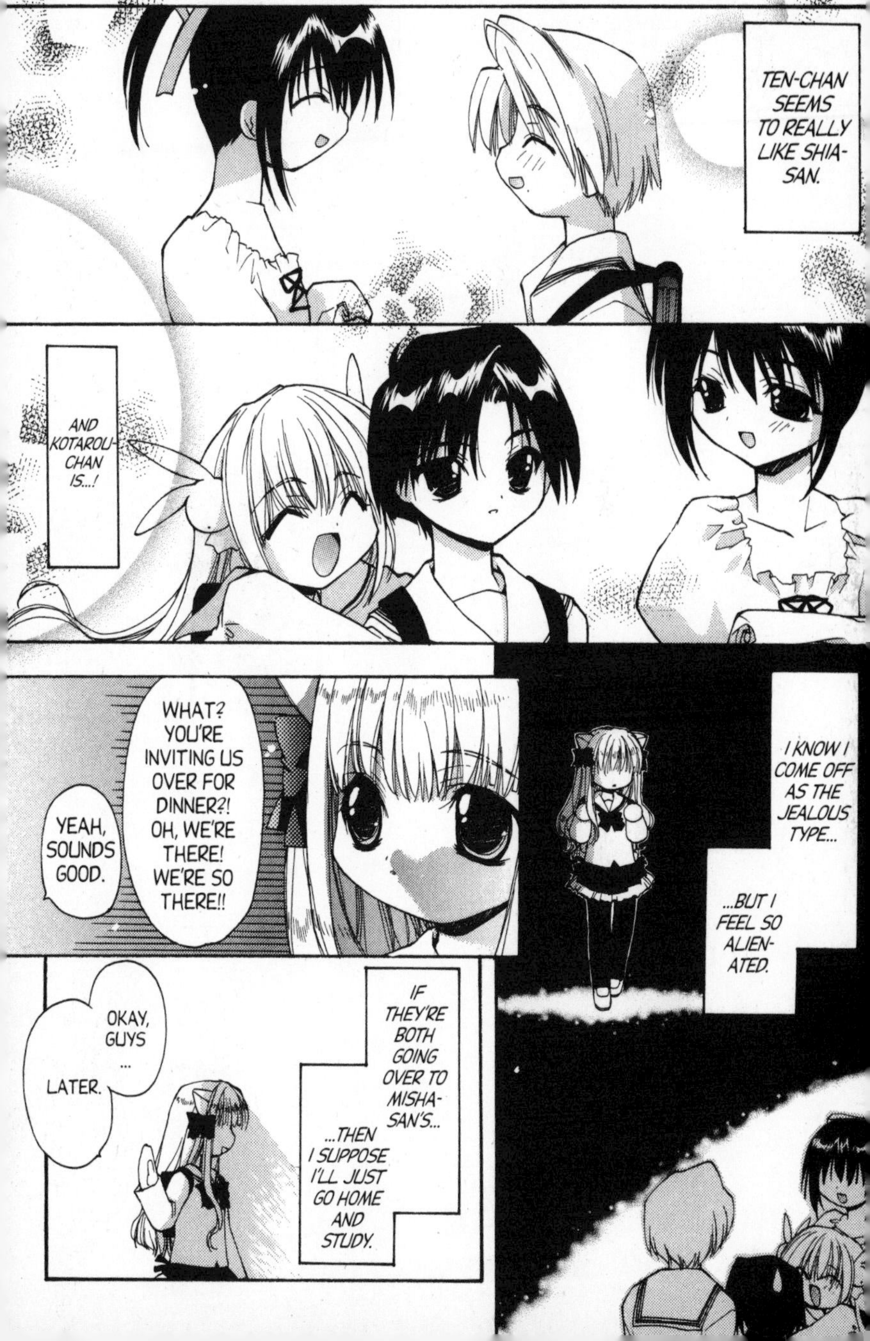
TEN-CHAN SEEMS TO REALLY LIKE SHIA-SAN.
AND KOTAROU-CHAN IS...!
I KNOW I COME OFF AS THE JEALOUS TYPE...
...BUT I FEEL SO ALIENATED.
WHAT? YOU'RE INVITING US OVER FOR DINNER?! OH, WE'RE THERE! WE'RE SO THERE!!
YEAH, SOUNDS GOOD.
IF THEY'RE BOTH GOING OVER TO MISHA-SAN'S...
...THEN I SUPPOSE I'LL JUST GO HOME AND STUDY.
OKAY, GUYS ... LATER.

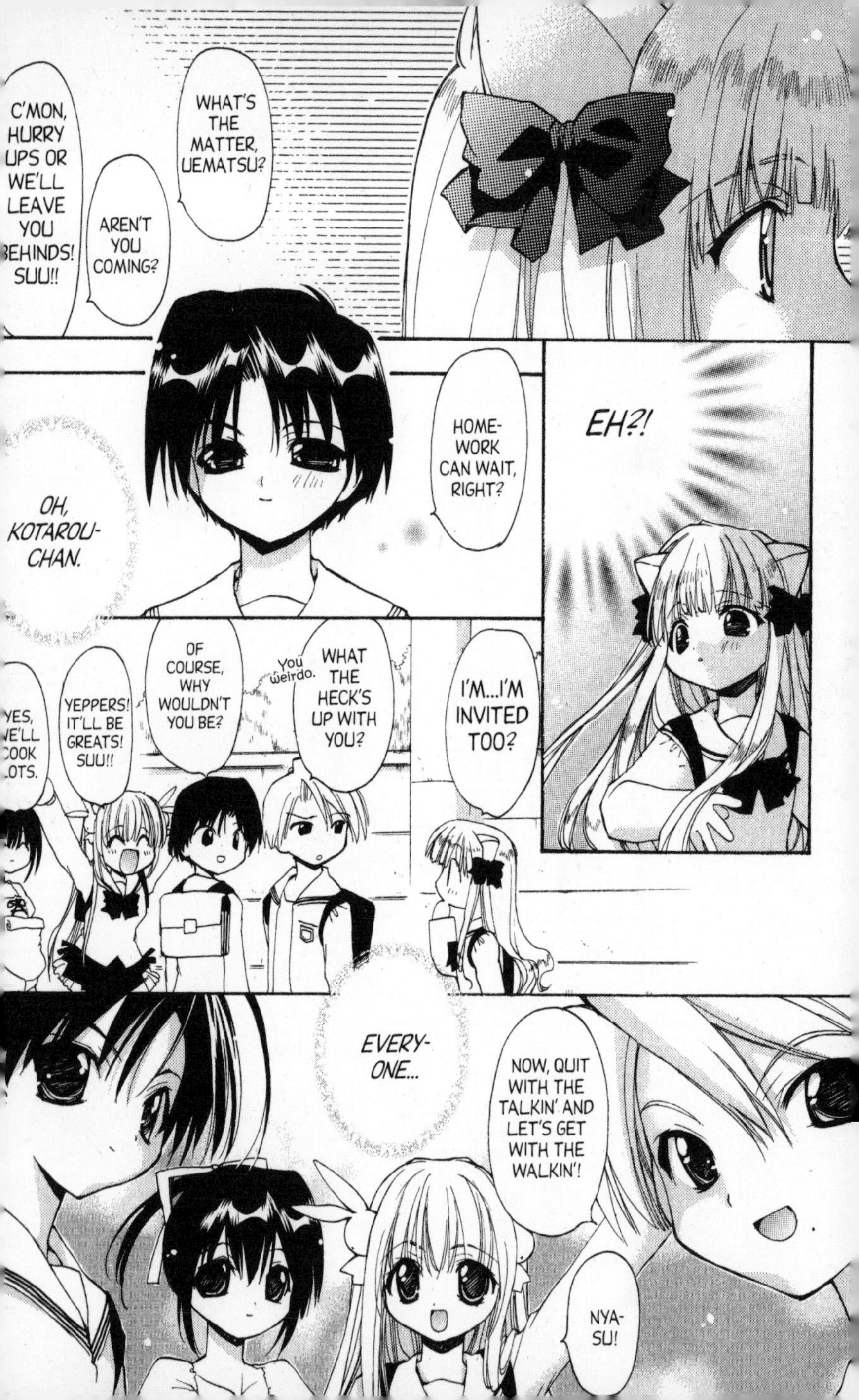
WHAT'S THE MATTER, UEMATSU?
AREN'T YOU COMING?
C'MON, HURRY UPS OR WE'LL LEAVE YOU BEHINDS! SUU!!
EH?!
HOME-WORK CAN WAIT, RIGHT?
OH, KOTAROU-CHAN.
I'M...I'M INVITED TOO?
WHAT THE HECK'S UP WITH YOU?
You weirdo.
OF COURSE, WHY WOULDN'T YOU BE?
YEPPERS! IT'LL BE GREATS! SUU!!
YES, WE'LL COOK LOTS.
NOW, QUIT WITH THE TALKIN' AND LET'S GET WITH THE WALKIN'!
NYA-SU!
EVERY-ONE...

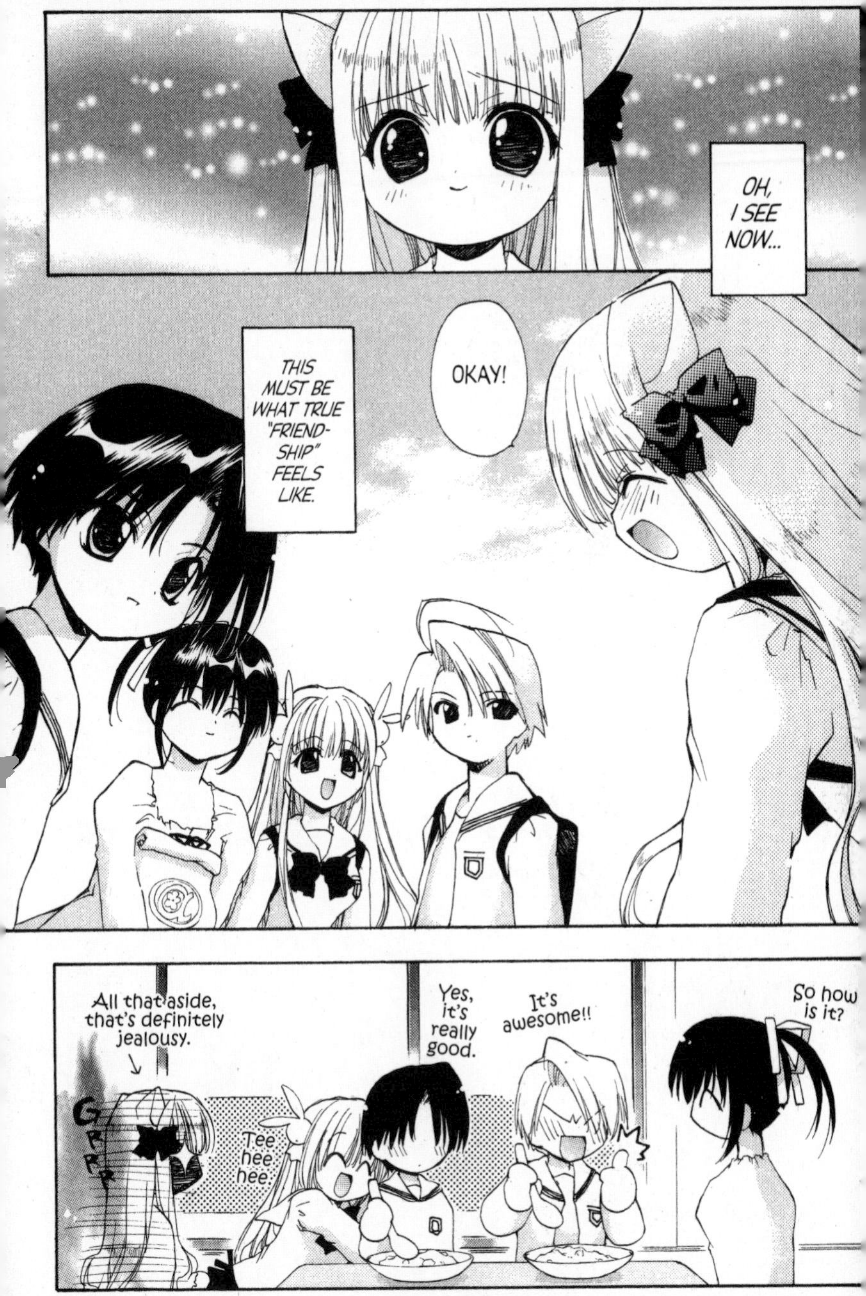
OH, I SEE NOW...
OKAY!
THIS MUST BE WHAT TRUE "FRIEND-SHIP" FEELS LIKE.
So how is it?
It's awesome!!
Yes, it's really good.
Tee hee hee.
All that aside, that's definitely jealousy.
GRRR

The End

Konata Hyura

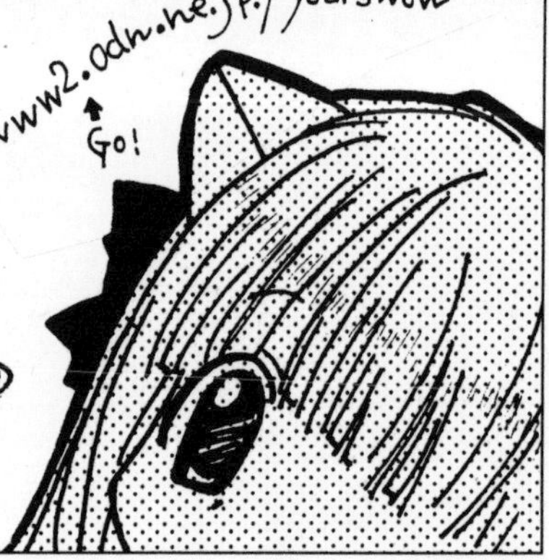
www2.odn.ne.jp./yourswon
Go!

Koboshi-chan is really cute.
I'm so happy that I got to draw her.
I'm a little disappointed that
I couldn't draw the boys
as much, though.

• Konata Hyuura '02 •

Writer's Talk

Umi Sugimoto

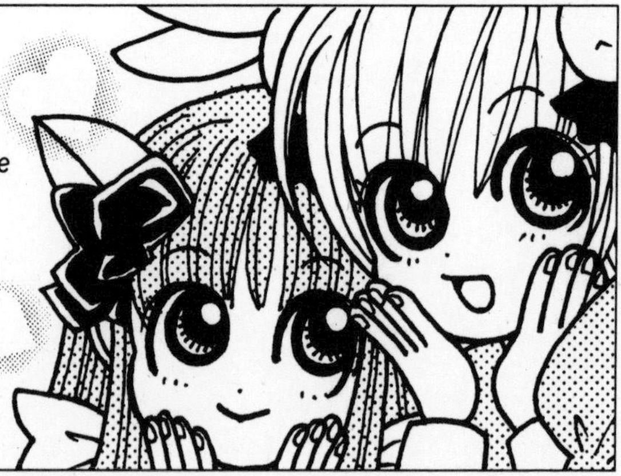

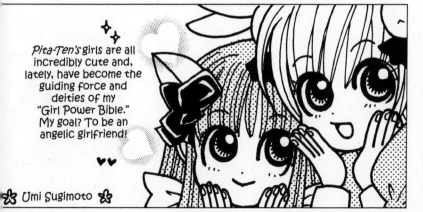

Pita-Ten's girls are all incredibly cute and, lately, have become the guiding force and deities of my "Girl Power Bible." My goal? To be an angelic girlfriend!

Umi Sugimoto

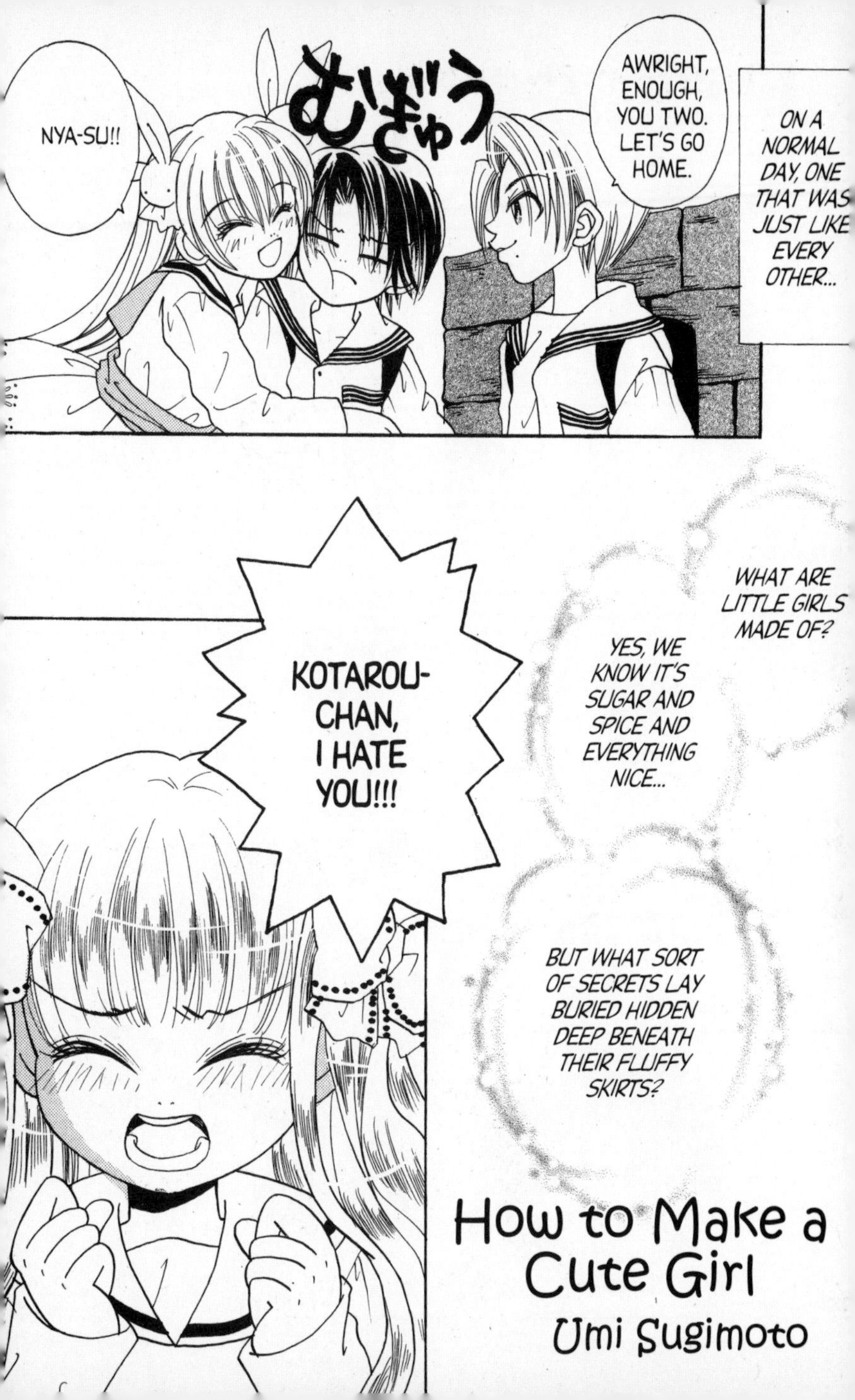
ON A NORMAL DAY, ONE THAT WAS JUST LIKE EVERY OTHER...
AWRIGHT, ENOUGH, YOU TWO. LET'S GO HOME.
むぎゅう
NYA-SU!!
WHAT ARE LITTLE GIRLS MADE OF?
YES, WE KNOW IT'S SUGAR AND SPICE AND EVERYTHING NICE...
BUT WHAT SORT OF SECRETS LAY BURIED HIDDEN DEEP BENEATH THEIR FLUFFY SKIRTS?
How to Make a Cute Girl
Umi Sugimoto
KOTAROU-CHAN, I HATE YOU!!!

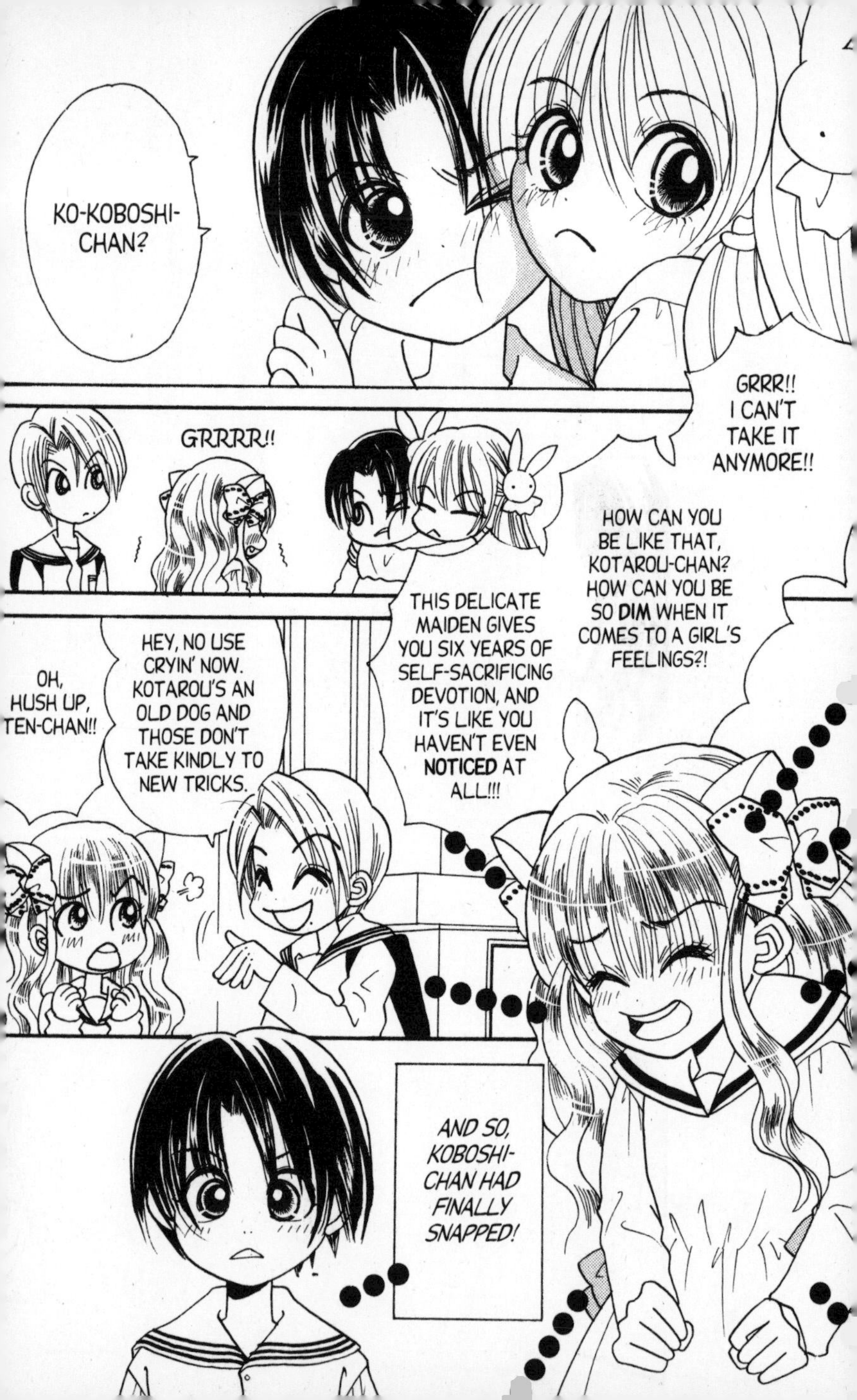
KO-KOBOSHI-CHAN?
GRRR!! I CAN'T TAKE IT ANYMORE!!
GRRRR!!
HOW CAN YOU BE LIKE THAT, KOTAROU-CHAN? HOW CAN YOU BE SO DIM WHEN IT COMES TO A GIRL'S FEELINGS?!
THIS DELICATE MAIDEN GIVES YOU SIX YEARS OF SELF-SACRIFICING DEVOTION, AND IT'S LIKE YOU HAVEN'T EVEN NOTICED AT ALL!!!
HEY, NO USE CRYIN' NOW. KOTAROU'S AN OLD DOG AND THOSE DON'T TAKE KINDLY TO NEW TRICKS.
OH, HUSH UP, TEN-CHAN!!
AND SO, KOBOSHI-CHAN HAD FINALLY SNAPPED!

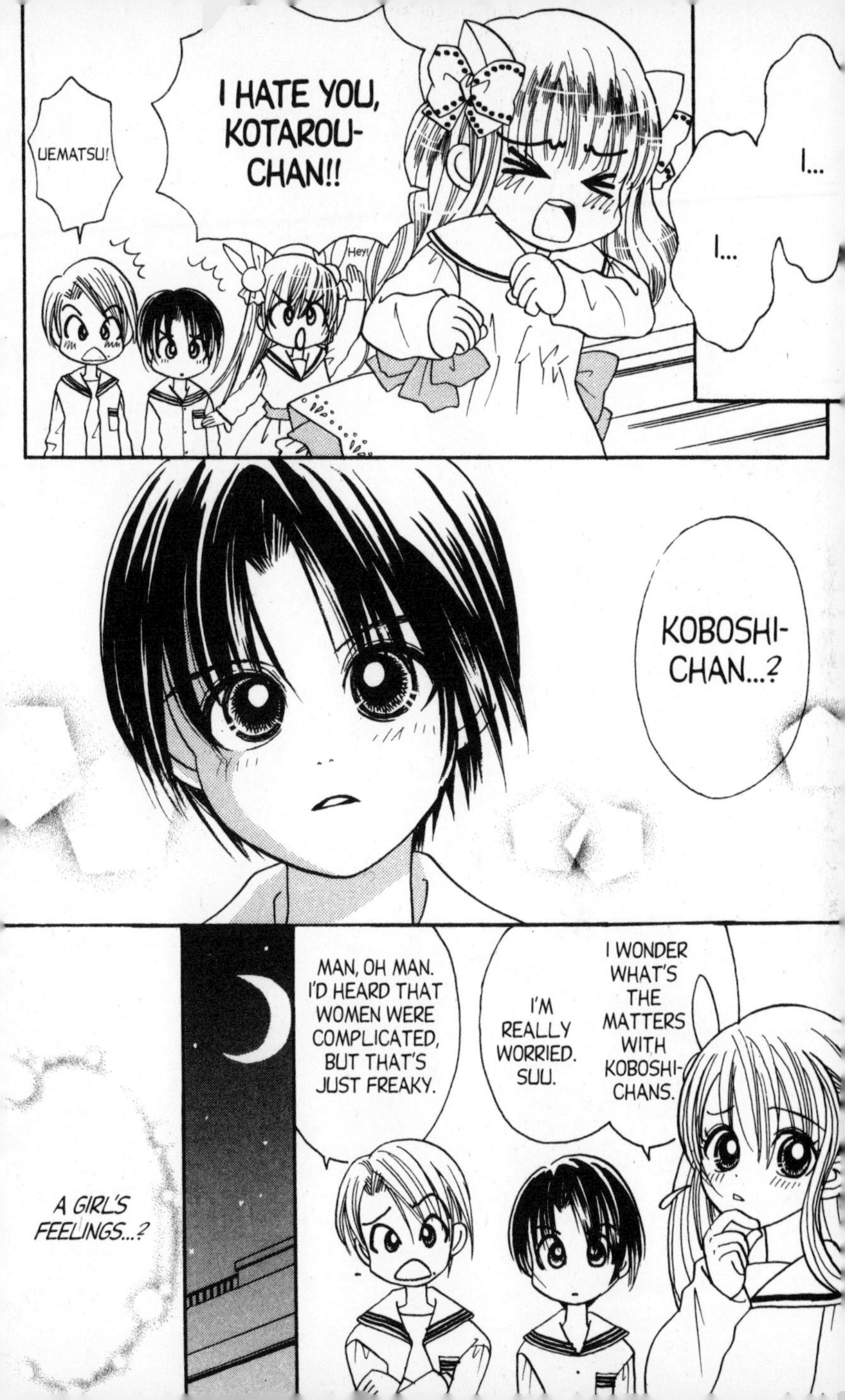
I...
I...
I HATE YOU, KOTAROU-CHAN!!
Hey!
UEMATSU!
KOBOSHI-CHAN...?
I WONDER WHAT'S THE MATTERS WITH KOBOSHI-CHANS.
I'M REALLY WORRIED. SUU.
MAN, OH MAN. I'D HEARD THAT WOMEN WERE COMPLICATED, BUT THAT'S JUST FREAKY.
A GIRL'S FEELINGS...?

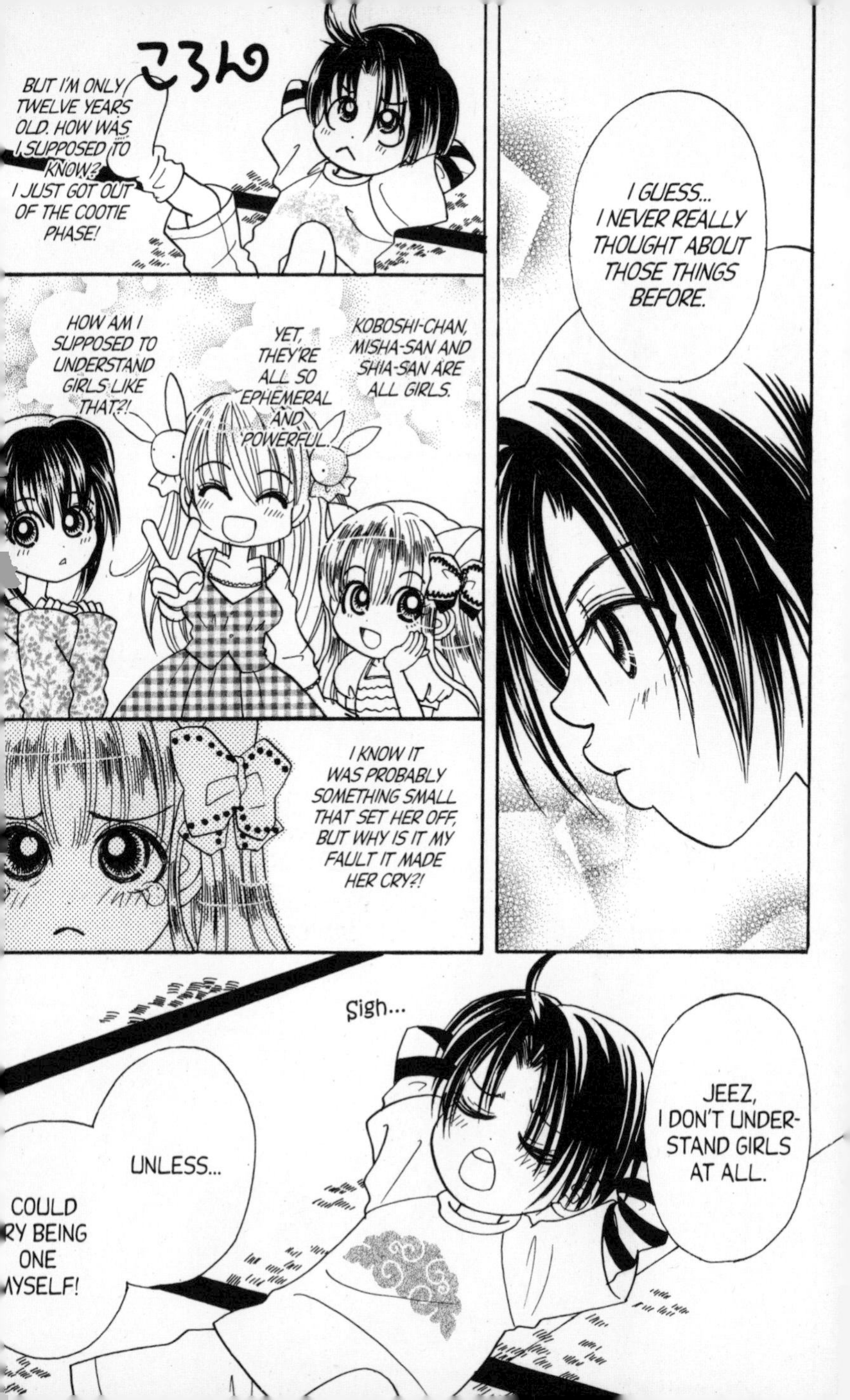
I GUESS... I NEVER REALLY THOUGHT ABOUT THOSE THINGS BEFORE.
ころん
BUT I'M ONLY TWELVE YEARS OLD. HOW WAS I SUPPOSED TO KNOW? I JUST GOT OUT OF THE COOTIE PHASE!
KOBOSHI-CHAN, MISHA-SAN AND SHIA-SAN ARE ALL GIRLS.
YET, THEY'RE ALL SO EPHEMERAL AND POWERFUL.
HOW AM I SUPPOSED TO UNDERSTAND GIRLS LIKE THAT?!
I KNOW IT WAS PROBABLY SOMETHING SMALL THAT SET HER OFF, BUT WHY IS IT MY FAULT IT MADE HER CRY?!
JEEZ, I DON'T UNDER-STAND GIRLS AT ALL.
Sigh...
UNLESS...
COULD RY BEING ONE MYSELF!

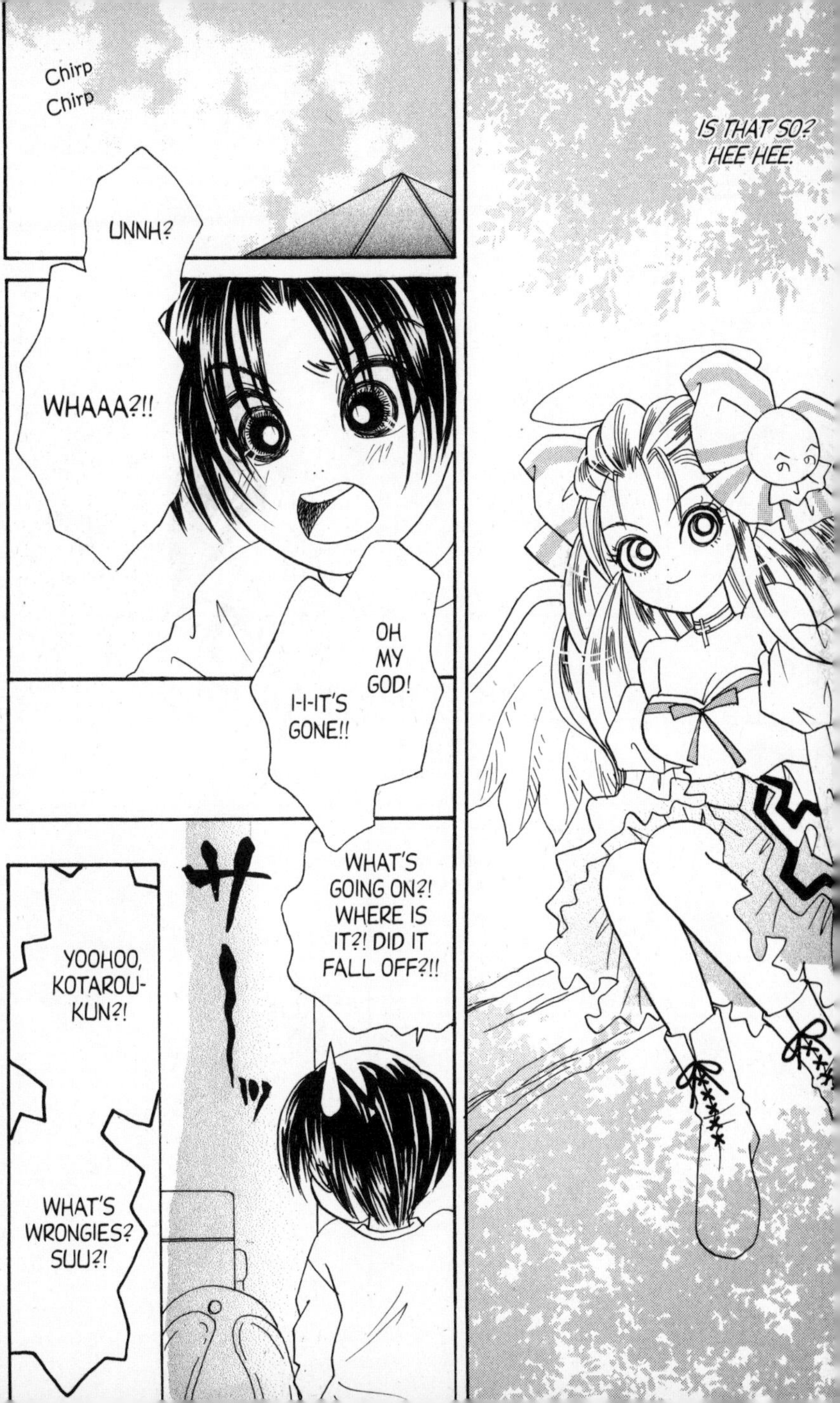
IS THAT SO? HEE HEE.
Chirp Chirp
UNNH?
WHAAA?!!
OH MY GOD!
I-I-IT'S GONE!!
WHAT'S GOING ON?! WHERE IS IT?! DID IT FALL OFF?!!
YOOHOO, KOTAROU-KUN?!
WHAT'S WRONGIES? SUU?!

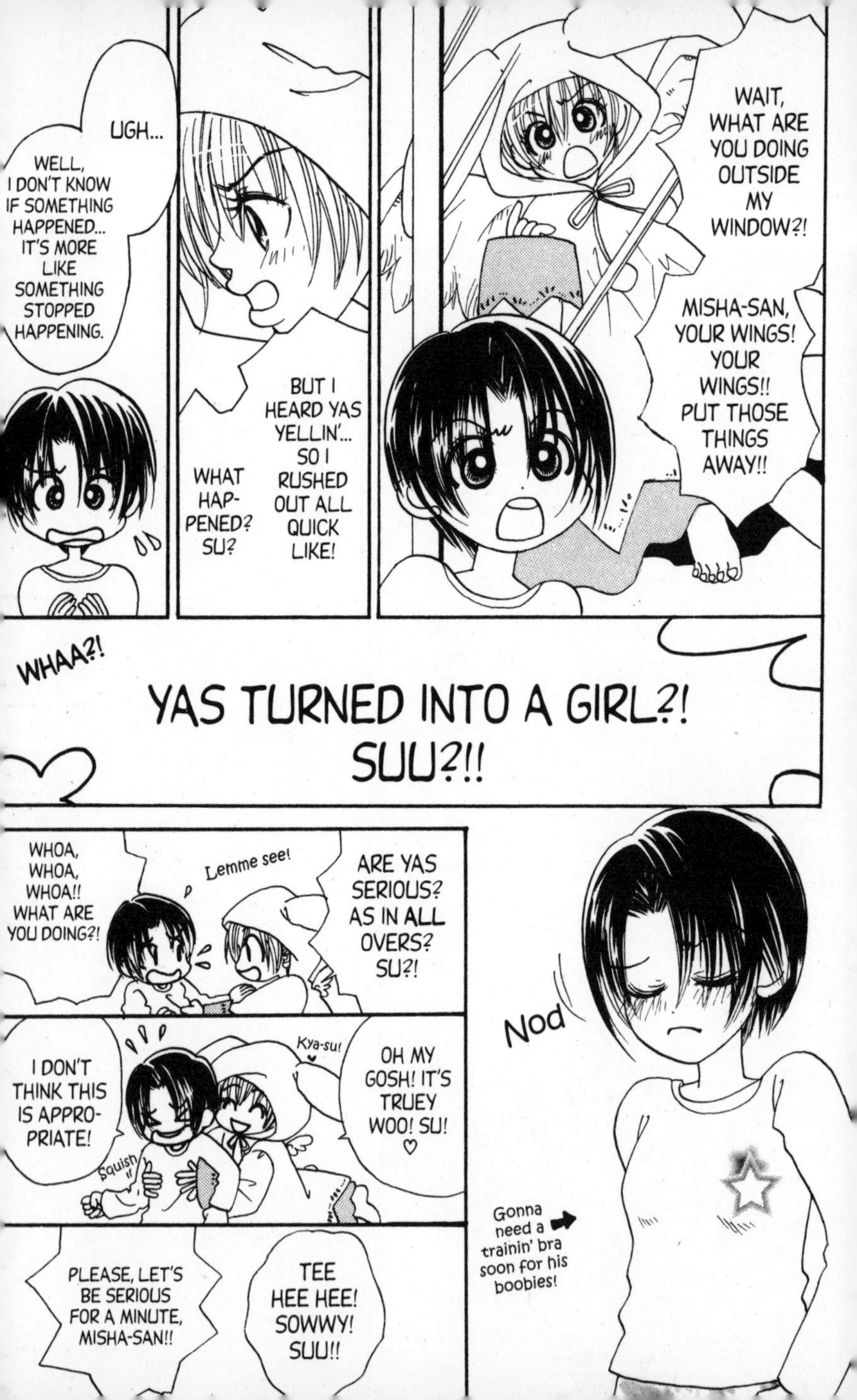
WAIT, WHAT ARE YOU DOING OUTSIDE MY WINDOW?!
MISHA-SAN, YOUR WINGS! YOUR WINGS!! PUT THOSE THINGS AWAY!!
BUT I HEARD YAS YELLIN'... SO I RUSHED OUT ALL QUICK LIKE!
WHAT HAP-PENED? SU?
UGH...
WELL, I DON'T KNOW IF SOMETHING HAPPENED... IT'S MORE LIKE SOMETHING STOPPED HAPPENING.
YAS TURNED INTO A GIRL?! SUU?!!
WHAA?!
Nod
Gonna need a trainin' bra soon for his boobies!
ARE YAS SERIOUS? AS IN ALL OVERS? SU?!
Lemme see!
WHOA, WHOA, WHOA!! WHAT ARE YOU DOING?!
OH MY GOSH! IT'S TRUEY WOO! SU! ♡
Kya-su!
I DON'T THINK THIS IS APPRO-PRIATE!
Squish
TEE HEE HEE! SOWWY! SUU!!
PLEASE, LET'S BE SERIOUS FOR A MINUTE, MISHA-SAN!!

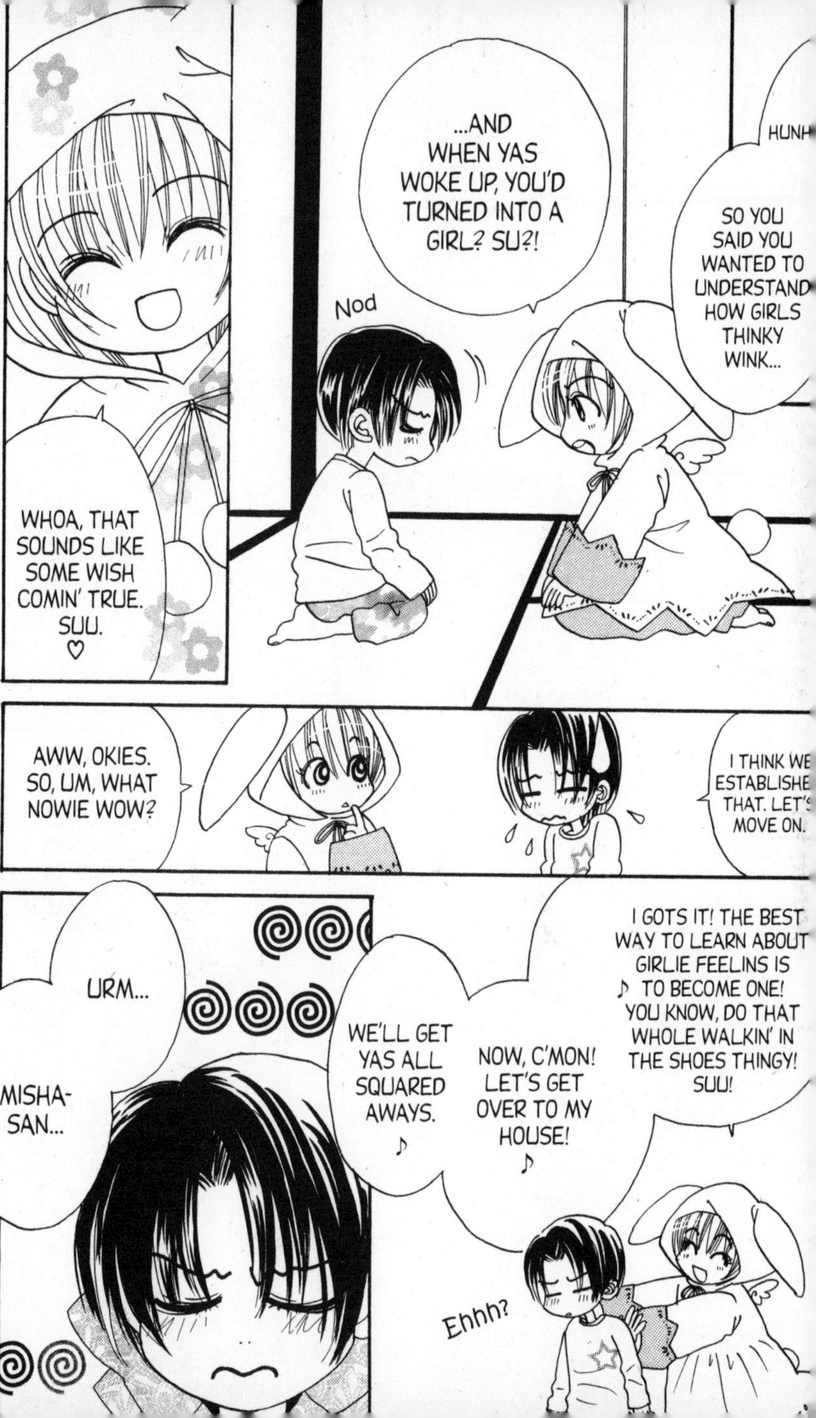
HUNH
SO YOU SAID YOU WANTED TO UNDERSTAND HOW GIRLS THINKY WINK...
...AND WHEN YAS WOKE UP, YOU'D TURNED INTO A GIRL? SU?!
Nod
WHOA, THAT SOUNDS LIKE SOME WISH COMIN' TRUE. SUU. ♡
I THINK WE ESTABLISHE THAT. LET'S MOVE ON.
AWW, OKIES. SO, UM, WHAT NOWIE WOW?
I GOTS IT! THE BEST WAY TO LEARN ABOUT GIRLIE FEELINS IS ♪ TO BECOME ONE! YOU KNOW, DO THAT WHOLE WALKIN' IN THE SHOES THINGY! SUU!
NOW, C'MON! LET'S GET OVER TO MY HOUSE! ♪
WE'LL GET YAS ALL SQUARED AWAYS. ♪
Ehhh?
URM...
MISHA-SAN...

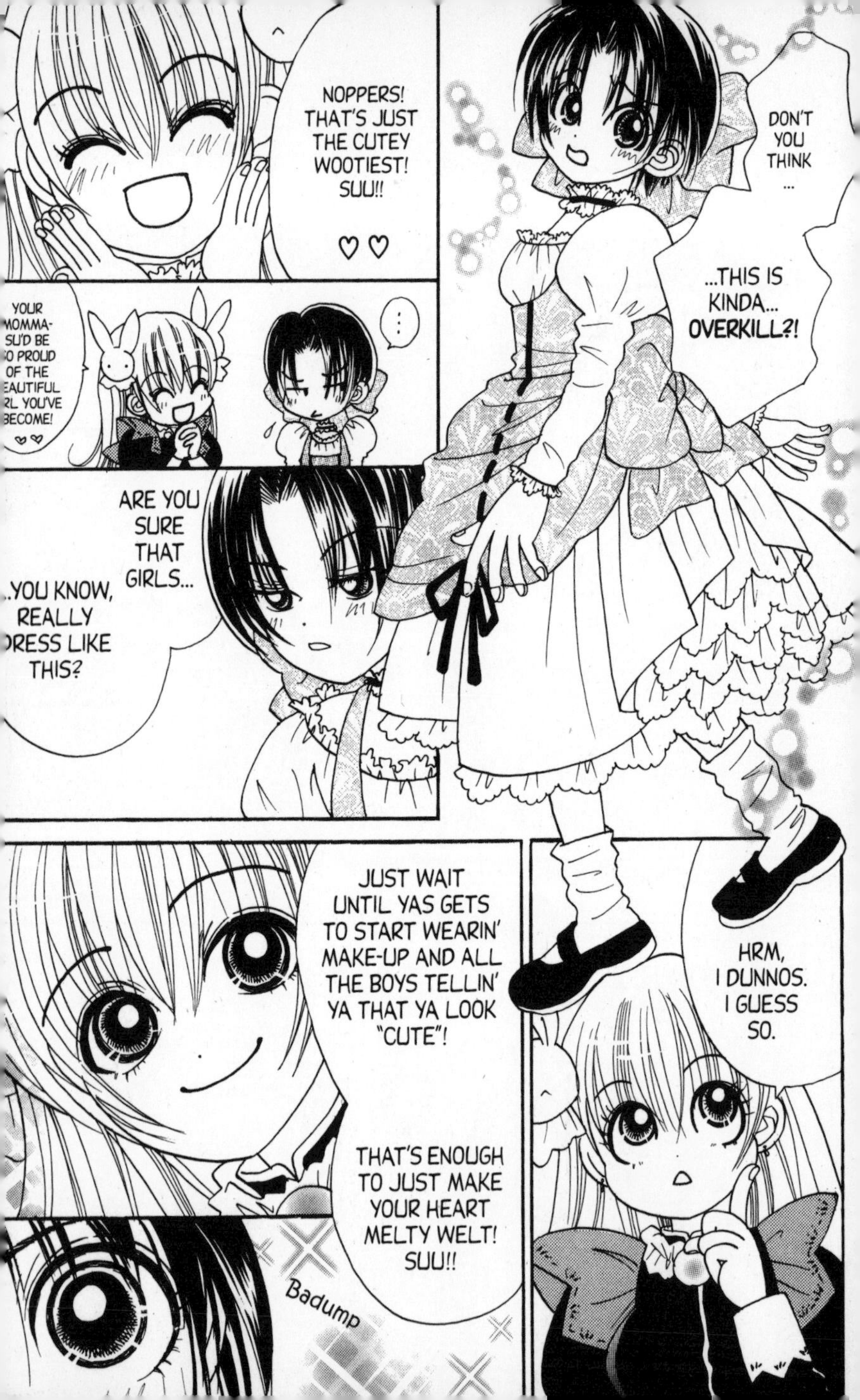

DON'T YOU THINK ...
...THIS IS KINDA... **OVERKILL?!**
NOPPERS! THAT'S JUST THE CUTEY WOOTIEST! SUU!! ♡ ♡
...
YOUR MOMMA-SU'D BE O PROUD OF THE EAUTIFUL RL YOU'VE BECOME! ♡♡
ARE YOU SURE THAT GIRLS...
.YOU KNOW, REALLY RESS LIKE THIS?
HRM, I DUNNOS. I GUESS SO.
JUST WAIT UNTIL YAS GETS TO START WEARIN' MAKE-UP AND ALL THE BOYS TELLIN' YA THAT YA LOOK "CUTE"!
THAT'S ENOUGH TO JUST MAKE YOUR HEART MELTY WELT! SUU!!
Badump

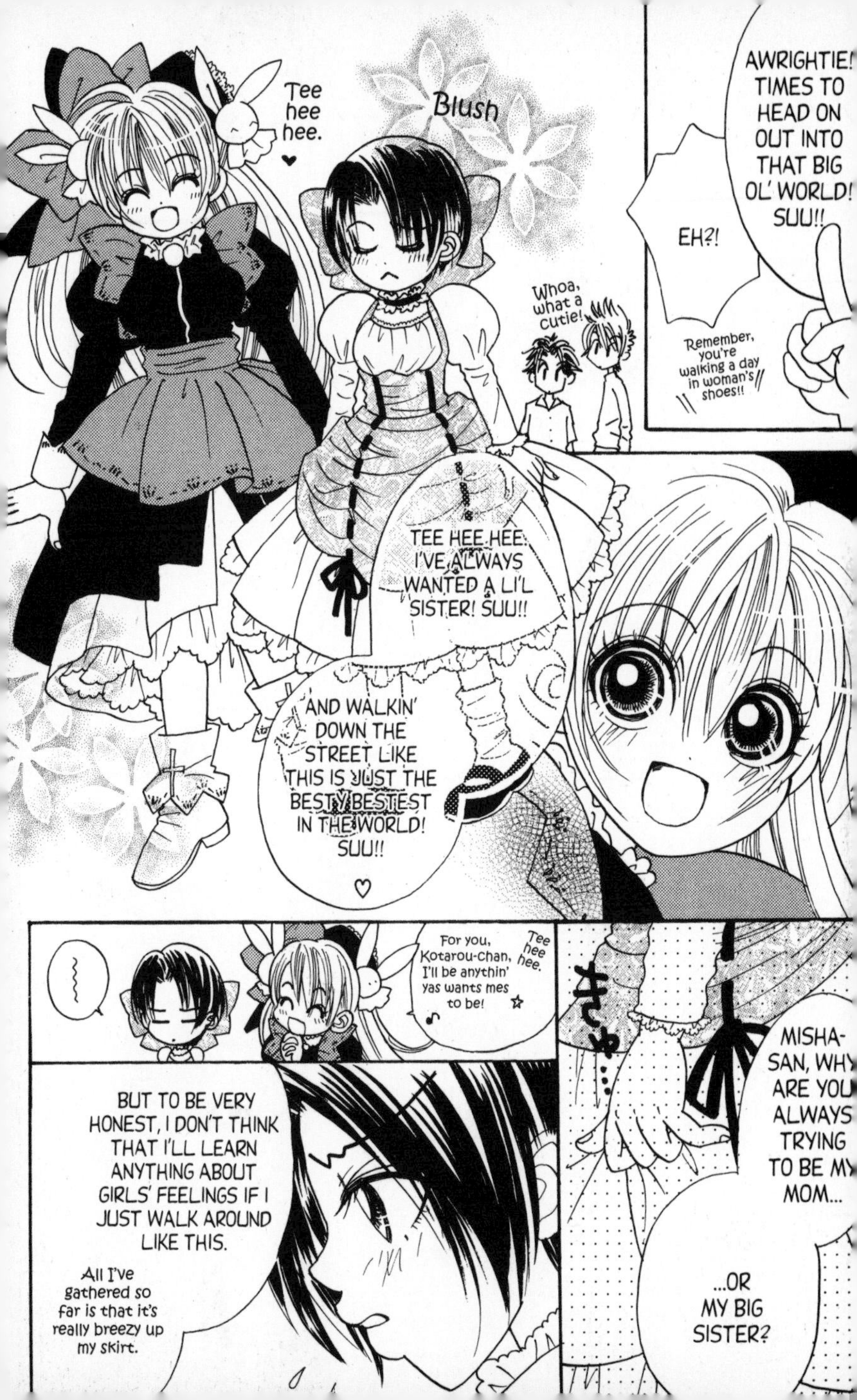
AWRIGHTIE! TIMES TO HEAD ON OUT INTO THAT BIG OL' WORLD! SUU!!
EH?!
Remember, you're walking a day in woman's shoes!!
TEE HEE HEE. I'VE ALWAYS WANTED A LI'L SISTER! SUU!!
AND WALKIN' DOWN THE STREET LIKE THIS IS JUST THE BESTY BESTEST IN THE WORLD! SUU!!
Tee hee hee.
Blush
Whoa, what a cutie!
MISHA-SAN, WHY ARE YOU ALWAYS TRYING TO BE MY MOM...
...OR MY BIG SISTER?
きゅ
Tee hee hee.
For you, Kotarou-chan, I'll be anythin' yas wants mes to be!
~~~
BUT TO BE VERY HONEST, I DON'T THINK THAT I'LL LEARN ANYTHING ABOUT GIRLS' FEELINGS IF I JUST WALK AROUND LIKE THIS.
All I've gathered so far is that it's really breezy up my skirt.
~~~

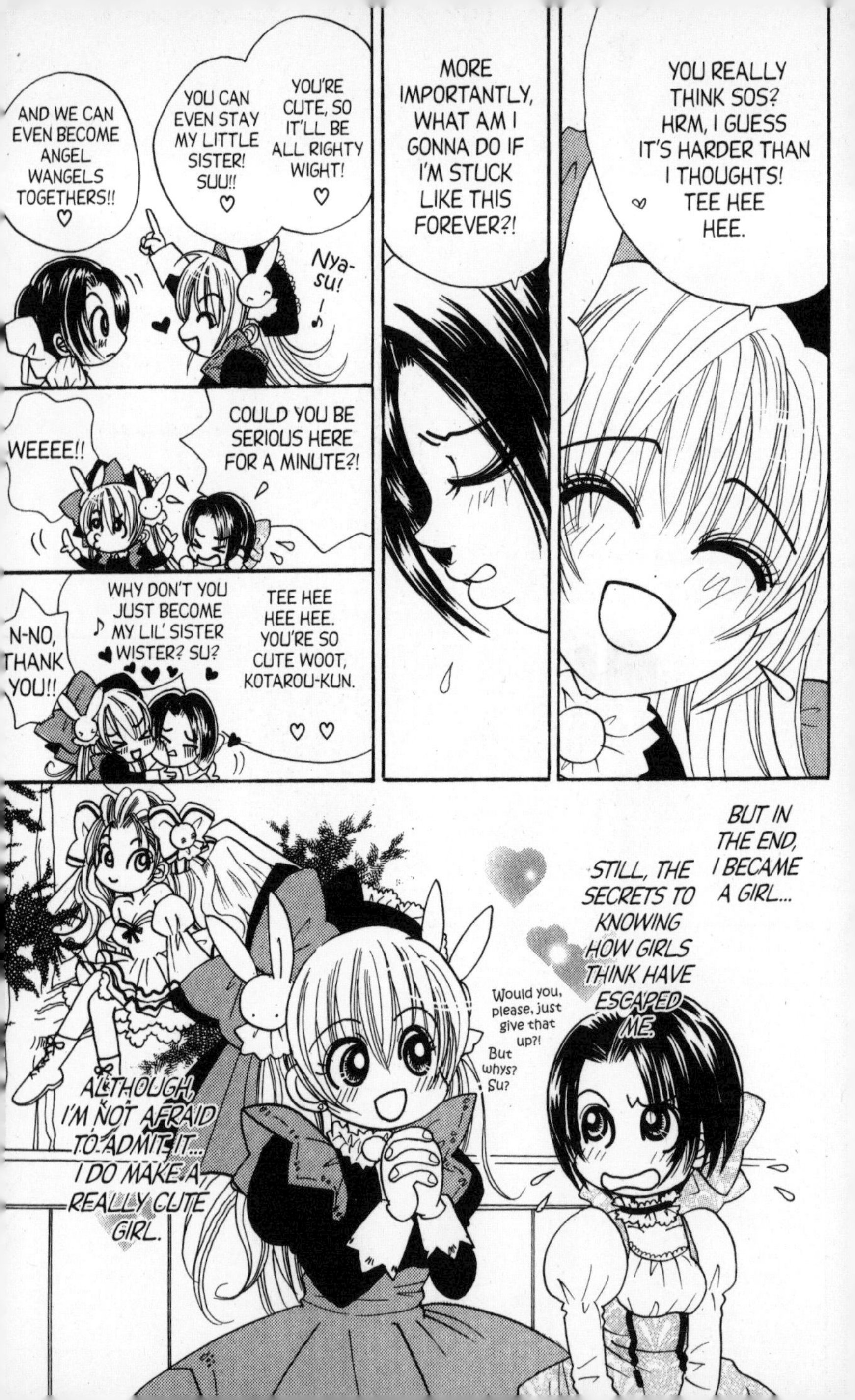
YOU REALLY THINK SOS? HRM, I GUESS IT'S HARDER THAN I THOUGHTS! TEE HEE HEE.
MORE IMPORTANTLY, WHAT AM I GONNA DO IF I'M STUCK LIKE THIS FOREVER?!
Nya-su!
YOU'RE CUTE, SO IT'LL BE ALL RIGHTY WIGHT!
YOU CAN EVEN STAY MY LITTLE SISTER! SUU!!
AND WE CAN EVEN BECOME ANGEL WANGELS TOGETHERS!!
COULD YOU BE SERIOUS HERE FOR A MINUTE?!
WEEEE!!
TEE HEE HEE HEE. YOU'RE SO CUTE WOOT, KOTAROU-KUN.
WHY DON'T YOU JUST BECOME MY LIL' SISTER WISTER? SU?
N-NO, THANK YOU!!
BUT IN THE END, I BECAME A GIRL...
STILL, THE SECRETS TO KNOWING HOW GIRLS THINK HAVE ESCAPED ME.
Would you, please, just give that up?!
But whys? Su?
ALTHOUGH, I'M NOT AFRAID TO ADMIT IT... I DO MAKE A REALLY CUTE GIRL.

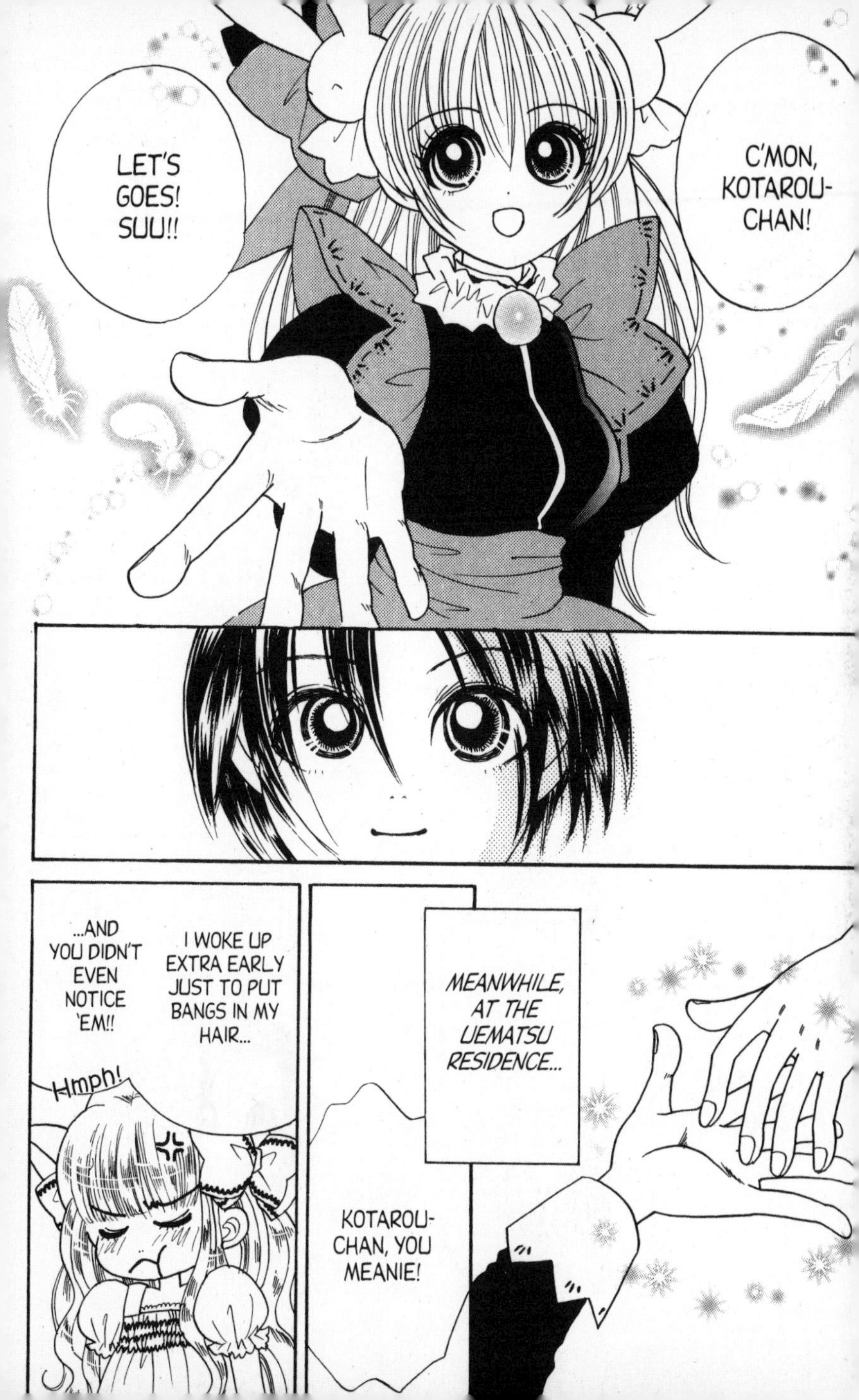
C'MON, KOTAROU-CHAN!
LET'S GOES! SUU!!
MEANWHILE, AT THE UEMATSU RESIDENCE...
KOTAROU-CHAN, YOU MEANIE!
I WOKE UP EXTRA EARLY JUST TO PUT BANGS IN MY HAIR...
...AND YOU DIDN'T EVEN NOTICE 'EM!!
Hmph!

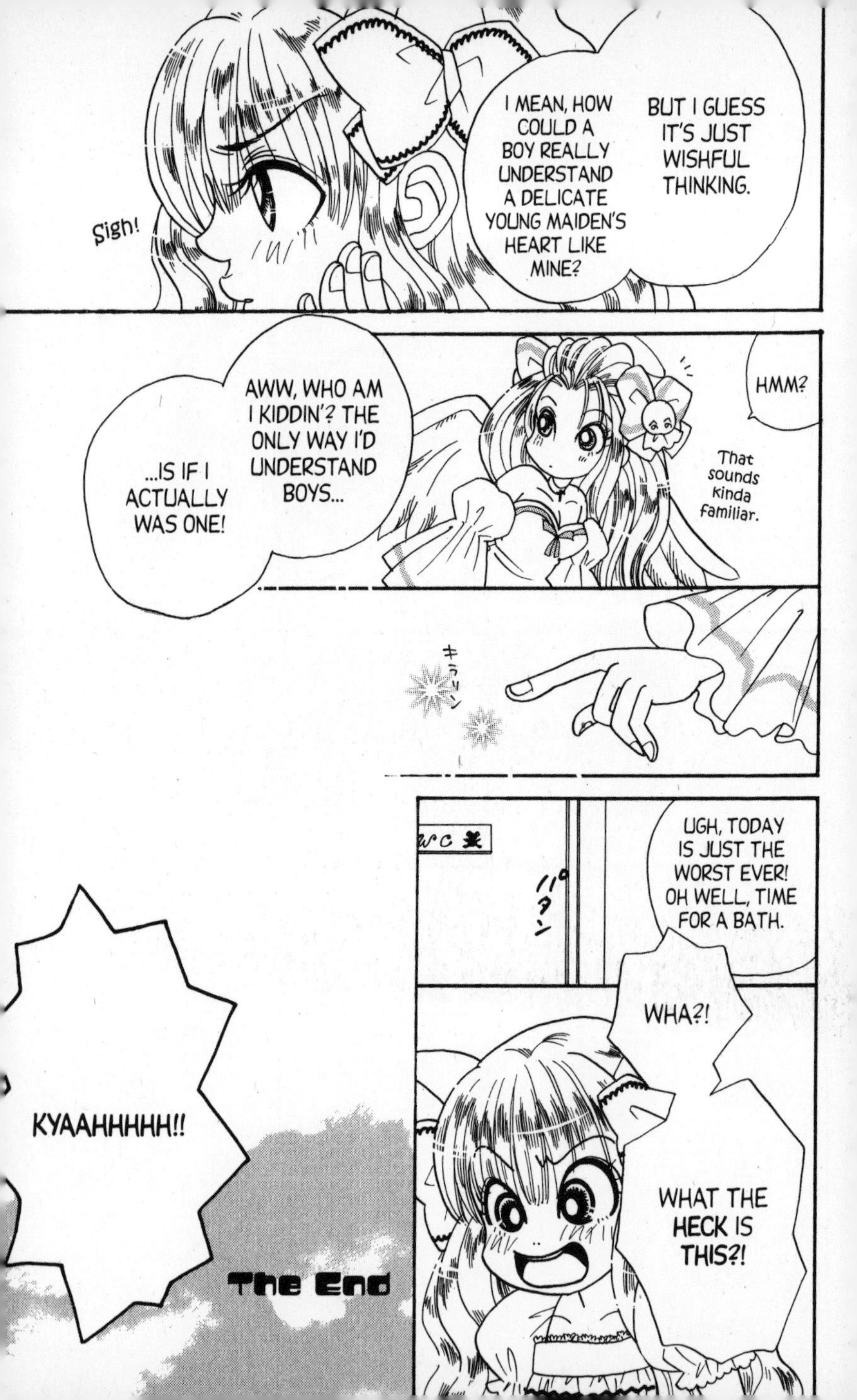
BUT I GUESS IT'S JUST WISHFUL THINKING.
I MEAN, HOW COULD A BOY REALLY UNDERSTAND A DELICATE YOUNG MAIDEN'S HEART LIKE MINE?
Sigh!
HMM?
That sounds kinda familiar.
AWW, WHO AM I KIDDIN'? THE ONLY WAY I'D UNDERSTAND BOYS...
...IS IF I ACTUALLY WAS ONE!
キラリン
UGH, TODAY IS JUST THE WORST EVER! OH WELL, TIME FOR A BATH.
パタン
WC
WHA?!
WHAT THE HECK IS THIS?!
KYAAHHHHH!!
The End

How to Become a Proper Adult

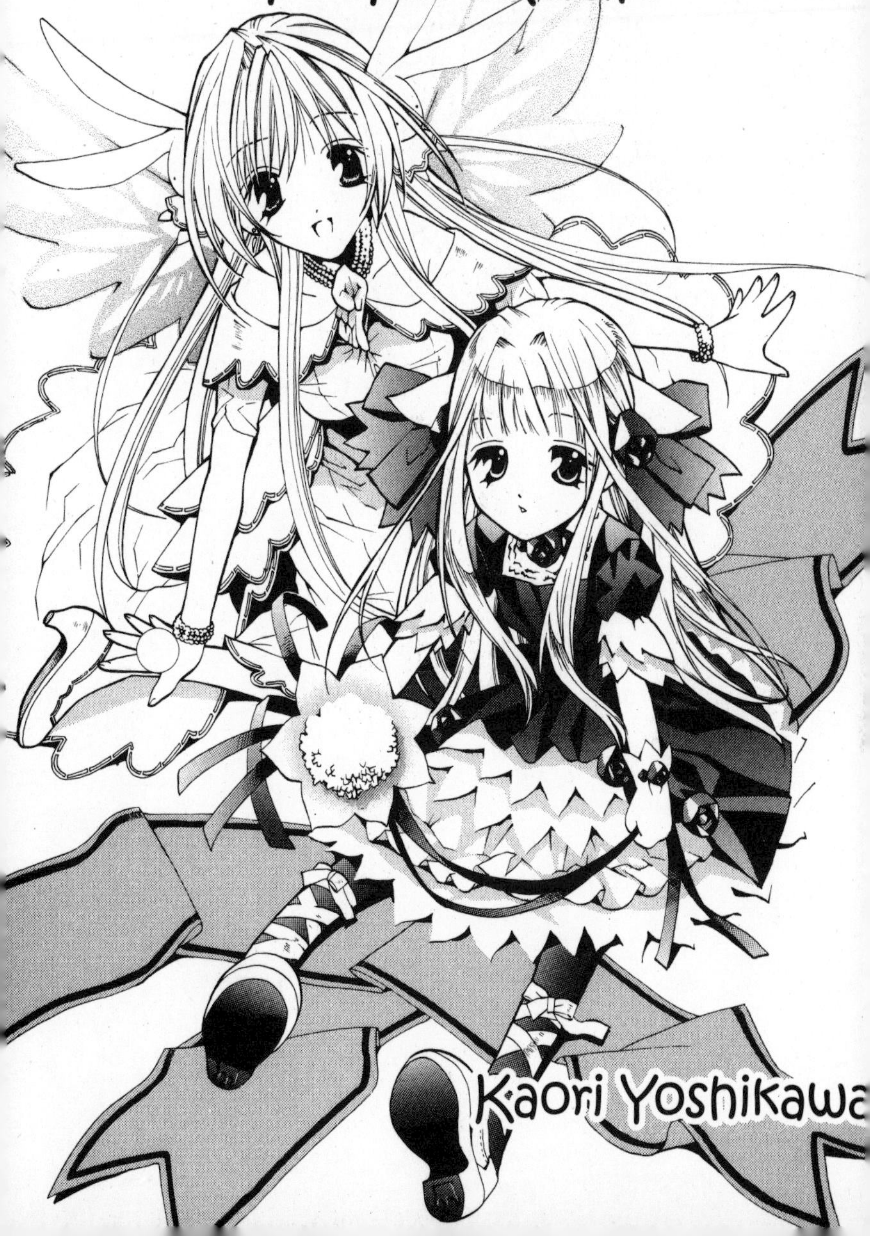
Kaori Yoshikawa

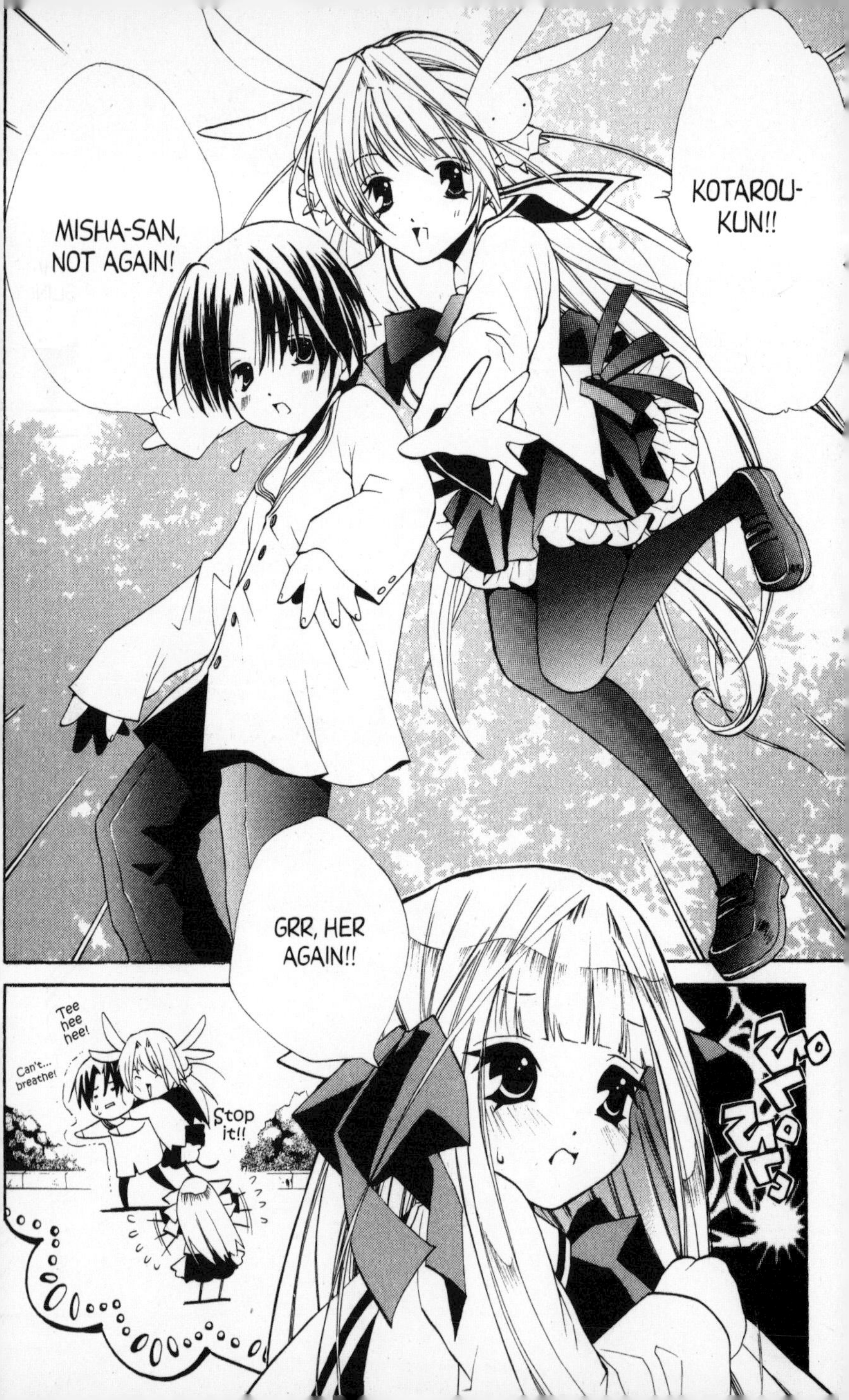
KOTAROU-KUN!!
MISHA-SAN, NOT AGAIN!
GRR, HER AGAIN!!
Tee hee hee!
Stop it!!
Can't... breathe!

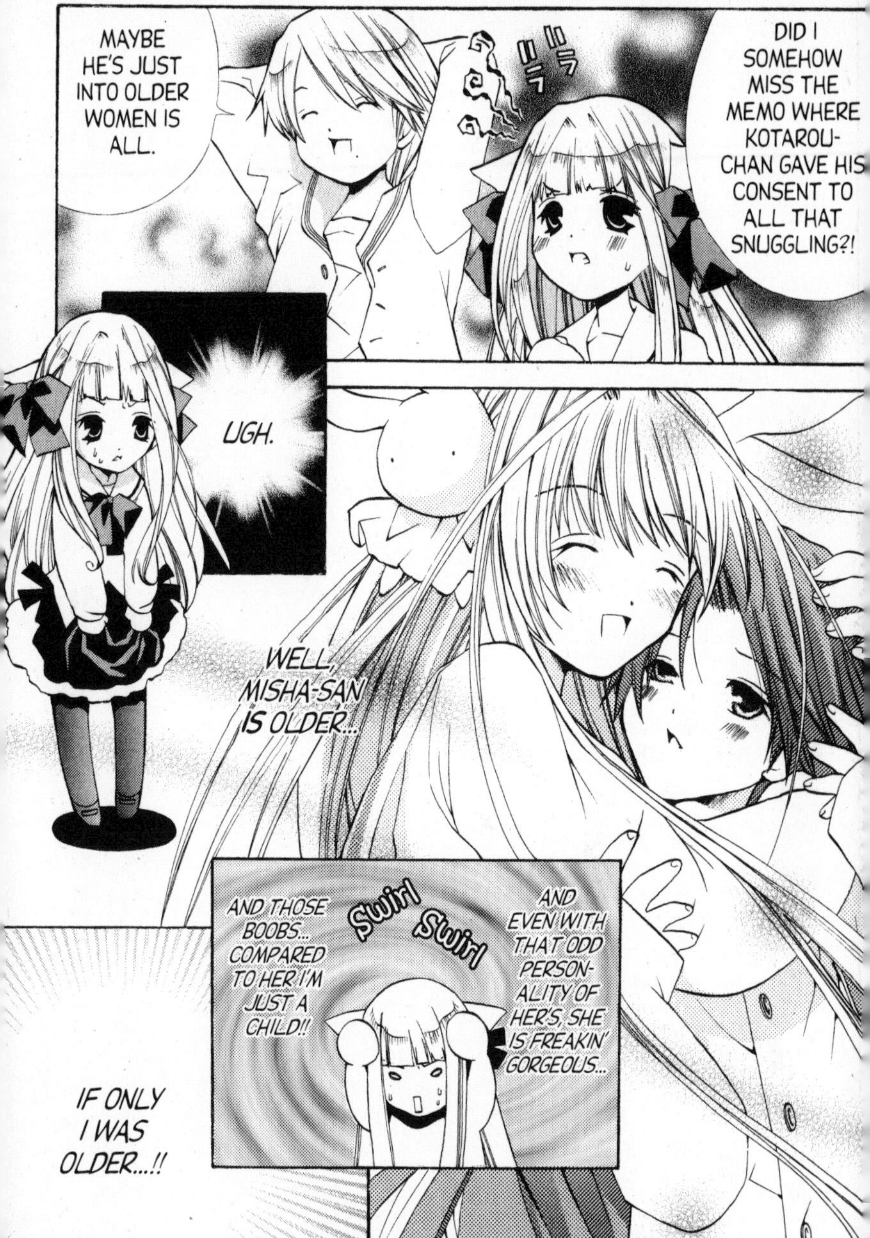
DID I SOMEHOW MISS THE MEMO WHERE KOTAROU-CHAN GAVE HIS CONSENT TO ALL THAT SNUGGLING?!
MAYBE HE'S JUST INTO OLDER WOMEN IS ALL.
UGH.
WELL, MISHA-SAN IS OLDER...
AND EVEN WITH THAT ODD PERSONALITY OF HER'S, SHE IS FREAKIN' GORGEOUS...
Swirl
Swirl
AND THOSE BOOBS... COMPARED TO HER I'M JUST A CHILD!!
IF ONLY I WAS OLDER...!!

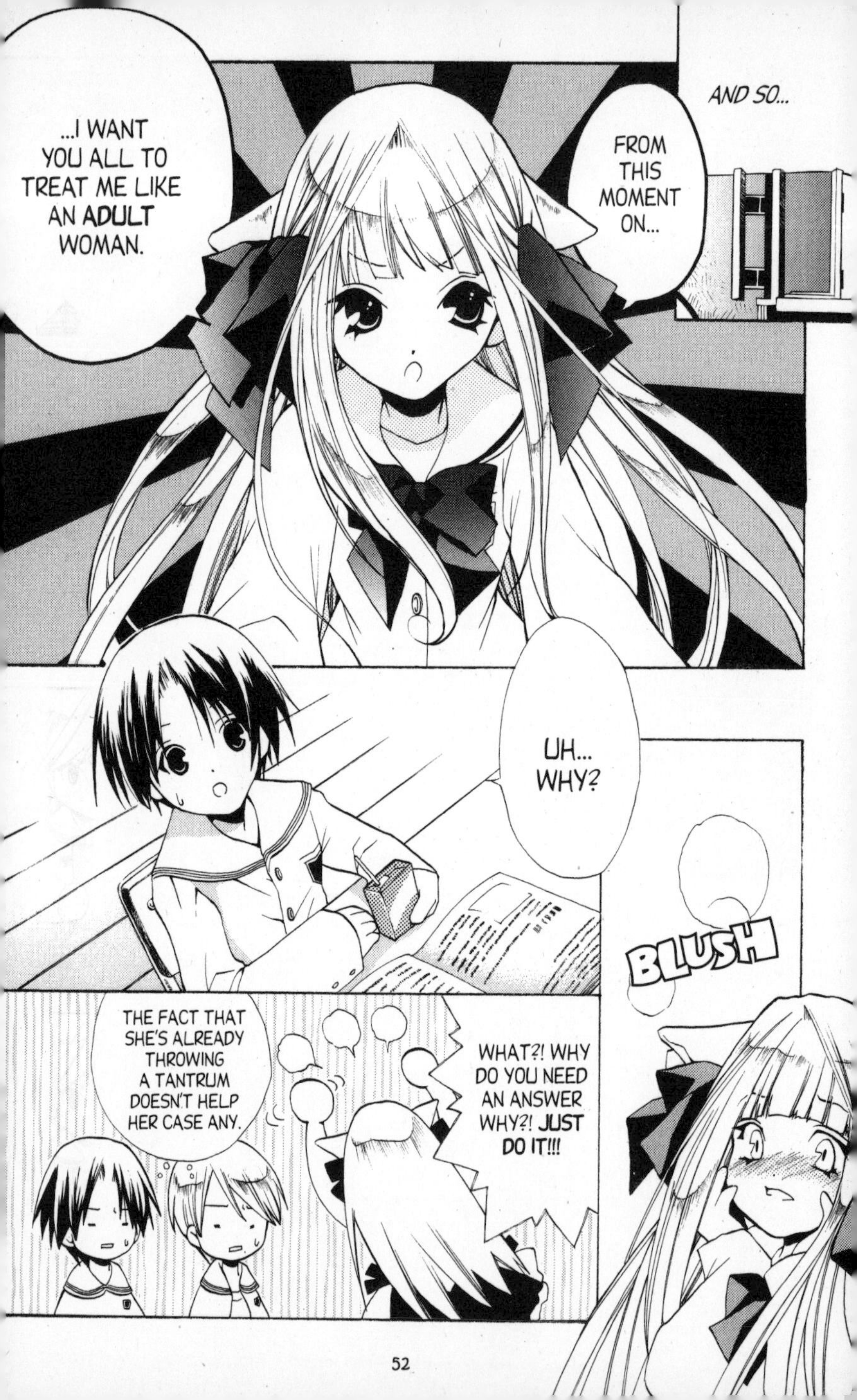

AND SO...
FROM THIS MOMENT ON...
...I WANT YOU ALL TO TREAT ME LIKE AN **ADULT** WOMAN.
UH... WHY?
BLUSH
WHAT?! WHY DO YOU NEED AN ANSWER WHY?! **JUST DO IT!!!**
THE FACT THAT SHE'S ALREADY THROWING A TANTRUM DOESN'T HELP HER CASE ANY.

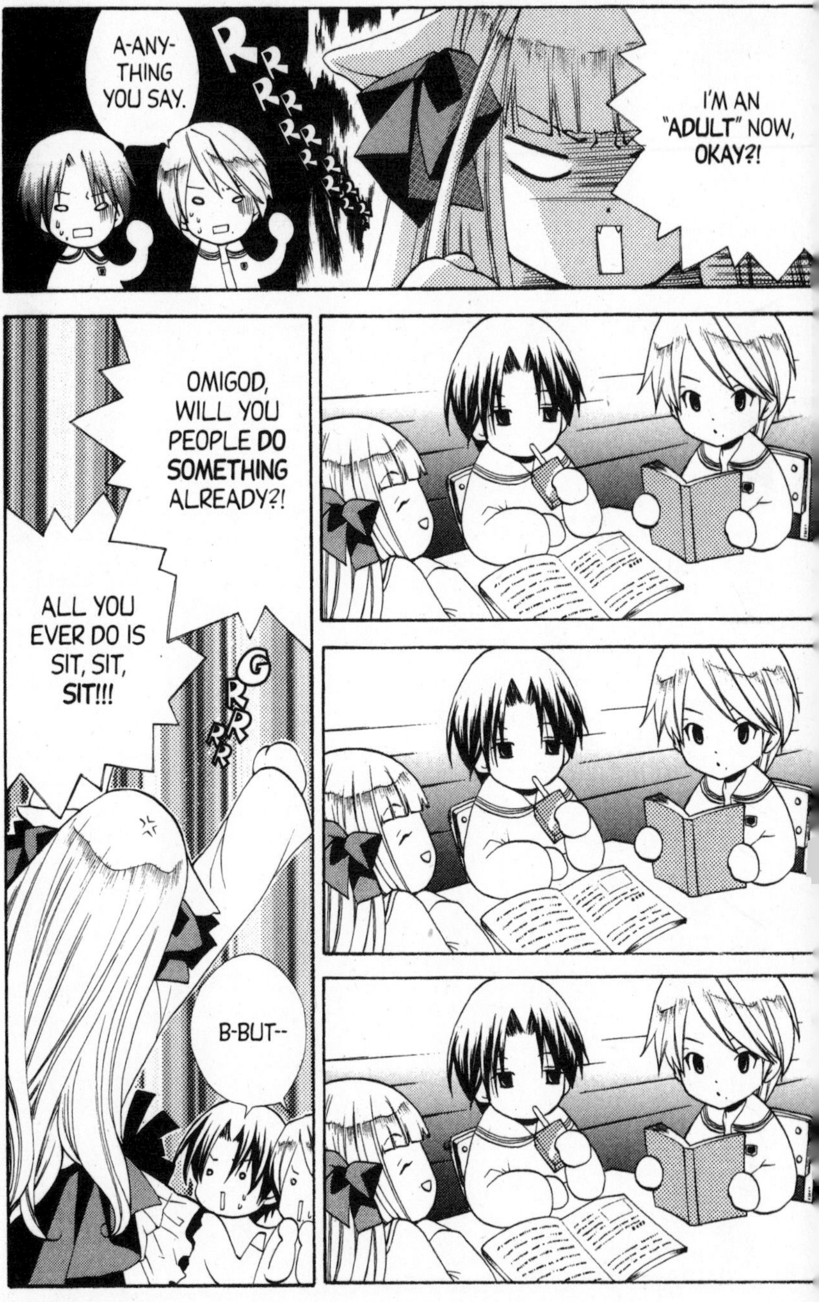
I'M AN "ADULT" NOW, OKAY?!
RRRRRRRRRRRR
A-ANY-THING YOU SAY.
OMIGOD, WILL YOU PEOPLE DO SOMETHING ALREADY?!
ALL YOU EVER DO IS SIT, SIT, SIT!!!
GRRRR
B-BUT--

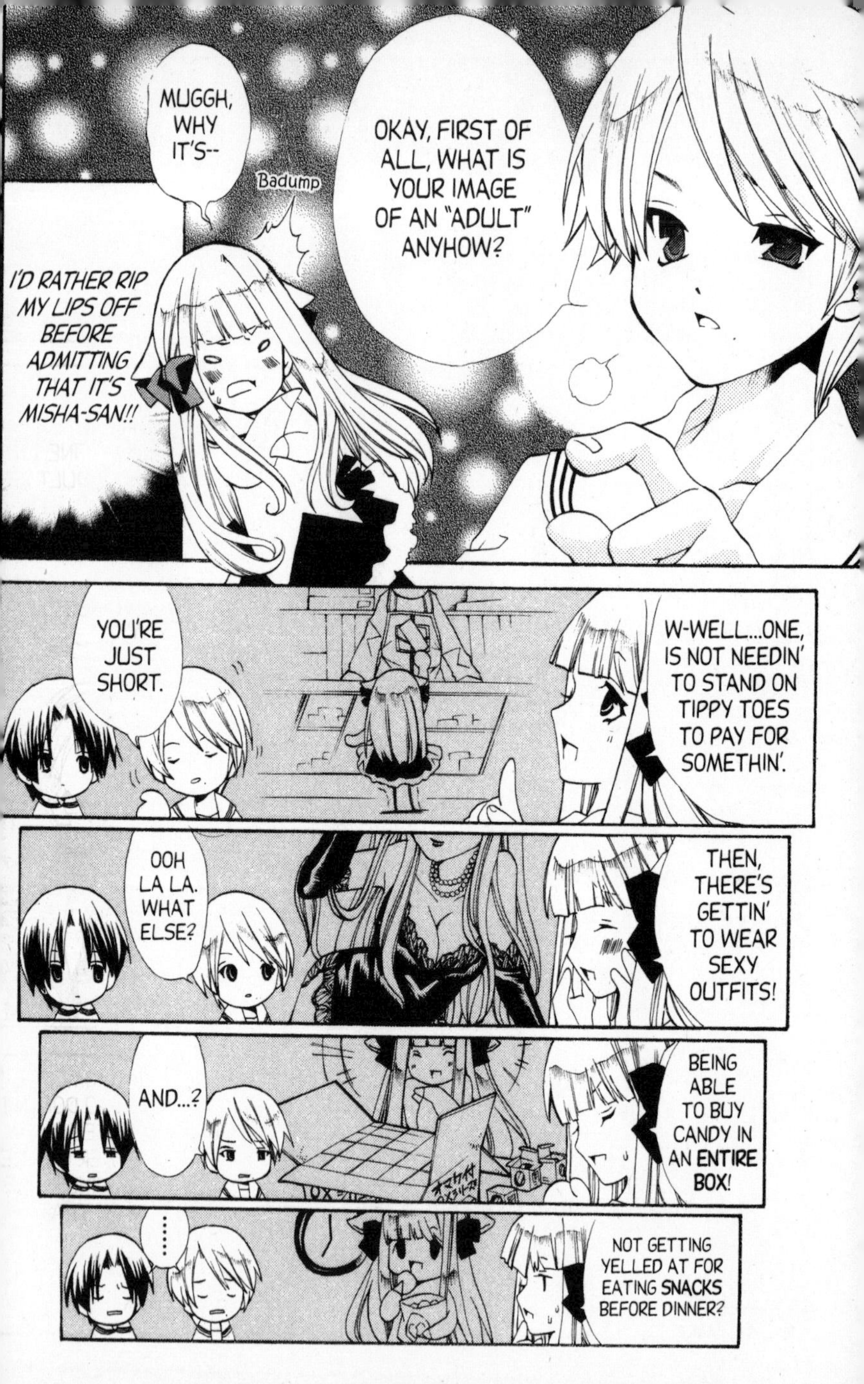
OKAY, FIRST OF ALL, WHAT IS YOUR IMAGE OF AN "ADULT" ANYHOW?
Badump
MUGGH, WHY IT'S--
I'D RATHER RIP MY LIPS OFF BEFORE ADMITTING THAT IT'S MISHA-SAN!!
W-WELL...ONE, IS NOT NEEDIN' TO STAND ON TIPPY TOES TO PAY FOR SOMETHIN'.
YOU'RE JUST SHORT.
THEN, THERE'S GETTIN' TO WEAR SEXY OUTFITS!
OOH LA LA. WHAT ELSE?
BEING ABLE TO BUY CANDY IN AN **ENTIRE BOX**!
AND...?
NOT GETTING YELLED AT FOR EATING **SNACKS** BEFORE DINNER?
......

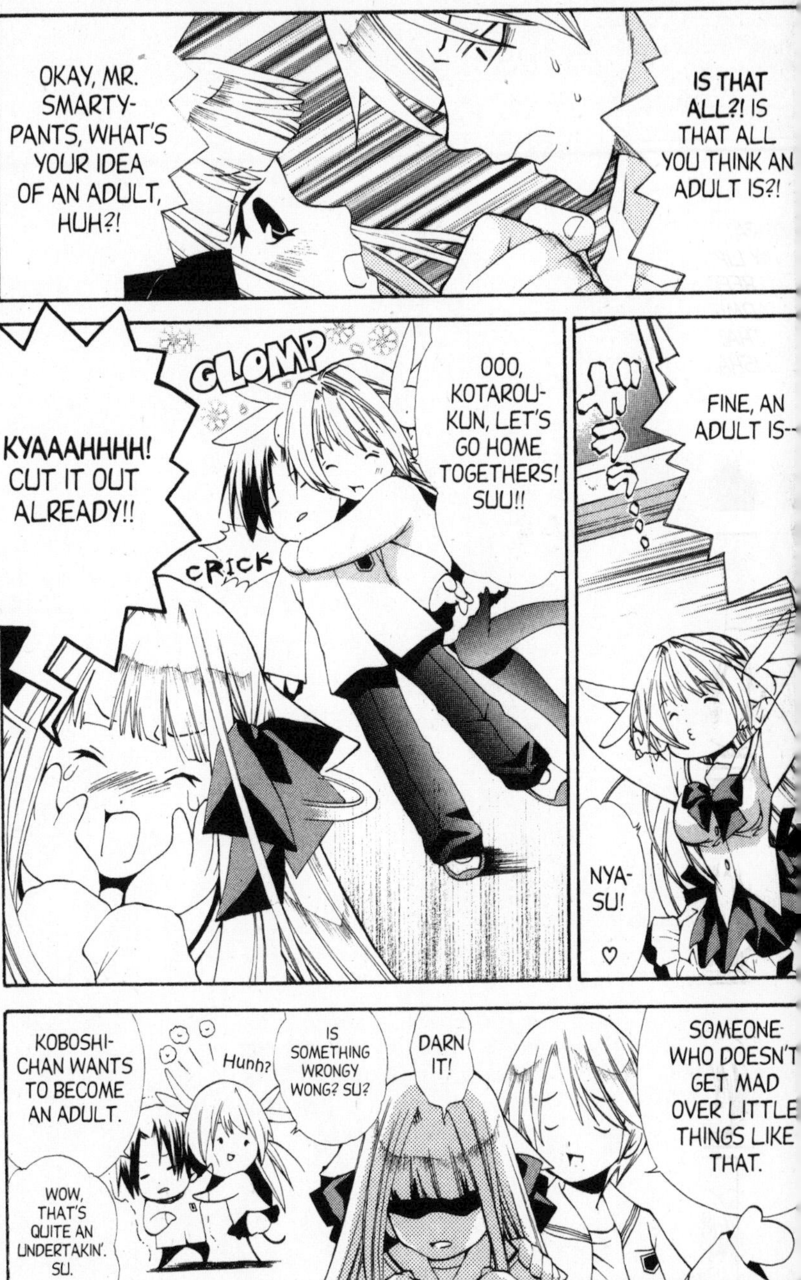
IS THAT ALL?! IS THAT ALL YOU THINK AN ADULT IS?!
OKAY, MR. SMARTY-PANTS, WHAT'S YOUR IDEA OF AN ADULT, HUH?!
FINE, AN ADULT IS--
NYA-SU! ♡
GLOMP
OOO, KOTAROU-KUN, LET'S GO HOME TOGETHERS! SUU!!
KYAAAHHHH! CUT IT OUT ALREADY!!
CRICK
SOMEONE WHO DOESN'T GET MAD OVER LITTLE THINGS LIKE THAT.
DARN IT!
IS SOMETHING WRONGY WONG? SU?
Hunh?
KOBOSHI-CHAN WANTS TO BECOME AN ADULT.
WOW, THAT'S QUITE AN UNDERTAKIN'. SU.

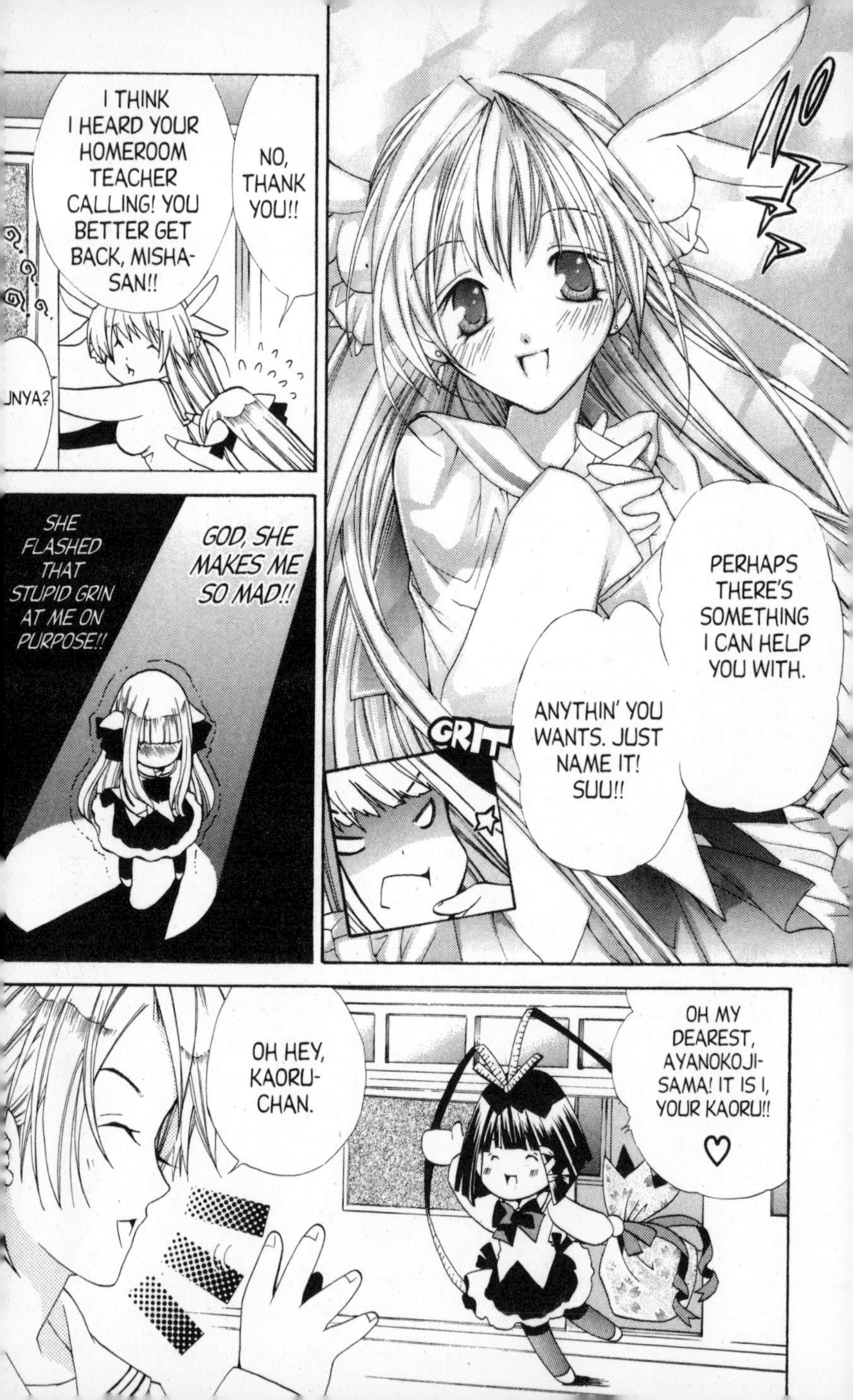
PERHAPS THERE'S SOMETHING I CAN HELP YOU WITH.
GRIT
ANYTHIN' YOU WANTS. JUST NAME IT! SUU!!
NO, THANK YOU!!
I THINK I HEARD YOUR HOMEROOM TEACHER CALLING! YOU BETTER GET BACK, MISHA-SAN!!
UNYA?
GOD, SHE MAKES ME SO MAD!!
SHE FLASHED THAT STUPID GRIN AT ME ON PURPOSE!!
OH MY DEAREST, AYANOKOJI-SAMA! IT IS I, YOUR KAORU!! ♡
OH HEY, KAORU-CHAN.

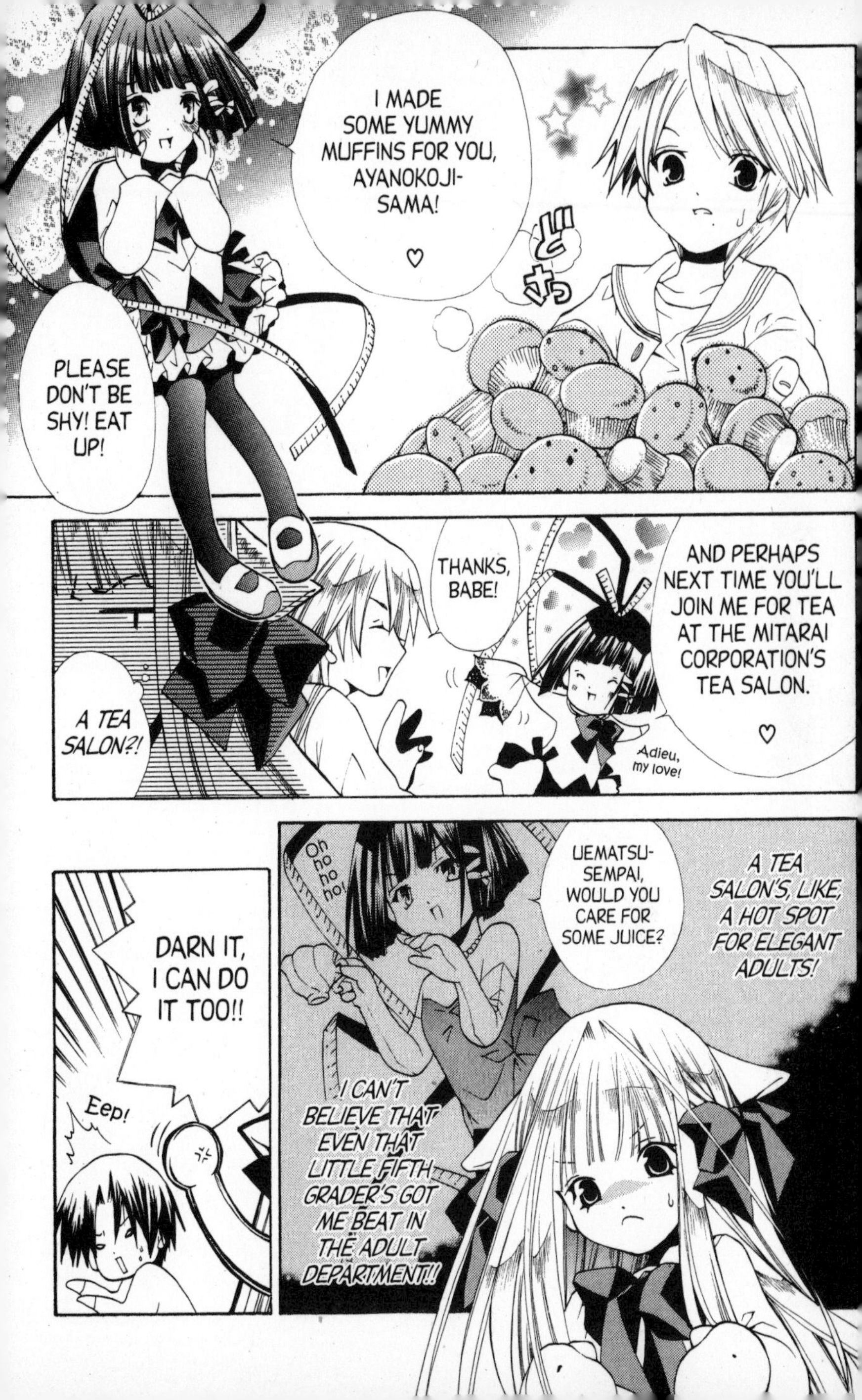

I MADE SOME YUMMY MUFFINS FOR YOU, AYANOKOJI-SAMA! ♡
どさっ
PLEASE DON'T BE SHY! EAT UP!
AND PERHAPS NEXT TIME YOU'LL JOIN ME FOR TEA AT THE MITARAI CORPORATION'S TEA SALON. ♡
Adieu, my love!
THANKS, BABE!
A TEA SALON?!
A TEA SALON'S, LIKE, A HOT SPOT FOR ELEGANT ADULTS!
UEMATSU-SEMPAI, WOULD YOU CARE FOR SOME JUICE?
Oh ho ho ho!
I CAN'T BELIEVE THAT EVEN THAT LITTLE FIFTH GRADER'S GOT ME BEAT IN THE ADULT DEPARTMENT!!
DARN IT, I CAN DO IT TOO!!
Eep!

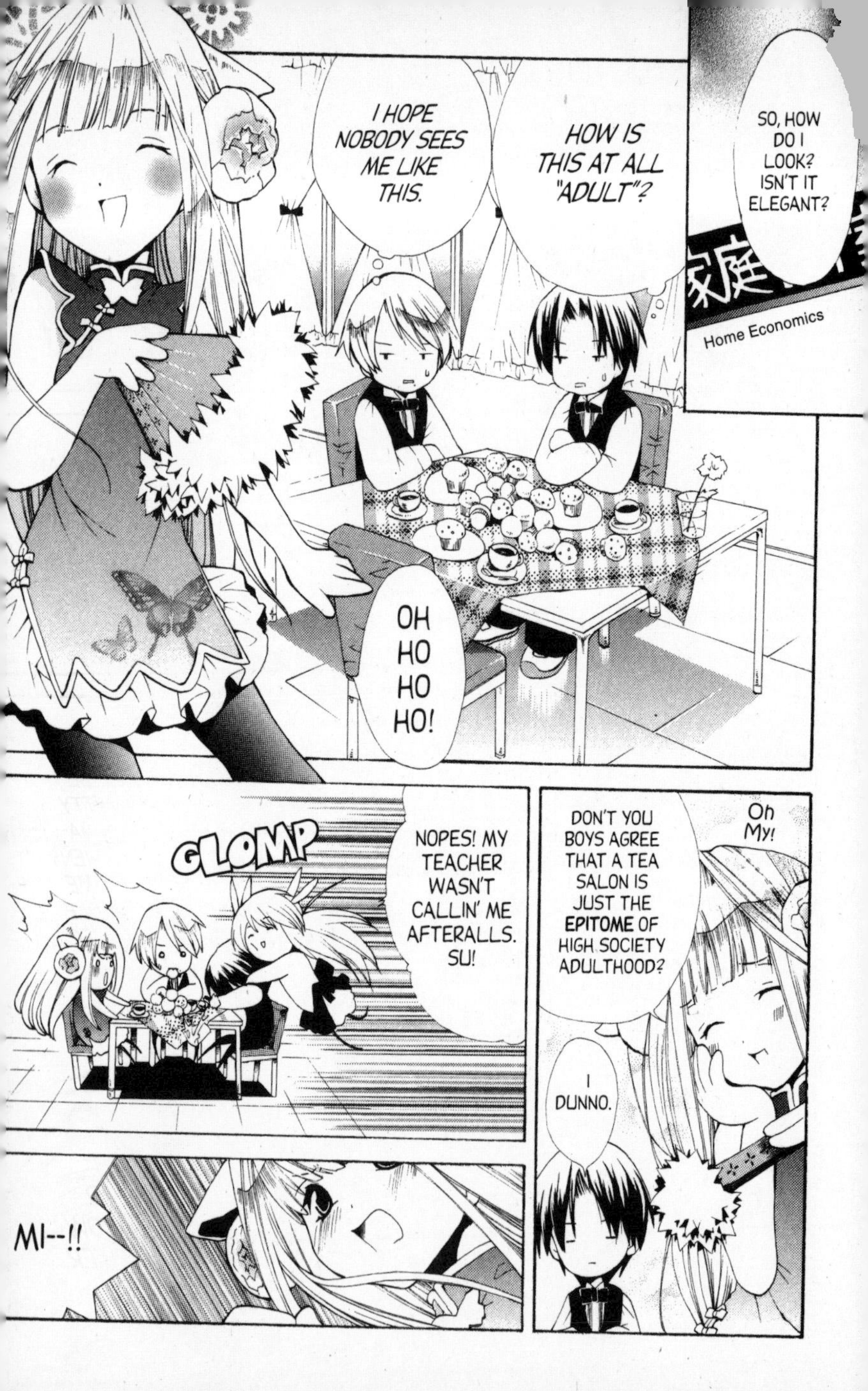
SO, HOW DO I LOOK? ISN'T IT ELEGANT?
家庭
Home Economics
HOW IS THIS AT ALL "ADULT"?
I HOPE NOBODY SEES ME LIKE THIS.
OH HO HO HO!
Oh My!
DON'T YOU BOYS AGREE THAT A TEA SALON IS JUST THE **EPITOME** OF HIGH SOCIETY ADULTHOOD?
I DUNNO.
GLOMP
NOPES! MY TEACHER WASN'T CALLIN' ME AFTERALLS. SU!
MI--!!

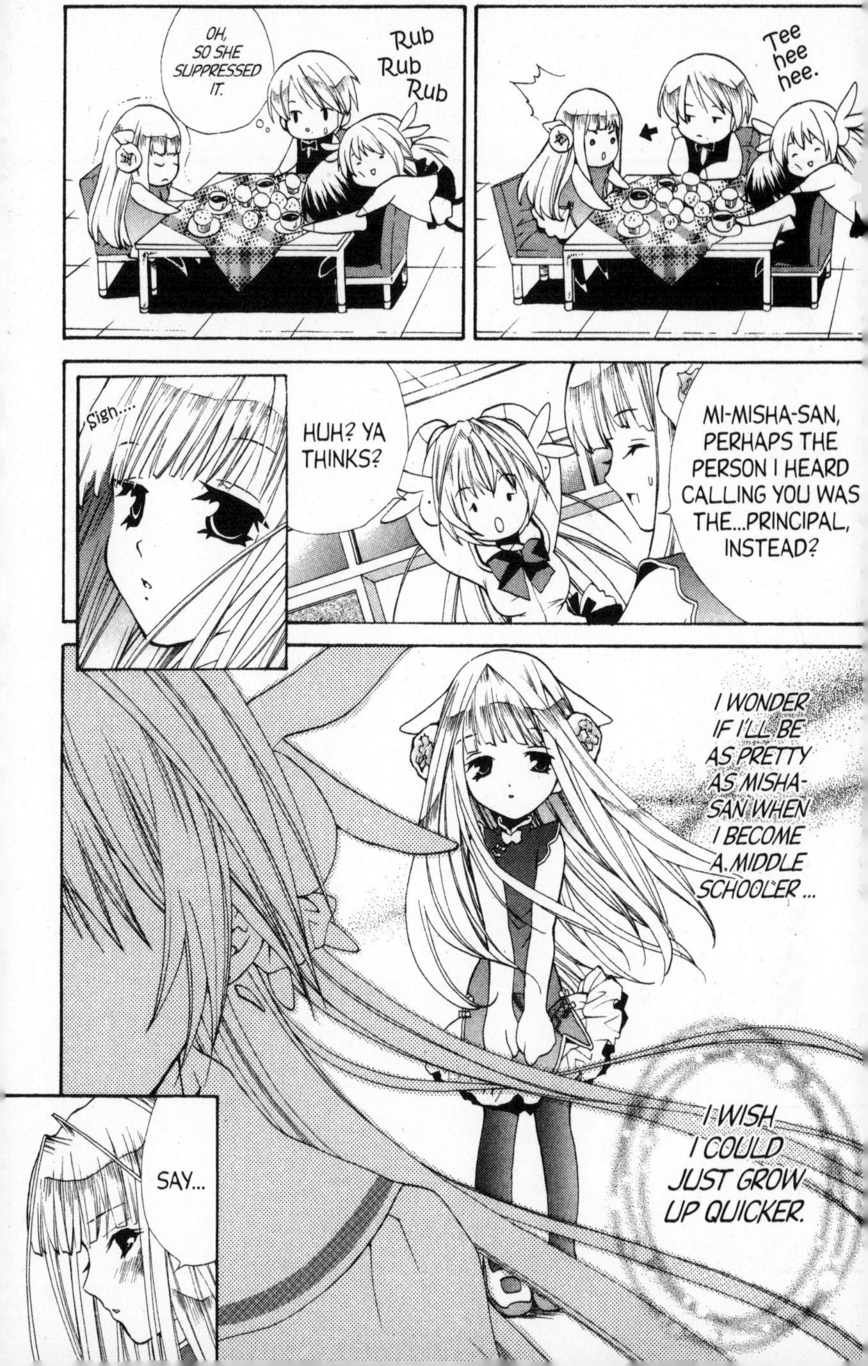
Tee hee hee.
OH, SO SHE SUPPRESSED IT.
Rub Rub Rub
MI-MISHA-SAN, PERHAPS THE PERSON I HEARD CALLING YOU WAS THE...PRINCIPAL, INSTEAD?
HUH? YA THINKS?
Sigh....
I WONDER IF I'LL BE AS PRETTY AS MISHA-SAN WHEN I BECOME A MIDDLE SCHOOLER ...
I WISH I COULD JUST GROW UP QUICKER.
SAY...

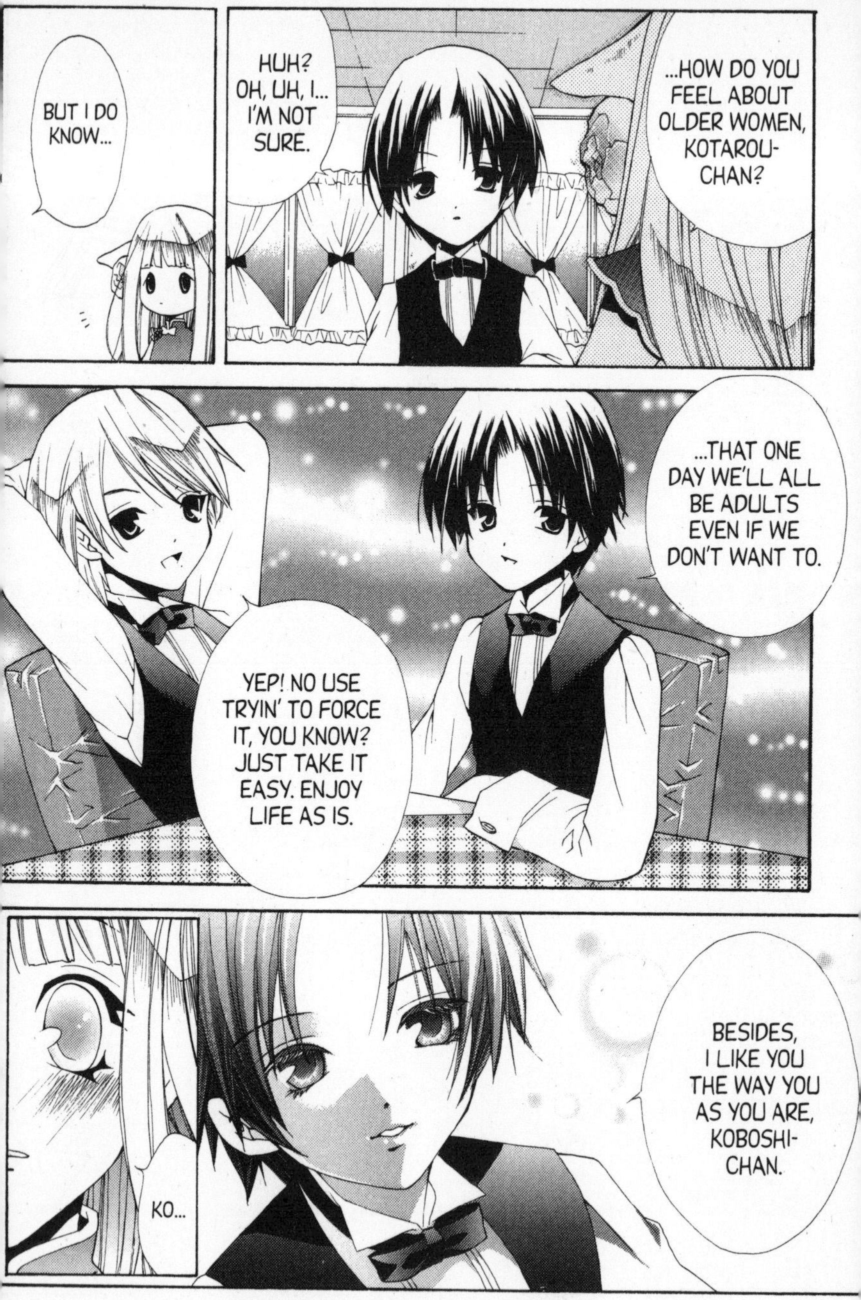
...HOW DO YOU FEEL ABOUT OLDER WOMEN, KOTAROU-CHAN?
HUH? OH, UH, I... I'M NOT SURE.
BUT I DO KNOW...
...THAT ONE DAY WE'LL ALL BE ADULTS EVEN IF WE DON'T WANT TO.
YEP! NO USE TRYIN' TO FORCE IT, YOU KNOW? JUST TAKE IT EASY. ENJOY LIFE AS IS.
BESIDES, I LIKE YOU THE WAY YOU AS YOU ARE, KOBOSHI-CHAN.
KO...

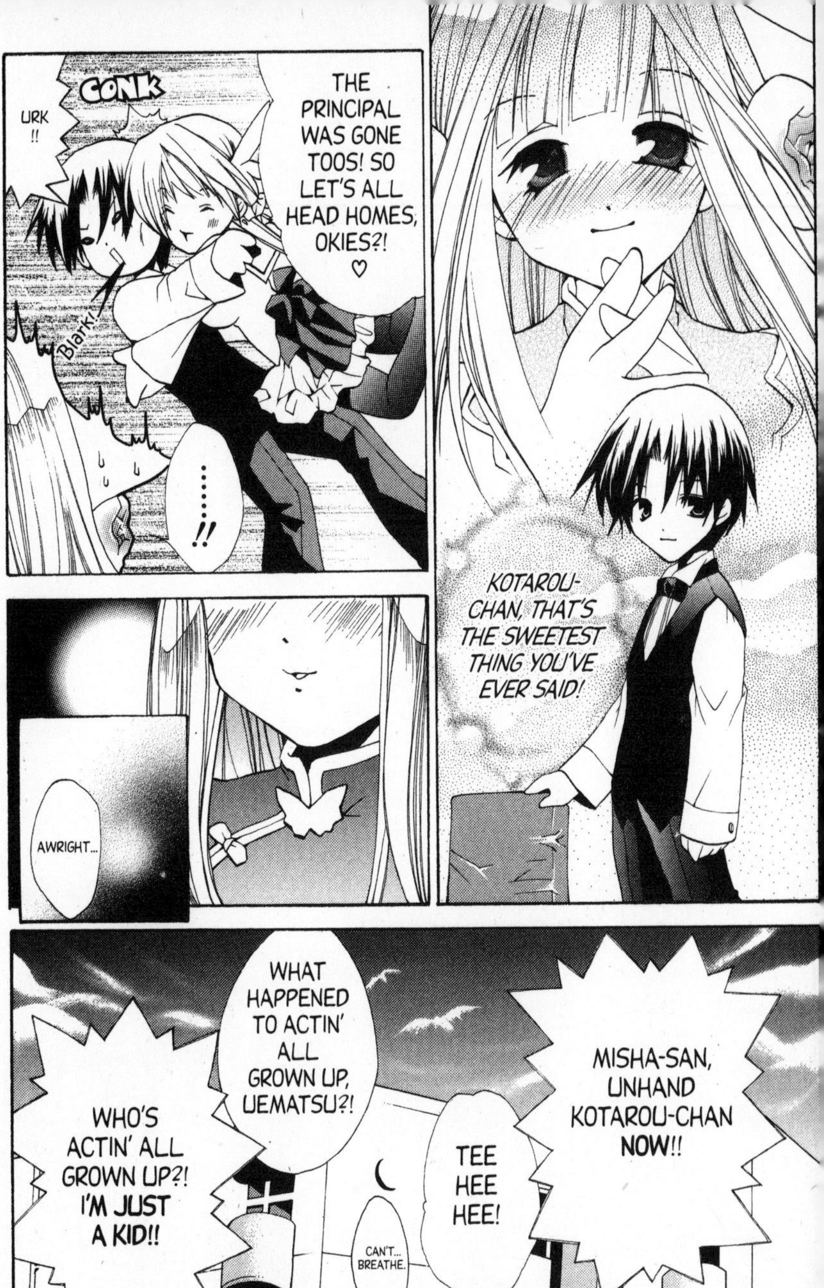
KOTAROU-CHAN, THAT'S THE SWEETEST THING YOU'VE EVER SAID!
THE PRINCIPAL WAS GONE TOOS! SO LET'S ALL HEAD HOMES, OKIES?! ♡
CONK
URK !!
Blark!
......!!
AWRIGHT...
MISHA-SAN, UNHAND KOTAROU-CHAN NOW!!
TEE HEE HEE!
WHAT HAPPENED TO ACTIN' ALL GROWN UP, UEMATSU?!
CAN'T... BREATHE.
WHO'S ACTIN' ALL GROWN UP?! I'M JUST A KID!!

The End

Kaori Yoshikawa

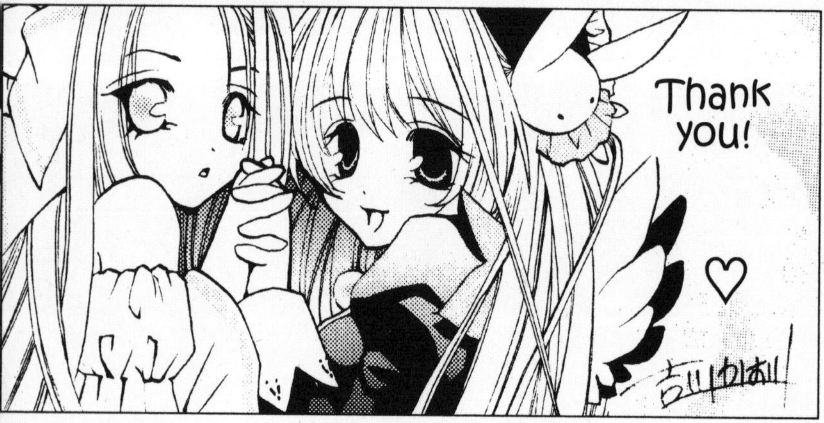
Thank you!
♡
吉川かおり

Writer's Talk

Asuka Izumi

Congratz on Volume 3!

Thank you very much for including me in this book. *Pita-Ten* is really getting exciting right now! But the anime's almost over!! It's gonna end soon!! What am I gonna wake up early for on Sunday mornings now?! (Sigh)

Whatever may happen,
I hope it happens with *Pita-Ten*!!
And with much happiness!!
(I have no idea what I'm saying anymore.)

I'm so happy to be part of this project.
Thank you so very, very much!!

2002.8 Asuka Izumi

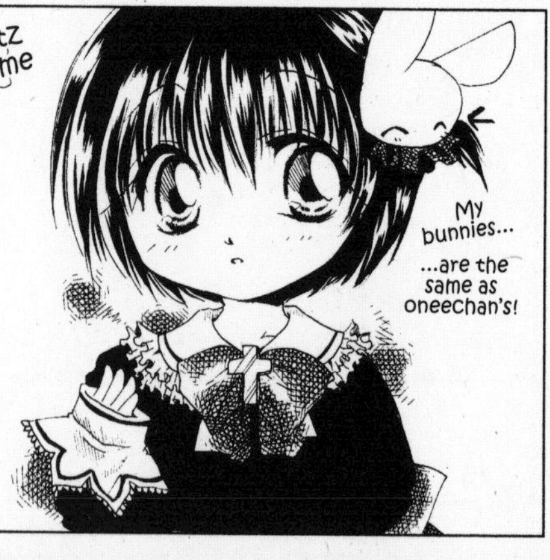
My bunnies...
...are the same as oneechan's!

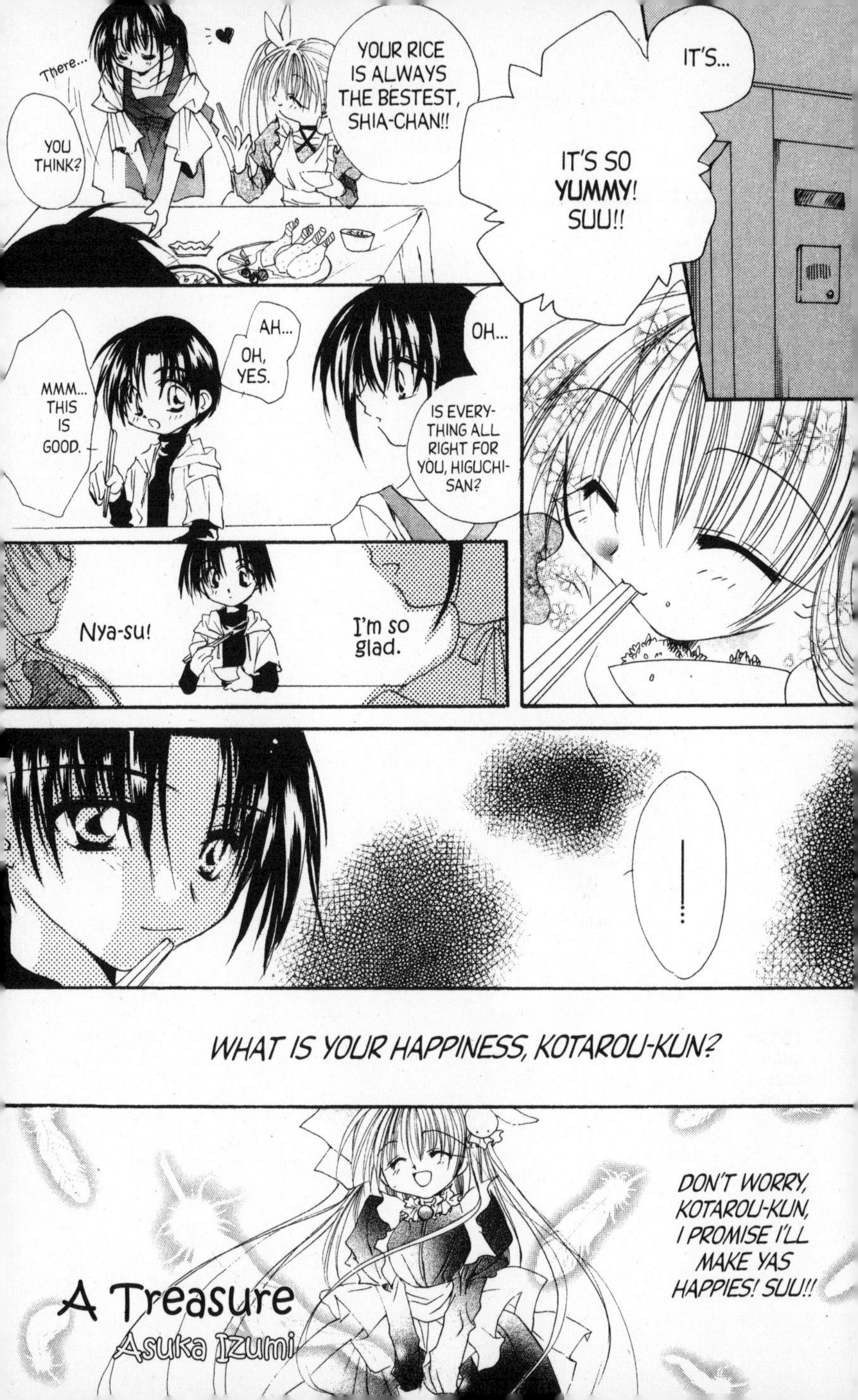
YOUR RICE IS ALWAYS THE BESTEST, SHIA-CHAN!!
There...
YOU THINK?
IT'S...
IT'S SO YUMMY! SUU!!
OH...
IS EVERYTHING ALL RIGHT FOR YOU, HIGUCHI-SAN?
AH... OH, YES.
MMM... THIS IS GOOD.
I'm so glad.
Nya-su!
!
WHAT IS YOUR HAPPINESS, KOTAROU-KUN?
DON'T WORRY, KOTAROU-KUN, I PROMISE I'LL MAKE YAS HAPPIES! SUU!!
A Treasure
Asuka Izumi

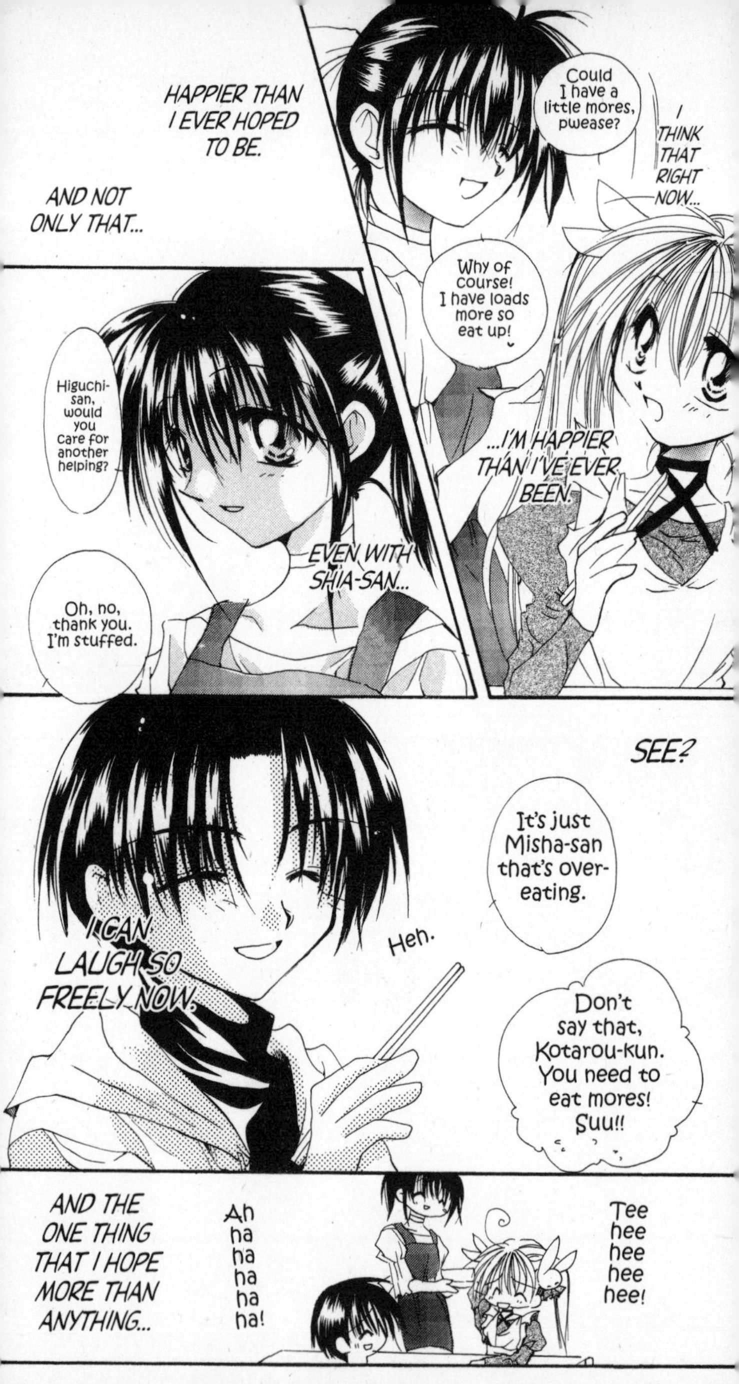
Could I have a little mores, pwease?
I THINK THAT RIGHT NOW...
Why of course! I have loads more so eat up!
...I'M HAPPIER THAN I'VE EVER BEEN.
HAPPIER THAN I EVER HOPED TO BE.
AND NOT ONLY THAT...
Higuchi-san, would you care for another helping?
EVEN WITH SHIA-SAN...
Oh, no, thank you. I'm stuffed.
SEE?
It's just Misha-san that's over-eating.
Heh.
I CAN LAUGH SO FREELY NOW.
Don't say that, Kotarou-kun. You need to eat mores! Suu!!
Tee hee hee hee hee!
Ah ha ha ha ha ha!
AND THE ONE THING THAT I HOPE MORE THAN ANYTHING...

TO NEVER LOSE MISHA-SAN.

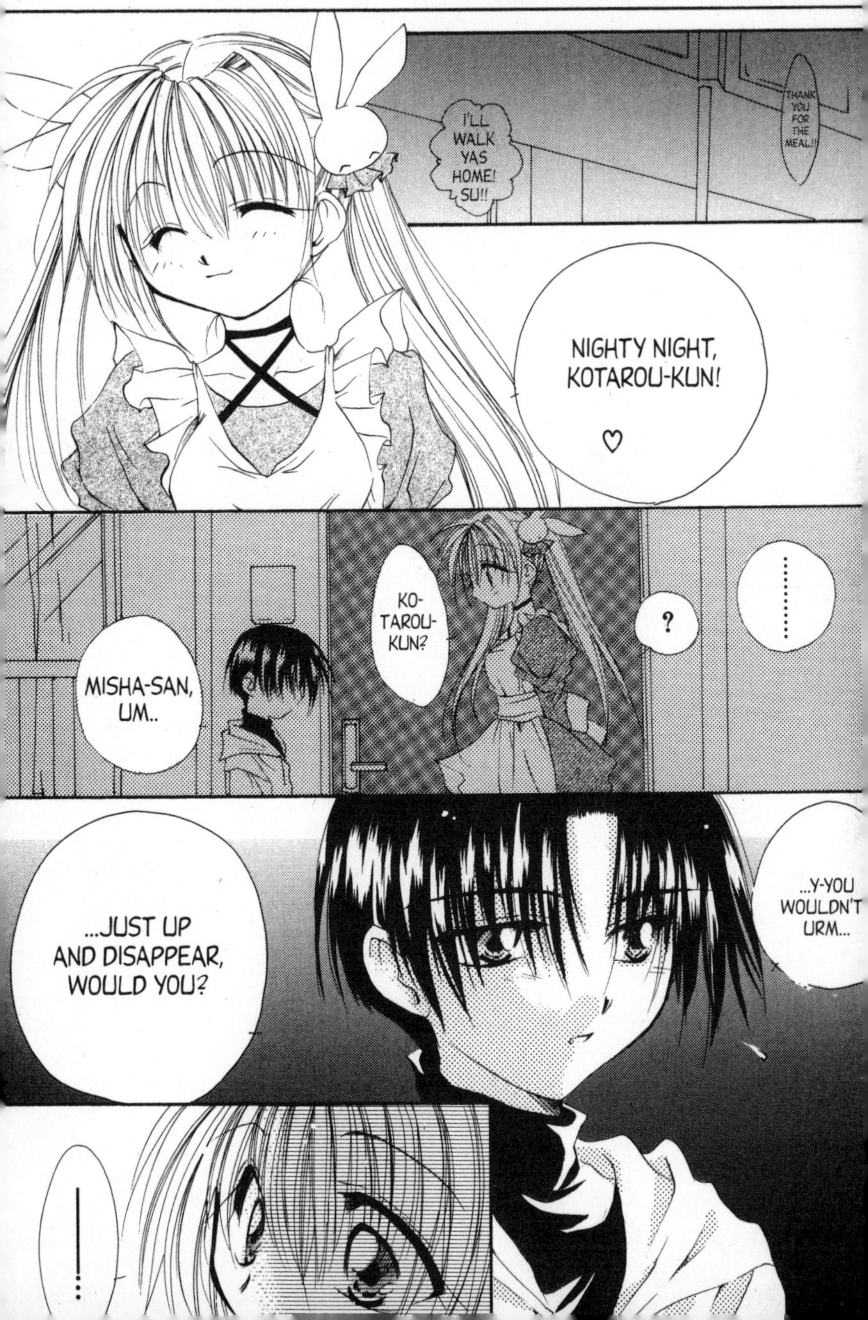
THANK YOU FOR THE MEAL!!
I'LL WALK YAS HOME! SU!!
NIGHTY NIGHT, KOTAROU-KUN! ♡
......
?
KO-TAROU-KUN?
MISHA-SAN, UM..
...Y-YOU WOULDN'T URM...
...JUST UP AND DISAPPEAR, WOULD YOU?
—......

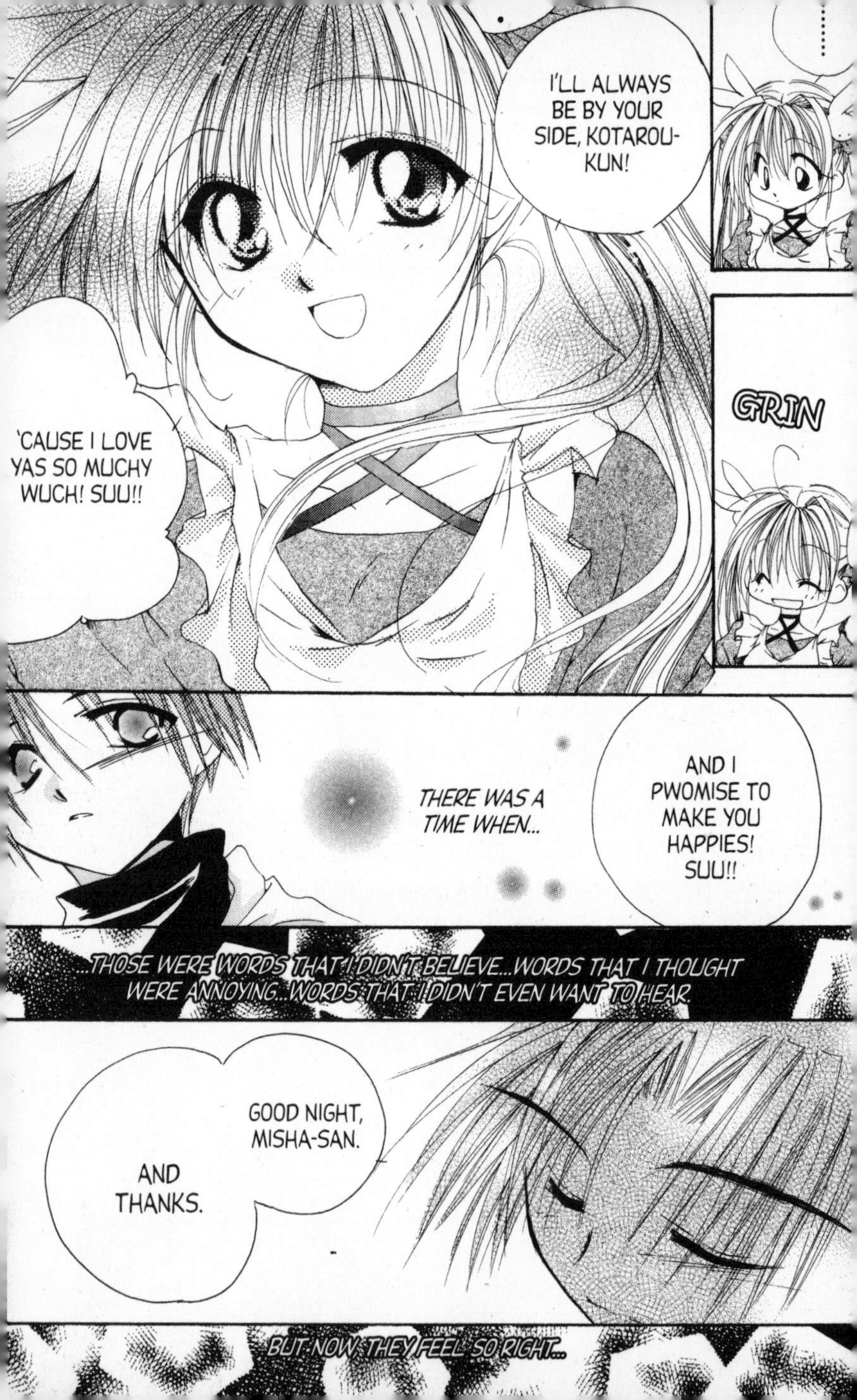
GRIN
I'LL ALWAYS BE BY YOUR SIDE, KOTAROU-KUN!
'CAUSE I LOVE YAS SO MUCHY WUCH! SUU!!
AND I PWOMISE TO MAKE YOU HAPPIES! SUU!!
THERE WAS A TIME WHEN...
...THOSE WERE WORDS THAT I DIDN'T BELIEVE...WORDS THAT I THOUGHT WERE ANNOYING...WORDS THAT I DIDN'T EVEN WANT TO HEAR.
GOOD NIGHT, MISHA-SAN.
AND THANKS.
BUT NOW, THEY FEEL SO RIGHT...

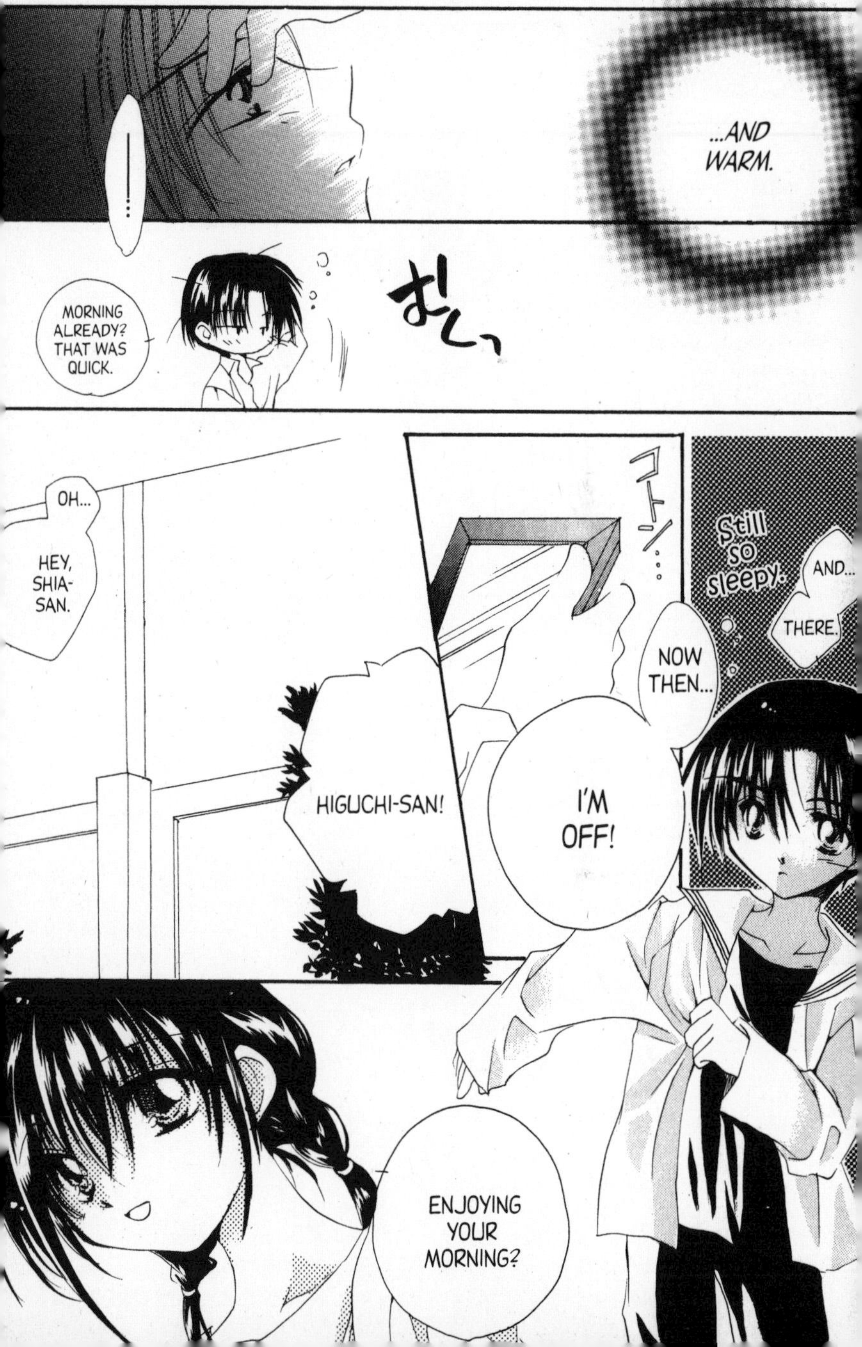
...AND WARM.
!...
MORNING ALREADY? THAT WAS QUICK.
Still so sleepy.
AND... THERE.
NOW THEN...
コトン...
I'M OFF!
HIGUCHI-SAN!
OH... HEY, SHIA-SAN.
ENJOYING YOUR MORNING?

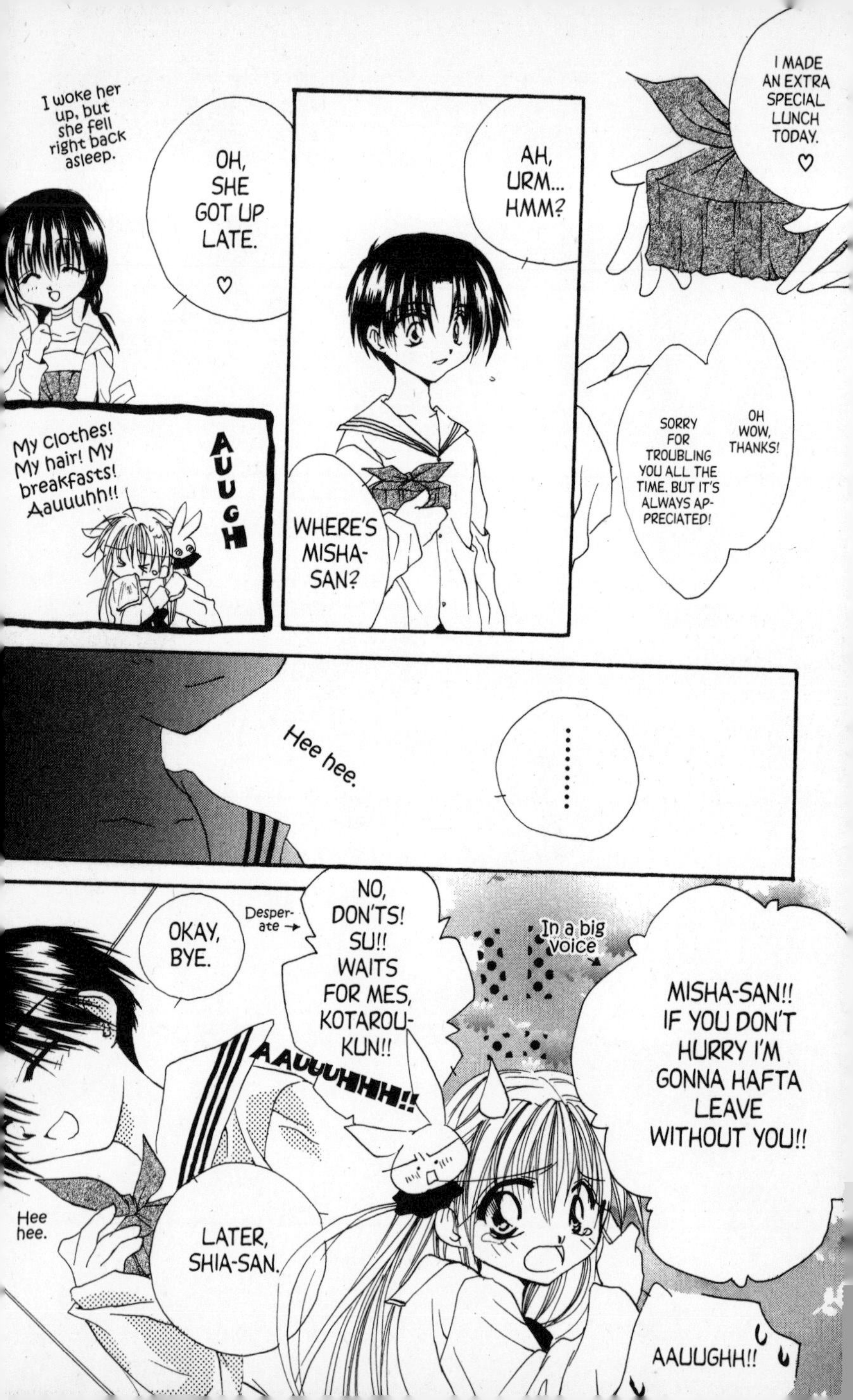

I MADE AN EXTRA SPECIAL LUNCH TODAY. ♡
OH WOW, THANKS!
SORRY FOR TROUBLING YOU ALL THE TIME. BUT IT'S ALWAYS AP-PRECIATED!
AH, URM... HMM?
WHERE'S MISHA-SAN?
OH, SHE GOT UP LATE. ♡
I woke her up, but she fell right back asleep.
AUUGH
My clothes! My hair! My breakfasts! Aauuuhh!!
……
Hee hee.
In a big voice
MISHA-SAN!! IF YOU DON'T HURRY I'M GONNA HAFTA LEAVE WITHOUT YOU!!
AAUUGHH!!
Desper-ate
NO, DON'TS! SU!! WAITS FOR MES, KOTAROU-KUN!!
AAUUUHHH!!
OKAY, BYE.
LATER, SHIA-SAN.
Hee hee.

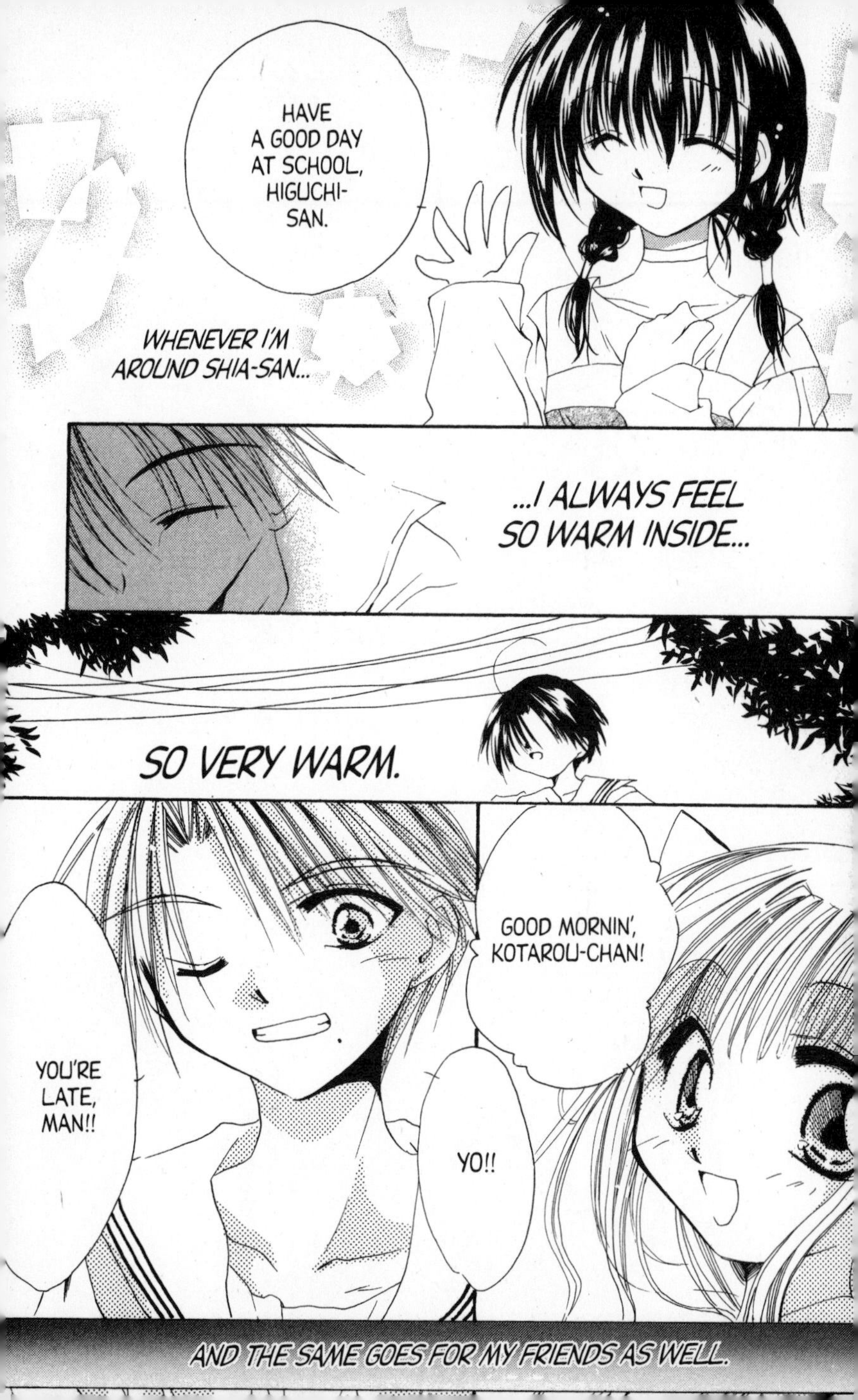
HAVE A GOOD DAY AT SCHOOL, HIGUCHI-SAN.
WHENEVER I'M AROUND SHIA-SAN...
...I ALWAYS FEEL SO WARM INSIDE...
SO VERY WARM.
GOOD MORNIN', KOTAROU-CHAN!
YOU'RE LATE, MAN!!
YO!!
AND THE SAME GOES FOR MY FRIENDS AS WELL.

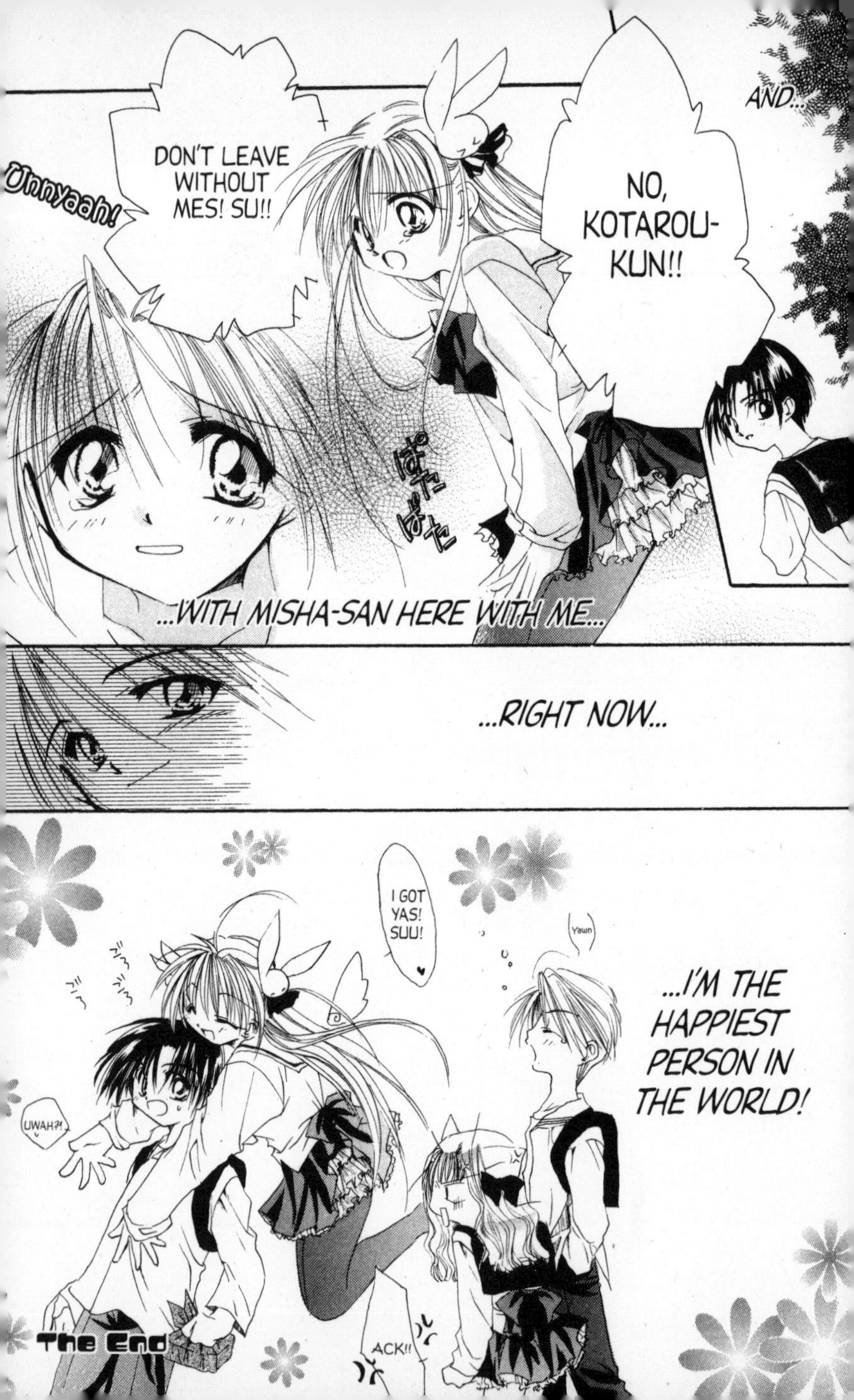
AND...
NO, KOTAROU-KUN!!
DON'T LEAVE WITHOUT MES! SU!!
Unnyaah!
ぱたぱた
...WITH MISHA-SAN HERE WITH ME...
...RIGHT NOW...
...I'M THE HAPPIEST PERSON IN THE WORLD!
Yawn
I GOT YAS! SUU!
UWAH?!
ACK!!
The End

How to Tell a Good Lie

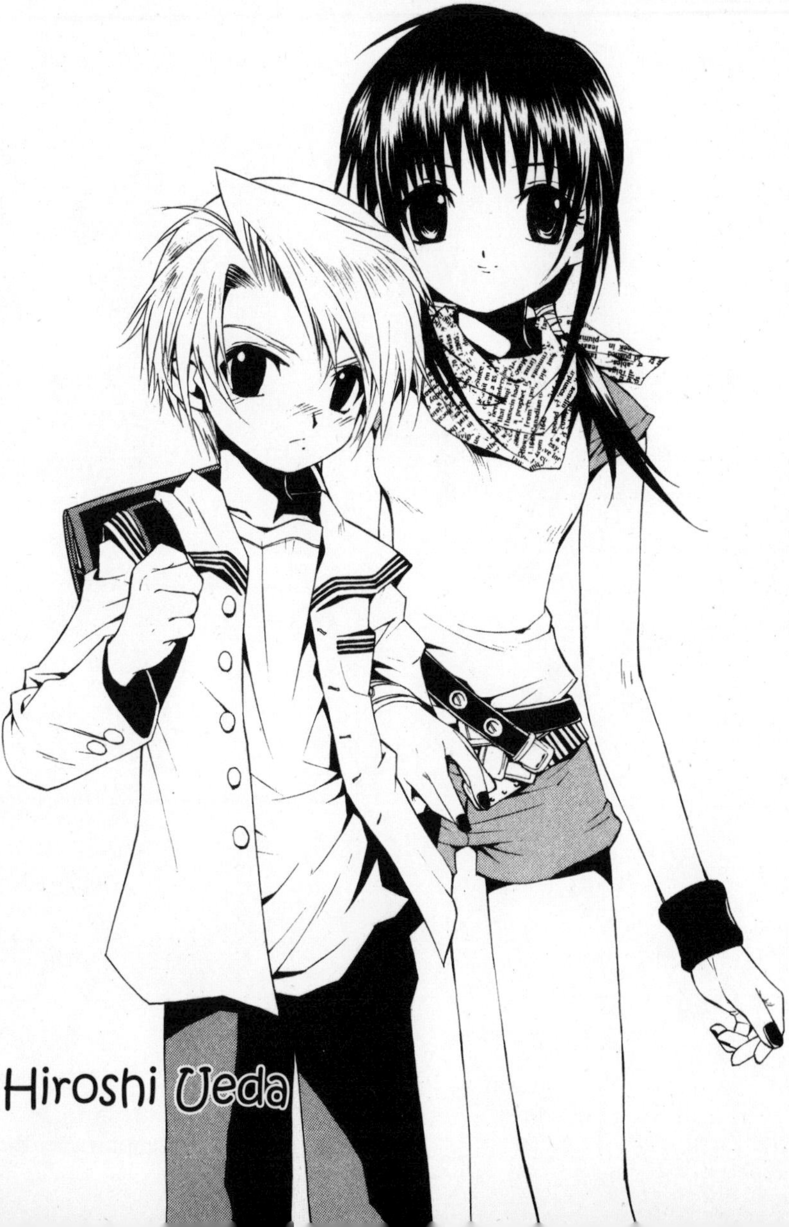

Hiroshi Ueda

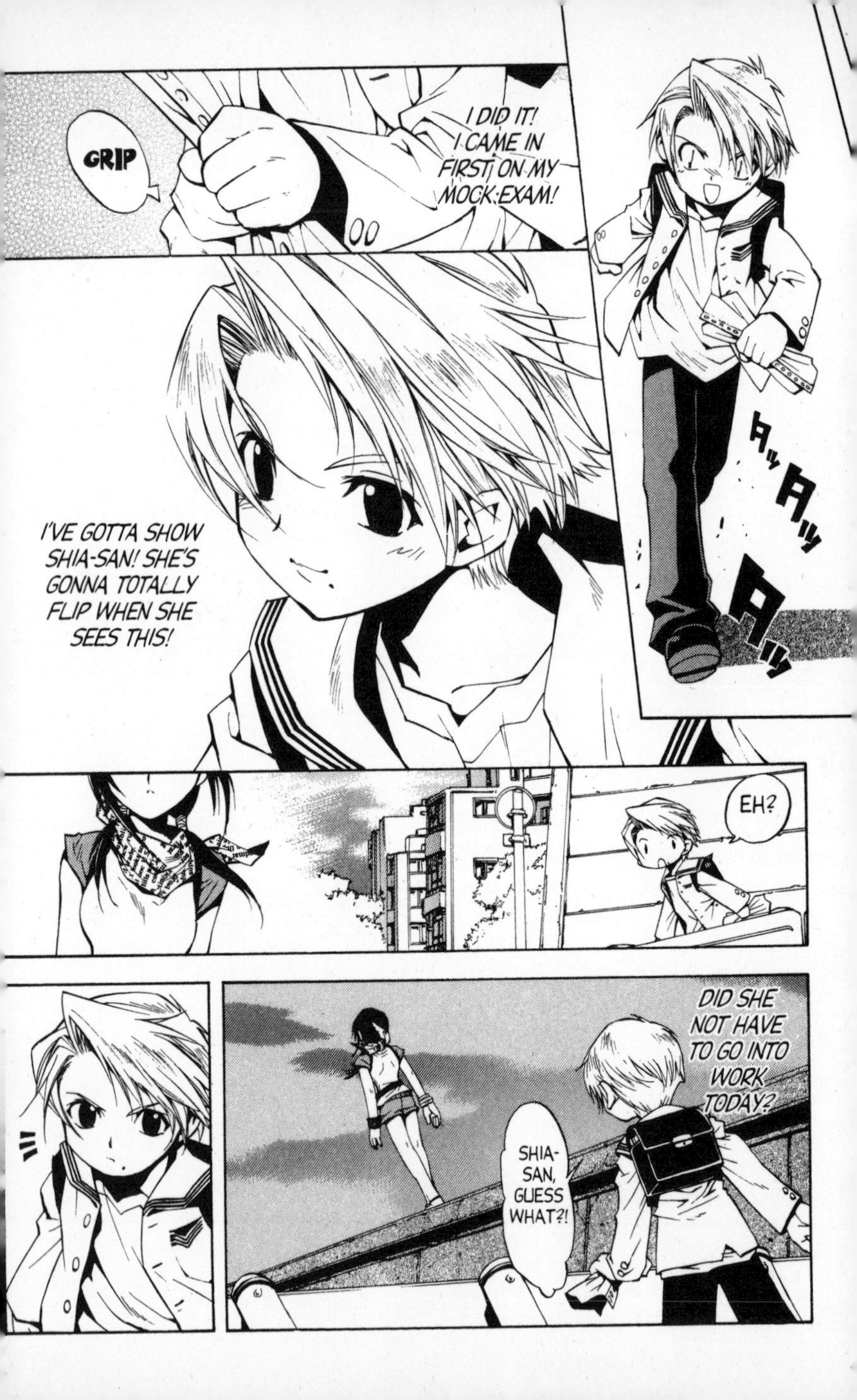
タッ
タッ
タッ
I DID IT! I CAME IN FIRST ON MY MOCK EXAM!
GRIP
I'VE GOTTA SHOW SHIA-SAN! SHE'S GONNA TOTALLY FLIP WHEN SHE SEES THIS!
EH?
DID SHE NOT HAVE TO GO INTO WORK TODAY?
SHIA-SAN, GUESS WHAT?!

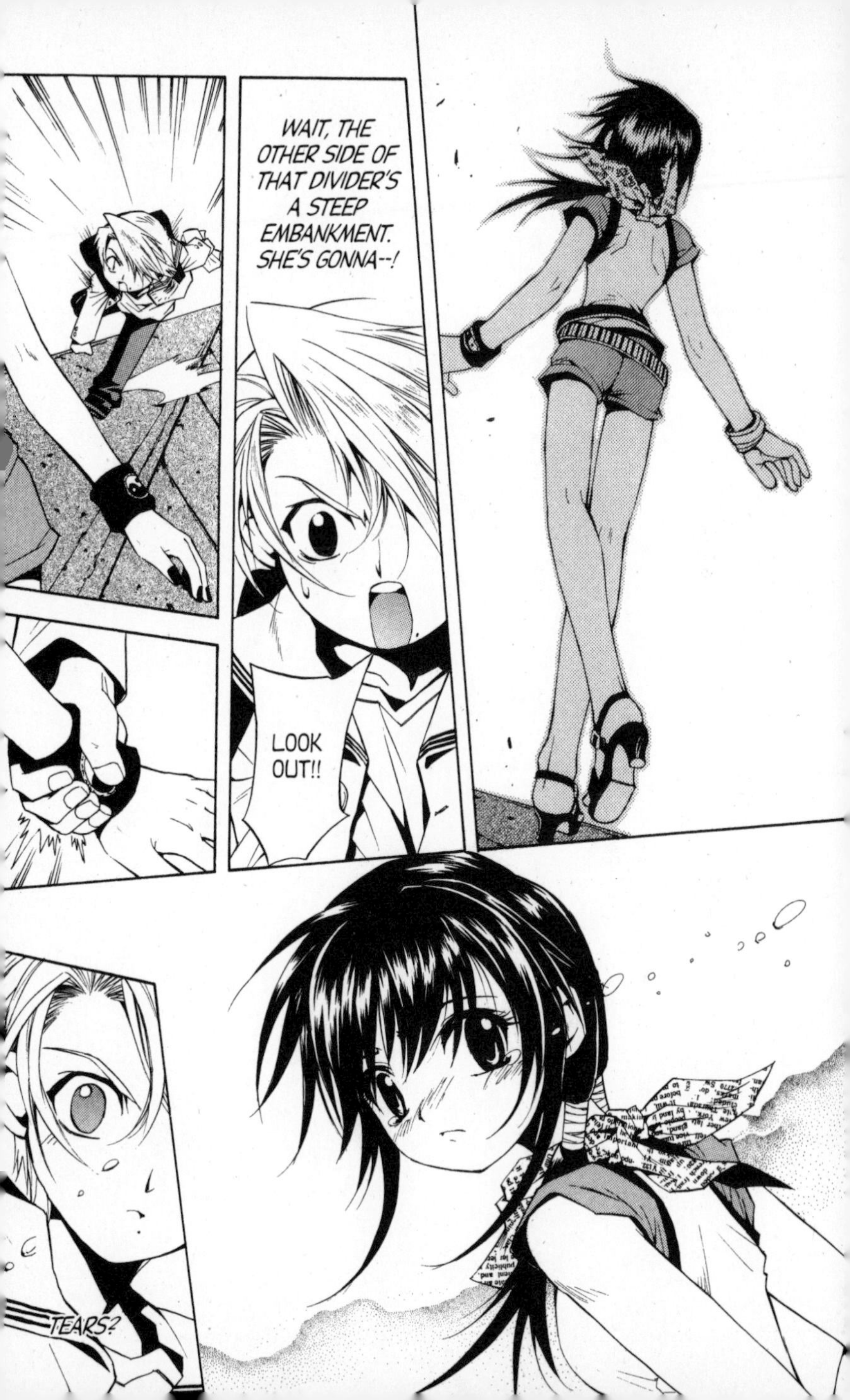
WAIT, THE OTHER SIDE OF THAT DIVIDER'S A STEEP EMBANKMENT. SHE'S GONNA--!
LOOK OUT!!
TEARS?

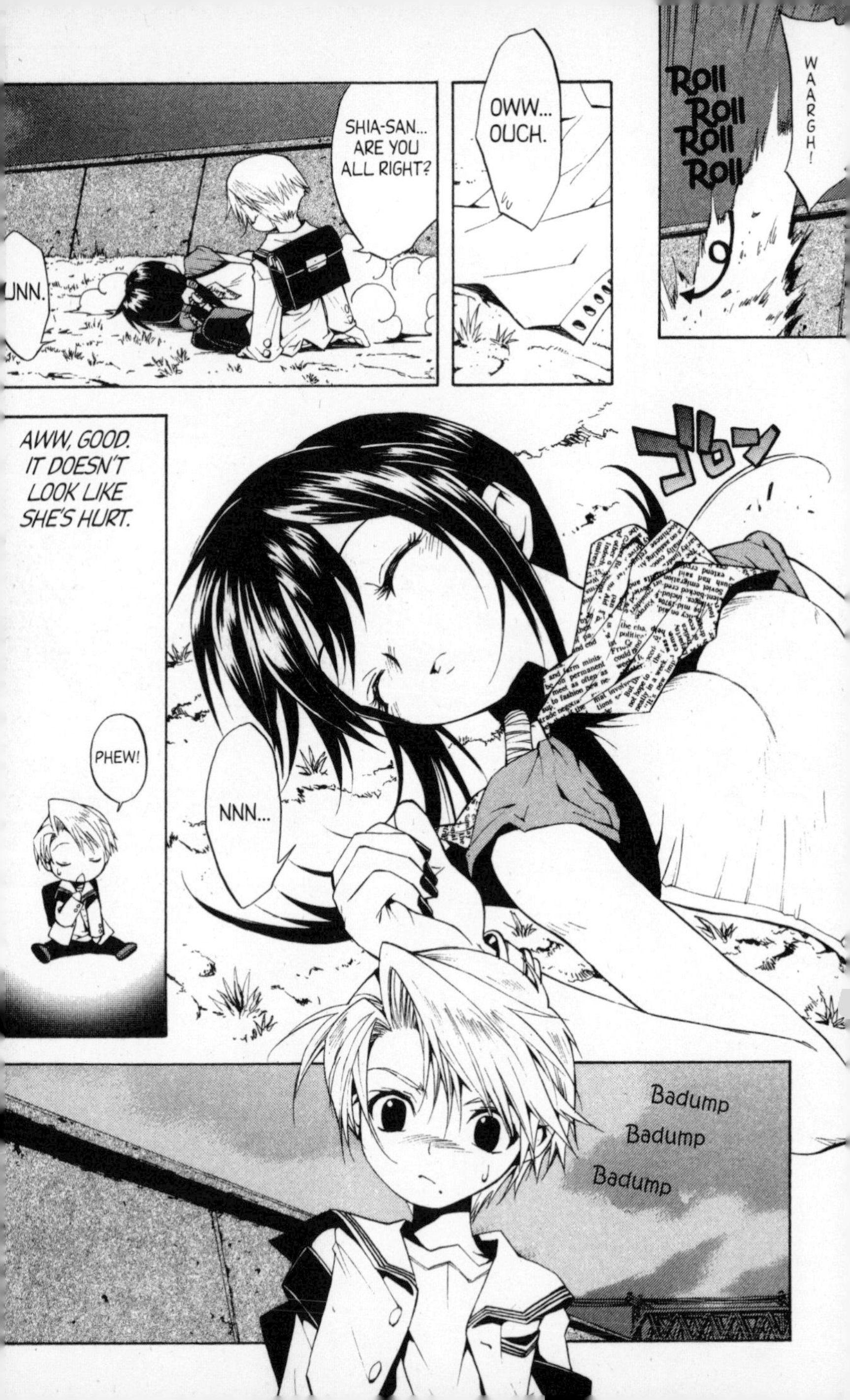
WAARGH!
Roll Roll Roll Roll
OWW... OUCH.
SHIA-SAN... ARE YOU ALL RIGHT?
UNN.
ゴロン
NNN...
AWW, GOOD. IT DOESN'T LOOK LIKE SHE'S HURT.
PHEW!
Badump
Badump
Badump

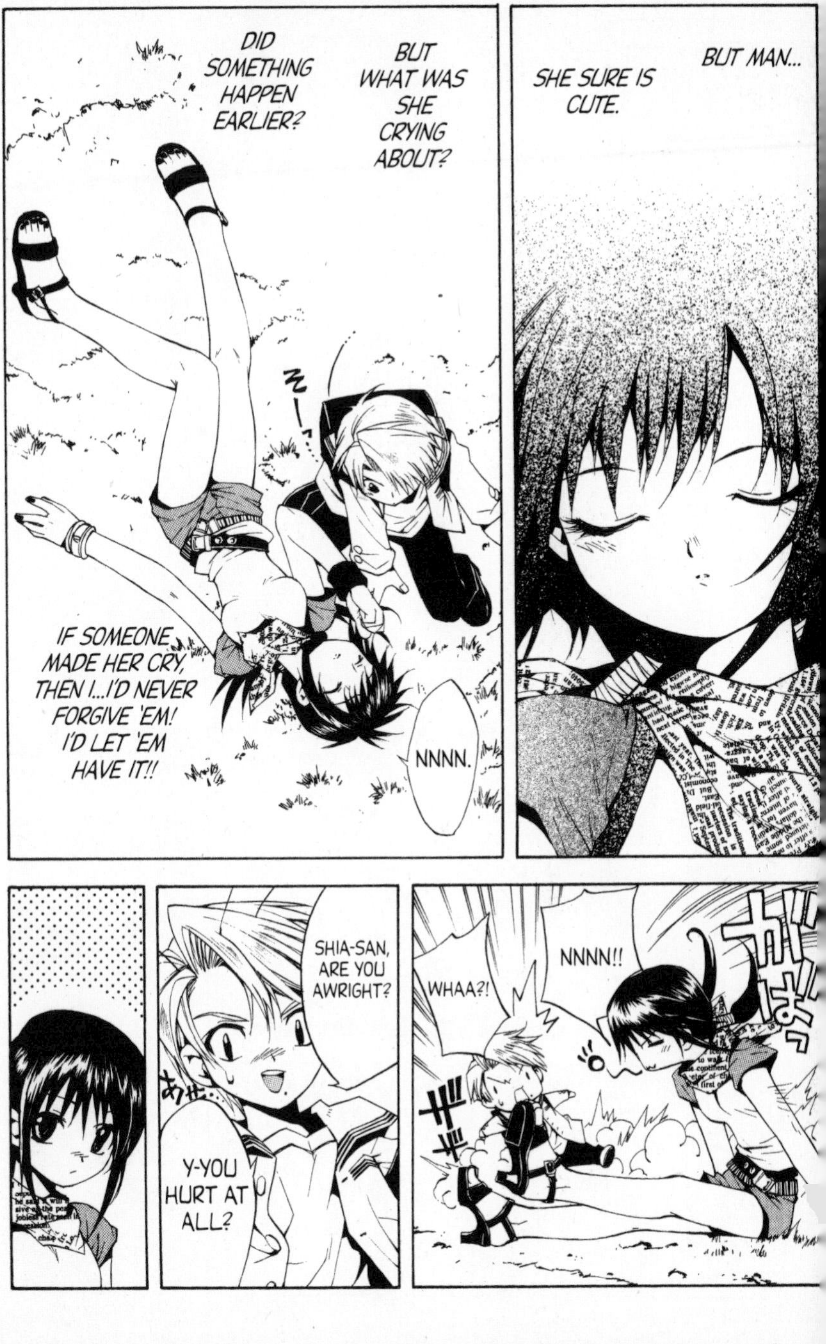
BUT MAN...
SHE SURE IS CUTE.
BUT WHAT WAS SHE CRYING ABOUT?
DID SOMETHING HAPPEN EARLIER?
IF SOMEONE MADE HER CRY, THEN I...I'D NEVER FORGIVE 'EM! I'D LET 'EM HAVE IT!!
NNNN.
NNNN!!
WHAA?!
SHIA-SAN, ARE YOU AWRIGHT?
Y-YOU HURT AT ALL?

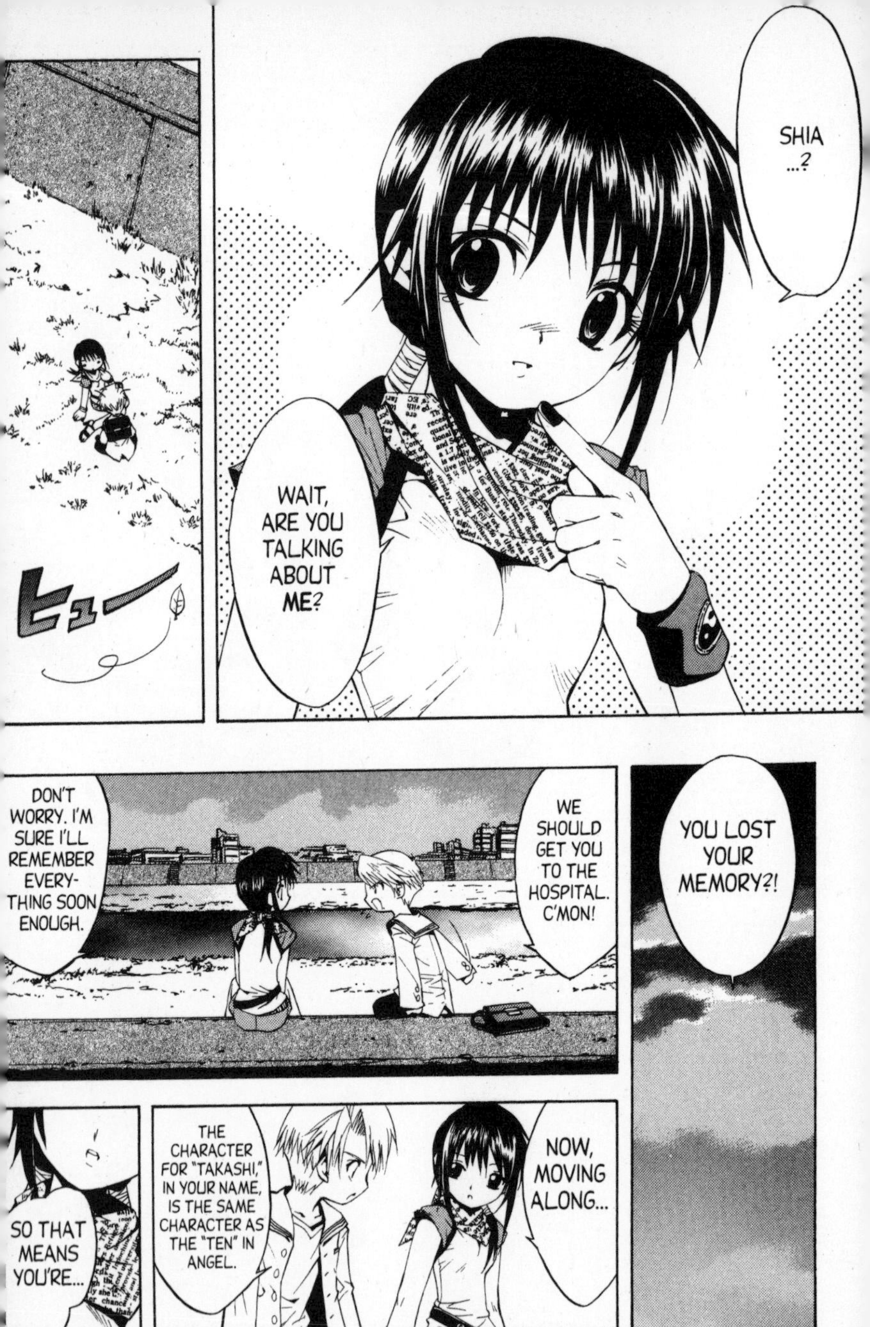
SHIA ...?
WAIT, ARE YOU TALKING ABOUT ME?
ヒュー
YOU LOST YOUR MEMORY?!
WE SHOULD GET YOU TO THE HOSPITAL. C'MON!
DON'T WORRY. I'M SURE I'LL REMEMBER EVERY-THING SOON ENOUGH.
NOW, MOVING ALONG...
THE CHARACTER FOR "TAKASHI," IN YOUR NAME, IS THE SAME CHARACTER AS THE "TEN" IN ANGEL.
SO THAT MEANS YOU'RE...

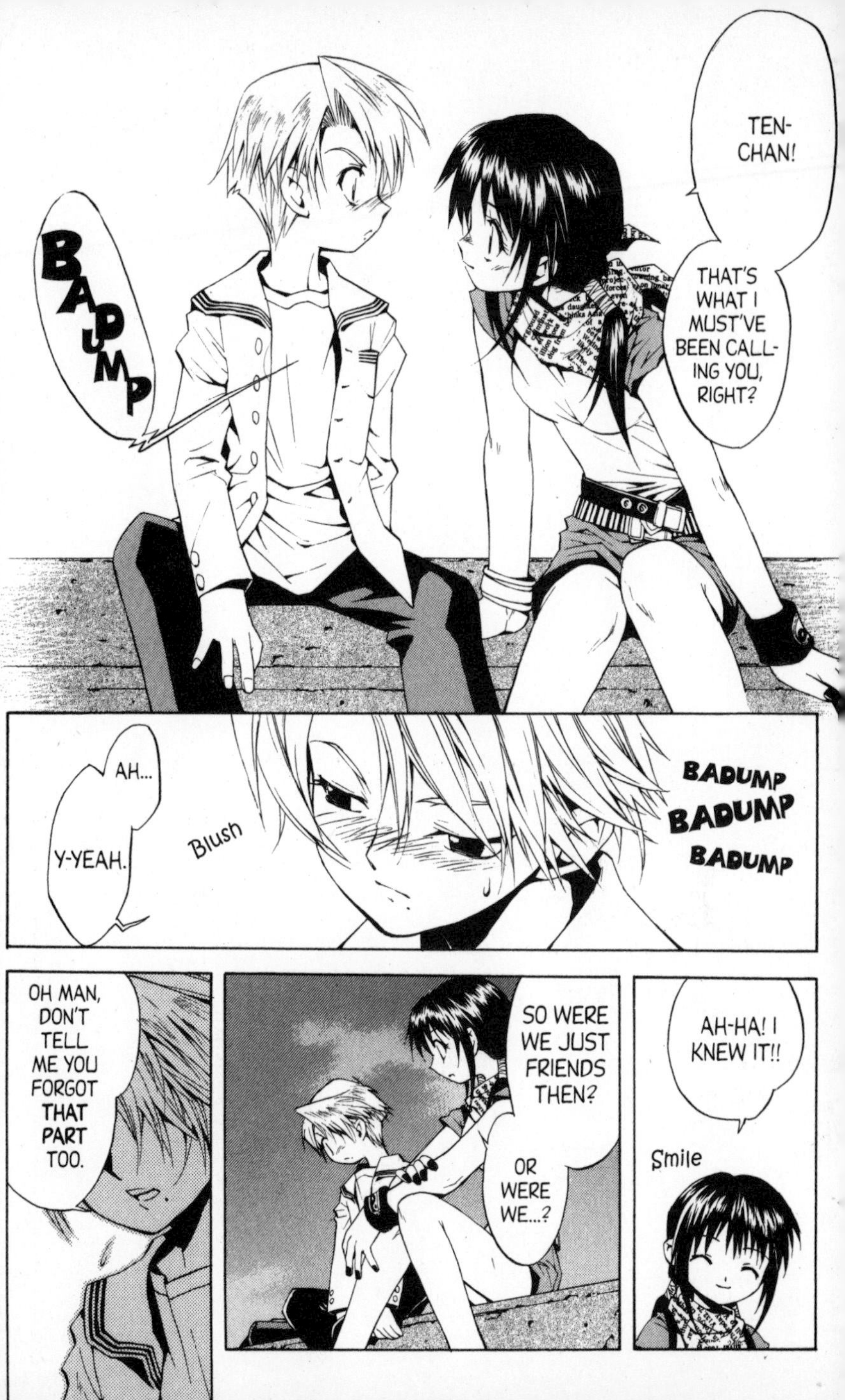

TEN-CHAN!
THAT'S WHAT I MUST'VE BEEN CALLING YOU, RIGHT?
BADUMP
BADUMP BADUMP BADUMP
Blush
AH... Y-YEAH.
AH-HA! I KNEW IT!!
Smile
SO WERE WE JUST FRIENDS THEN?
OR WERE WE...?
OH MAN, DON'T TELL ME YOU FORGOT **THAT PART** TOO.

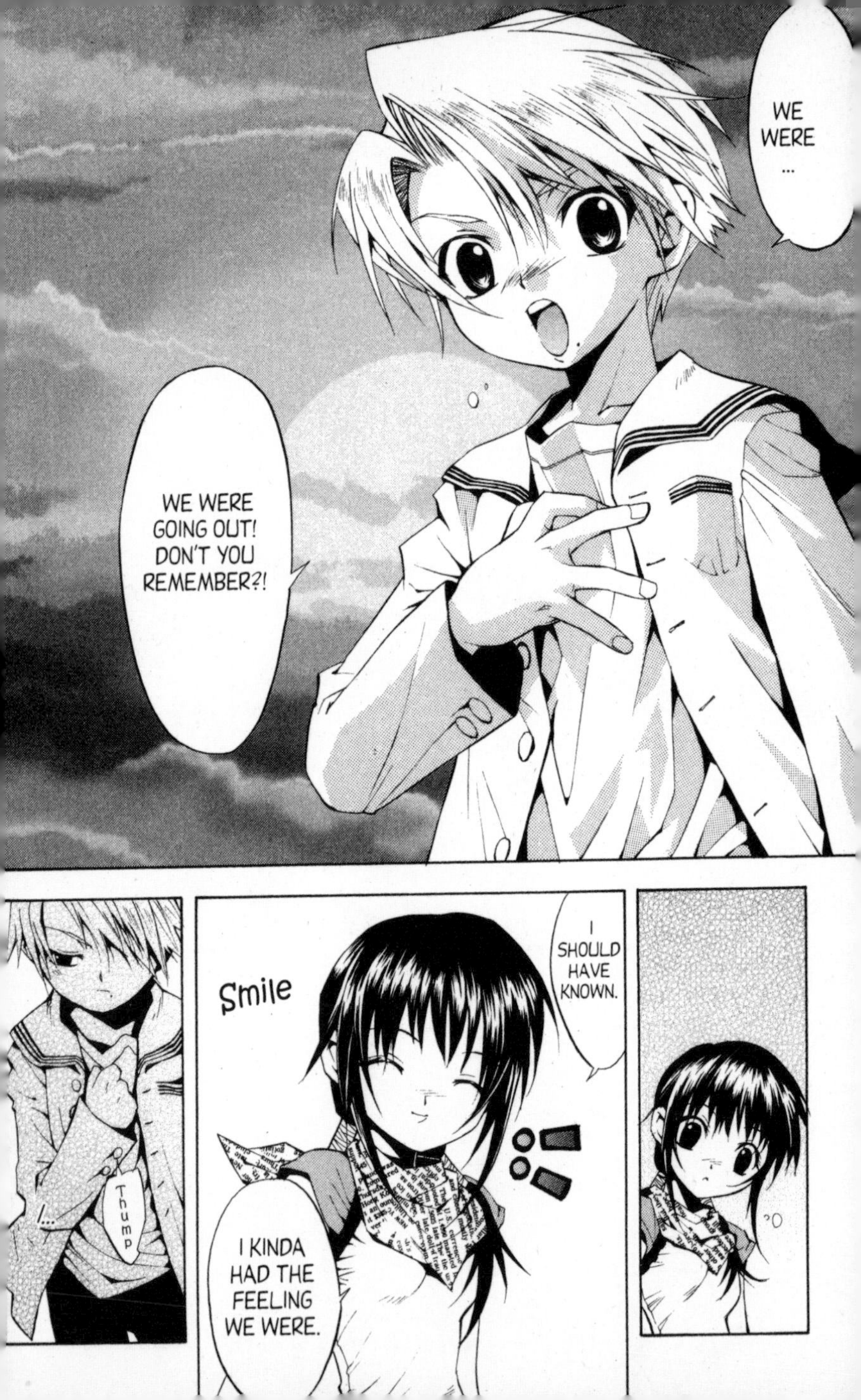
WE WERE ...
WE WERE GOING OUT! DON'T YOU REMEMBER?!
I SHOULD HAVE KNOWN.
Smile
I KINDA HAD THE FEELING WE WERE.
Thump
I...

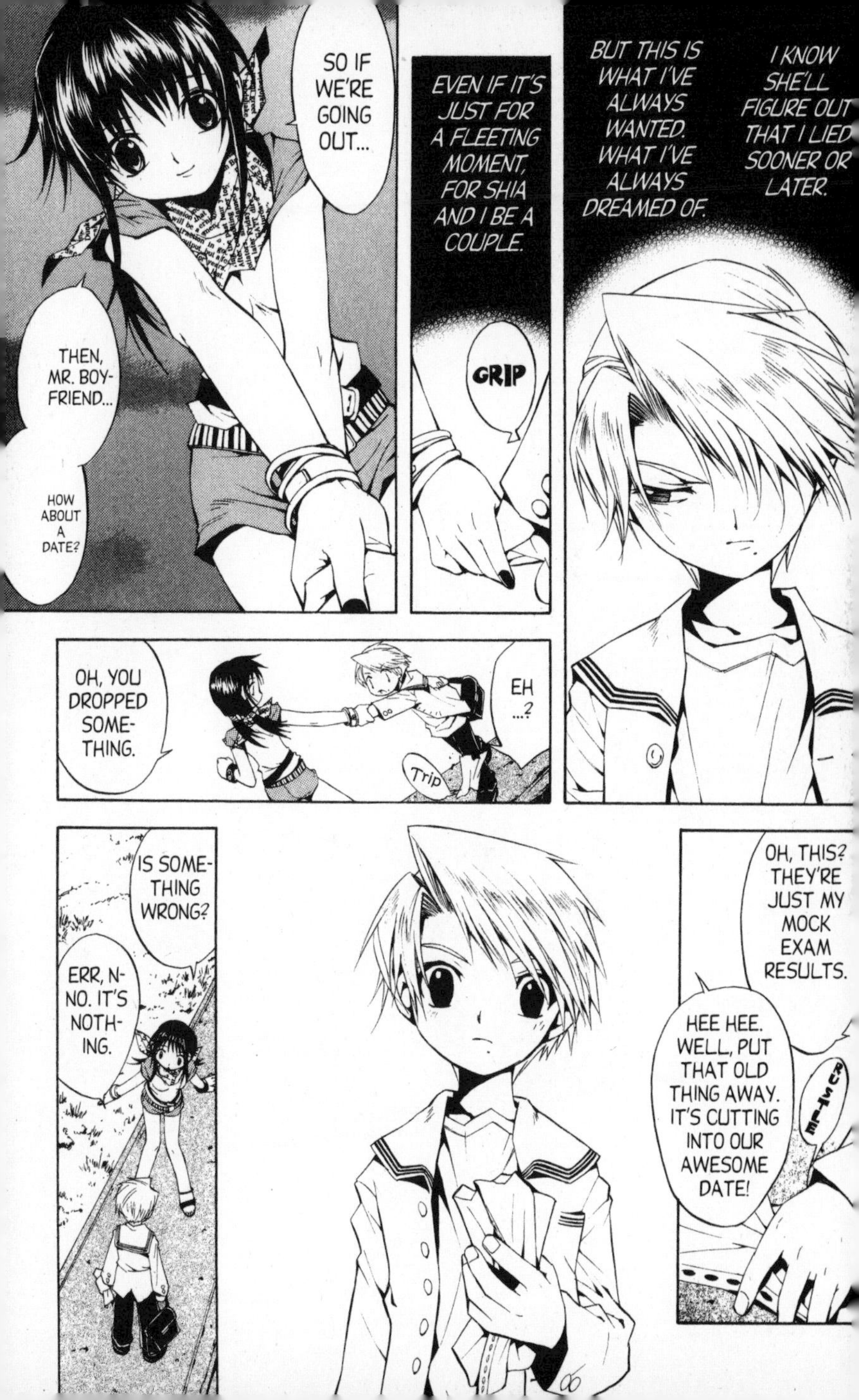
I KNOW SHE'LL FIGURE OUT THAT I LIED SOONER OR LATER.
BUT THIS IS WHAT I'VE ALWAYS WANTED. WHAT I'VE ALWAYS DREAMED OF.
EVEN IF IT'S JUST FOR A FLEETING MOMENT, FOR SHIA AND I BE A COUPLE.
GRIP
SO IF WE'RE GOING OUT...
THEN, MR. BOY-FRIEND...
HOW ABOUT A DATE?
EH ...?
OH, YOU DROPPED SOME-THING.
Trip
OH, THIS? THEY'RE JUST MY MOCK EXAM RESULTS.
RUSTLE
HEE HEE. WELL, PUT THAT OLD THING AWAY. IT'S CUTTING INTO OUR AWESOME DATE!
IS SOME-THING WRONG?
ERR, N-NO. IT'S NOTH-ING.

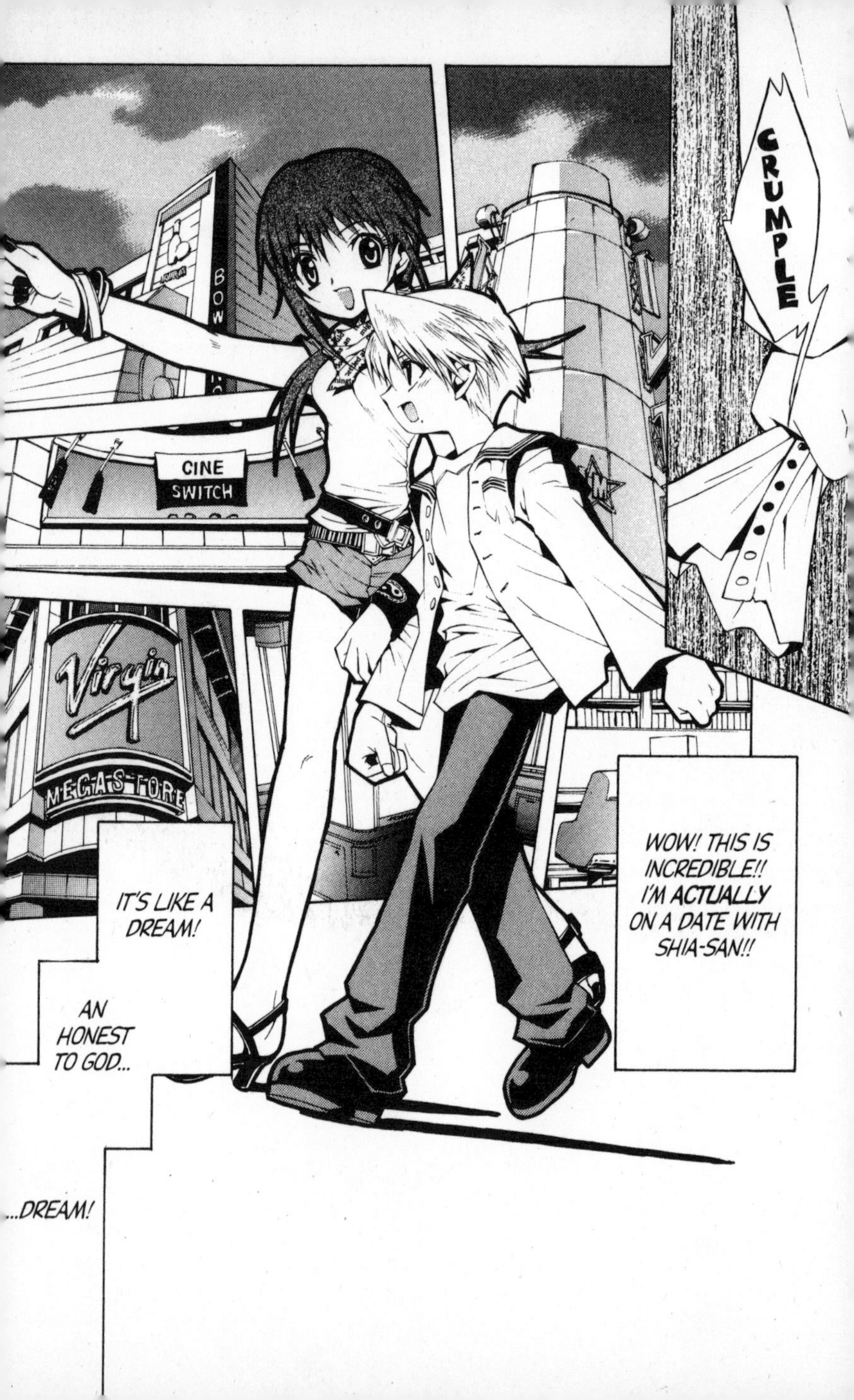
CRUMPLE
BOW
CINE SWITCH
Virgin
MEGASTORE
WOW! THIS IS INCREDIBLE!! I'M ACTUALLY ON A DATE WITH SHIA-SAN!!
IT'S LIKE A DREAM!
AN HONEST TO GOD...
...DREAM!

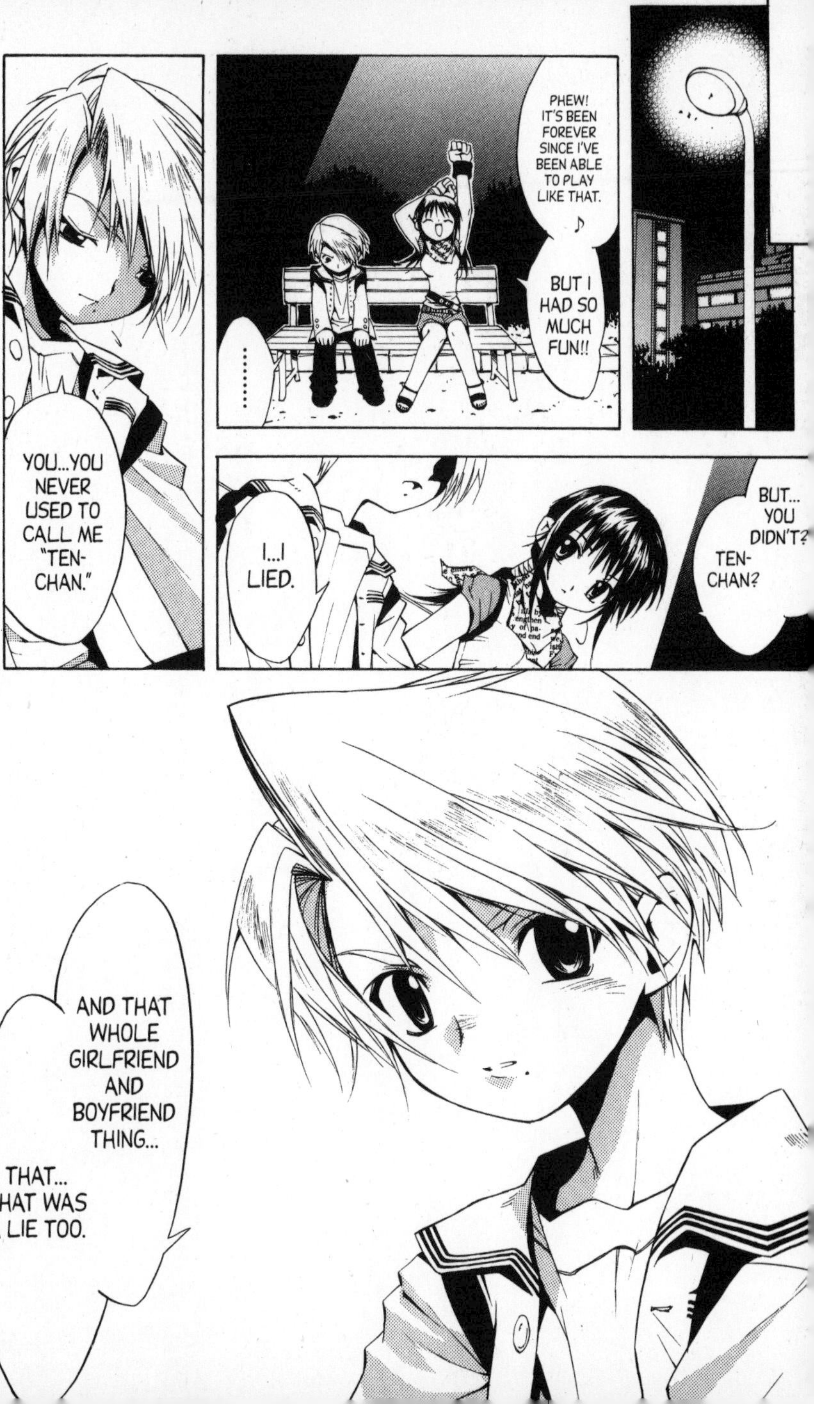
PHEW! IT'S BEEN FOREVER SINCE I'VE BEEN ABLE TO PLAY LIKE THAT. ♪
BUT I HAD SO MUCH FUN!!
......
BUT... YOU DIDN'T? TEN-CHAN?
I...I LIED.
YOU...YOU NEVER USED TO CALL ME "TEN-CHAN."
AND THAT WHOLE GIRLFRIEND AND BOYFRIEND THING...
THAT... THAT WAS A LIE TOO.

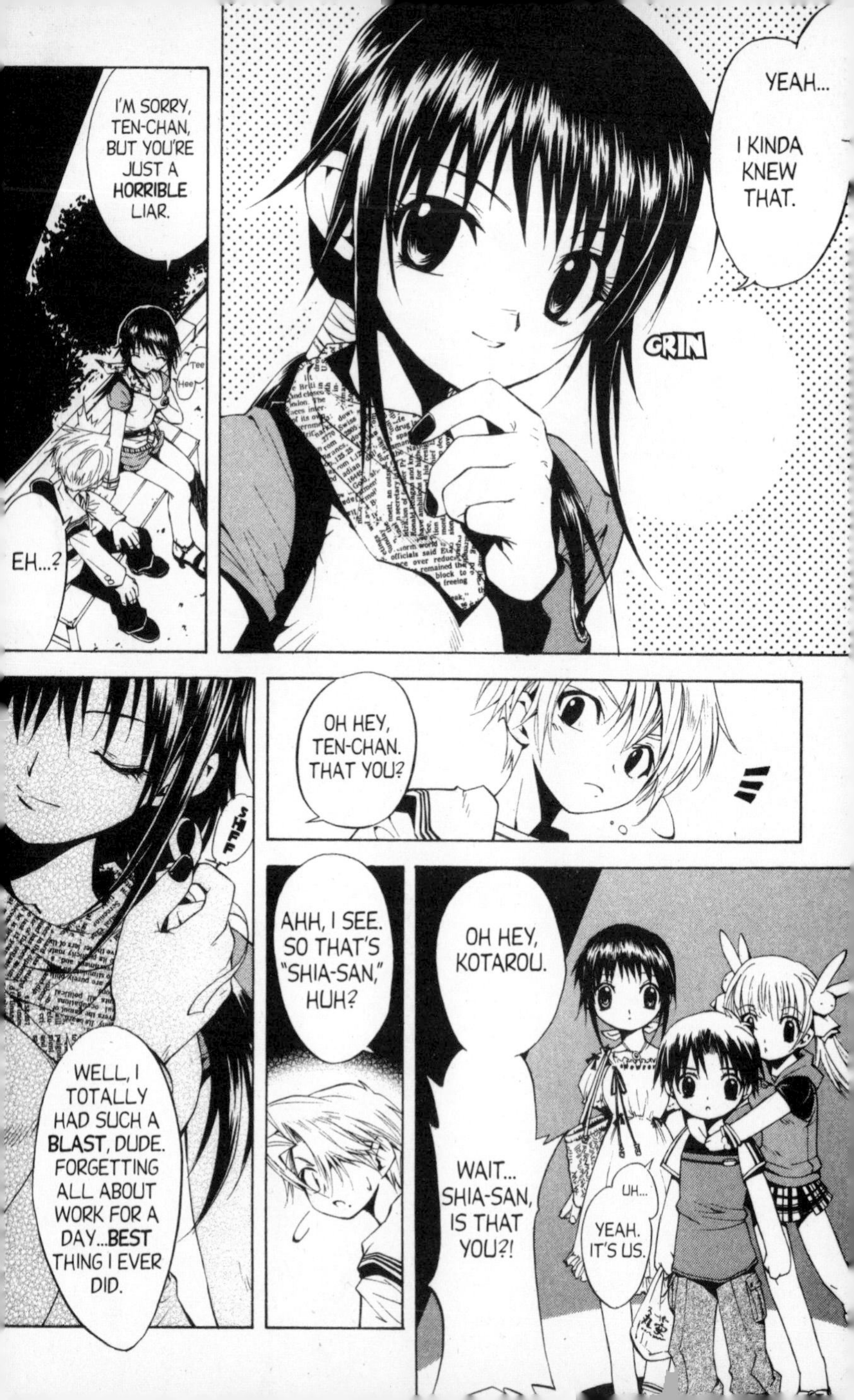

YEAH...
I KINDA KNEW THAT.
GRIN
I'M SORRY, TEN-CHAN, BUT YOU'RE JUST A **HORRIBLE** LIAR.
Tee Hee
EH...?
OH HEY, TEN-CHAN. THAT YOU?
OH HEY, KOTAROU.
WAIT... SHIA-SAN, IS THAT YOU?!
UH...
YEAH. IT'S US.
AHH, I SEE. SO THAT'S "SHIA-SAN," HUH?
WELL, I TOTALLY HAD SUCH A **BLAST**, DUDE. FORGETTING ALL ABOUT WORK FOR A DAY...**BEST** THING I EVER DID.

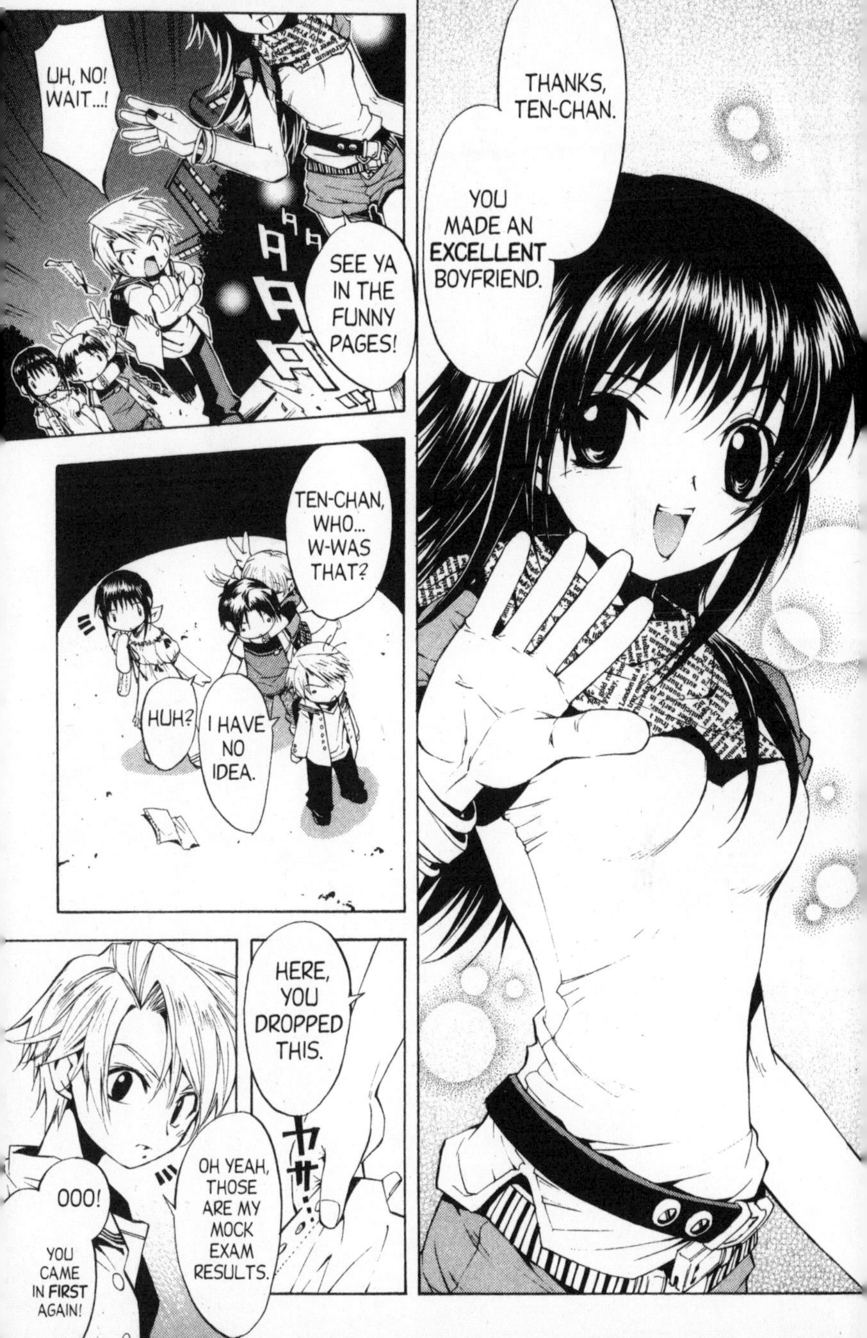
THANKS, TEN-CHAN.
YOU MADE AN **EXCELLENT** BOYFRIEND.
SEE YA IN THE FUNNY PAGES!
UH, NO! WAIT...!
TEN-CHAN, WHO... W-WAS THAT?
I HAVE NO IDEA.
HUH?
HERE, YOU DROPPED THIS.
OH YEAH, THOSE ARE MY MOCK EXAM RESULTS.
OOO!
YOU CAME IN **FIRST** AGAIN!

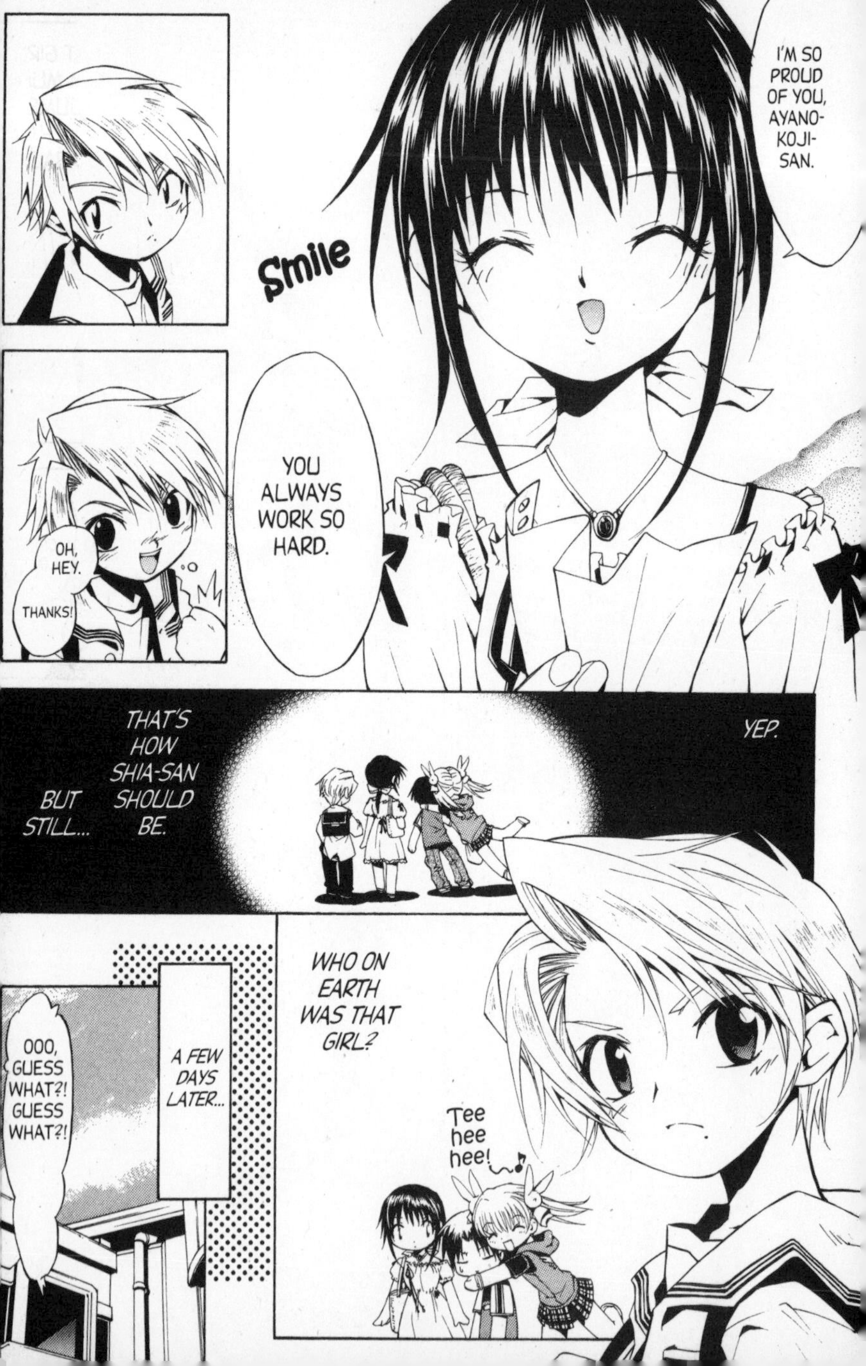
I'M SO PROUD OF YOU, AYANO-KOJI-SAN.
Smile
YOU ALWAYS WORK SO HARD.
OH, HEY.
THANKS!
YEP.
THAT'S HOW SHIA-SAN SHOULD BE.
BUT STILL...
WHO ON EARTH WAS THAT GIRL?
Tee hee hee!
A FEW DAYS LATER...
OOO, GUESS WHAT?! GUESS WHAT?!

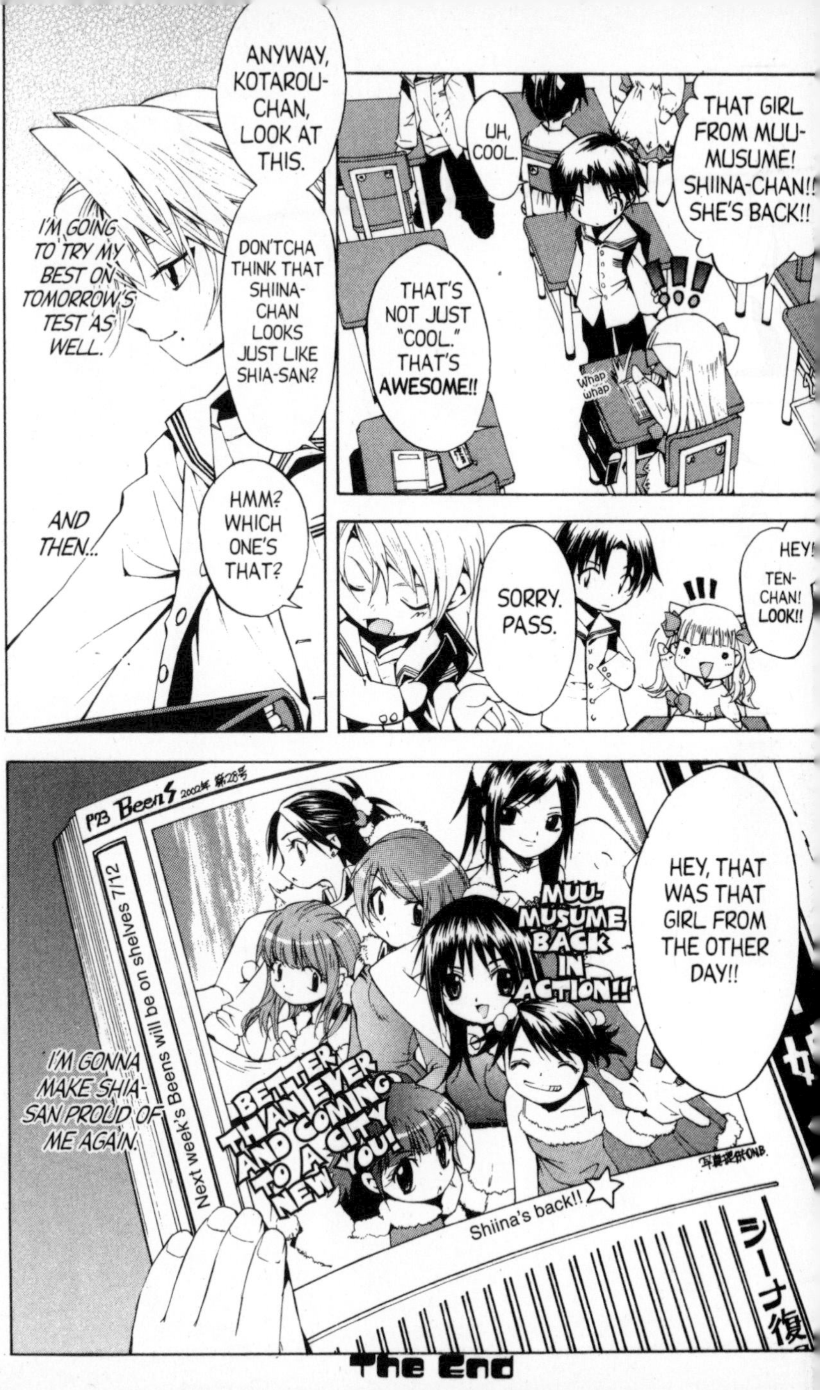
THAT GIRL FROM MUU-MUSUME! SHIINA-CHAN!! SHE'S BACK!!
UH, COOL.
THAT'S NOT JUST "COOL." THAT'S AWESOME!!
Whap whap
HEY! TEN-CHAN! LOOK!!
SORRY. PASS.
ANYWAY, KOTAROU-CHAN, LOOK AT THIS.
DON'TCHA THINK THAT SHIINA-CHAN LOOKS JUST LIKE SHIA-SAN?
HMM? WHICH ONE'S THAT?
I'M GOING TO TRY MY BEST ON TOMORROW'S TEST AS WELL.
AND THEN...
HEY, THAT WAS THAT GIRL FROM THE OTHER DAY!!
P73 BeenS 2002年 第28号
MUU-MUSUME BACK IN ACTION!!
BETTER THAN EVER AND COMING TO A CITY NEW YOU!
Next week's Beens will be on shelves 7/12
Shiina's back!!
シーナ復
I'M GONNA MAKE SHIA-SAN PROUD OF ME AGAIN.

The End

Hiroshi Ueda

Gratz on Anthology Volume 3!!

This piece was for all of you Ten-chan lovers out there! ☆

If you liked Shiina also, then I couldn't be happier.

By Ueda

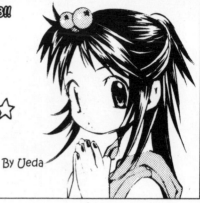

Writer's Talk

Muca Tonami

I'm so happy for being given the opportunity to participate in the Pinnacle of *Pita-Ten* Fandom-- The Official Comic Fan-Book!

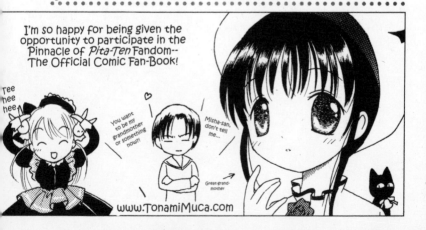

Misha-san, don't tell me...
You want to be my grandmother or something now?!
Tee hee hee.
Great-grand-mother

www.TonamiMuca.com

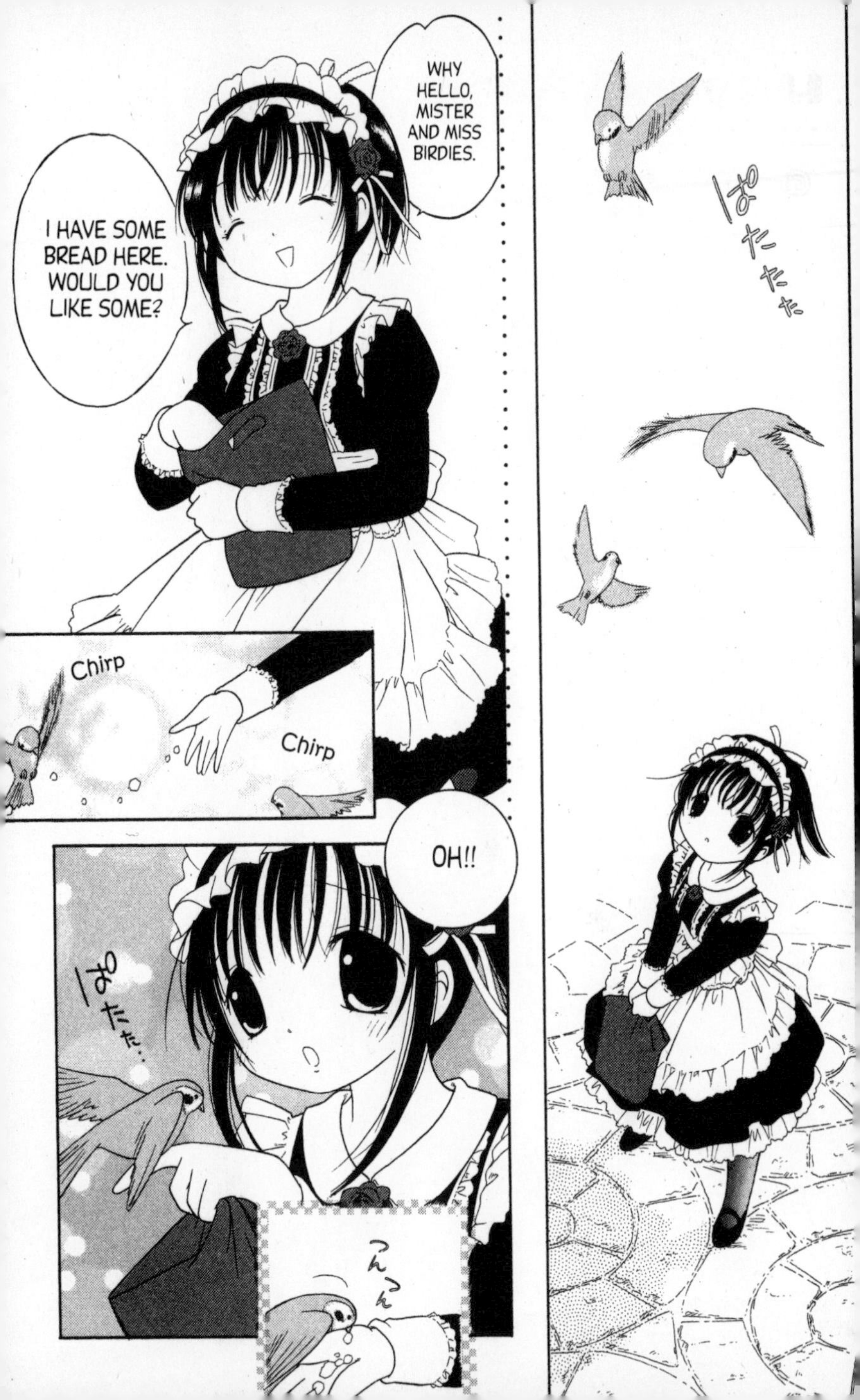
ぱたたた
WHY HELLO, MISTER AND MISS BIRDIES.
I HAVE SOME BREAD HERE. WOULD YOU LIKE SOME?
Chirp
Chirp
OH!!
ぱたた…
つんつん

How to Convey Warmth

Muca Tonami

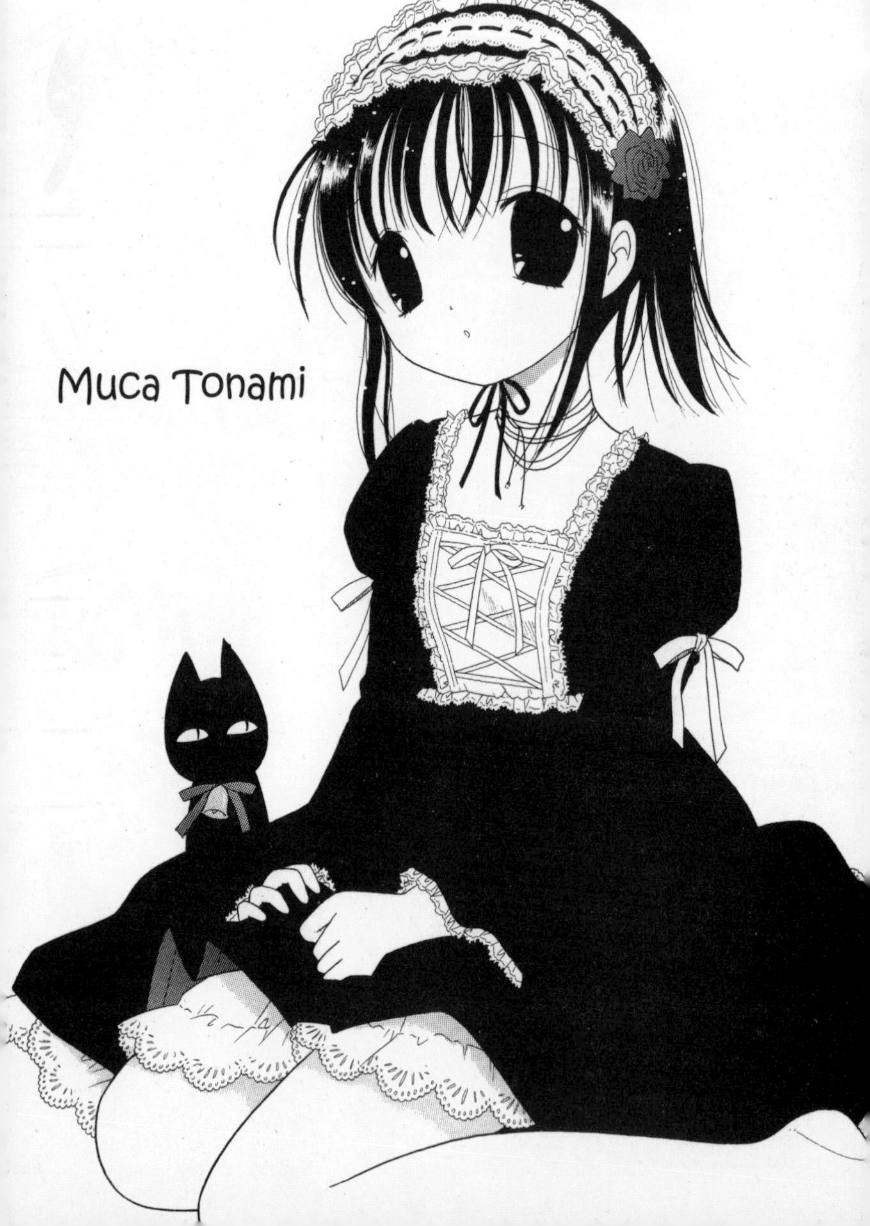

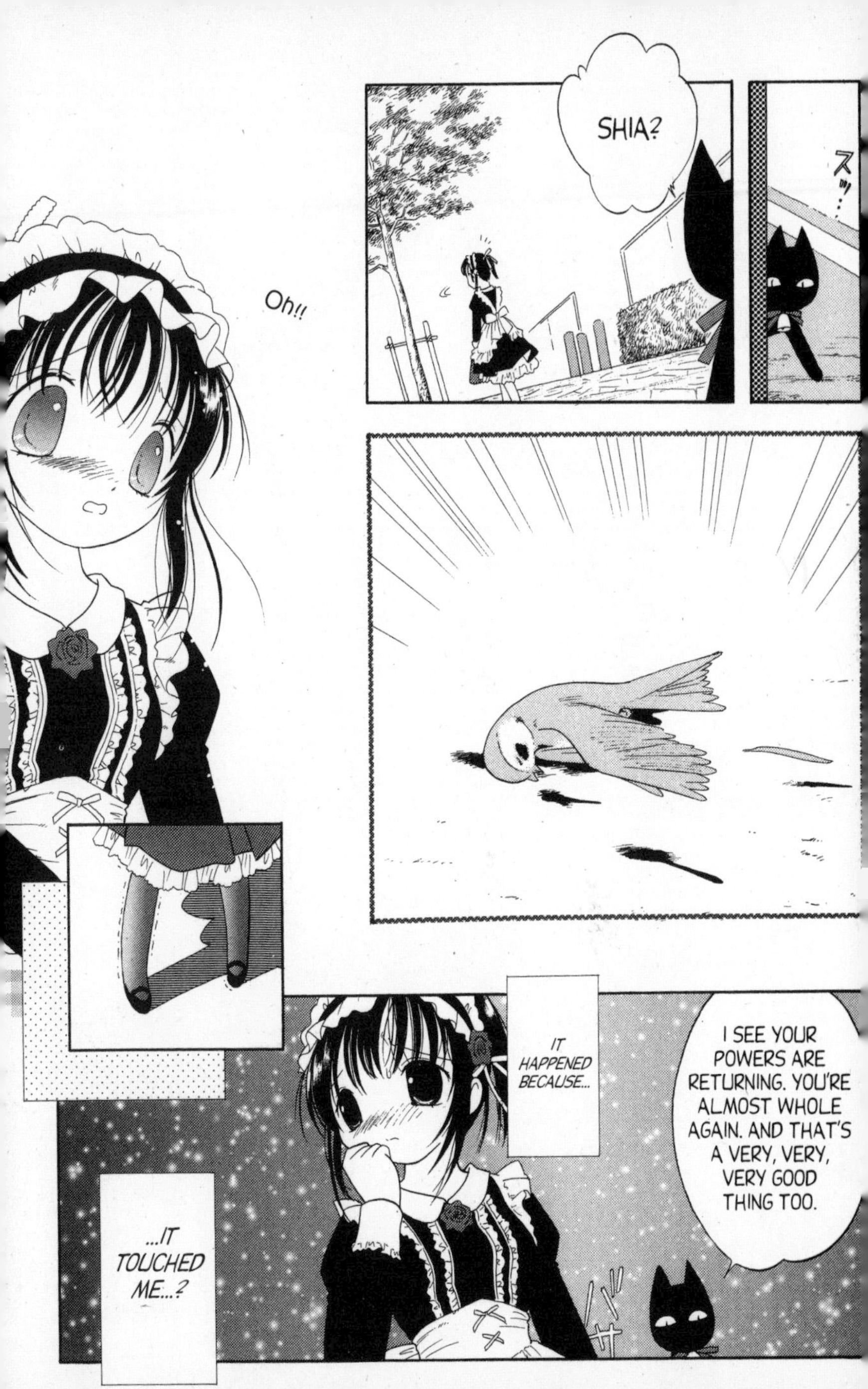
スッ…
SHIA?
Oh!!
I SEE YOUR POWERS ARE RETURNING. YOU'RE ALMOST WHOLE AGAIN. AND THAT'S A VERY, VERY, VERY GOOD THING TOO.
IT HAPPENED BECAUSE...
...IT TOUCHED ME...?

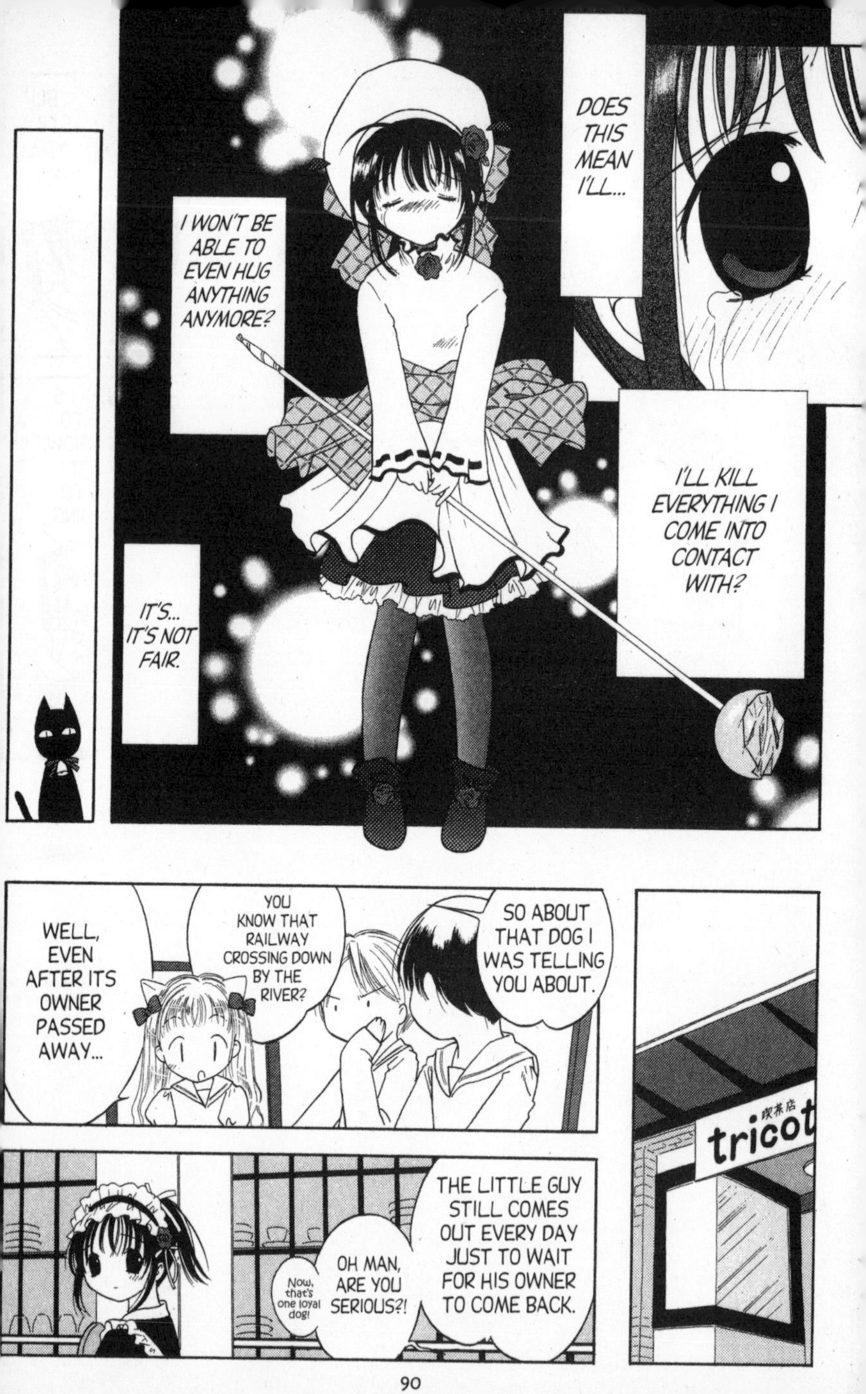
DOES THIS MEAN I'LL...
I'LL KILL EVERYTHING I COME INTO CONTACT WITH?
I WON'T BE ABLE TO EVEN HUG ANYTHING ANYMORE?
IT'S... IT'S NOT FAIR.
喫茶店
tricot
SO ABOUT THAT DOG I WAS TELLING YOU ABOUT.
YOU KNOW THAT RAILWAY CROSSING DOWN BY THE RIVER?
WELL, EVEN AFTER ITS OWNER PASSED AWAY...
THE LITTLE GUY STILL COMES OUT EVERY DAY JUST TO WAIT FOR HIS OWNER TO COME BACK.
OH MAN, ARE YOU SERIOUS?!
Now, that's one loyal dog!

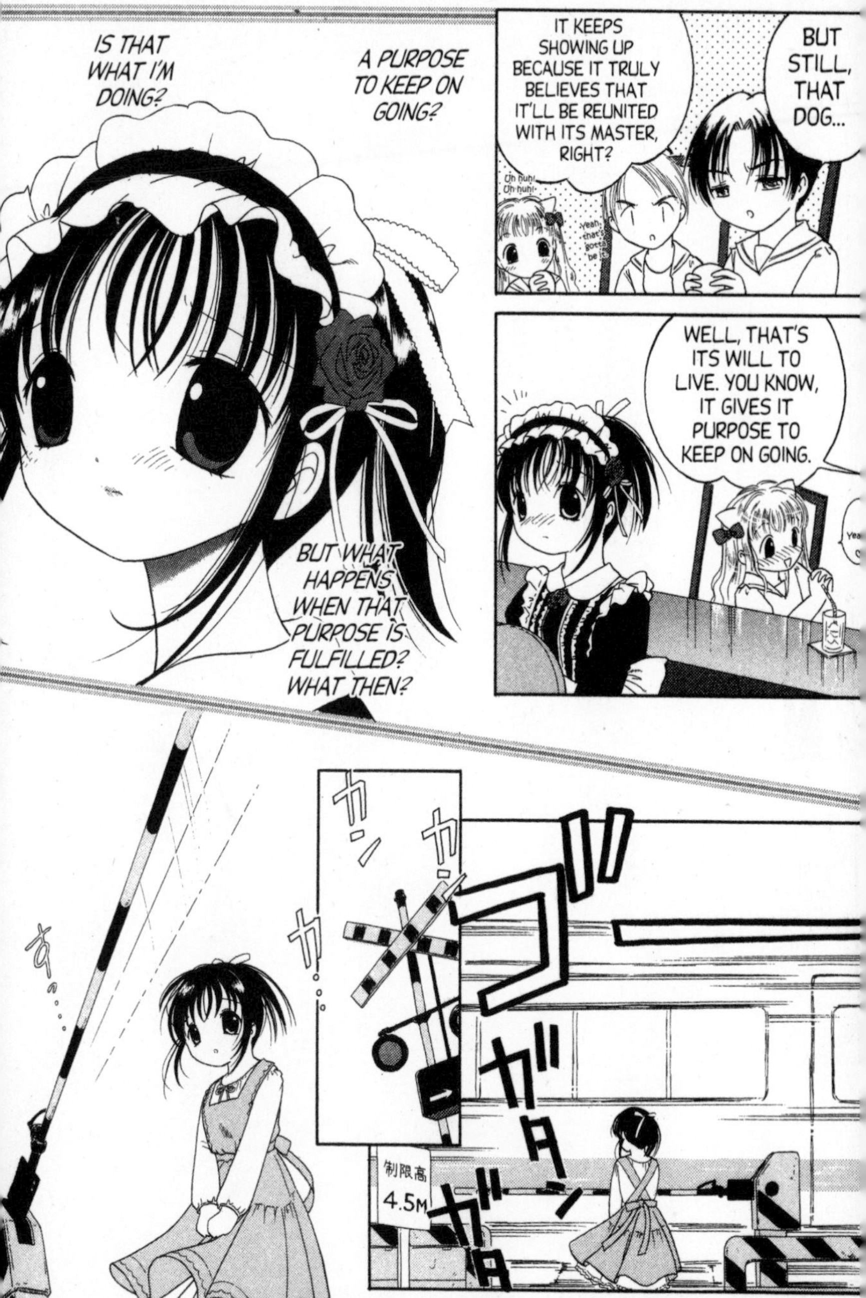
BUT STILL, THAT DOG...
IT KEEPS SHOWING UP BECAUSE IT TRULY BELIEVES THAT IT'LL BE REUNITED WITH ITS MASTER, RIGHT?
Yeah, that's gotta be it.
Uh huh! Uh huh!
WELL, THAT'S ITS WILL TO LIVE. YOU KNOW, IT GIVES IT PURPOSE TO KEEP ON GOING.
A PURPOSE TO KEEP ON GOING?
IS THAT WHAT I'M DOING?
BUT WHAT HAPPENS WHEN THAT PURPOSE IS FULFILLED? WHAT THEN?
カン
カン
ゴー
ガタン
ガタ
制限高
4.5M

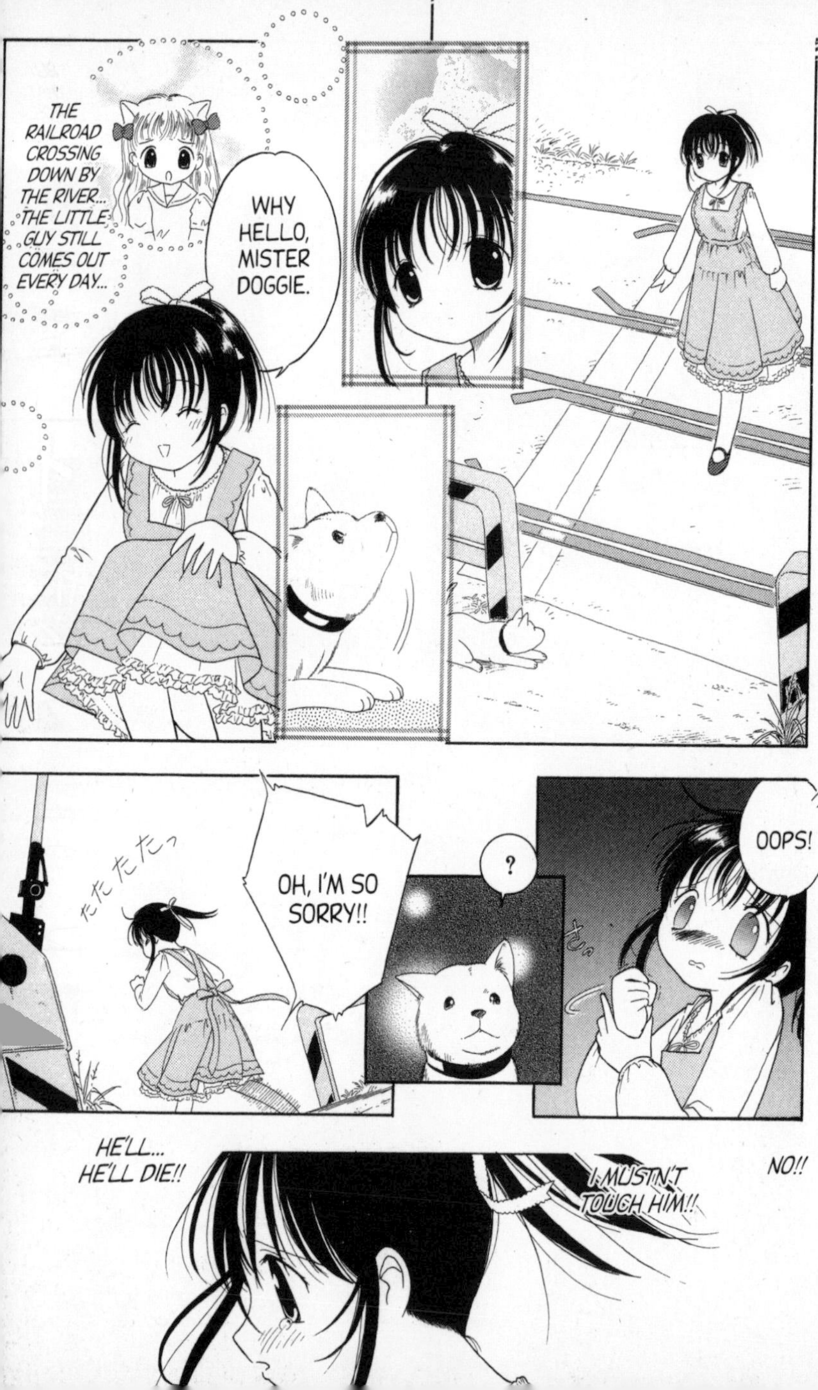
THE RAILROAD CROSSING DOWN BY THE RIVER... THE LITTLE GUY STILL COMES OUT EVERY DAY...
WHY HELLO, MISTER DOGGIE.
OOPS!
?
OH, I'M SO SORRY!!
たたたたっ
NO!!
I MUSTN'T TOUCH HIM!!
HE'LL... HE'LL DIE!!

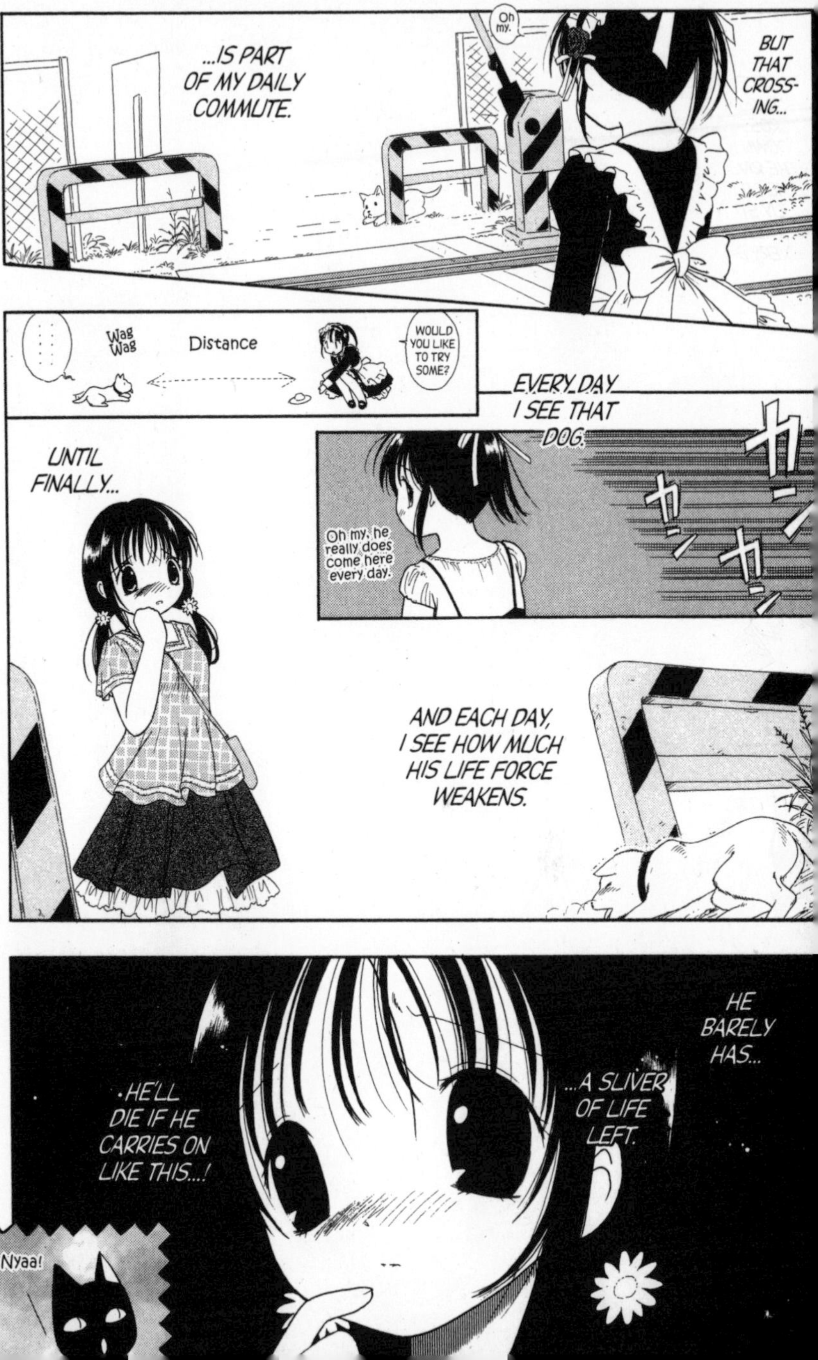
BUT THAT CROSSING...
Oh my.
...IS PART OF MY DAILY COMMUTE.
WOULD YOU LIKE TO TRY SOME?
Distance
Wag Wag
...
EVERY DAY I SEE THAT DOG.
カン
カン
カン
Oh my, he really does come here every day.
AND EACH DAY, I SEE HOW MUCH HIS LIFE FORCE WEAKENS.
UNTIL FINALLY...
HE BARELY HAS...
...A SLIVER OF LIFE LEFT.
HE'LL DIE IF HE CARRIES ON LIKE THIS...!
Nyaa!

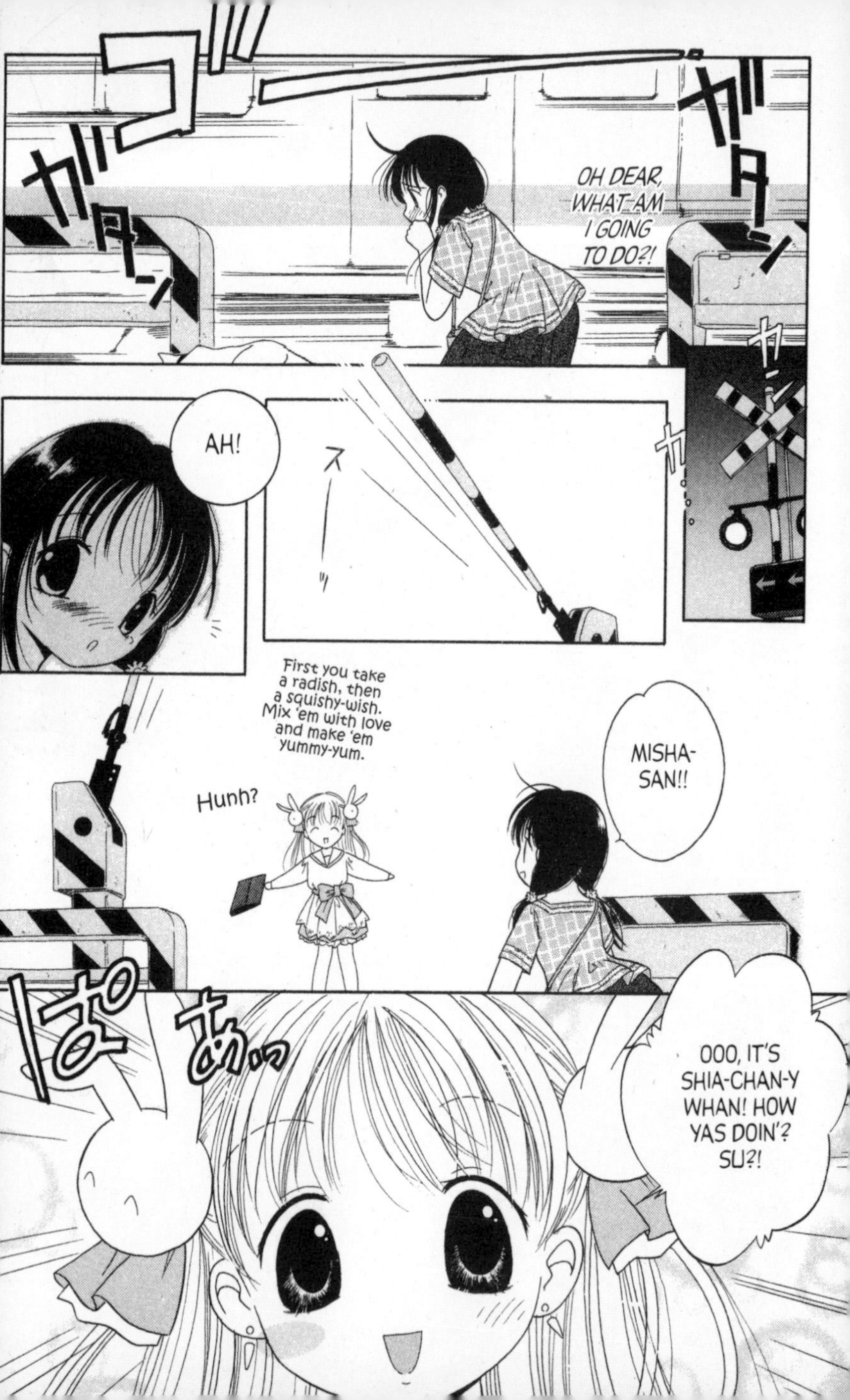
OH DEAR, WHAT AM I GOING TO DO?!
AH!
MISHA-SAN!!
First you take a radish, then a squishy-wish. Mix 'em with love and make 'em yummy-yum.
Hunh?
OOO, IT'S SHIA-CHAN-Y WHAN! HOW YAS DOIN'? SU?!

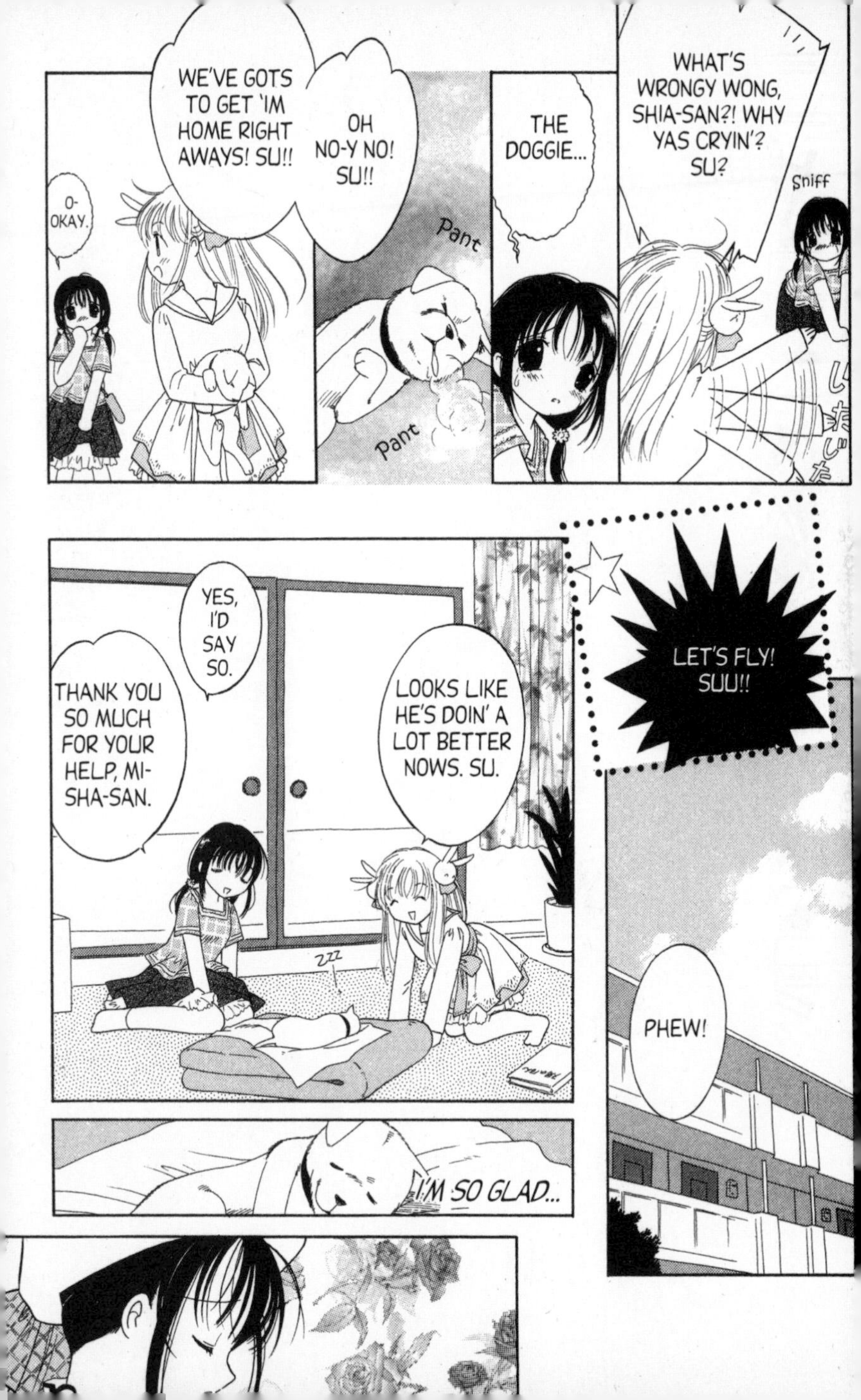
WHAT'S WRONGY WONG, SHIA-SAN?! WHY YAS CRYIN'? SU?
Sniff
THE DOGGIE...
Pant
Pant
OH NO-Y NO! SU!!
WE'VE GOTS TO GET 'IM HOME RIGHT AWAYS! SU!!
O-OKAY.
LET'S FLY! SUU!!
PHEW!
LOOKS LIKE HE'S DOIN' A LOT BETTER NOWS. SU.
YES, I'D SAY SO.
THANK YOU SO MUCH FOR YOUR HELP, MI-SHA-SAN.
ZZZ
I'M SO GLAD...

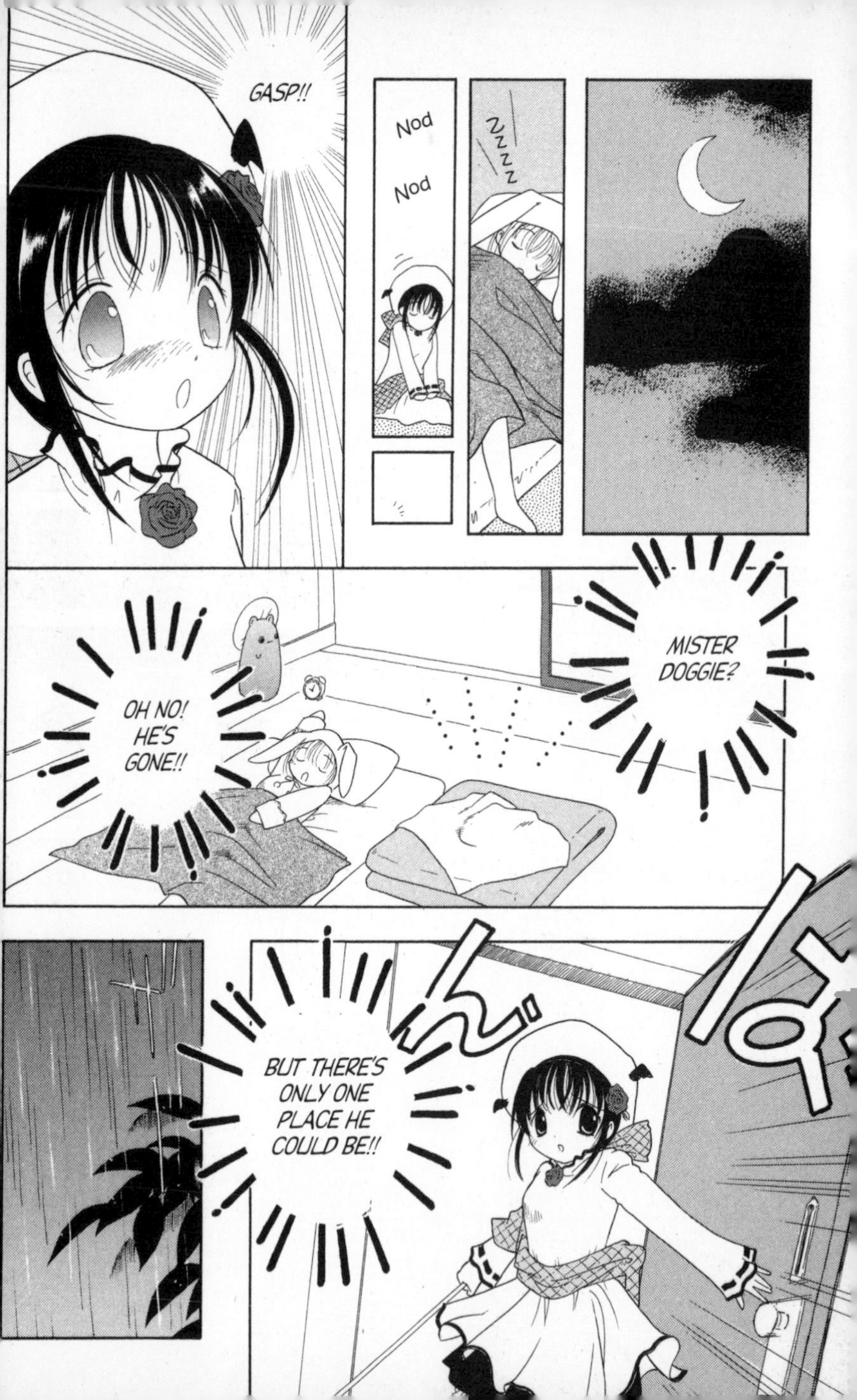
ZZZZ
Nod
Nod
GASP!!
MISTER DOGGIE?
OH NO! HE'S GONE!!
BUT THERE'S ONLY ONE PLACE HE COULD BE!!

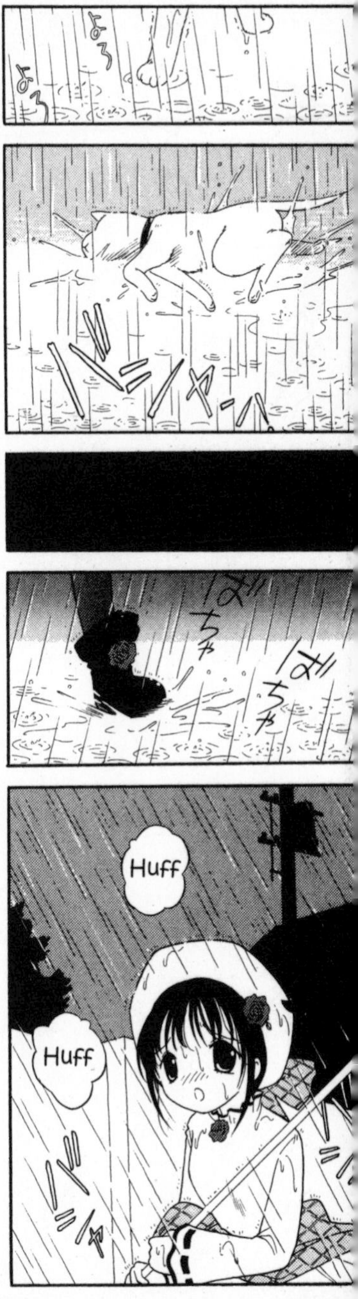
よろ
よろ
ぱちゃ
ぱちゃ
Huff
Huff
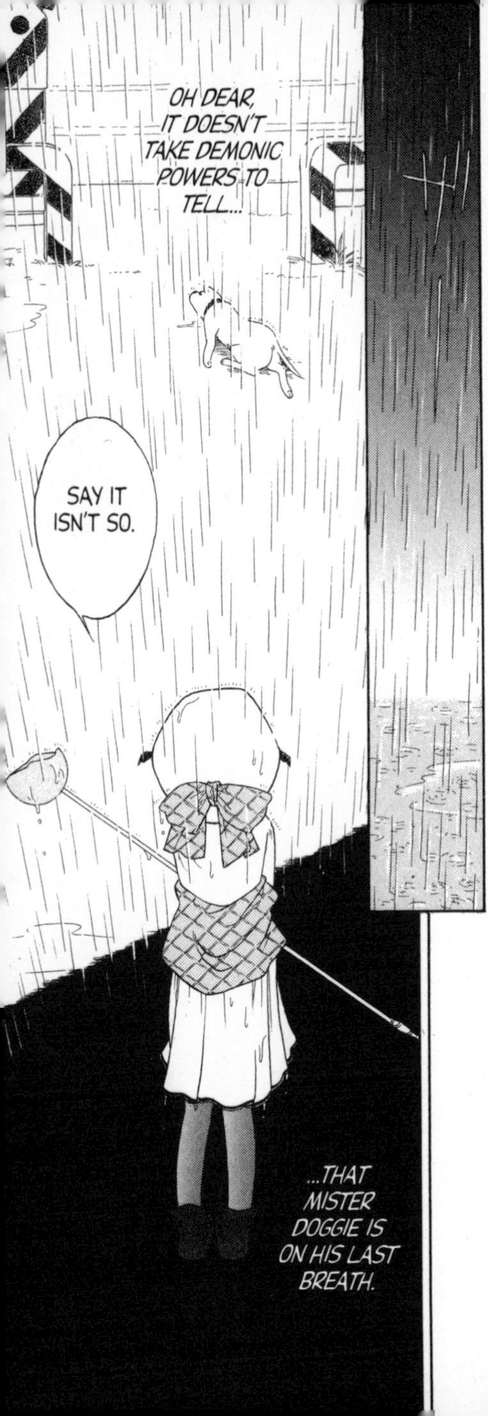
OH DEAR, IT DOESN'T TAKE DEMONIC POWERS TO TELL...
SAY IT ISN'T SO.
...THAT MISTER DOGGIE IS ON HIS LAST BREATH.

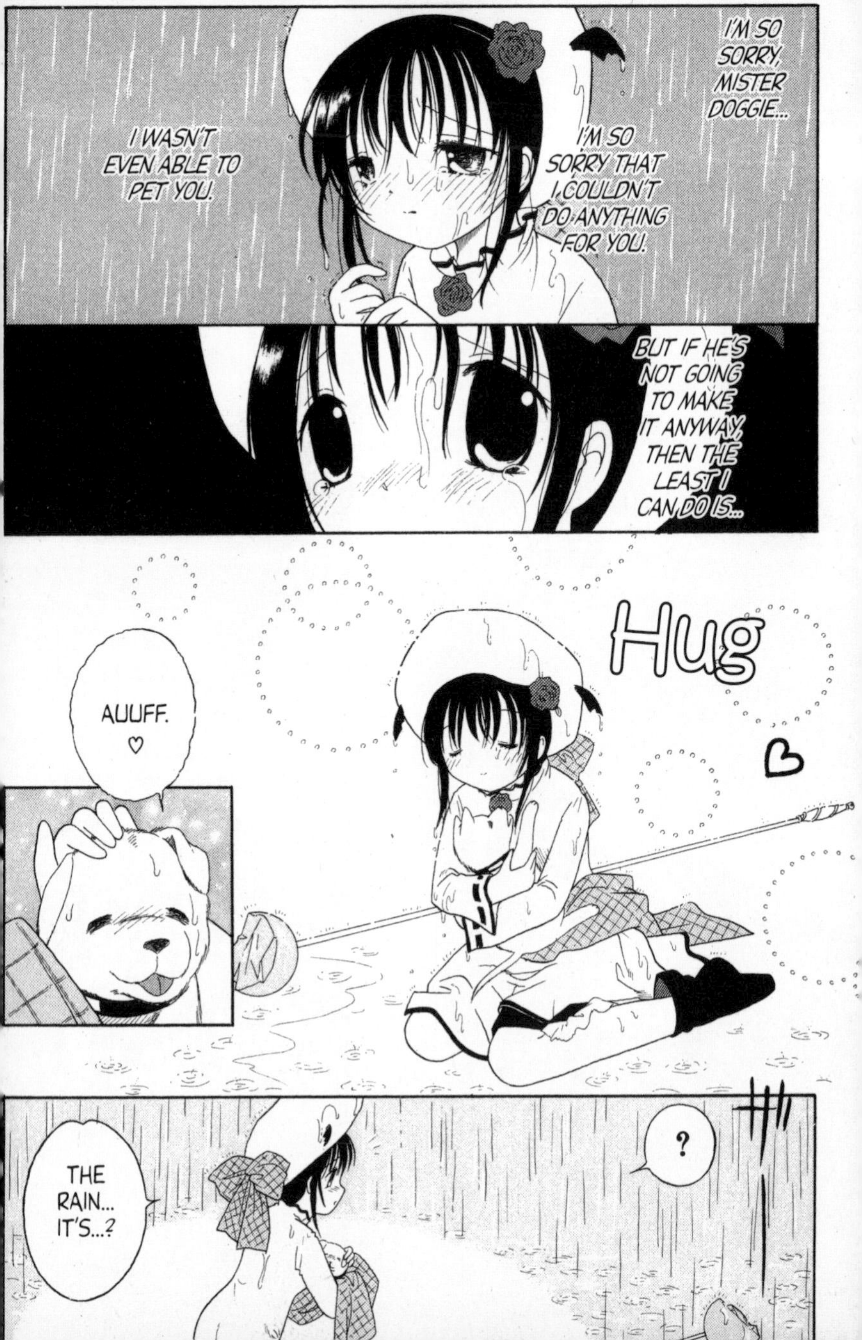
I'M SO SORRY, MISTER DOGGIE...
I'M SO SORRY THAT I COULDN'T DO ANYTHING FOR YOU.
I WASN'T EVEN ABLE TO PET YOU.
BUT IF HE'S NOT GOING TO MAKE IT ANYWAY, THEN THE LEAST I CAN DO IS...
Hug
♡
AUUFF. ♡
?
THE RAIN... IT'S...?

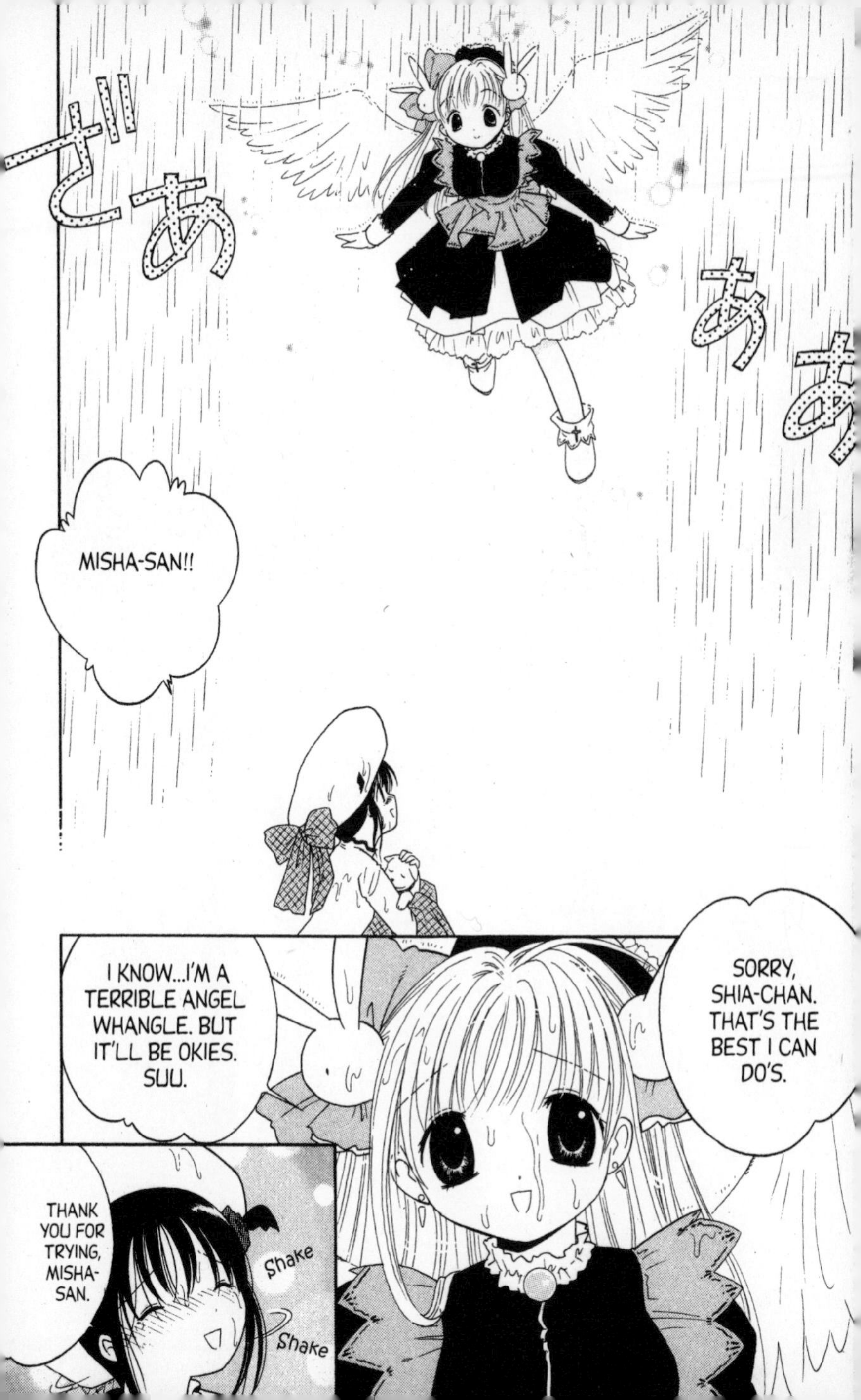
ざあ
ああ
MISHA-SAN!!
SORRY, SHIA-CHAN. THAT'S THE BEST I CAN DO'S.
I KNOW...I'M A TERRIBLE ANGEL WHANGLE. BUT IT'LL BE OKIES. SUU.
THANK YOU FOR TRYING, MISHA-SAN.
Shake
Shake

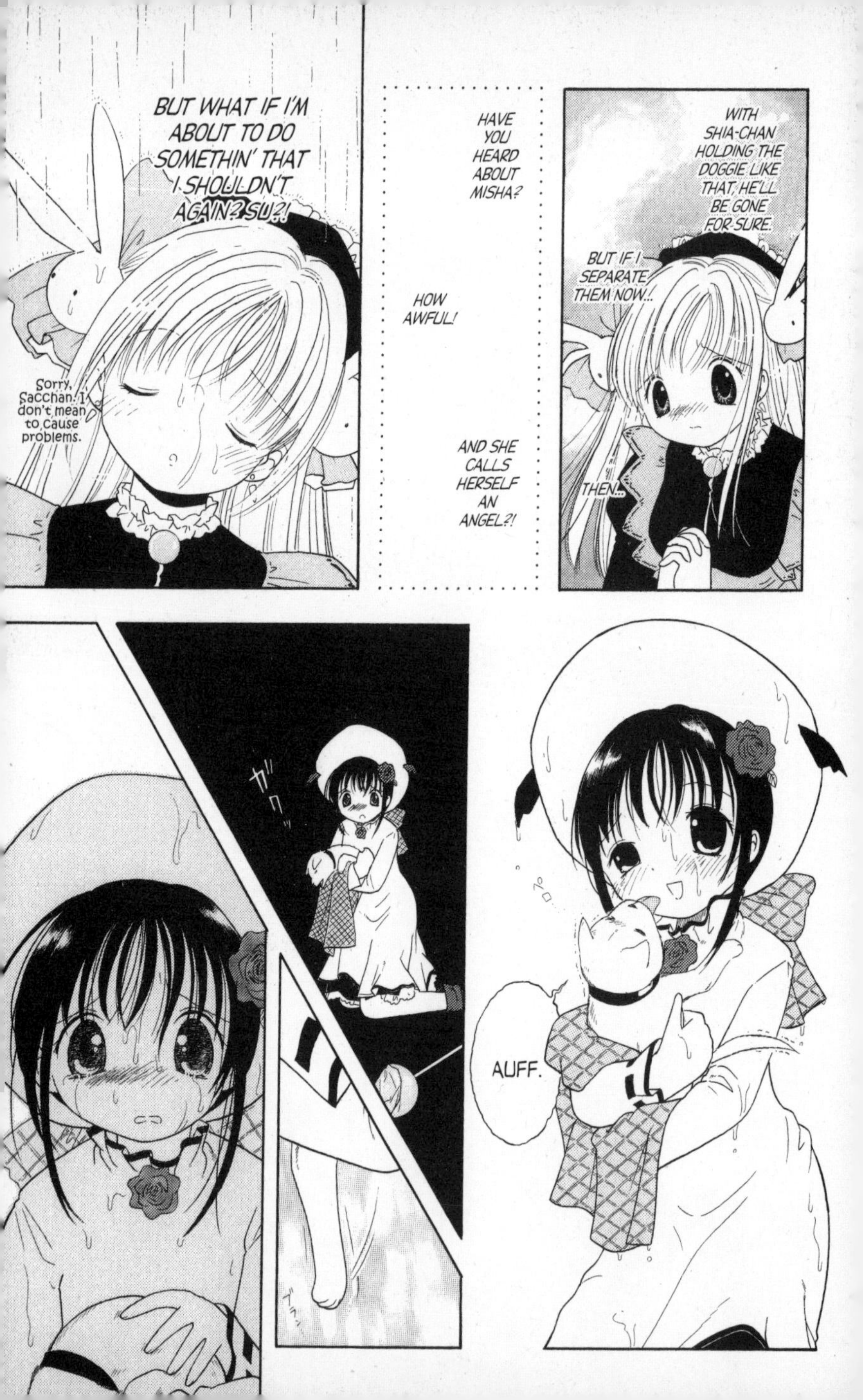
WITH SHIA-CHAN HOLDING THE DOGGIE LIKE THAT, HE'LL BE GONE FOR SURE.
BUT IF I SEPARATE THEM NOW...
THEN...
HAVE YOU HEARD ABOUT MISHA?
HOW AWFUL!
AND SHE CALLS HERSELF AN ANGEL?!
BUT WHAT IF I'M ABOUT TO DO SOMETHIN' THAT I SHOULDN'T AGAIN? SU?!
Sorry, Sacchan. I don't mean to cause problems.
AUFF.

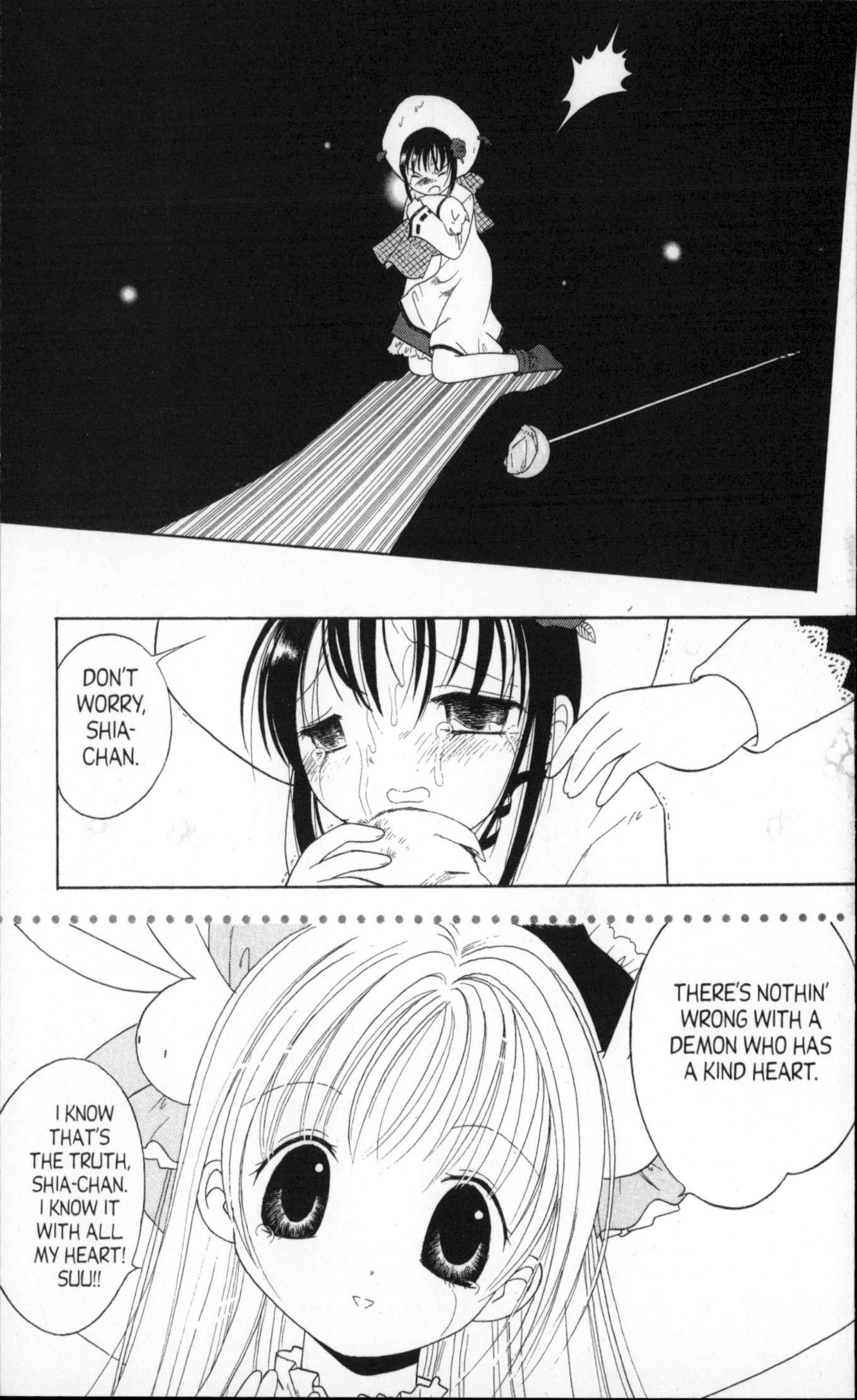
DON'T WORRY, SHIA-CHAN.
THERE'S NOTHIN' WRONG WITH A DEMON WHO HAS A KIND HEART.
I KNOW THAT'S THE TRUTH, SHIA-CHAN. I KNOW IT WITH ALL MY HEART! SUU!!

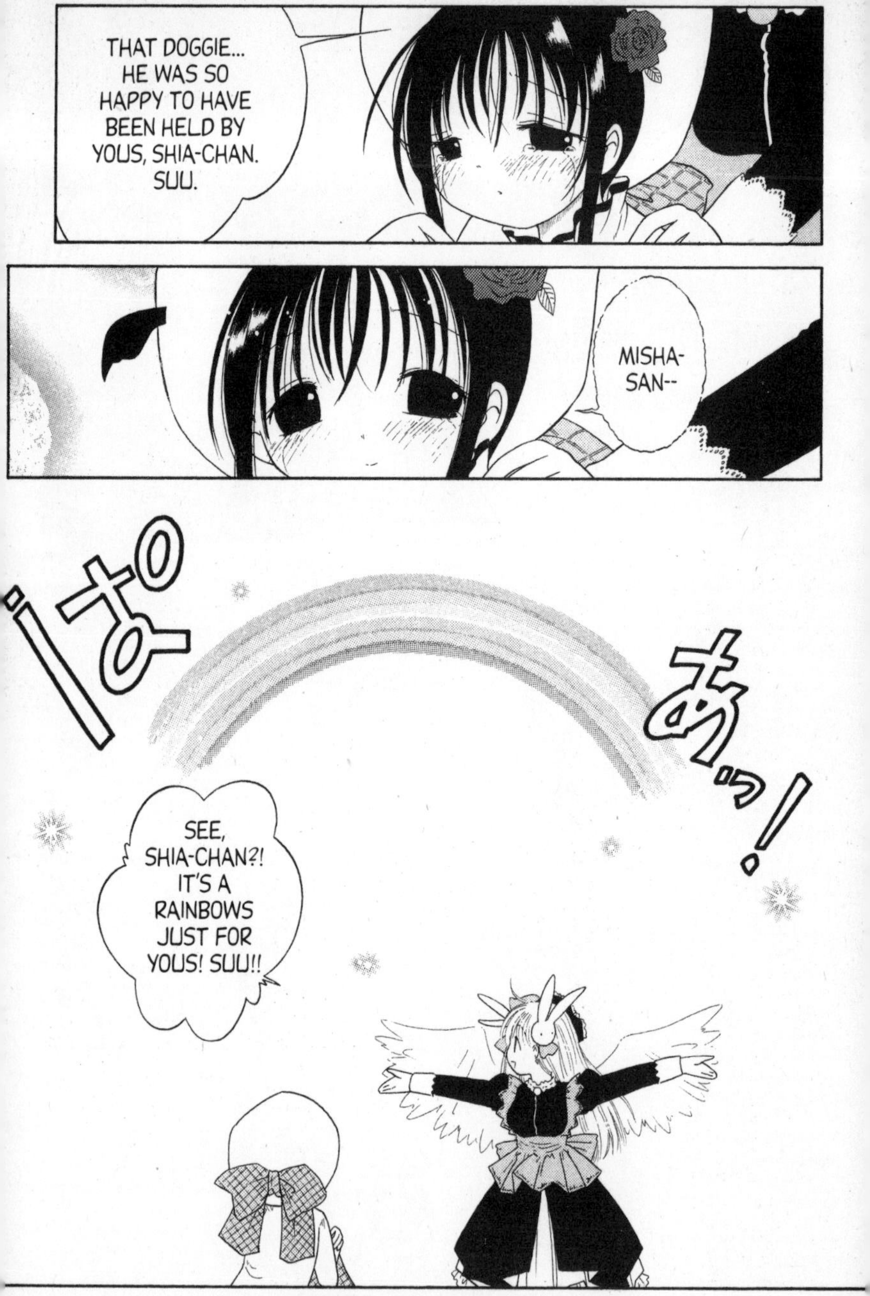
THAT DOGGIE... HE WAS SO HAPPY TO HAVE BEEN HELD BY YOUS, SHIA-CHAN. SUU.
MISHA-SAN--
ぱあっ!
SEE, SHIA-CHAN?! IT'S A RAINBOWS JUST FOR YOUS! SUU!!

The End

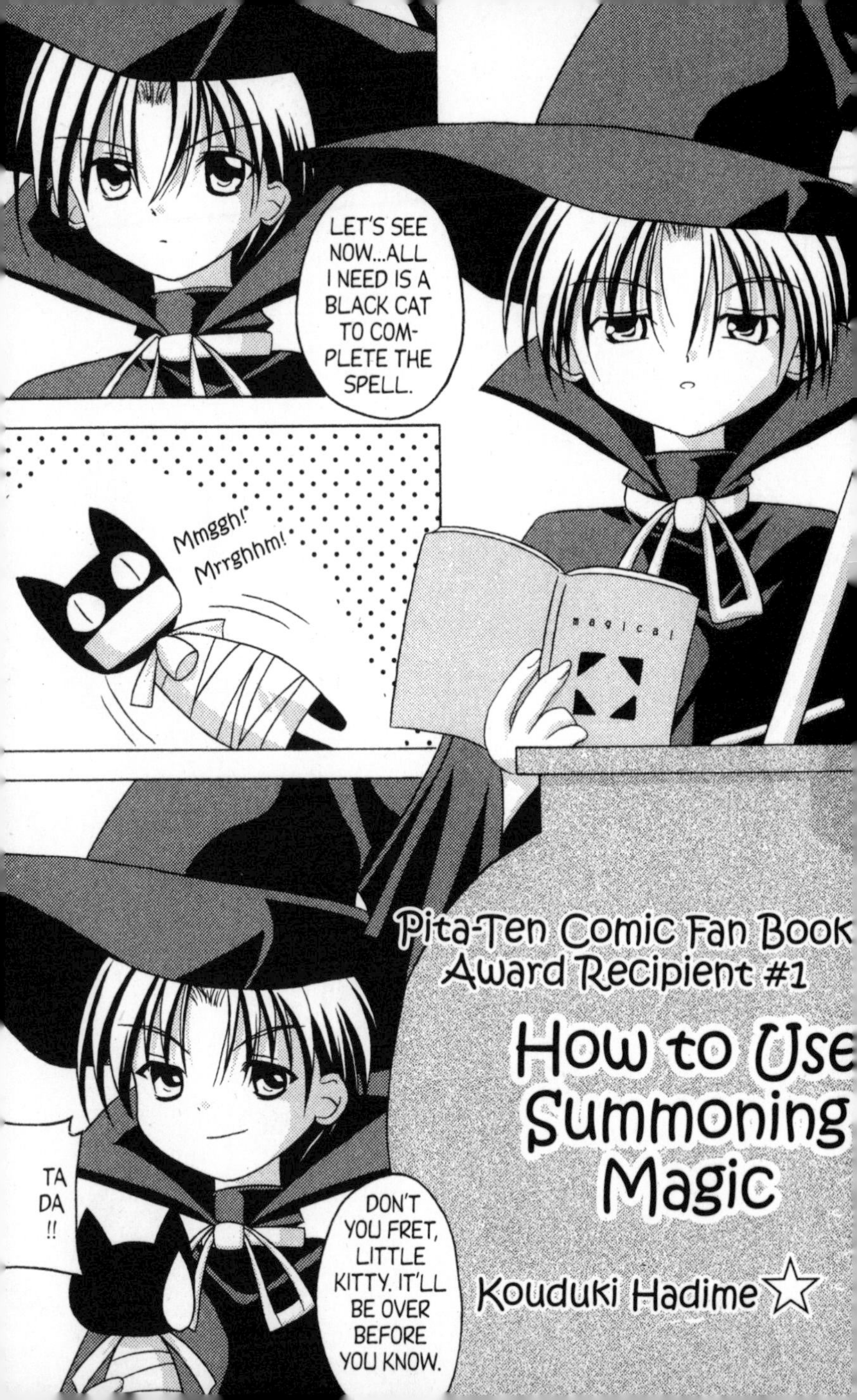
LET'S SEE NOW...ALL I NEED IS A BLACK CAT TO COMPLETE THE SPELL.
magical
Mmggh! Mrrghhm!
Pita-Ten Comic Fan Book Award Recipient #1
How to Use Summoning Magic
Kouduki Hadime ☆
TA DA !!
DON'T YOU FRET, LITTLE KITTY. IT'LL BE OVER BEFORE YOU KNOW.

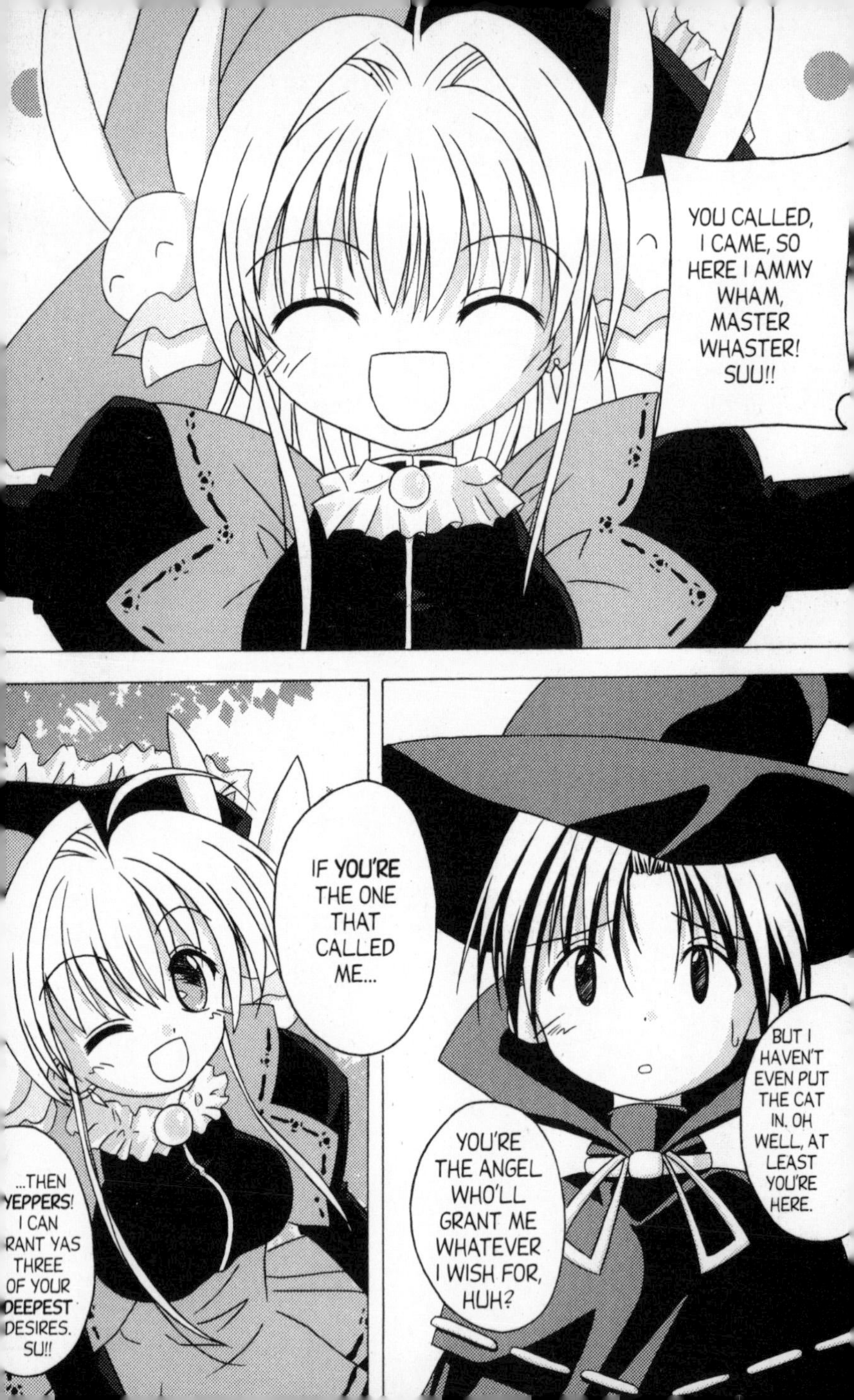
YOU CALLED, I CAME, SO HERE I AMMY WHAM, MASTER WHASTER! SUU!!
BUT I HAVEN'T EVEN PUT THE CAT IN. OH WELL, AT LEAST YOU'RE HERE.
YOU'RE THE ANGEL WHO'LL GRANT ME WHATEVER I WISH FOR, HUH?
IF **YOU'RE** THE ONE THAT CALLED ME...
...THEN **YEPPERS!** I CAN RANT YAS THREE OF YOUR **DEEPEST** DESIRES. SU!!

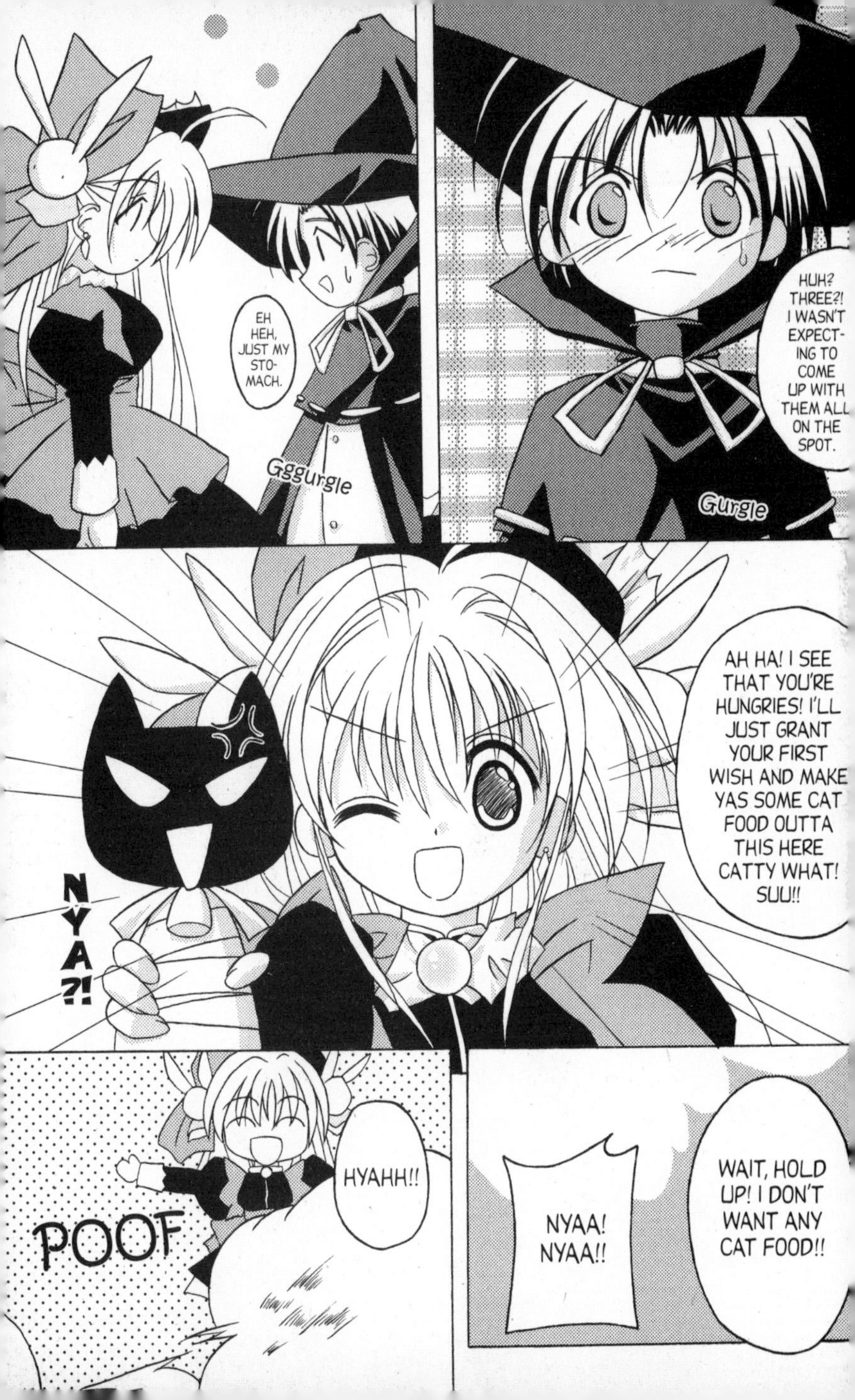
HUH? THREE?! I WASN'T EXPECTING TO COME UP WITH THEM ALL ON THE SPOT.
Gurgle
EH HEH, JUST MY STOMACH.
Gggurgle
AH HA! I SEE THAT YOU'RE HUNGRIES! I'LL JUST GRANT YOUR FIRST WISH AND MAKE YAS SOME CAT FOOD OUTTA THIS HERE CATTY WHAT! SUU!!
NYA?!
WAIT, HOLD UP! I DON'T WANT ANY CAT FOOD!!
NYAA! NYAA!!
HYAHH!!
POOF

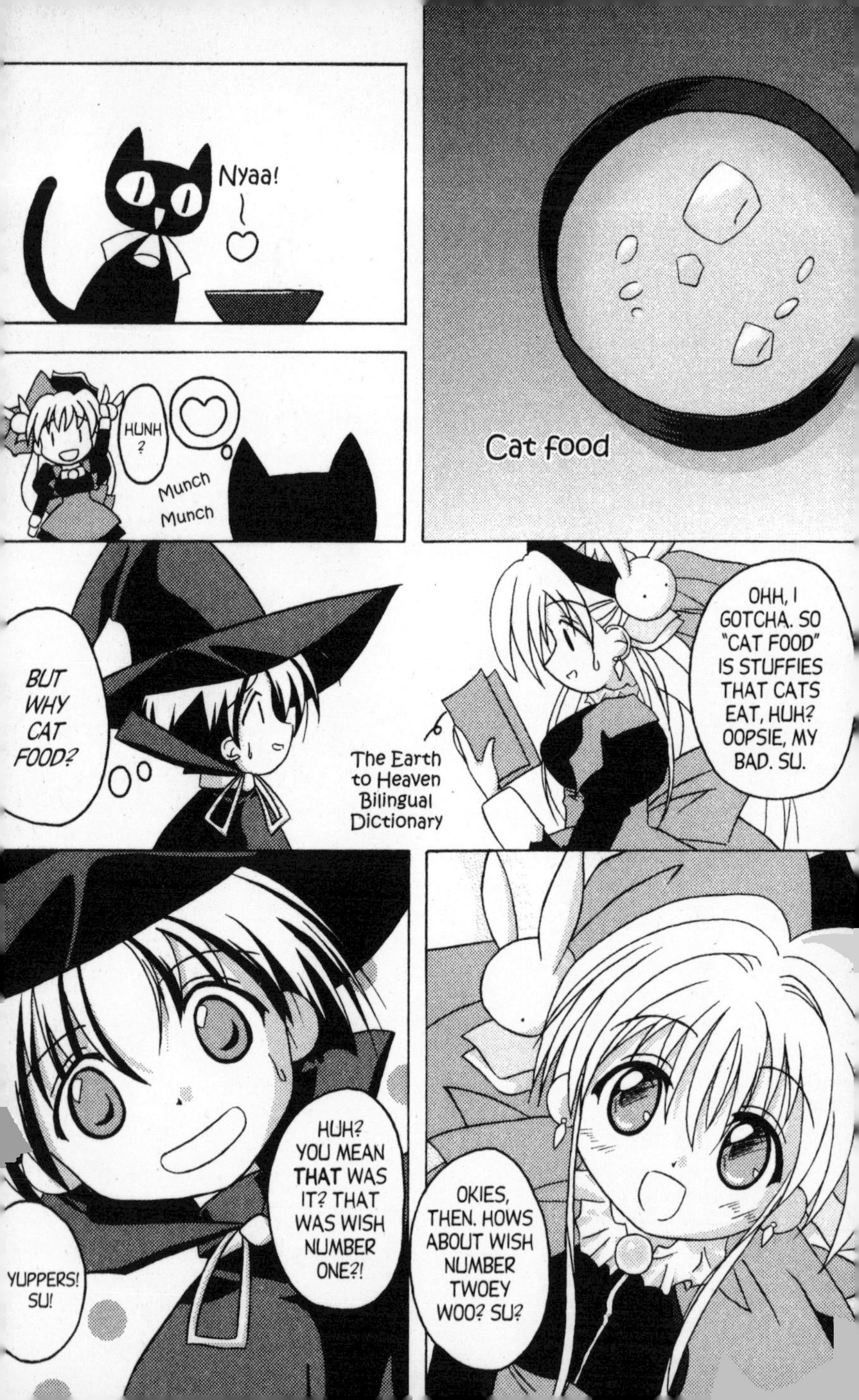
Cat food
Nyaa!
HUNH ?
Munch Munch
OHH, I GOTCHA. SO "CAT FOOD" IS STUFFIES THAT CATS EAT, HUH? OOPSIE, MY BAD. SU.
The Earth to Heaven Bilingual Dictionary
BUT WHY CAT FOOD?
OKIES, THEN. HOWS ABOUT WISH NUMBER TWOEY WOO? SU?
HUH? YOU MEAN THAT WAS IT? THAT WAS WISH NUMBER ONE?!
YUPPERS! SU!

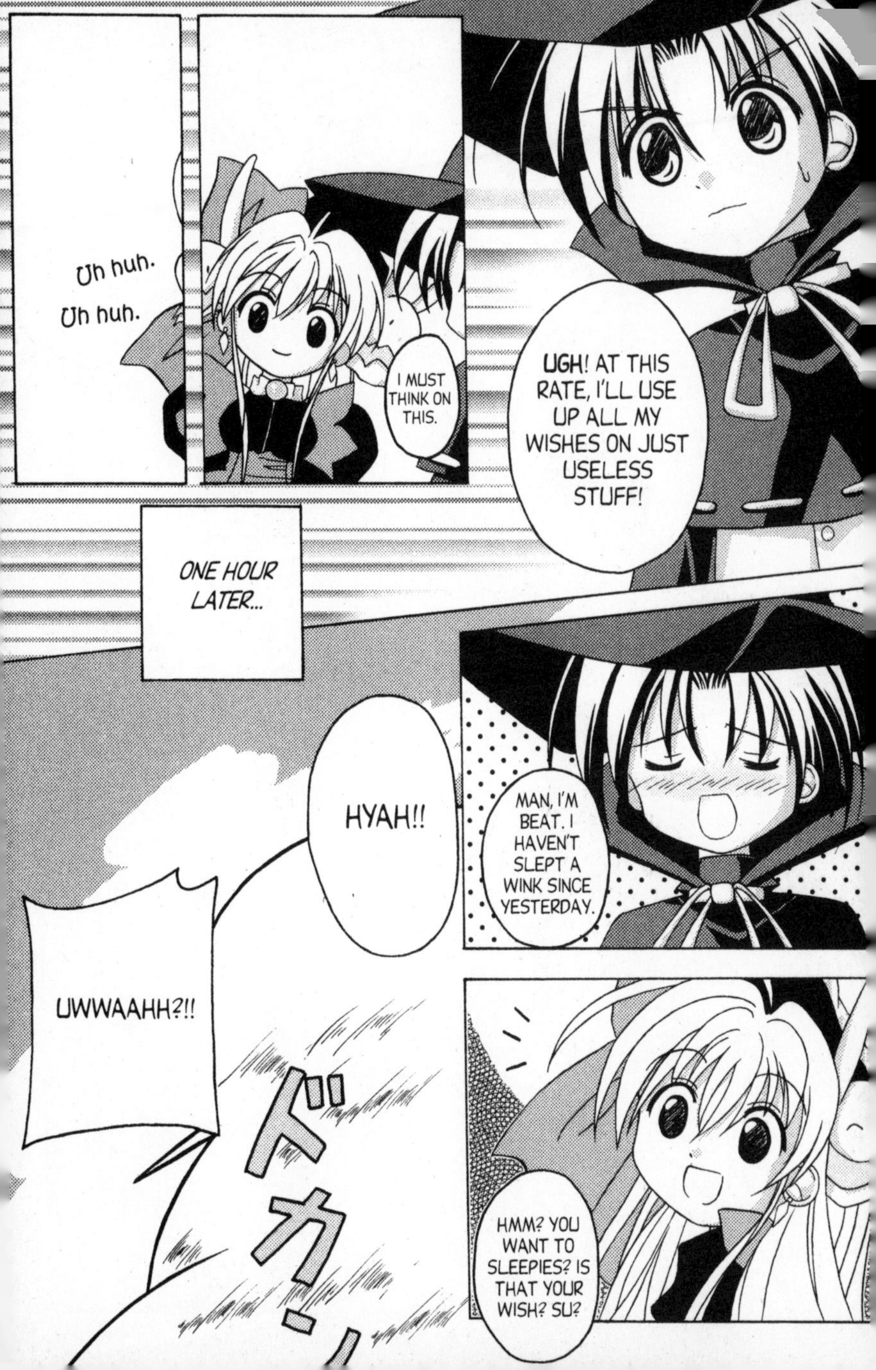
UGH! AT THIS RATE, I'LL USE UP ALL MY WISHES ON JUST USELESS STUFF!
I MUST THINK ON THIS.
Uh huh.
Uh huh.
ONE HOUR LATER...
MAN, I'M BEAT. I HAVEN'T SLEPT A WINK SINCE YESTERDAY.
HMM? YOU WANT TO SLEEPIES? IS THAT YOUR WISH? SU?
HYAH!!
UWWAAHH?!!
ドカッ

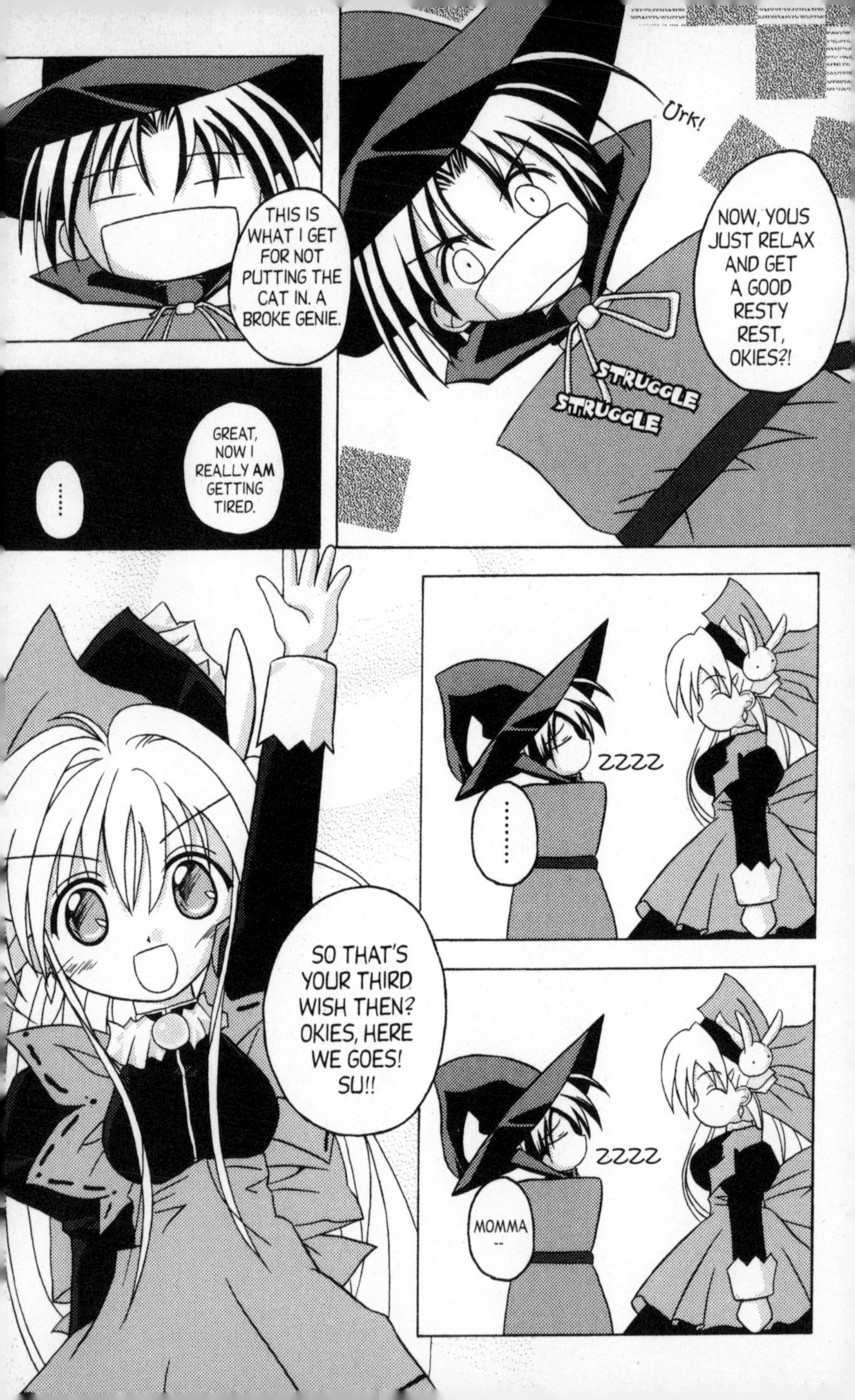
Urk!
NOW, YOUS JUST RELAX AND GET A GOOD RESTY REST, OKIES?!
STRUGGLE
STRUGGLE
THIS IS WHAT I GET FOR NOT PUTTING THE CAT IN. A BROKE GENIE.
GREAT, NOW I REALLY **AM** GETTING TIRED.
......
ZZZZ
......
ZZZZ
MOMMA --
SO THAT'S YOUR THIRD WISH THEN? OKIES, HERE WE GOES! SU!!

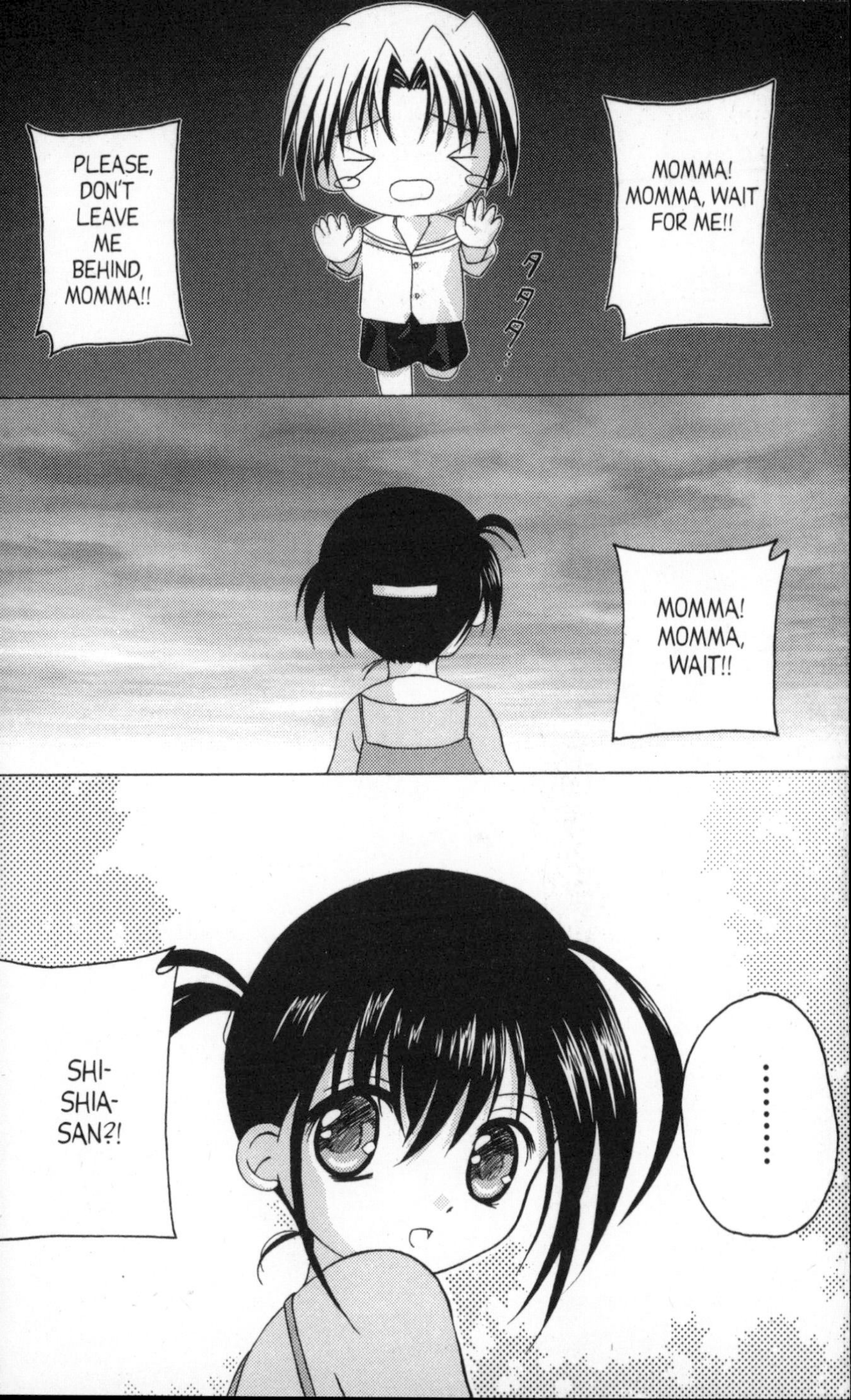
MOMMA! MOMMA, WAIT FOR ME!!
PLEASE, DON'T LEAVE ME BEHIND, MOMMA!!
MOMMA! MOMMA, WAIT!!
....
SHI-SHIA-SAN?!

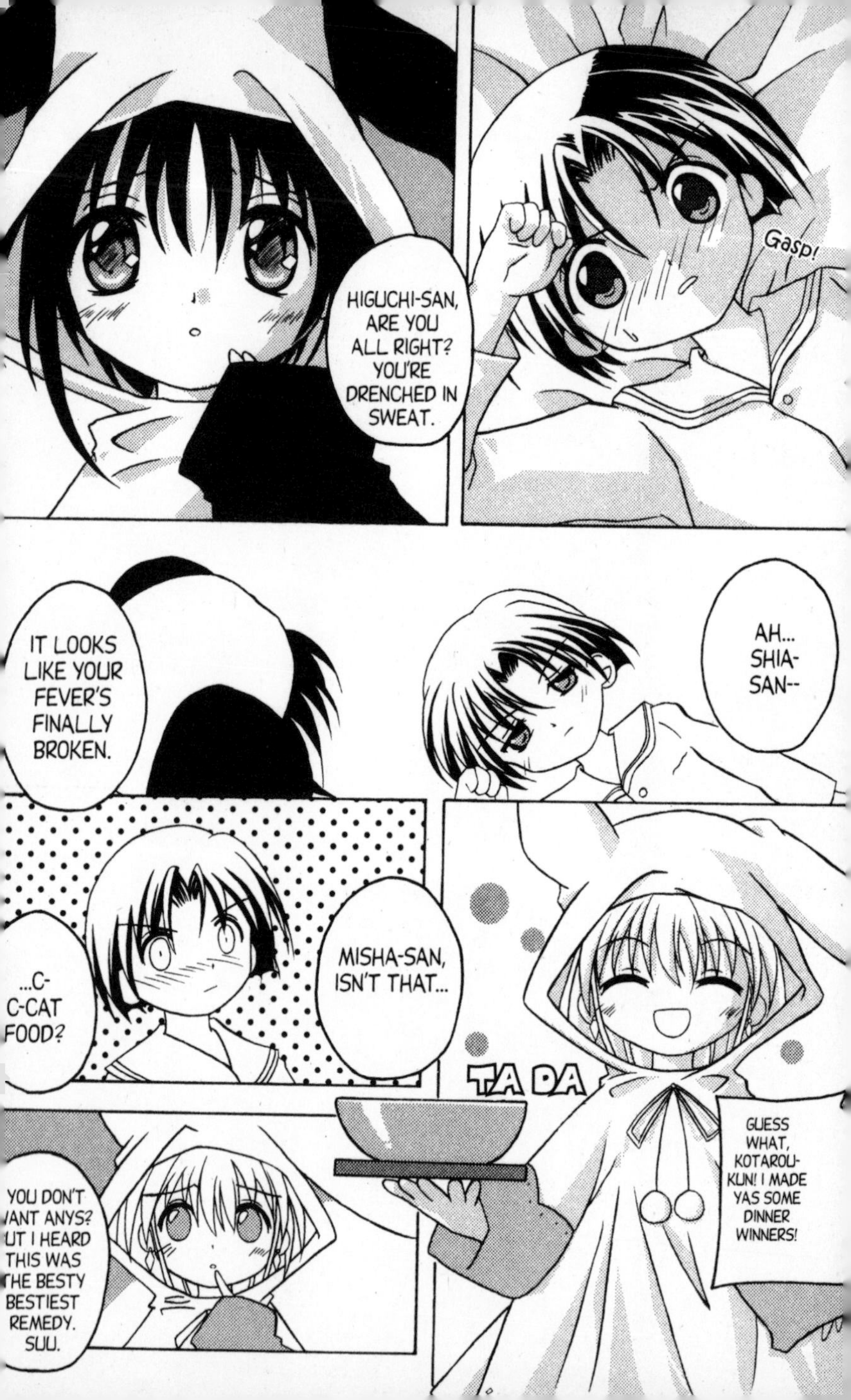
Gasp!
HIGUCHI-SAN, ARE YOU ALL RIGHT? YOU'RE DRENCHED IN SWEAT.
AH... SHIA-SAN--
IT LOOKS LIKE YOUR FEVER'S FINALLY BROKEN.
TA DA
GUESS WHAT, KOTAROU-KUN! I MADE YAS SOME DINNER WINNERS!
MISHA-SAN, ISN'T THAT...
...C-C-CAT FOOD?
YOU DON'T ANT ANYS? UT I HEARD THIS WAS HE BESTY BESTIEST REMEDY. SUU.

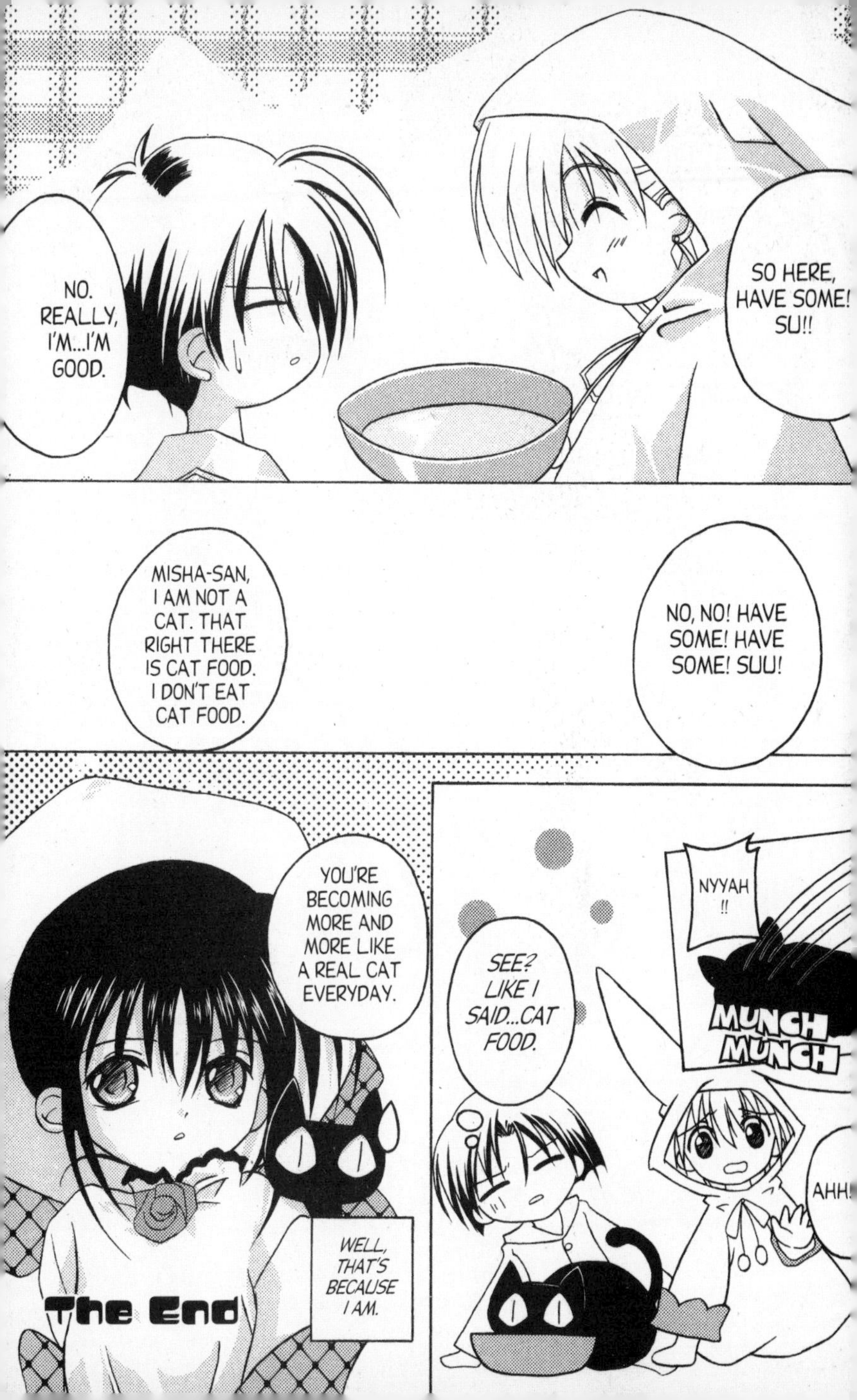

SO HERE, HAVE SOME! SU!!
NO. REALLY, I'M...I'M GOOD.
NO, NO! HAVE SOME! HAVE SOME! SUU!
MISHA-SAN, I AM NOT A CAT. THAT RIGHT THERE IS CAT FOOD. I DON'T EAT CAT FOOD.
NYYAH !!
MUNCH MUNCH
AHH!
SEE? LIKE I SAID...CAT FOOD.
YOU'RE BECOMING MORE AND MORE LIKE A REAL CAT EVERYDAY.
WELL, THAT'S BECAUSE I AM.
The End

Pita-Ten Comic Fan Award Recipients

Miya Hazuki

To be very honest, it had been eight months since my last comic. So now that I look over this particular work, I'm quite embarrassed. D'oh!

But still, I love you, Misha-san!! So there!

Hee hee.

Kouduki Hadime

I love *Pita-Ten*!! And I'm so grateful for receiving the Comic Fan Award!! I'm so incredibly happy! Thank you so very much!! http://www.din.or.jp/~momitan

If you'd be so kind as to post your thoughts about the comic, I'd be even more grateful!!

-Kouduki Hadime

I love Nya!

Pita-Ten Comic Fan Award Recipient #2

How to Wish Upon a Star

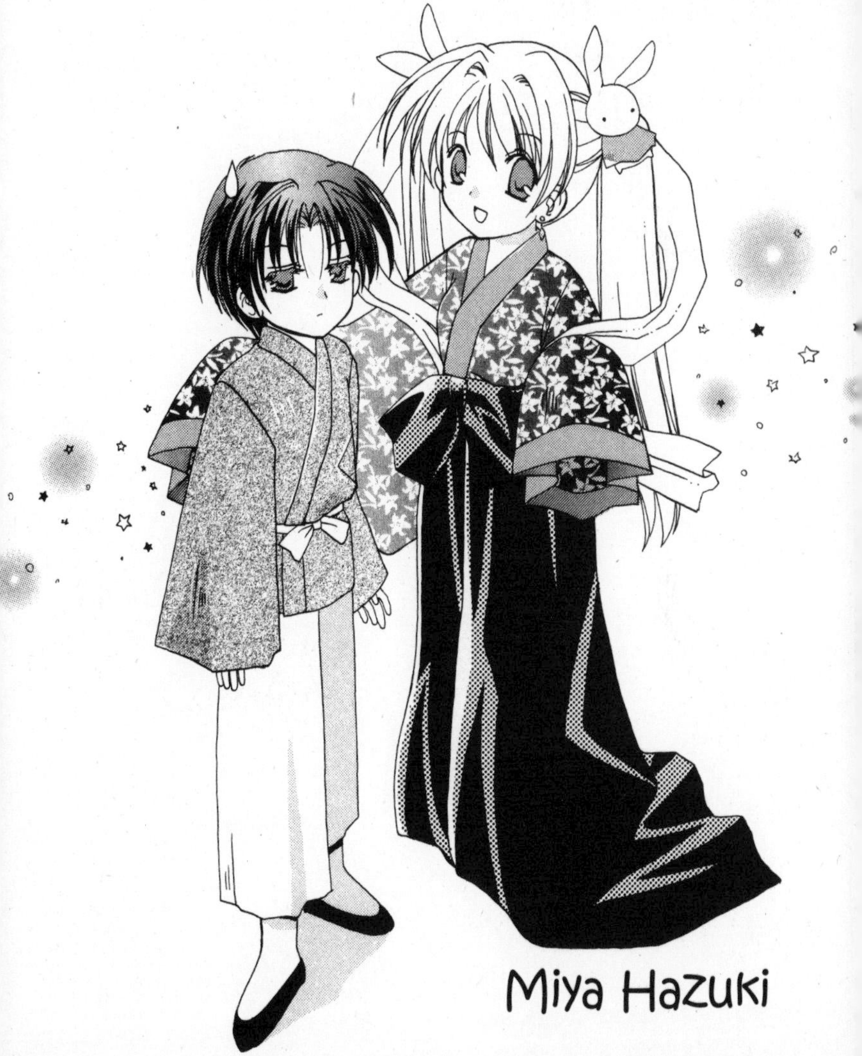

Miya Hazuki

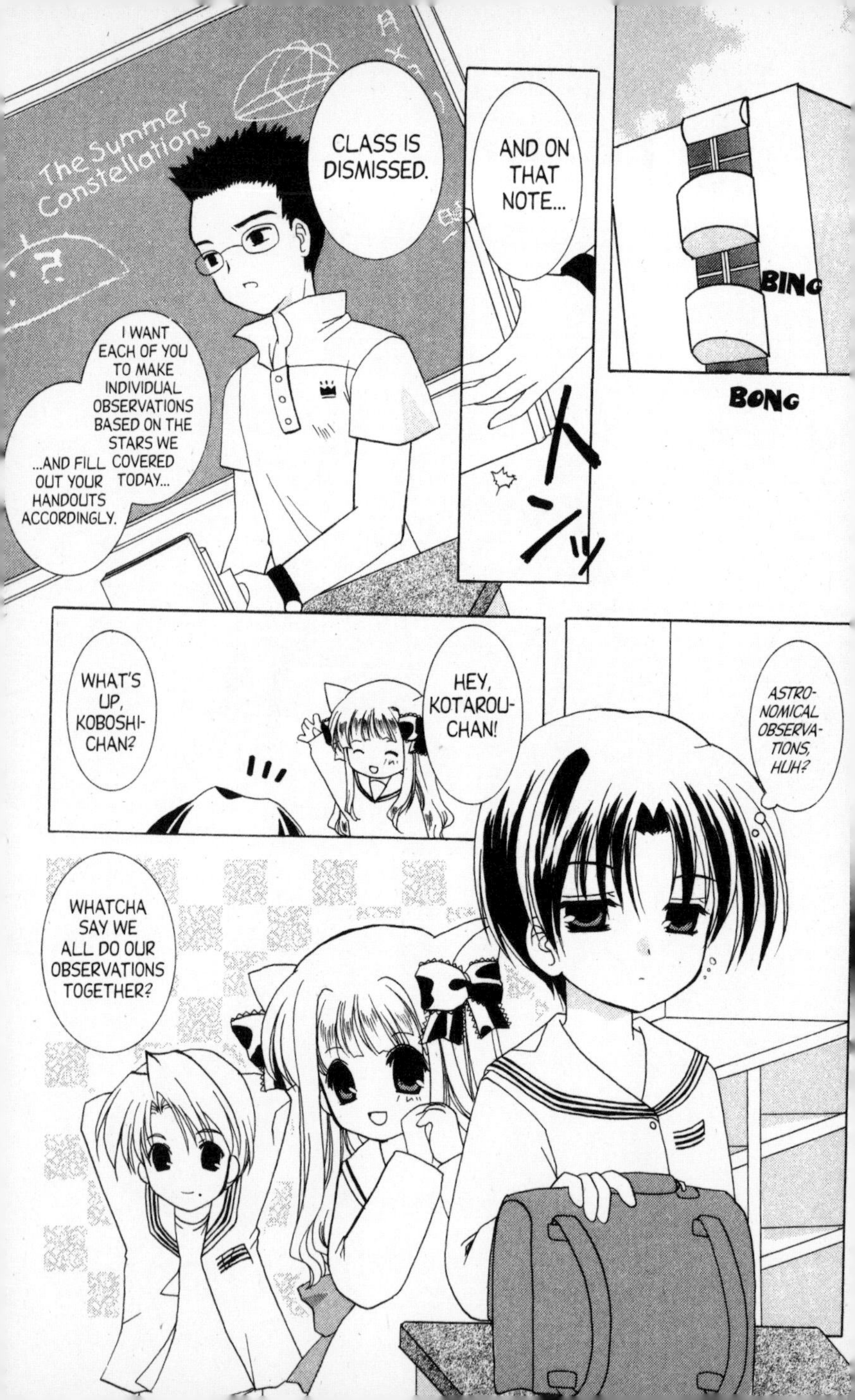
BING
BONG
AND ON THAT NOTE...
トンッ
CLASS IS DISMISSED.
The Summer Constellations
I WANT EACH OF YOU TO MAKE INDIVIDUAL OBSERVATIONS BASED ON THE STARS WE COVERED TODAY... ...AND FILL OUT YOUR HANDOUTS ACCORDINGLY.
ASTRONOMICAL OBSERVATIONS, HUH?
HEY, KOTAROU-CHAN!
WHAT'S UP, KOBOSHI-CHAN?
WHATCHA SAY WE ALL DO OUR OBSERVATIONS TOGETHER?

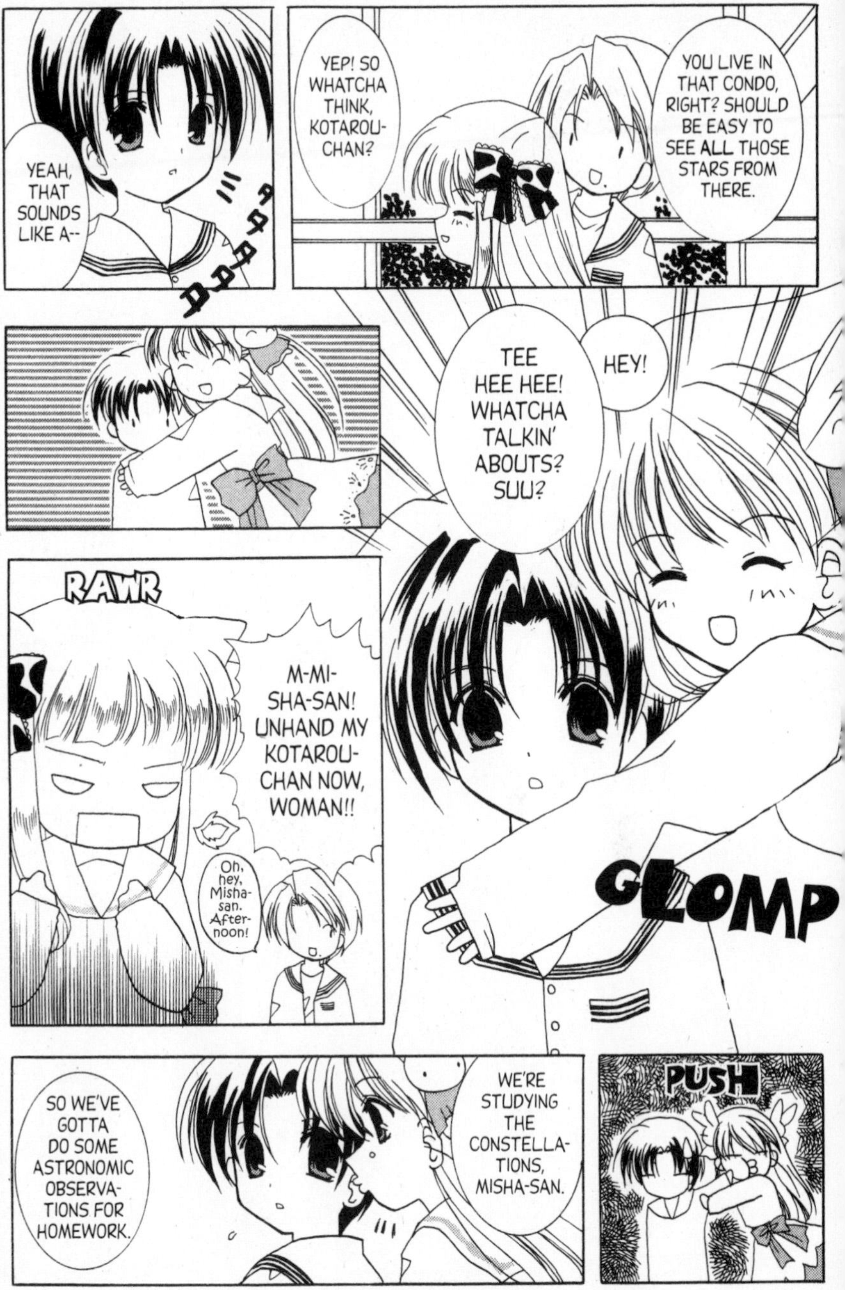
YOU LIVE IN THAT CONDO, RIGHT? SHOULD BE EASY TO SEE **ALL** THOSE STARS FROM THERE.
YEP! SO WHATCHA THINK, KOTAROU-CHAN?
YEAH, THAT SOUNDS LIKE A--
HEY!
TEE HEE HEE! WHATCHA TALKIN' ABOUTS? SUU?
GLOMP
RAWR
M-MI-SHA-SAN! UNHAND MY KOTAROU-CHAN NOW, WOMAN!!
Oh, hey, Misha-san. Afternoon!
PUSH
WE'RE STUDYING THE CONSTELLATIONS, MISHA-SAN.
SO WE'VE GOTTA DO SOME ASTRONOMIC OBSERVATIONS FOR HOMEWORK.

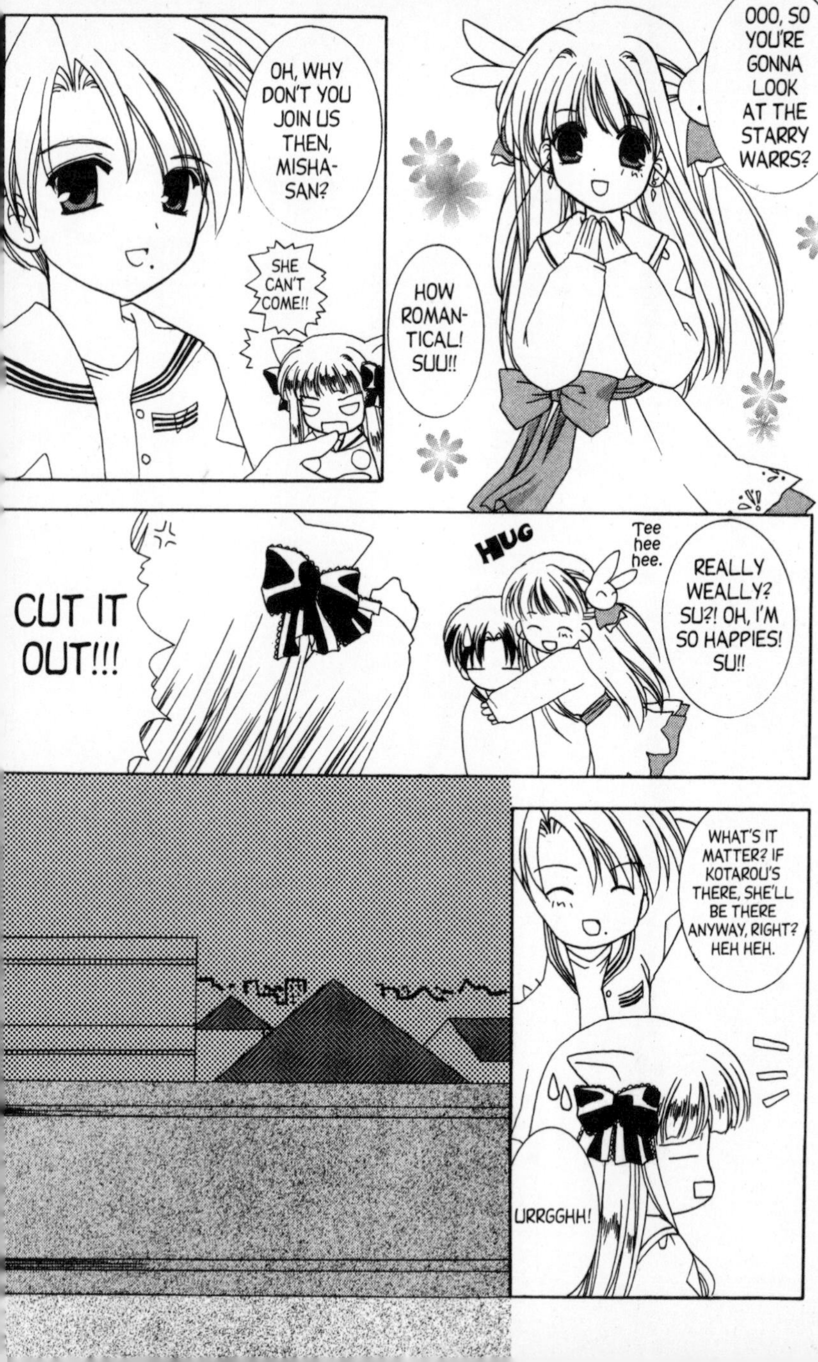
OOO, SO YOU'RE GONNA LOOK AT THE STARRY WARRS?
HOW ROMAN-TICAL! SUU!!
OH, WHY DON'T YOU JOIN US THEN, MISHA-SAN?
SHE CAN'T COME!!
REALLY WEALLY? SU?! OH, I'M SO HAPPIES! SU!!
Tee hee hee.
HUG
CUT IT OUT!!!
WHAT'S IT MATTER? IF KOTAROU'S THERE, SHE'LL BE THERE ANYWAY, RIGHT? HEH HEH.
URRGGHH!

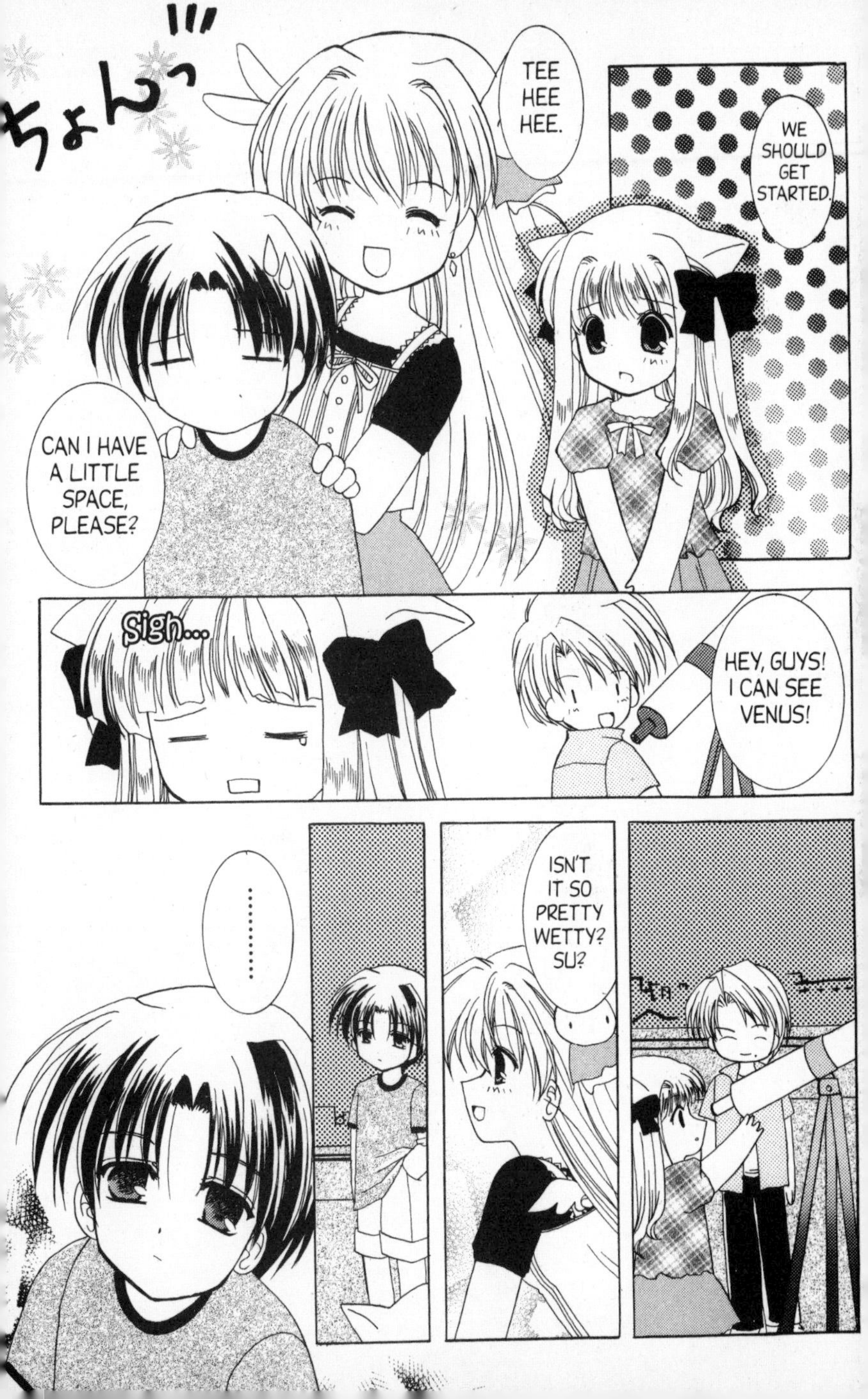

WE SHOULD GET STARTED.
TEE HEE HEE.
ちょんっ
CAN I HAVE A LITTLE SPACE, PLEASE?
HEY, GUYS! I CAN SEE VENUS!
Sigh...
ISN'T IT SO PRETTY WETTY? SU?
....

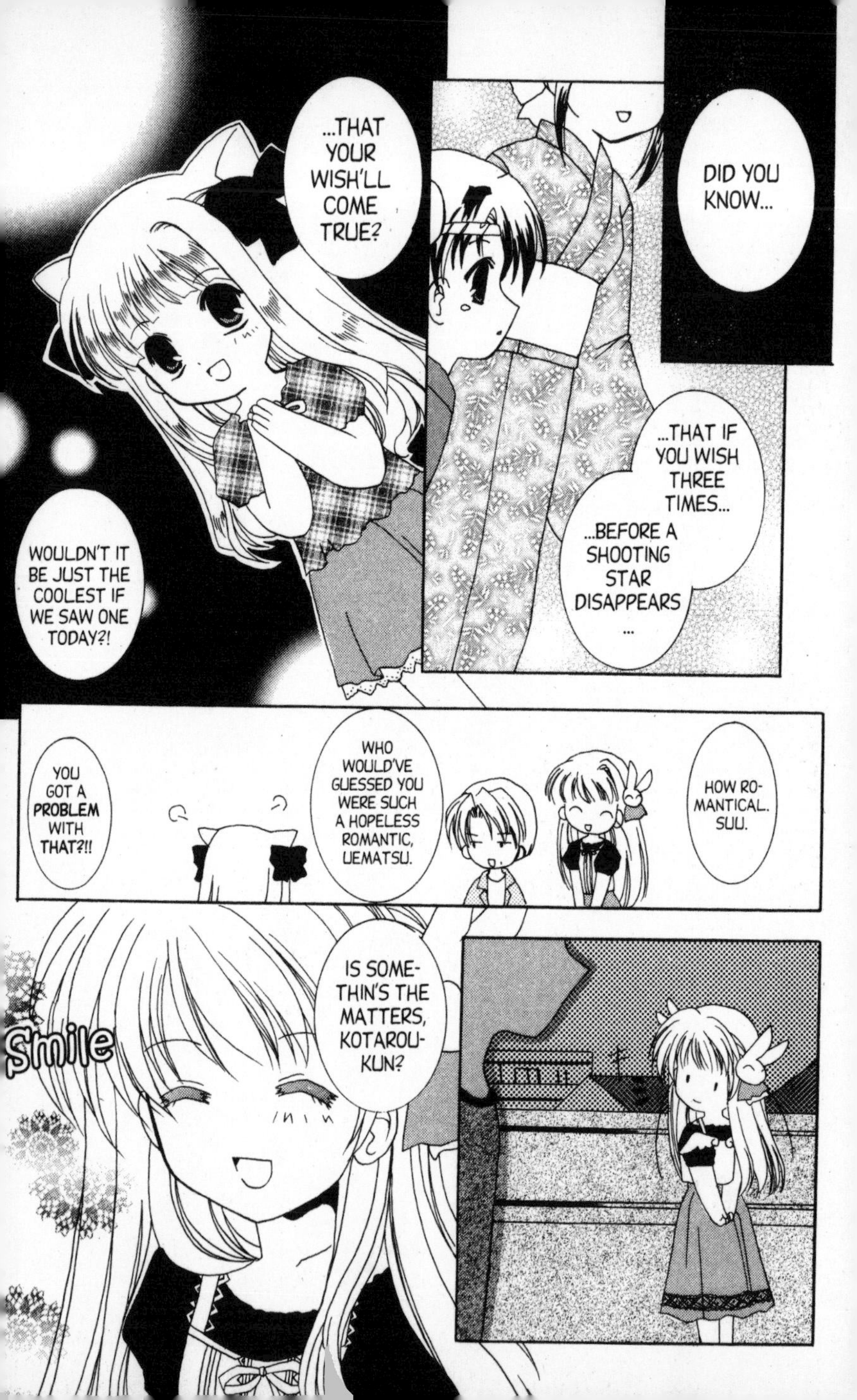
DID YOU KNOW...
...THAT IF YOU WISH THREE TIMES...
...BEFORE A SHOOTING STAR DISAPPEARS ...
...THAT YOUR WISH'LL COME TRUE?
WOULDN'T IT BE JUST THE COOLEST IF WE SAW ONE TODAY?!
HOW RO-MANTICAL. SUU.
WHO WOULD'VE GUESSED YOU WERE SUCH A HOPELESS ROMANTIC, UEMATSU.
YOU GOT A **PROBLEM** WITH **THAT?!!**
IS SOME-THIN'S THE MATTERS, KOTAROU-KUN?
Smile

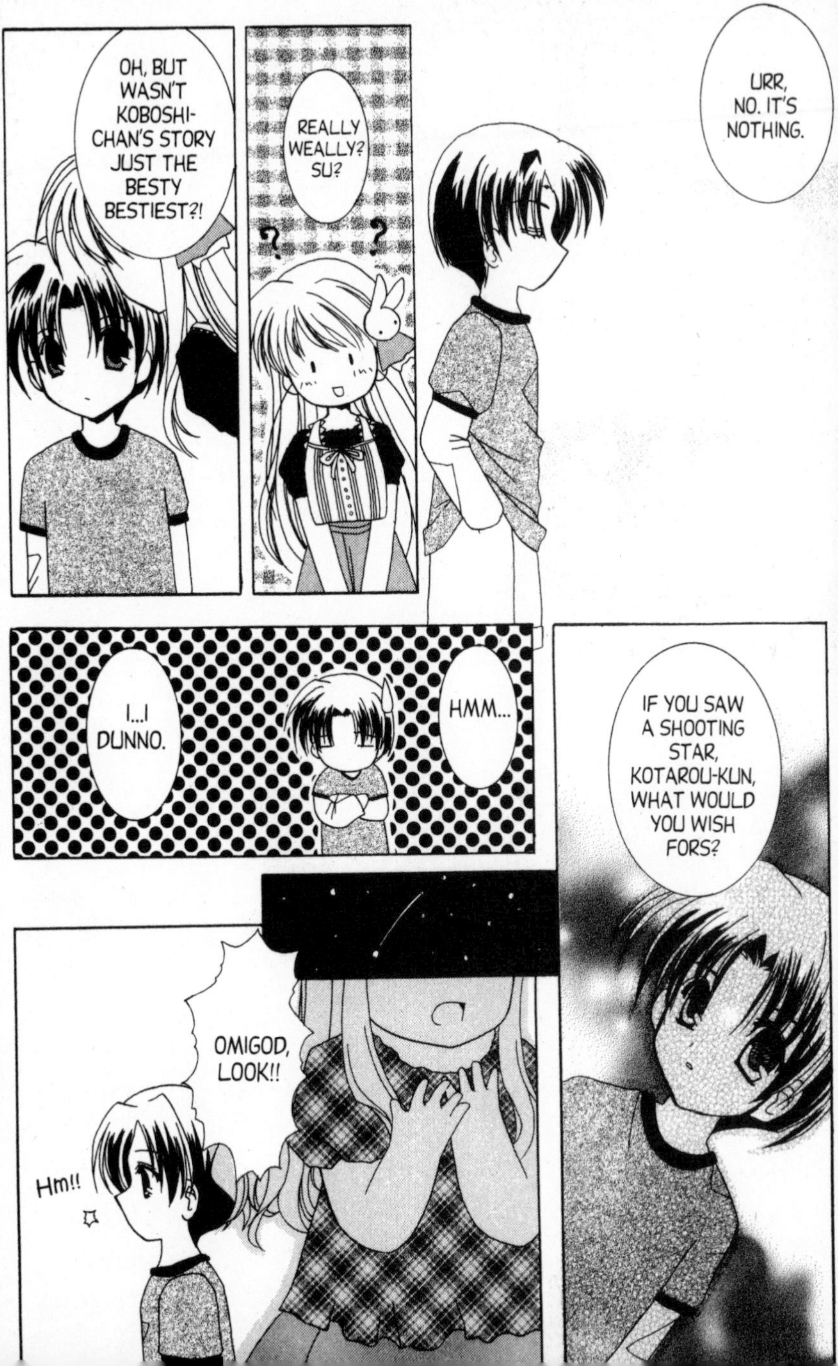
URR, NO. IT'S NOTHING.
REALLY WEALLY? SU?
OH, BUT WASN'T KOBOSHI-CHAN'S STORY JUST THE BESTY BESTIEST?!
IF YOU SAW A SHOOTING STAR, KOTAROU-KUN, WHAT WOULD YOU WISH FORS?
HMM...
I...I DUNNO.
OMIGOD, LOOK!!
Hm!!

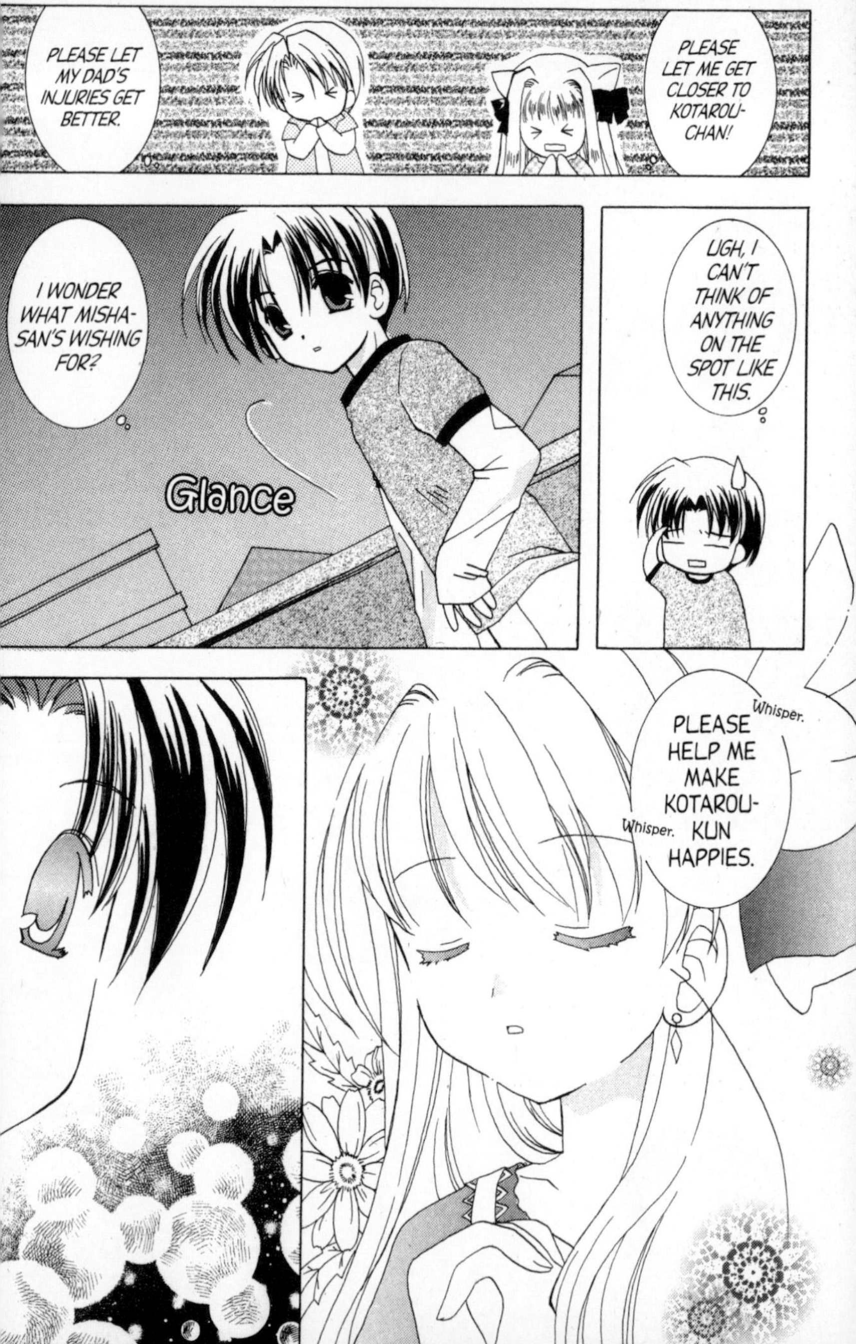
PLEASE LET ME GET CLOSER TO KOTAROU-CHAN!
PLEASE LET MY DAD'S INJURIES GET BETTER.
UGH, I CAN'T THINK OF ANYTHING ON THE SPOT LIKE THIS.
I WONDER WHAT MISHA-SAN'S WISHING FOR?
Glance
Whisper.
PLEASE HELP ME MAKE KOTAROU-KUN HAPPIES.
Whisper.

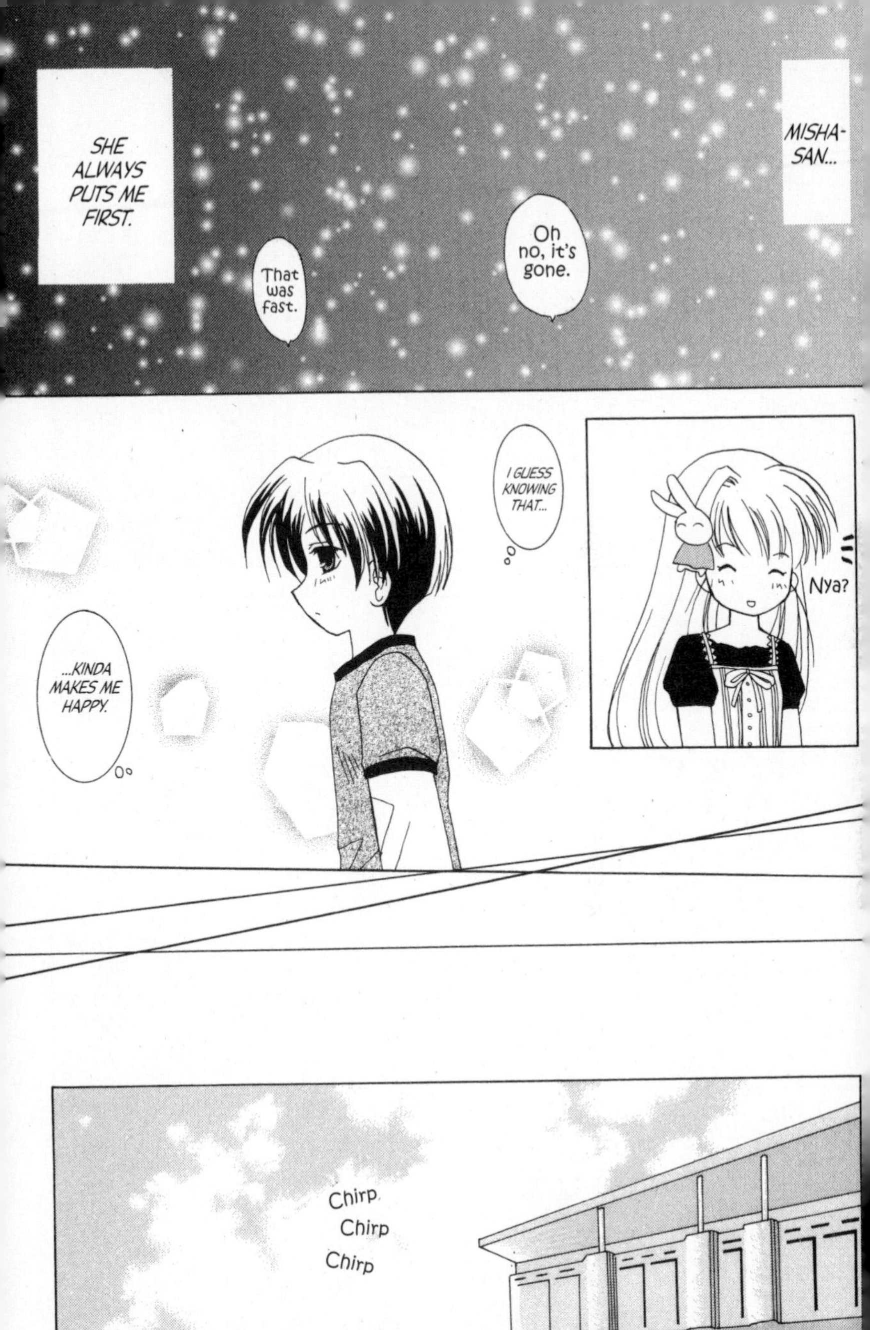
MISHA-SAN...
Oh no, it's gone.
That was fast.
SHE ALWAYS PUTS ME FIRST.
Nya?
I GUESS KNOWING THAT...
...KINDA MAKES ME HAPPY.
Chirp
Chirp
Chirp

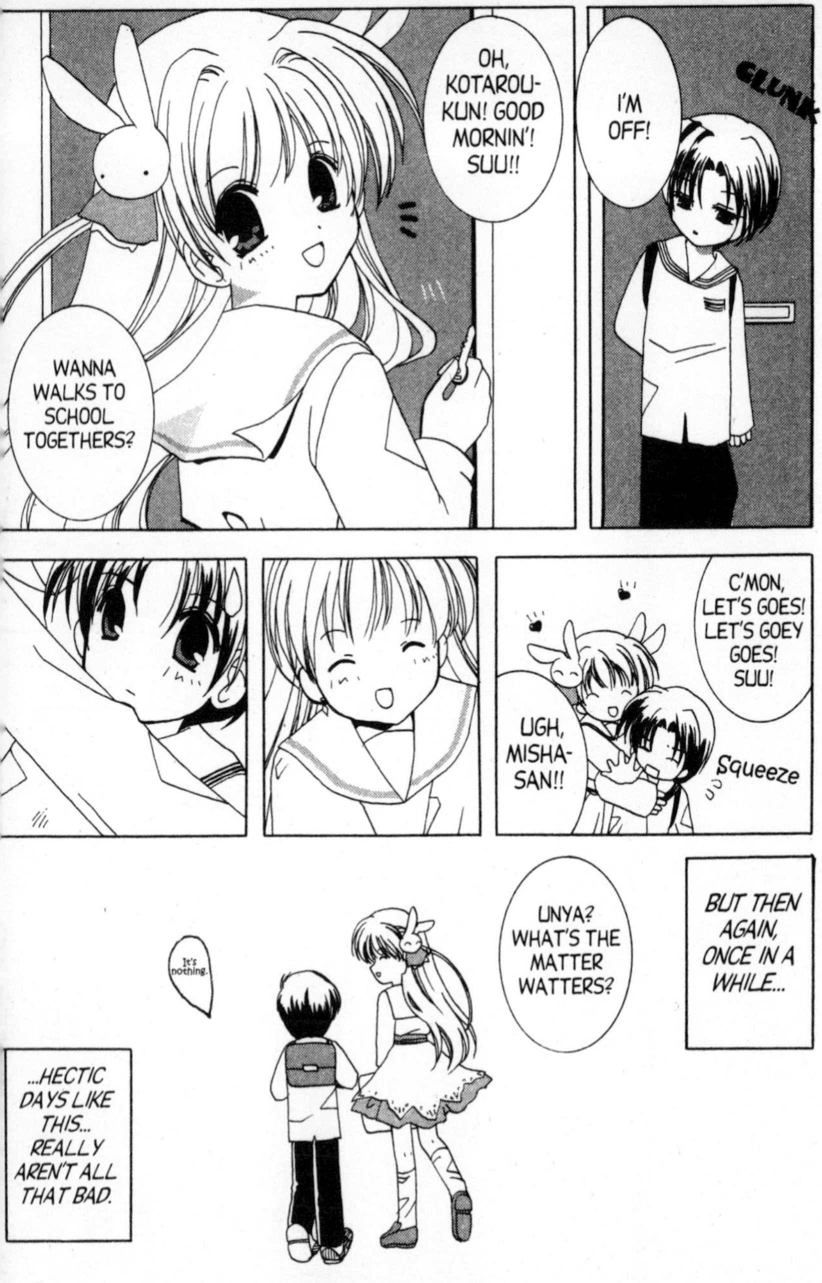
CLUNK
I'M OFF!
OH, KOTAROU-KUN! GOOD MORNIN'! SUU!!
WANNA WALKS TO SCHOOL TOGETHERS?
C'MON, LET'S GOES! LET'S GOEY GOES! SUU!
UGH, MISHA-SAN!!
Squeeze
BUT THEN AGAIN, ONCE IN A WHILE...
UNYA? WHAT'S THE MATTER WATTERS?
It's nothing.
...HECTIC DAYS LIKE THIS... REALLY AREN'T ALL THAT BAD.

The End

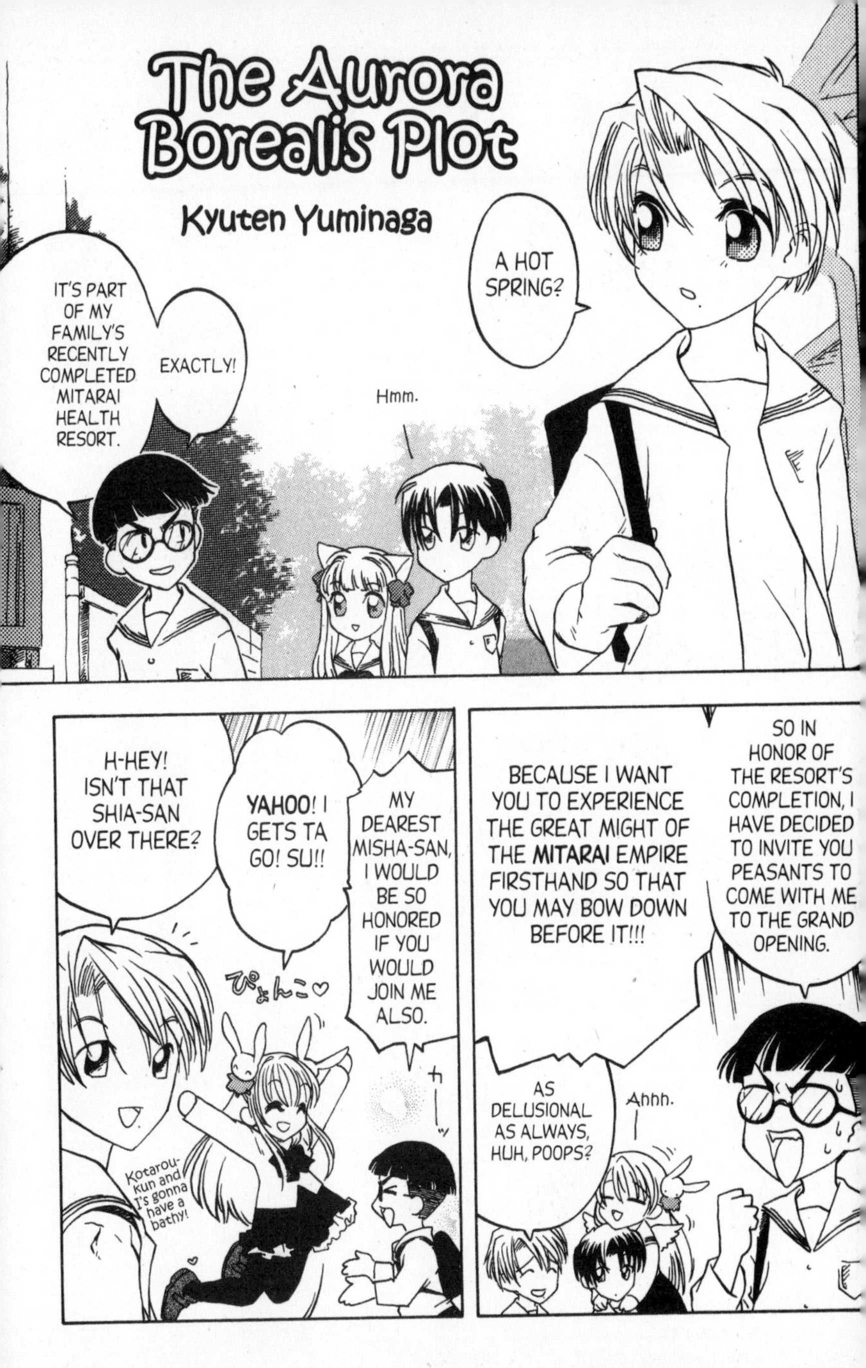
The Aurora Borealis Plot
Kyuten Yuminaga
A HOT SPRING?
EXACTLY!
IT'S PART OF MY FAMILY'S RECENTLY COMPLETED MITARAI HEALTH RESORT.
Hmm.
SO IN HONOR OF THE RESORT'S COMPLETION, I HAVE DECIDED TO INVITE YOU PEASANTS TO COME WITH ME TO THE GRAND OPENING.
BECAUSE I WANT YOU TO EXPERIENCE THE GREAT MIGHT OF THE **MITARAI** EMPIRE FIRSTHAND SO THAT YOU MAY BOW DOWN BEFORE IT!!!
Ahhh.
AS DELUSIONAL AS ALWAYS, HUH, POOPS?
MY DEAREST MISHA-SAN, I WOULD BE SO HONORED IF YOU WOULD JOIN ME ALSO.
YAHOO! I GETS TA GO! SU!!
H-HEY! ISN'T THAT SHIA-SAN OVER THERE?
ぴょんこ♡
カー…ッ
Kotarou-kun and I's gonna have a bathy!

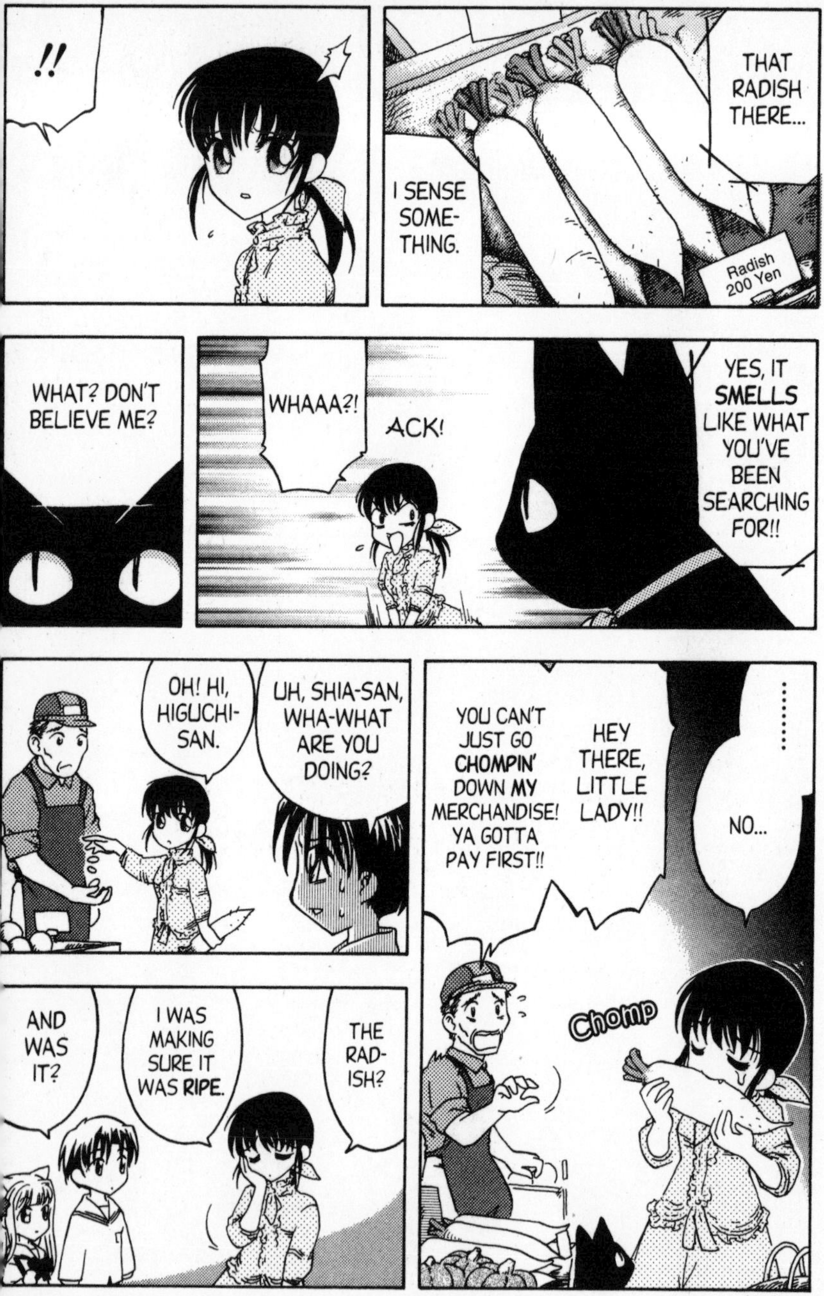
THAT RADISH THERE...
I SENSE SOMETHING.
Radish 200 Yen
!!
YES, IT SMELLS LIKE WHAT YOU'VE BEEN SEARCHING FOR!!
WHAAA?!
ACK!
WHAT? DON'T BELIEVE ME?
......
NO...
HEY THERE, LITTLE LADY!!
YOU CAN'T JUST GO CHOMPIN' DOWN MY MERCHANDISE! YA GOTTA PAY FIRST!!
Chomp
UH, SHIA-SAN, WHA-WHAT ARE YOU DOING?
OH! HI, HIGUCHI-SAN.
THE RADISH?
I WAS MAKING SURE IT WAS RIPE.
AND WAS IT?

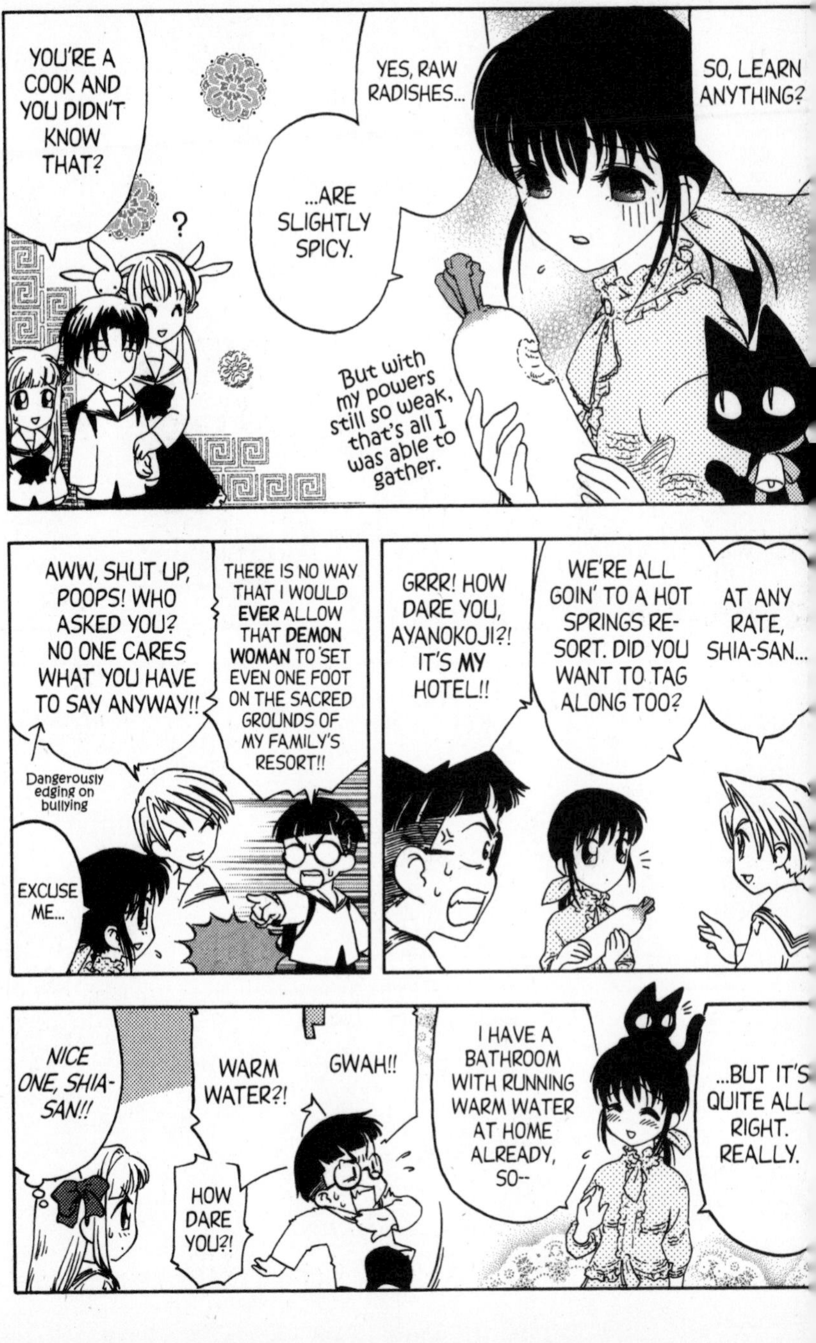
SO, LEARN ANYTHING?
YES, RAW RADISHES...
...ARE SLIGHTLY SPICY.
But with my powers still so weak, that's all I was able to gather.
YOU'RE A COOK AND YOU DIDN'T KNOW THAT?
?
AT ANY RATE, SHIA-SAN...
WE'RE ALL GOIN' TO A HOT SPRINGS RE-SORT. DID YOU WANT TO TAG ALONG TOO?
GRRR! HOW DARE YOU, AYANOKOJI?! IT'S MY HOTEL!!
THERE IS NO WAY THAT I WOULD EVER ALLOW THAT DEMON WOMAN TO SET EVEN ONE FOOT ON THE SACRED GROUNDS OF MY FAMILY'S RESORT!!
AWW, SHUT UP, POOPS! WHO ASKED YOU? NO ONE CARES WHAT YOU HAVE TO SAY ANYWAY!!
Dangerously edging on bullying
EXCUSE ME...
...BUT IT'S QUITE ALL RIGHT. REALLY.
I HAVE A BATHROOM WITH RUNNING WARM WATER AT HOME ALREADY, SO--
GWAH!!
WARM WATER?!
HOW DARE YOU?!
NICE ONE, SHIA-SAN!!

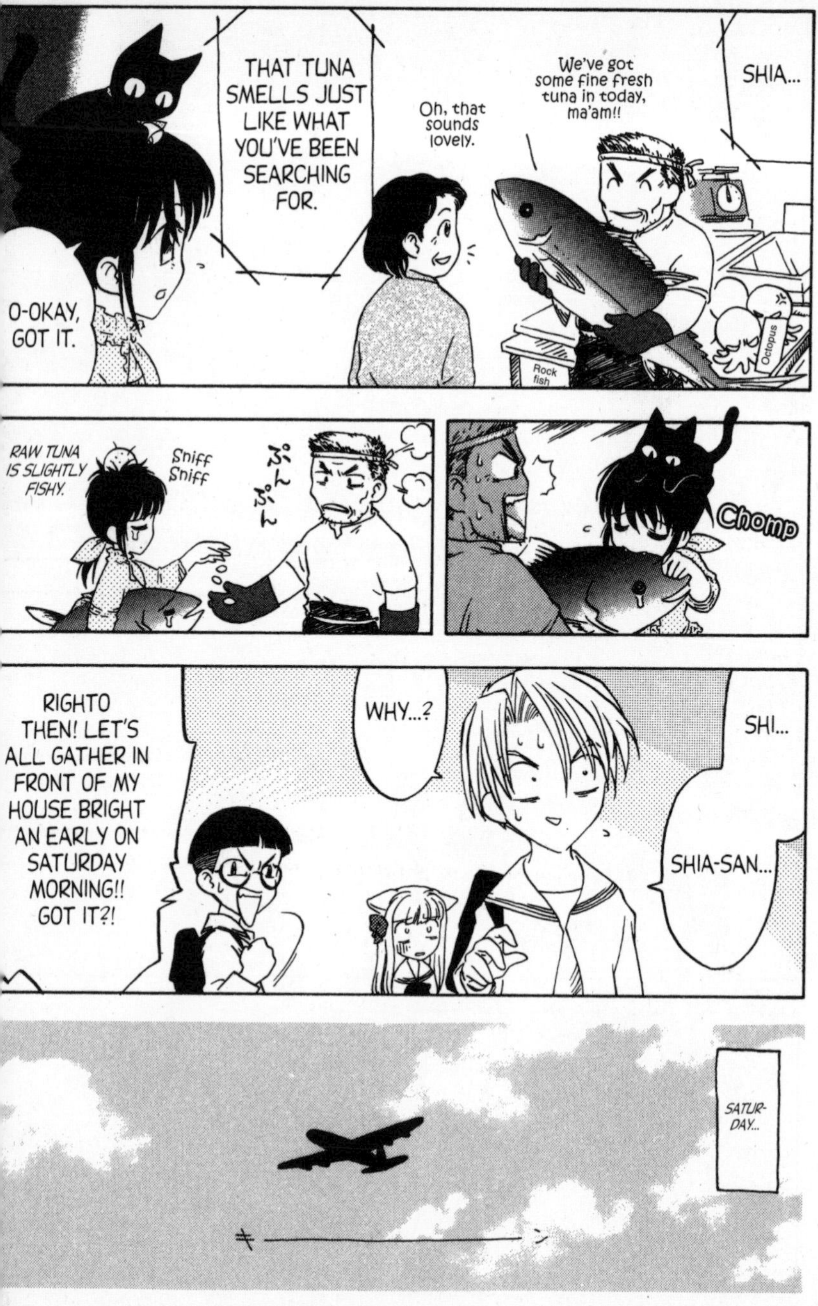
SHIA...
We've got some fine fresh tuna in today, ma'am!!
Oh, that sounds lovely.
THAT TUNA SMELLS JUST LIKE WHAT YOU'VE BEEN SEARCHING FOR.
Octopus
Rock fish
O-OKAY, GOT IT.
Chomp
ぷんぷん
Sniff Sniff
RAW TUNA IS SLIGHTLY FISHY.
SHI...
SHIA-SAN...
WHY...?
RIGHTO THEN! LET'S ALL GATHER IN FRONT OF MY HOUSE BRIGHT AN EARLY ON SATURDAY MORNING!! GOT IT?!
SATURDAY...
キーン

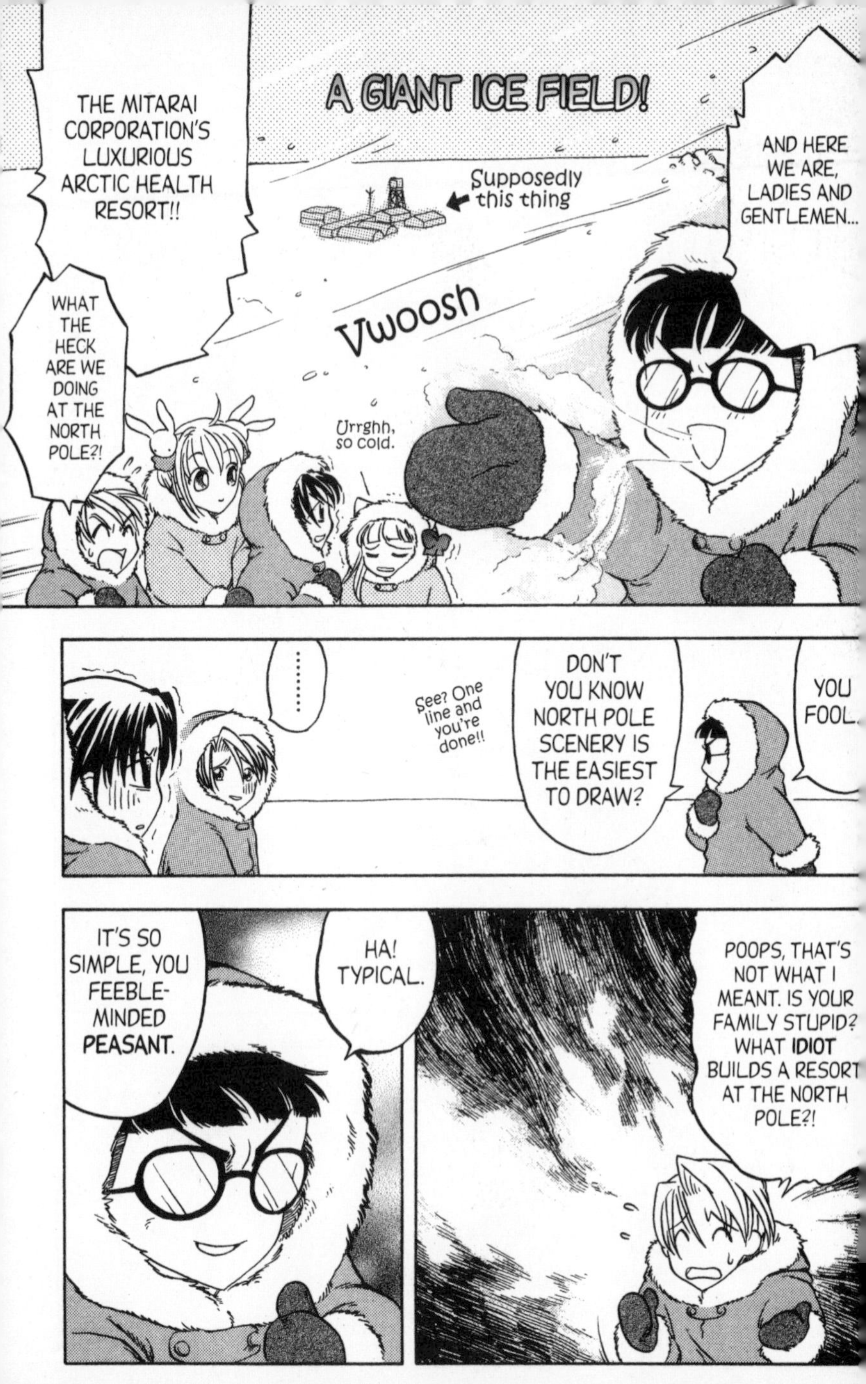
AND HERE WE ARE, LADIES AND GENTLEMEN...
A GIANT ICE FIELD!
THE MITARAI CORPORATION'S LUXURIOUS ARCTIC HEALTH RESORT!!
Supposedly this thing
Vwoosh
Urrghh, so cold.
WHAT THE HECK ARE WE DOING AT THE NORTH POLE?!
YOU FOOL.
DON'T YOU KNOW NORTH POLE SCENERY IS THE EASIEST TO DRAW?
See? One line and you're done!!
....
POOPS, THAT'S NOT WHAT I MEANT. IS YOUR FAMILY STUPID? WHAT **IDIOT** BUILDS A RESORT AT THE NORTH POLE?!
HA! TYPICAL.
IT'S SO SIMPLE, YOU FEEBLE-MINDED **PEASANT**.

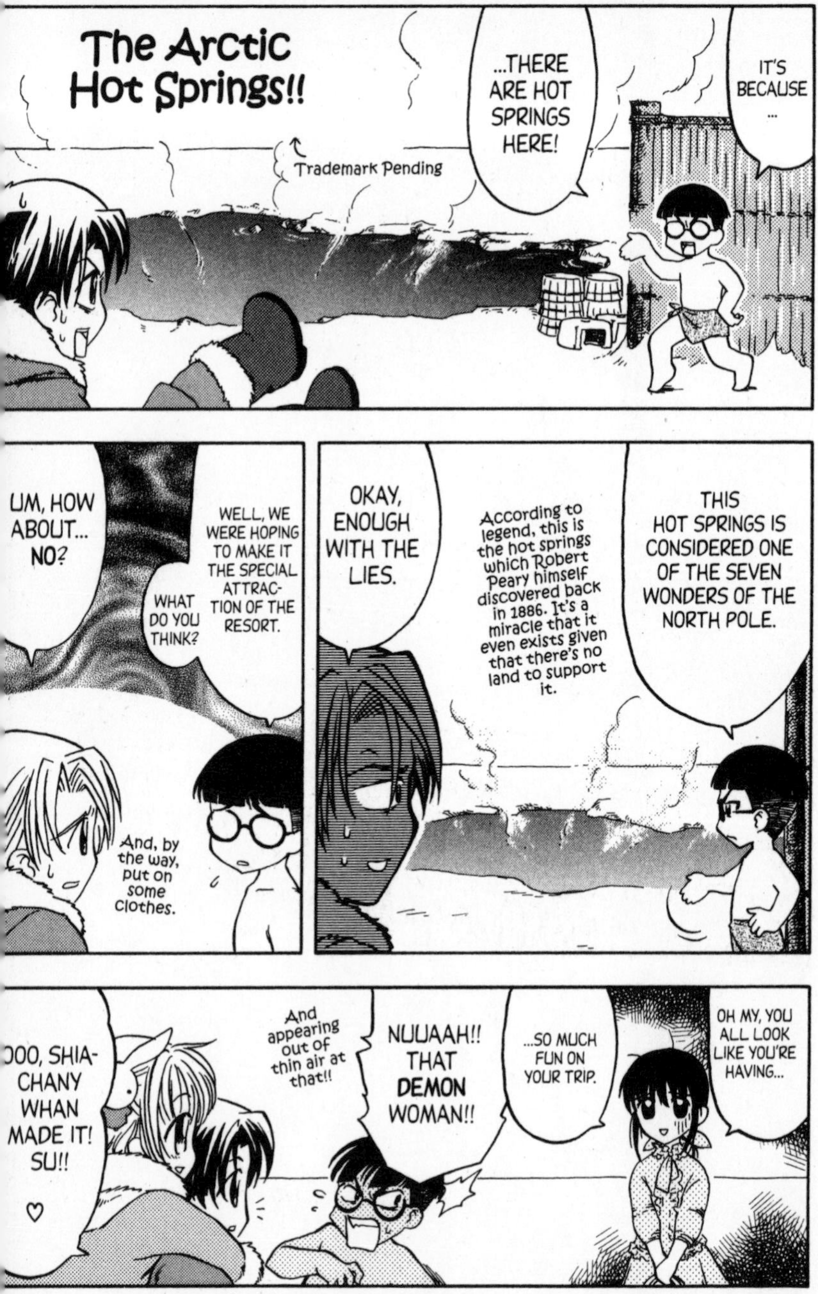
IT'S BECAUSE ...
...THERE ARE HOT SPRINGS HERE!
The Arctic Hot Springs!!
Trademark Pending
THIS HOT SPRINGS IS CONSIDERED ONE OF THE SEVEN WONDERS OF THE NORTH POLE.
According to legend, this is the hot springs which Robert Peary himself discovered back in 1886. It's a miracle that it even exists given that there's no land to support it.
OKAY, ENOUGH WITH THE LIES.
WELL, WE WERE HOPING TO MAKE IT THE SPECIAL ATTRACTION OF THE RESORT.
WHAT DO YOU THINK?
UM, HOW ABOUT... **NO?**
And, by the way, put on some clothes.
OH MY, YOU ALL LOOK LIKE YOU'RE HAVING...
...SO MUCH FUN ON YOUR TRIP.
NUUAAH!! THAT **DEMON** WOMAN!!
And appearing out of thin air at that!!
OOO, SHIA-CHANY WHAN MADE IT! SU!! ♡

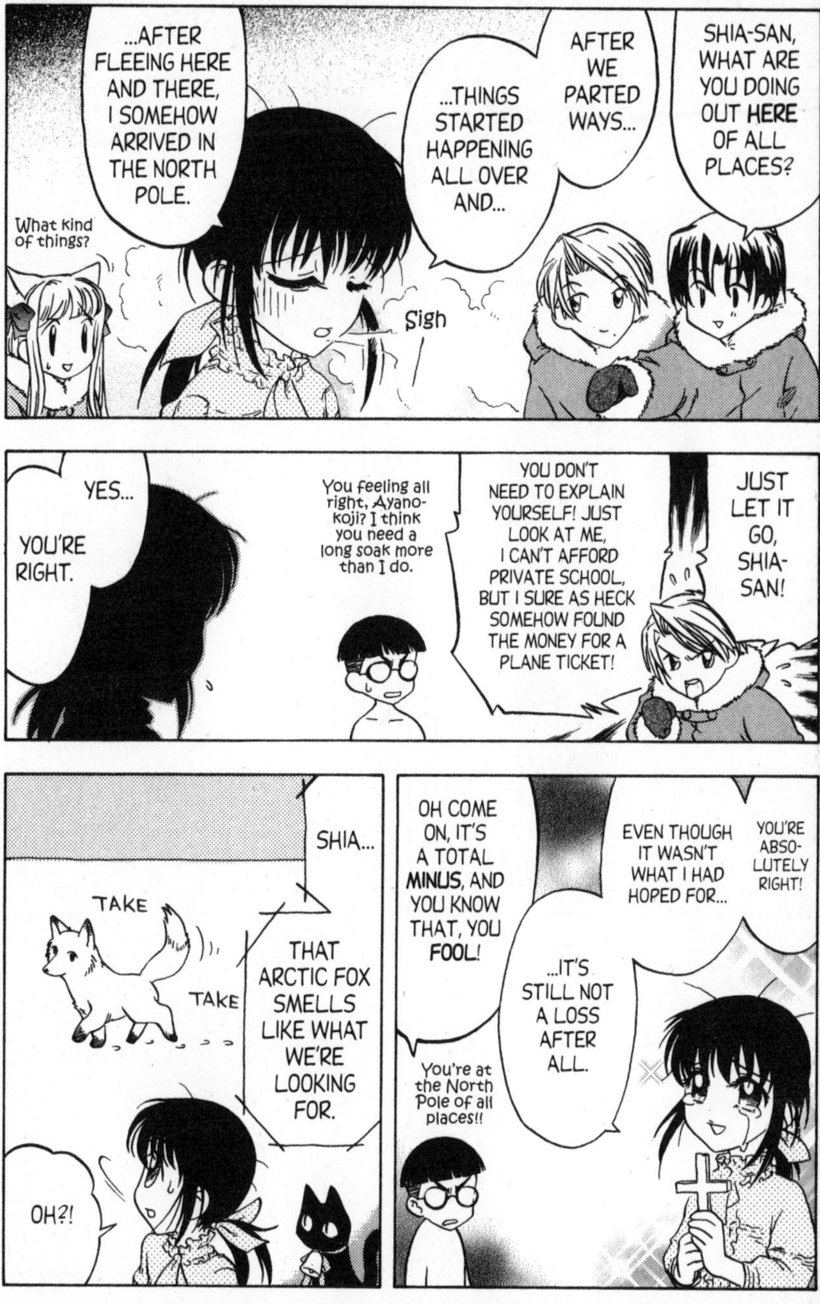
SHIA-SAN, WHAT ARE YOU DOING OUT HERE OF ALL PLACES?
AFTER WE PARTED WAYS...
...THINGS STARTED HAPPENING ALL OVER AND...
Sigh
...AFTER FLEEING HERE AND THERE, I SOMEHOW ARRIVED IN THE NORTH POLE.
What kind of things?
JUST LET IT GO, SHIA-SAN!
YOU DON'T NEED TO EXPLAIN YOURSELF! JUST LOOK AT ME, I CAN'T AFFORD PRIVATE SCHOOL, BUT I SURE AS HECK SOMEHOW FOUND THE MONEY FOR A PLANE TICKET!
You feeling all right, Ayano-koji? I think you need a long soak more than I do.
YES... YOU'RE RIGHT.
YOU'RE ABSOLUTELY RIGHT!
EVEN THOUGH IT WASN'T WHAT I HAD HOPED FOR...
...IT'S STILL NOT A LOSS AFTER ALL.
OH COME ON, IT'S A TOTAL MINUS, AND YOU KNOW THAT, YOU FOOL!
You're at the North Pole of all places!!
SHIA...
THAT ARCTIC FOX SMELLS LIKE WHAT WE'RE LOOKING FOR.
TAKE
TAKE
OH?!

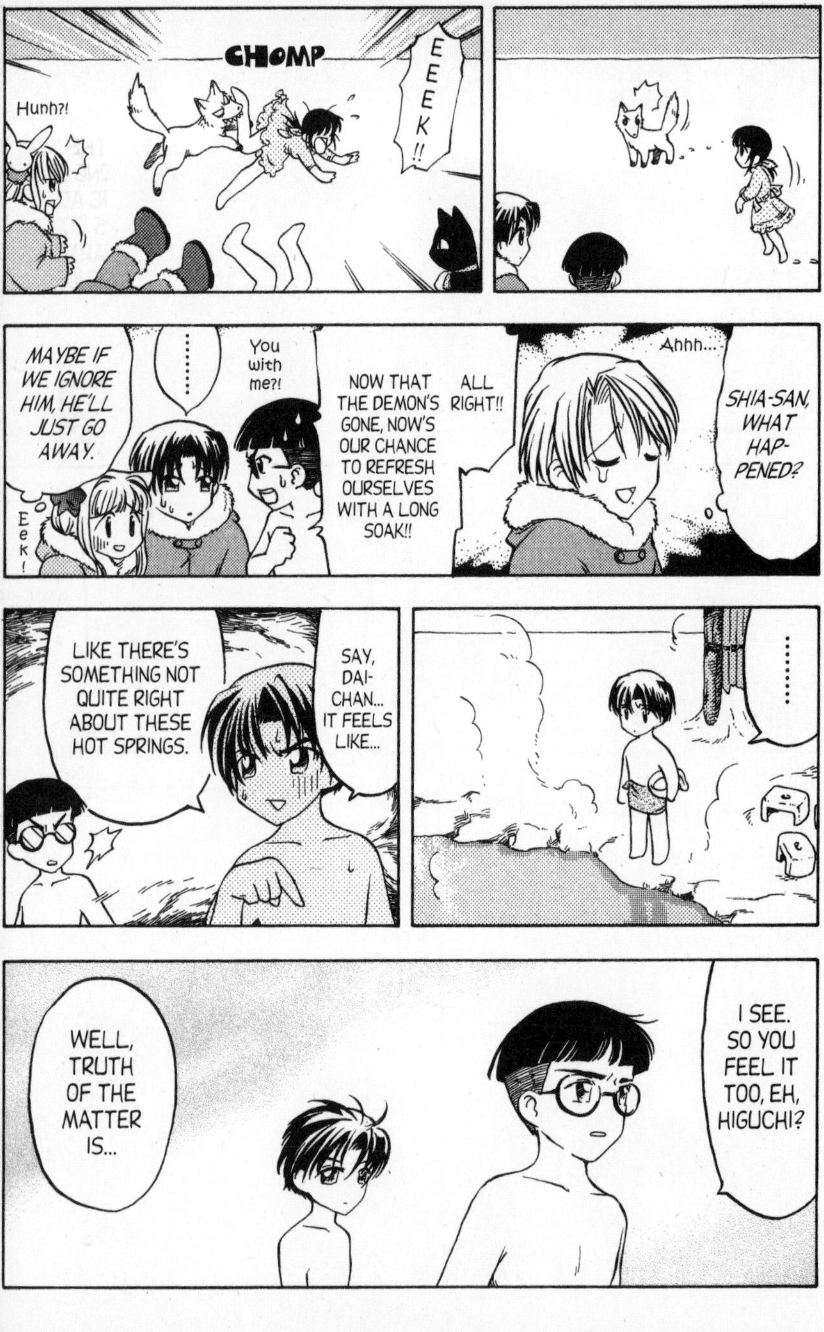
EEEEK!!
CHOMP
Hunh?!
SHIA-SAN, WHAT HAP-PENED?
Ahhh...
ALL RIGHT!!
NOW THAT THE DEMON'S GONE, NOW'S OUR CHANCE TO REFRESH OURSELVES WITH A LONG SOAK!!
You with me?!
....
MAYBE IF WE IGNORE HIM, HE'LL JUST GO AWAY.
Eek!
....
SAY, DAI-CHAN... IT FEELS LIKE...
LIKE THERE'S SOMETHING NOT QUITE RIGHT ABOUT THESE HOT SPRINGS.
I SEE. SO YOU FEEL IT TOO, EH, HIGUCHI?
WELL, TRUTH OF THE MATTER IS...

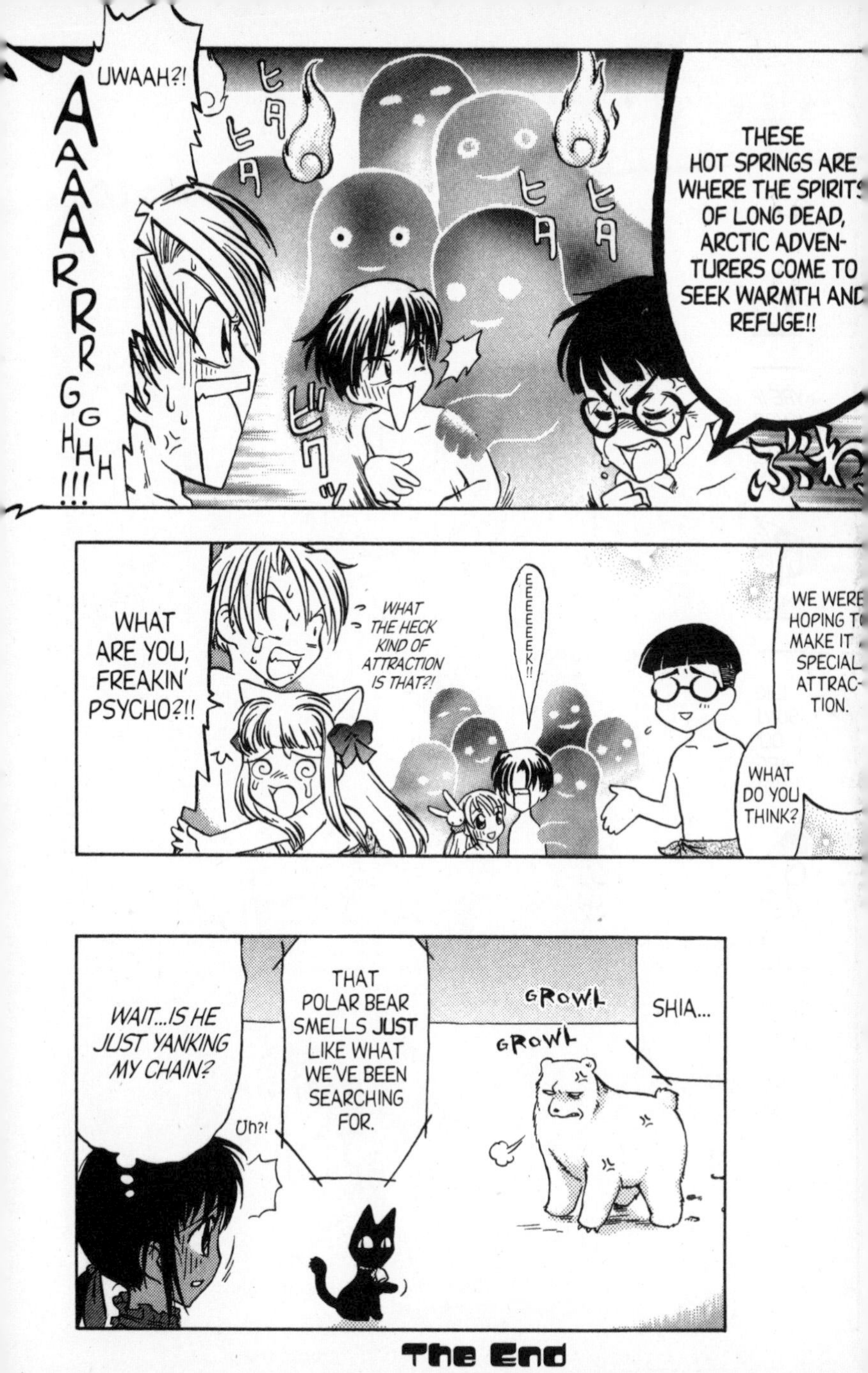
THESE HOT SPRINGS ARE WHERE THE SPIRITS OF LONG DEAD, ARCTIC ADVENTURERS COME TO SEEK WARMTH AND REFUGE!!
ヒタ ヒタ
ビクッ
ヒタ ヒタ
UWAAH?!
AAAARRRGGHHH!!!
WE WERE HOPING TO MAKE IT A SPECIAL ATTRACTION.
WHAT DO YOU THINK?
EEEEEEEK!!
WHAT THE HECK KIND OF ATTRACTION IS THAT?!
WHAT ARE YOU, FREAKIN' PSYCHO?!!
SHIA...
GROWL
GROWL
THAT POLAR BEAR SMELLS **JUST** LIKE WHAT WE'VE BEEN SEARCHING FOR.
Uh?!
WAIT...IS HE JUST YANKING MY CHAIN?

The End

Kyuten Yuminaga

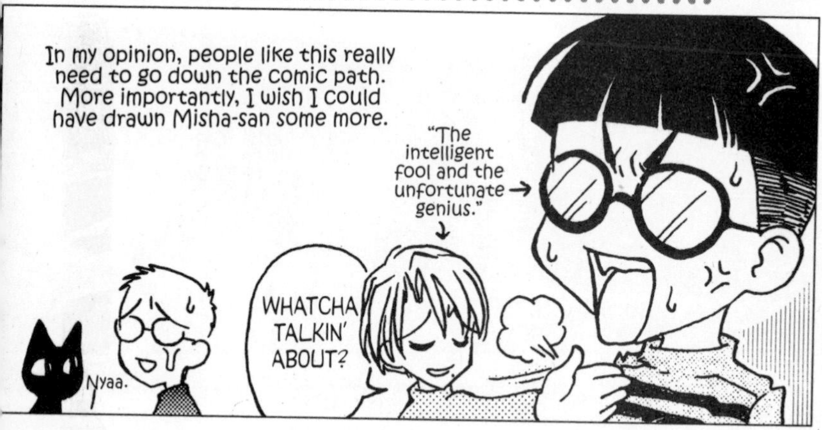
In my opinion, people like this really need to go down the comic path. More importantly, I wish I could have drawn Misha-san some more.
"The intelligent fool and the unfortunate genius."
WHATCHA TALKIN' ABOUT?
Nyaa.

Writer's Talk

Eiki Sibusawa

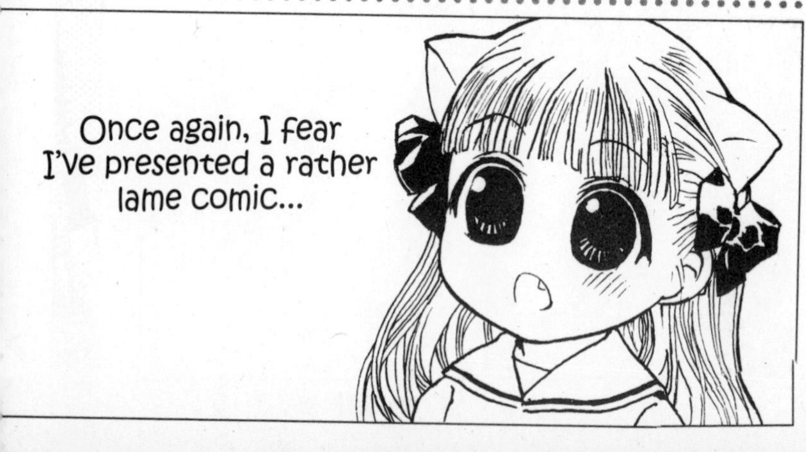
Once again, I fear I've presented a rather lame comic...

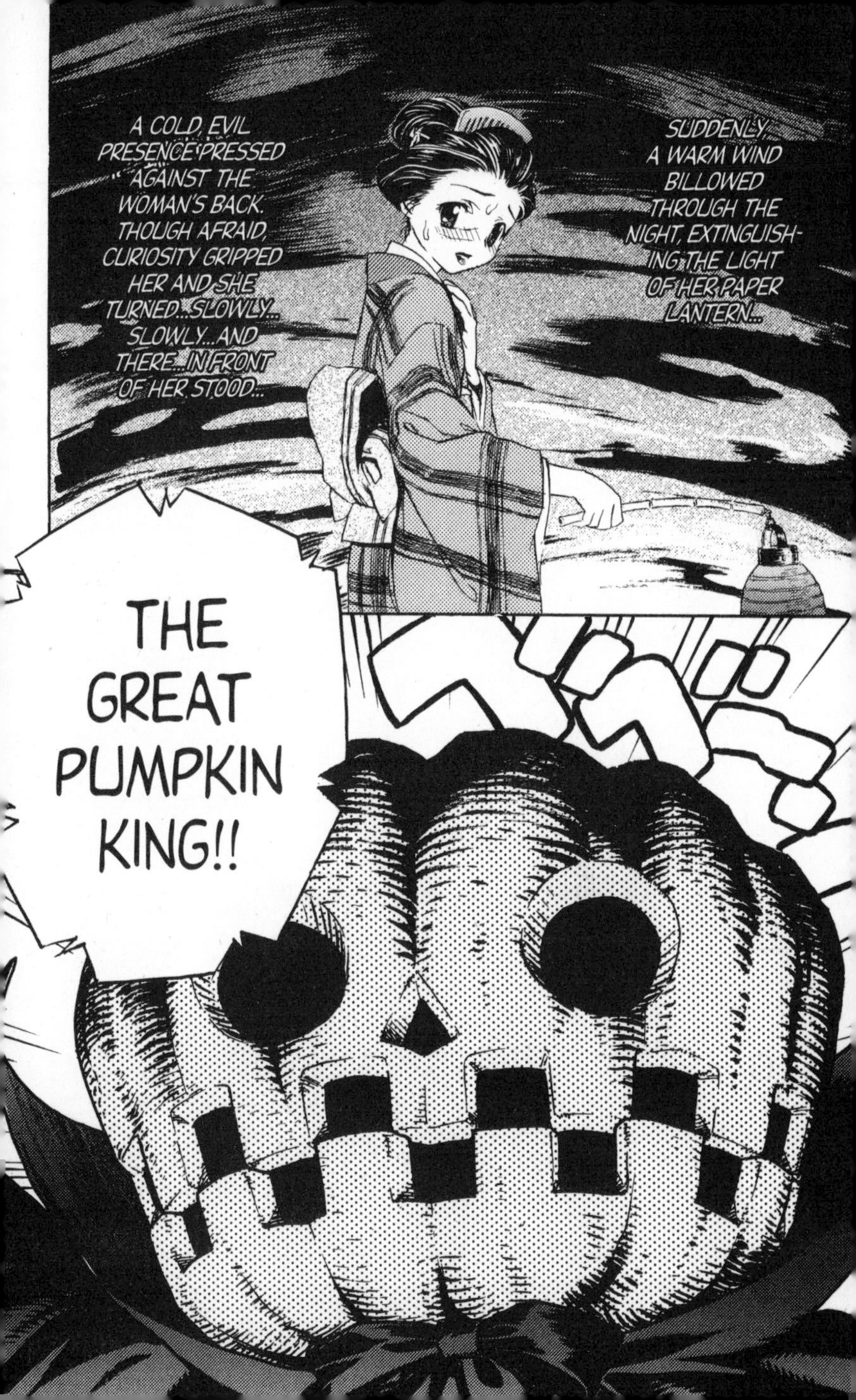
SUDDENLY, A WARM WIND BILLOWED THROUGH THE NIGHT, EXTINGUISH-ING THE LIGHT OF HER PAPER LANTERN...
A COLD, EVIL PRESENCE PRESSED AGAINST THE WOMAN'S BACK. THOUGH AFRAID, CURIOSITY GRIPPED HER AND SHE TURNED...SLOWLY... SLOWLY...AND THERE...IN FRONT OF HER STOOD...
THE GREAT PUMPKIN KING!!

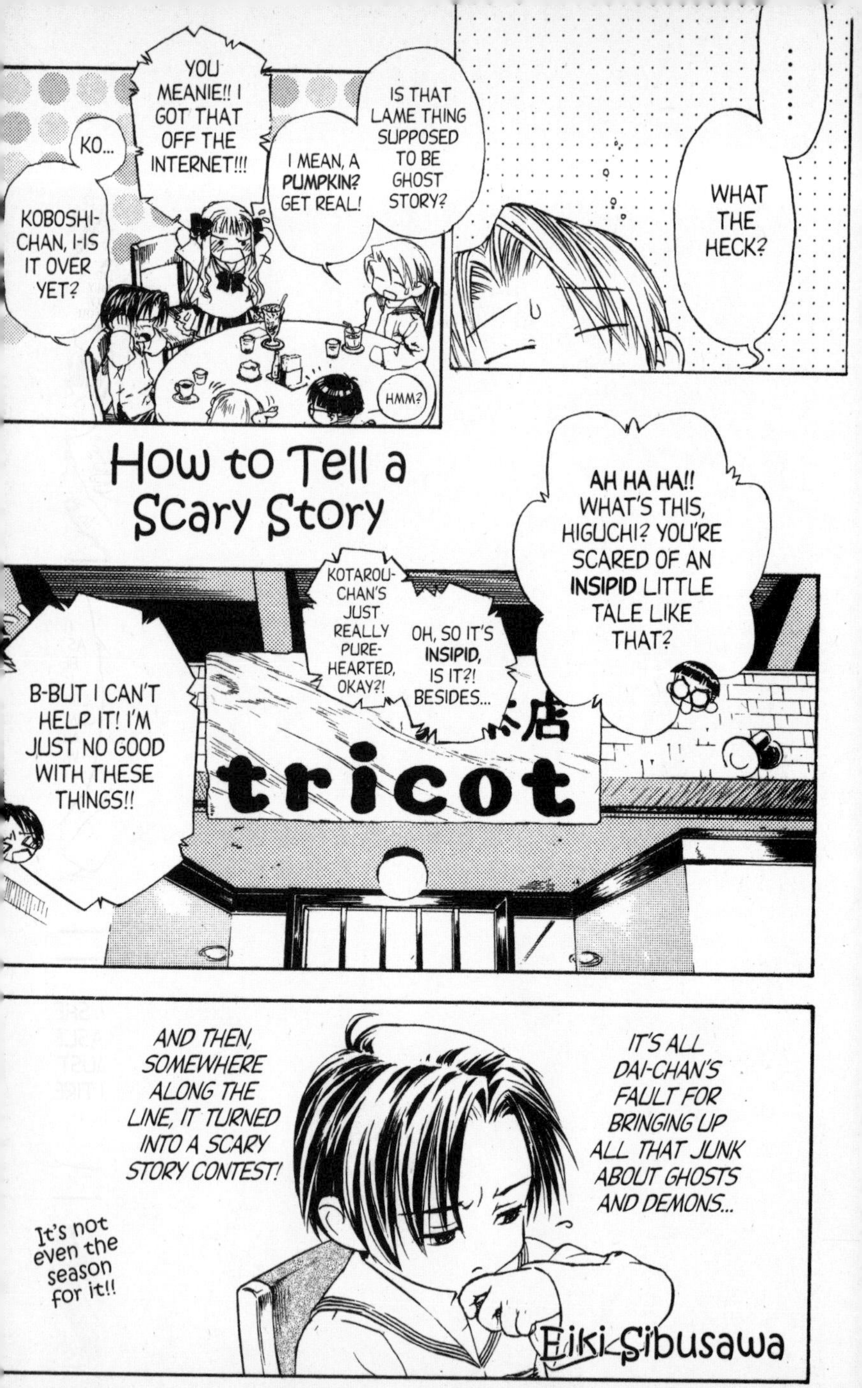
WHAT THE HECK?
IS THAT LAME THING SUPPOSED TO BE GHOST STORY?
I MEAN, A PUMPKIN? GET REAL!
YOU MEANIE!! I GOT THAT OFF THE INTERNET!!!
KO...
KOBOSHI-CHAN, I-IS IT OVER YET?
HMM?
How to Tell a Scary Story
AH HA HA!! WHAT'S THIS, HIGUCHI? YOU'RE SCARED OF AN INSIPID LITTLE TALE LIKE THAT?
OH, SO IT'S INSIPID, IS IT?! BESIDES...
KOTAROU-CHAN'S JUST REALLY PURE-HEARTED, OKAY?!
tricot
B-BUT I CAN'T HELP IT! I'M JUST NO GOOD WITH THESE THINGS!!
IT'S ALL DAI-CHAN'S FAULT FOR BRINGING UP ALL THAT JUNK ABOUT GHOSTS AND DEMONS...
AND THEN, SOMEWHERE ALONG THE LINE, IT TURNED INTO A SCARY STORY CONTEST!
It's not even the season for it!!
Eiki Sibusawa

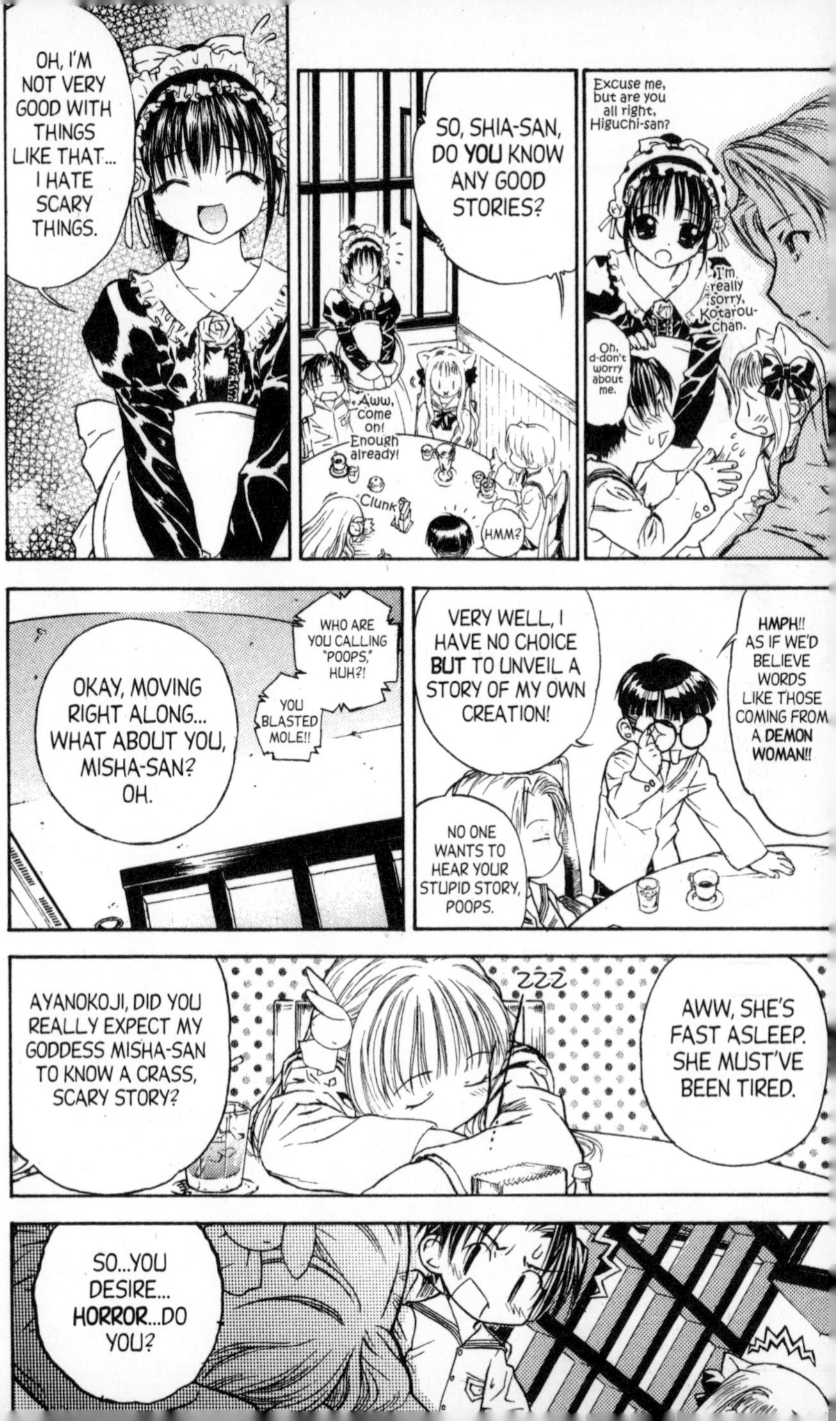
Excuse me, but are you all right, Higuchi-san?
I'm really sorry, Kotarou-chan.
Oh, d-don't worry about me.
SO, SHIA-SAN, DO **YOU** KNOW ANY GOOD STORIES?
Aww, come on! Enough already!
Clunk
HMM?
OH, I'M NOT VERY GOOD WITH THINGS LIKE THAT... I HATE SCARY THINGS.
VERY WELL, I HAVE NO CHOICE **BUT** TO UNVEIL A STORY OF MY OWN CREATION!
HMPH!! AS IF WE'D BELIEVE WORDS LIKE THOSE COMING FROM A **DEMON WOMAN!!**
NO ONE WANTS TO HEAR YOUR STUPID STORY, POOPS.
WHO ARE YOU CALLING "POOPS," HUH?!
YOU BLASTED MOLE!!
OKAY, MOVING RIGHT ALONG... WHAT ABOUT YOU, MISHA-SAN? OH.
AWW, SHE'S FAST ASLEEP. SHE MUST'VE BEEN TIRED.
ZZZ
AYANOKOJI, DID YOU REALLY EXPECT MY GODDESS MISHA-SAN TO KNOW A CRASS, SCARY STORY?
SO...YOU DESIRE... **HORROR**...DO YOU?

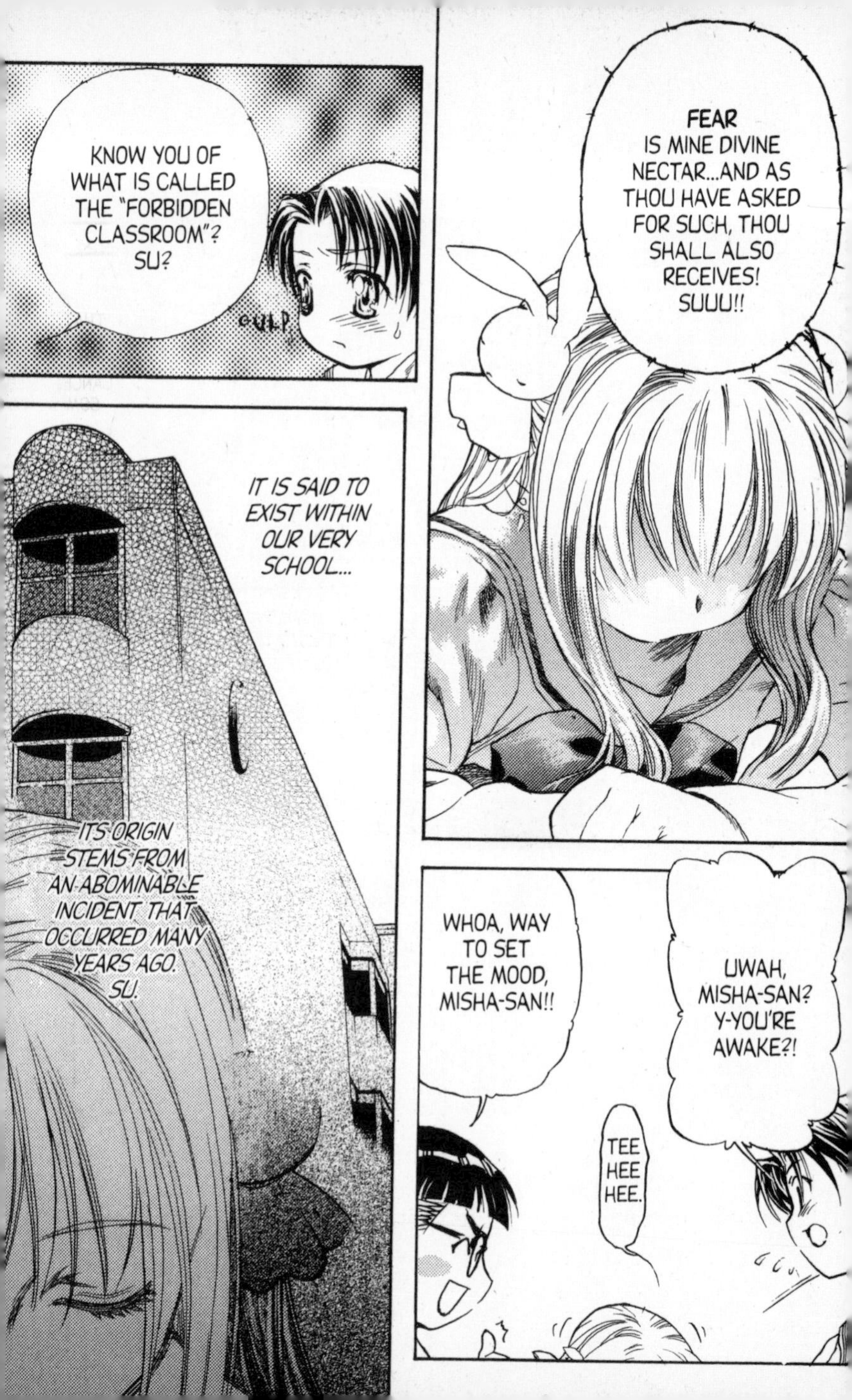
FEAR IS MINE DIVINE NECTAR...AND AS THOU HAVE ASKED FOR SUCH, THOU SHALL ALSO RECEIVES! SUUU!!
KNOW YOU OF WHAT IS CALLED THE "FORBIDDEN CLASSROOM"? SU?
GULP
IT IS SAID TO EXIST WITHIN OUR VERY SCHOOL...
ITS ORIGIN STEMS FROM AN ABOMINABLE INCIDENT THAT OCCURRED MANY YEARS AGO. SU.
UWAH, MISHA-SAN? Y-YOU'RE AWAKE?!
WHOA, WAY TO SET THE MOOD, MISHA-SAN!!
TEE HEE HEE.

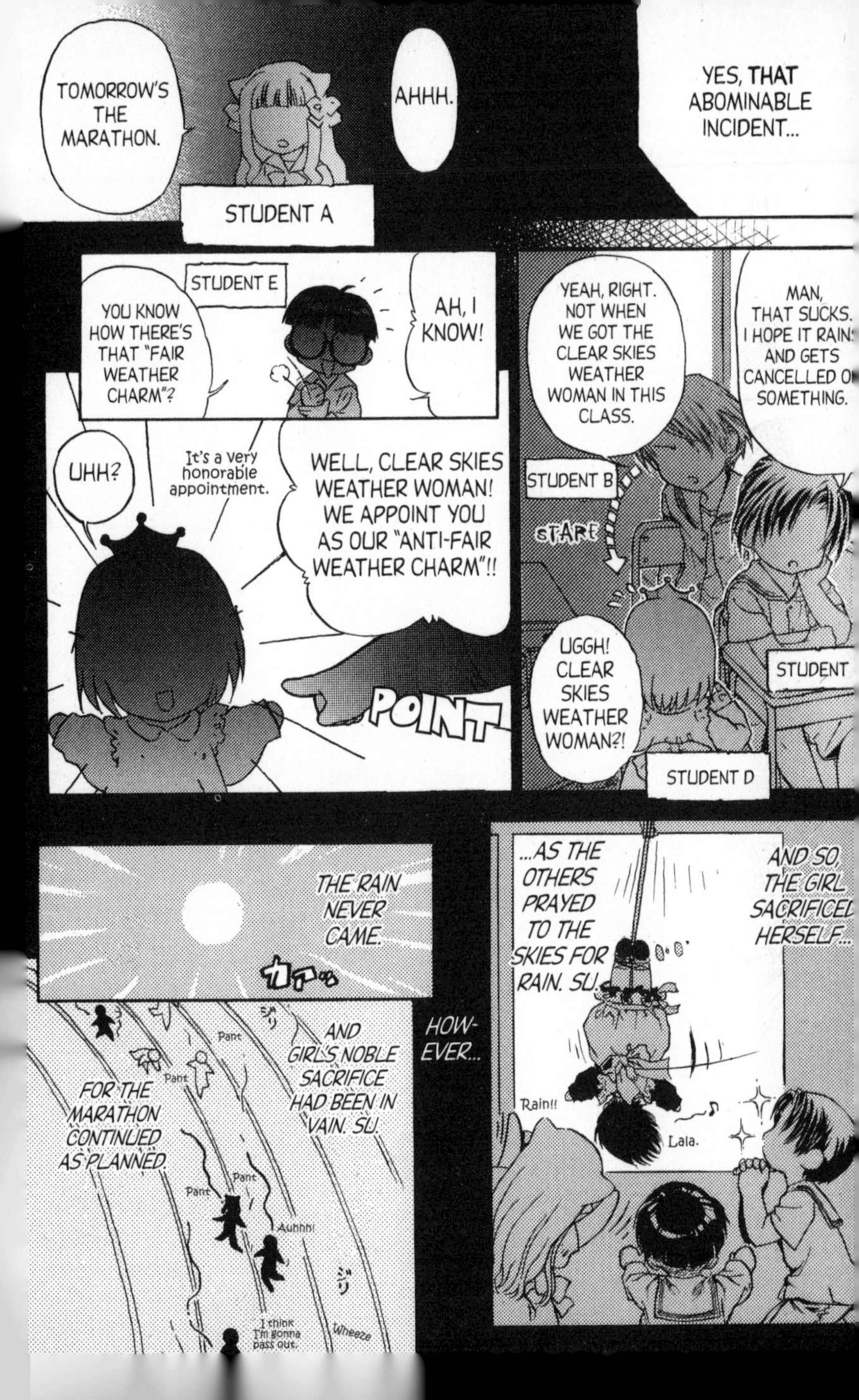
YES, THAT ABOMINABLE INCIDENT...
AHHH.
TOMORROW'S THE MARATHON.
STUDENT A
MAN, THAT SUCKS. I HOPE IT RAINS AND GETS CANCELLED OR SOMETHING.
YEAH, RIGHT. NOT WHEN WE GOT THE CLEAR SKIES WEATHER WOMAN IN THIS CLASS.
STUDENT B
STARE
STUDENT
UGGH! CLEAR SKIES WEATHER WOMAN?!
STUDENT D
AH, I KNOW!
STUDENT E
YOU KNOW HOW THERE'S THAT "FAIR WEATHER CHARM"?
WELL, CLEAR SKIES WEATHER WOMAN! WE APPOINT YOU AS OUR "ANTI-FAIR WEATHER CHARM"!!
It's a very honorable appointment.
UHH?
POINT
AND SO, THE GIRL SACRIFICED HERSELF...
...AS THE OTHERS PRAYED TO THE SKIES FOR RAIN. SU.
Rain!!
Lala.
HOW-EVER...
THE RAIN NEVER CAME.
AND GIRL'S NOBLE SACRIFICE HAD BEEN IN VAIN. SU.
FOR THE MARATHON CONTINUED AS PLANNED.
Pant
Pant
Pant
Pant
Auhhh!
I think I'm gonna pass out.
Wheeze

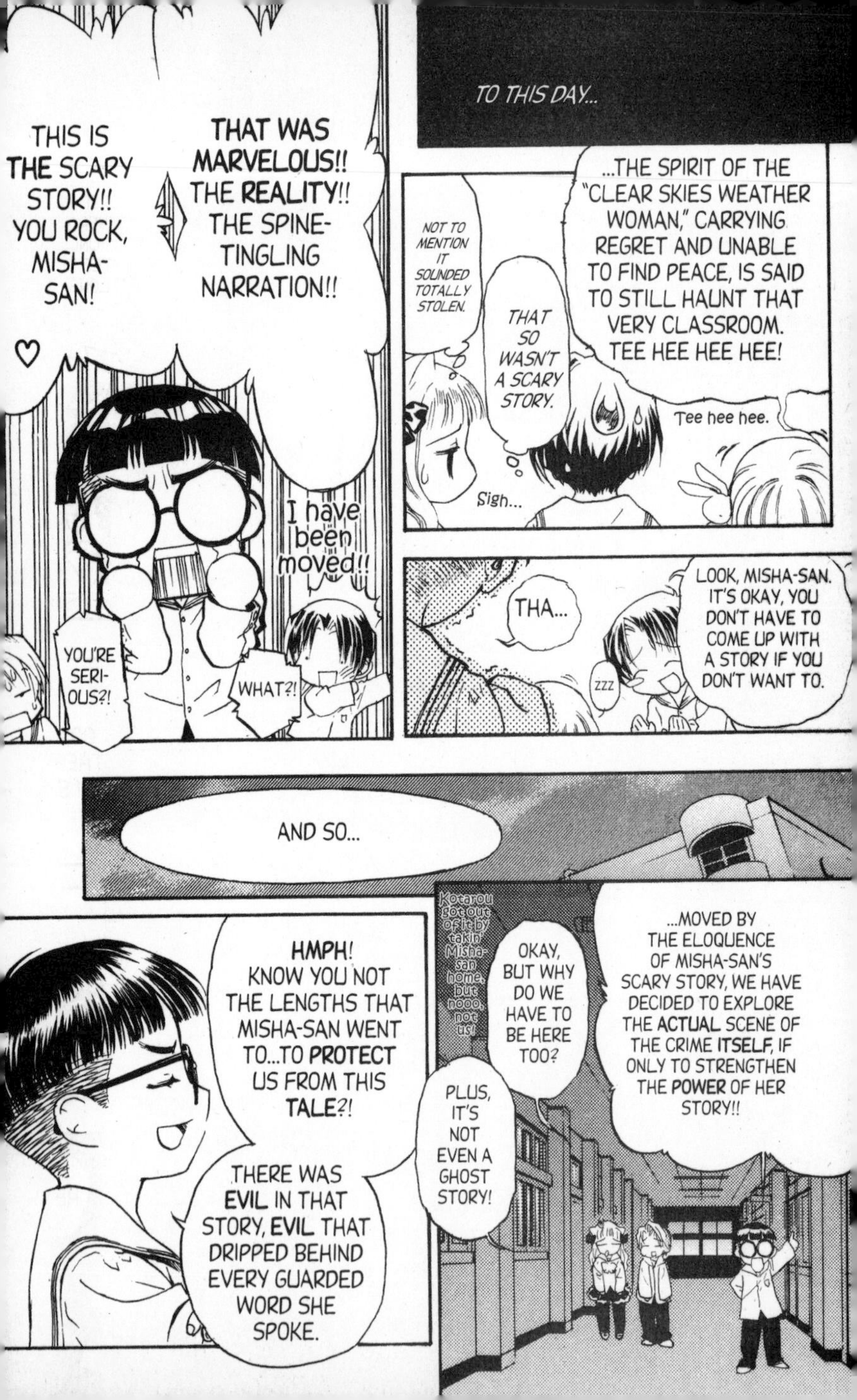

TO THIS DAY...
...THE SPIRIT OF THE "CLEAR SKIES WEATHER WOMAN," CARRYING REGRET AND UNABLE TO FIND PEACE, IS SAID TO STILL HAUNT THAT VERY CLASSROOM. TEE HEE HEE HEE!
Tee hee hee.
THAT SO WASN'T A SCARY STORY.
NOT TO MENTION IT SOUNDED TOTALLY STOLEN.
Sigh...
LOOK, MISHA-SAN. IT'S OKAY, YOU DON'T HAVE TO COME UP WITH A STORY IF YOU DON'T WANT TO.
THA...
ZZZ
THAT WAS MARVELOUS!! THE REALITY!! THE SPINE-TINGLING NARRATION!!
THIS IS THE SCARY STORY!! YOU ROCK, MISHA-SAN! ♡
I have been moved!!
WHAT?!
YOU'RE SERIOUS?!
AND SO...
...MOVED BY THE ELOQUENCE OF MISHA-SAN'S SCARY STORY, WE HAVE DECIDED TO EXPLORE THE ACTUAL SCENE OF THE CRIME ITSELF, IF ONLY TO STRENGTHEN THE POWER OF HER STORY!!
OKAY, BUT WHY DO WE HAVE TO BE HERE TOO?
Kotarou got out of it by takin' Misha-san home, but nooo, not us!
PLUS, IT'S NOT EVEN A GHOST STORY!
HMPH! KNOW YOU NOT THE LENGTHS THAT MISHA-SAN WENT TO...TO PROTECT US FROM THIS TALE?!
THERE WAS EVIL IN THAT STORY, EVIL THAT DRIPPED BEHIND EVERY GUARDED WORD SHE SPOKE.

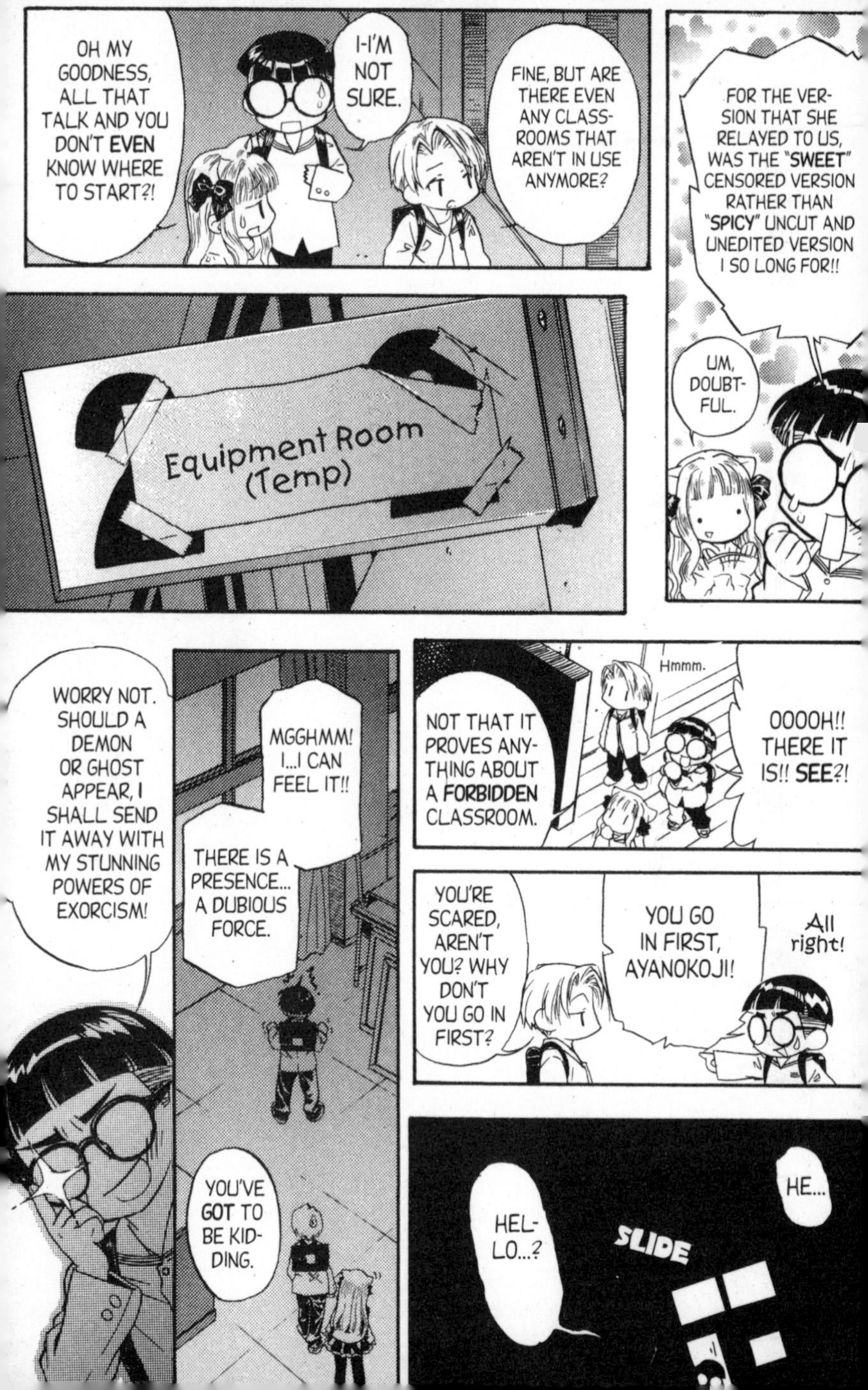

FOR THE VERSION THAT SHE RELAYED TO US, WAS THE "SWEET" CENSORED VERSION RATHER THAN "SPICY" UNCUT AND UNEDITED VERSION I SO LONG FOR!!
UM, DOUBTFUL.
FINE, BUT ARE THERE EVEN ANY CLASSROOMS THAT AREN'T IN USE ANYMORE?
I-I'M NOT SURE.
OH MY GOODNESS, ALL THAT TALK AND YOU DON'T EVEN KNOW WHERE TO START?!
Equipment Room (Temp)
OOOOH!! THERE IT IS!! SEE?!
Hmmm.
NOT THAT IT PROVES ANYTHING ABOUT A FORBIDDEN CLASSROOM.
All right!
YOU GO IN FIRST, AYANOKOJI!
YOU'RE SCARED, AREN'T YOU? WHY DON'T YOU GO IN FIRST?
HE...
SLIDE
HELLO...?
MGGHMM! I...I CAN FEEL IT!!
THERE IS A PRESENCE... A DUBIOUS FORCE.
YOU'VE GOT TO BE KIDDING.
WORRY NOT. SHOULD A DEMON OR GHOST APPEAR, I SHALL SEND IT AWAY WITH MY STUNNING POWERS OF EXORCISM!

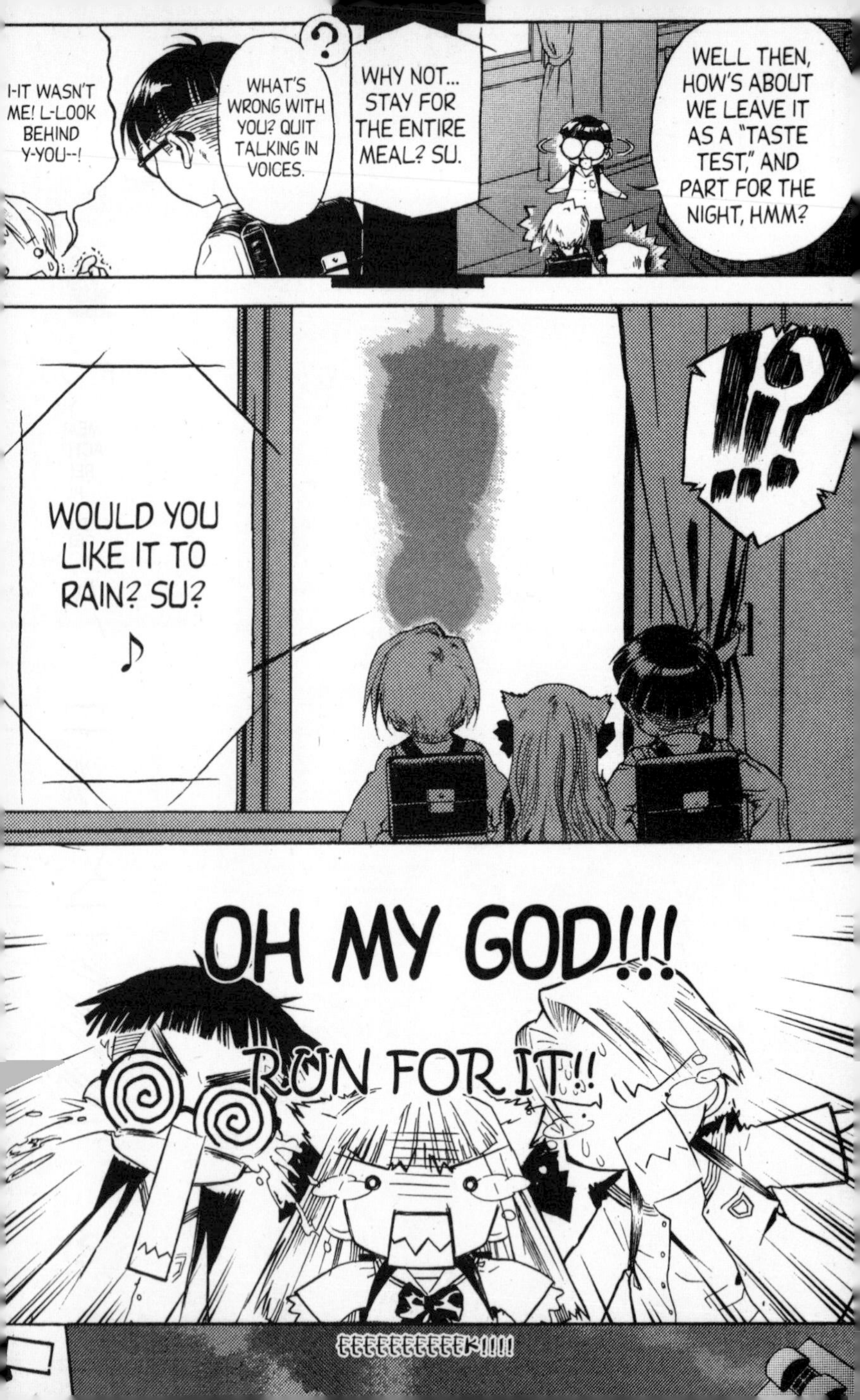
WELL THEN, HOW'S ABOUT WE LEAVE IT AS A "TASTE TEST," AND PART FOR THE NIGHT, HMM?
WHY NOT... STAY FOR THE ENTIRE MEAL? SU.
?
WHAT'S WRONG WITH YOU? QUIT TALKING IN VOICES.
I-IT WASN'T ME! L-LOOK BEHIND Y-YOU--!
!?
WOULD YOU LIKE IT TO RAIN? SU? ♪
OH MY GOD!!!
RUN FOR IT!!
EEEEEEEEEEEK!!!!

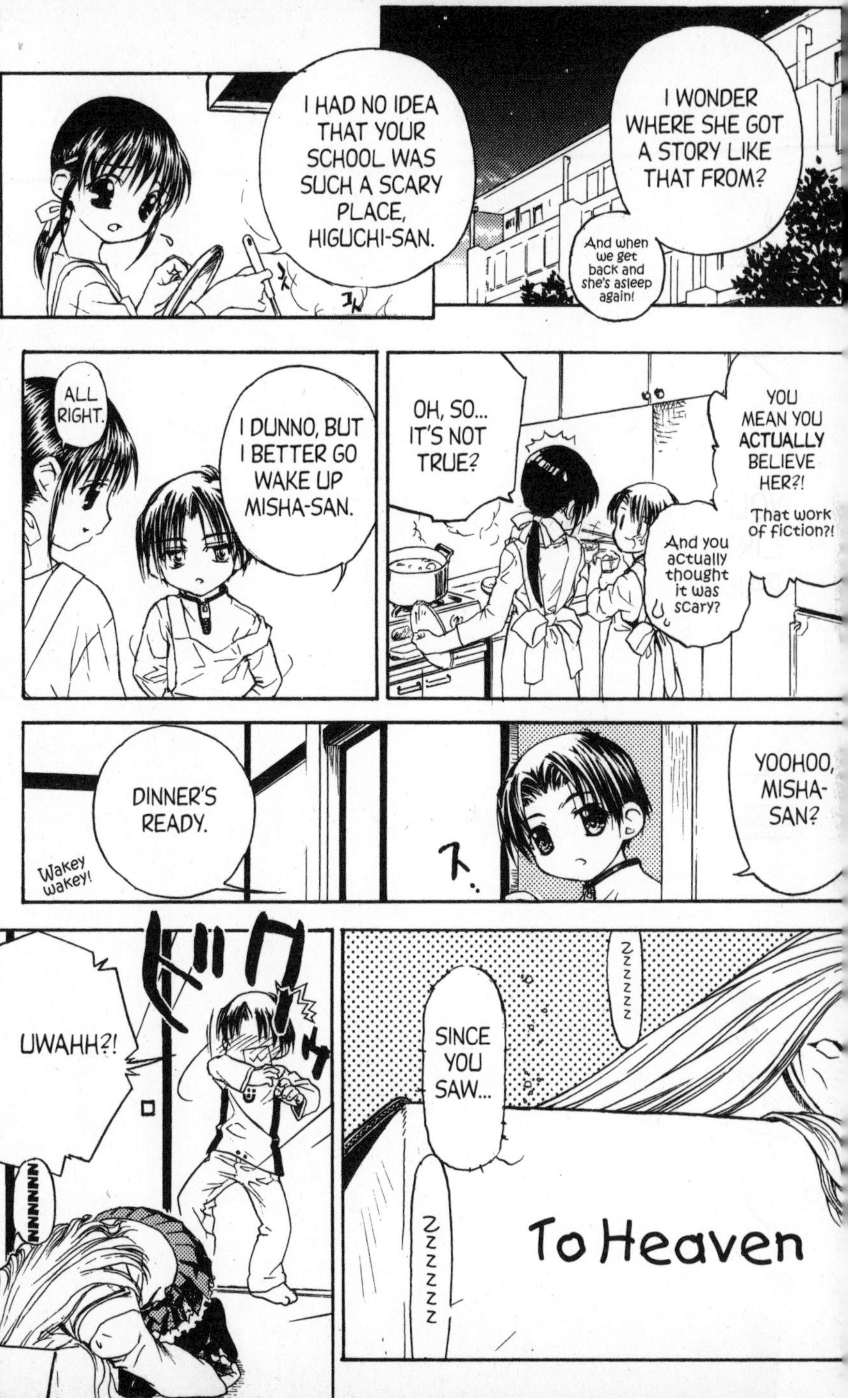
I WONDER WHERE SHE GOT A STORY LIKE THAT FROM?
And when we get back and she's asleep again!
I HAD NO IDEA THAT YOUR SCHOOL WAS SUCH A SCARY PLACE, HIGUCHI-SAN.
YOU MEAN YOU **ACTUALLY** BELIEVE HER?!
That work of fiction?!
And you actually thought it was scary?
OH, SO... IT'S NOT TRUE?
I DUNNO, BUT I BETTER GO WAKE UP MISHA-SAN.
ALL RIGHT.
YOOHOO, MISHA-SAN?
DINNER'S READY.
Wakey wakey!
ZZZZZZ
SINCE YOU SAW...
ZZZZZZ
To Heaven
UWAHH?!
NNNNNN

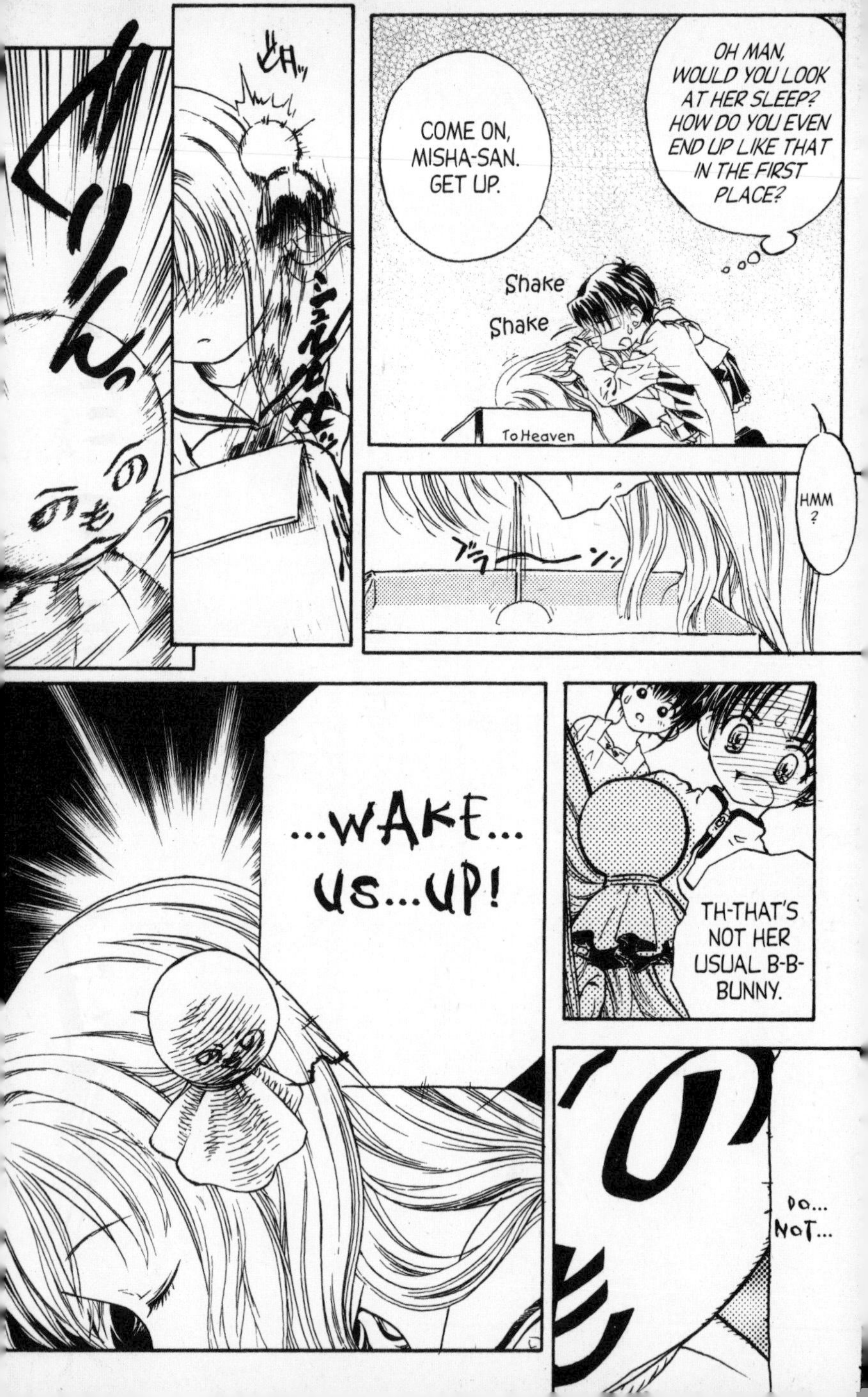
OH MAN, WOULD YOU LOOK AT HER SLEEP? HOW DO YOU EVEN END UP LIKE THAT IN THE FIRST PLACE?
COME ON, MISHA-SAN. GET UP.
Shake
Shake
To Heaven
HMM ?
TH-THAT'S NOT HER USUAL B-B-BUNNY.
DO... NOT...
...WAKE... US...UP!

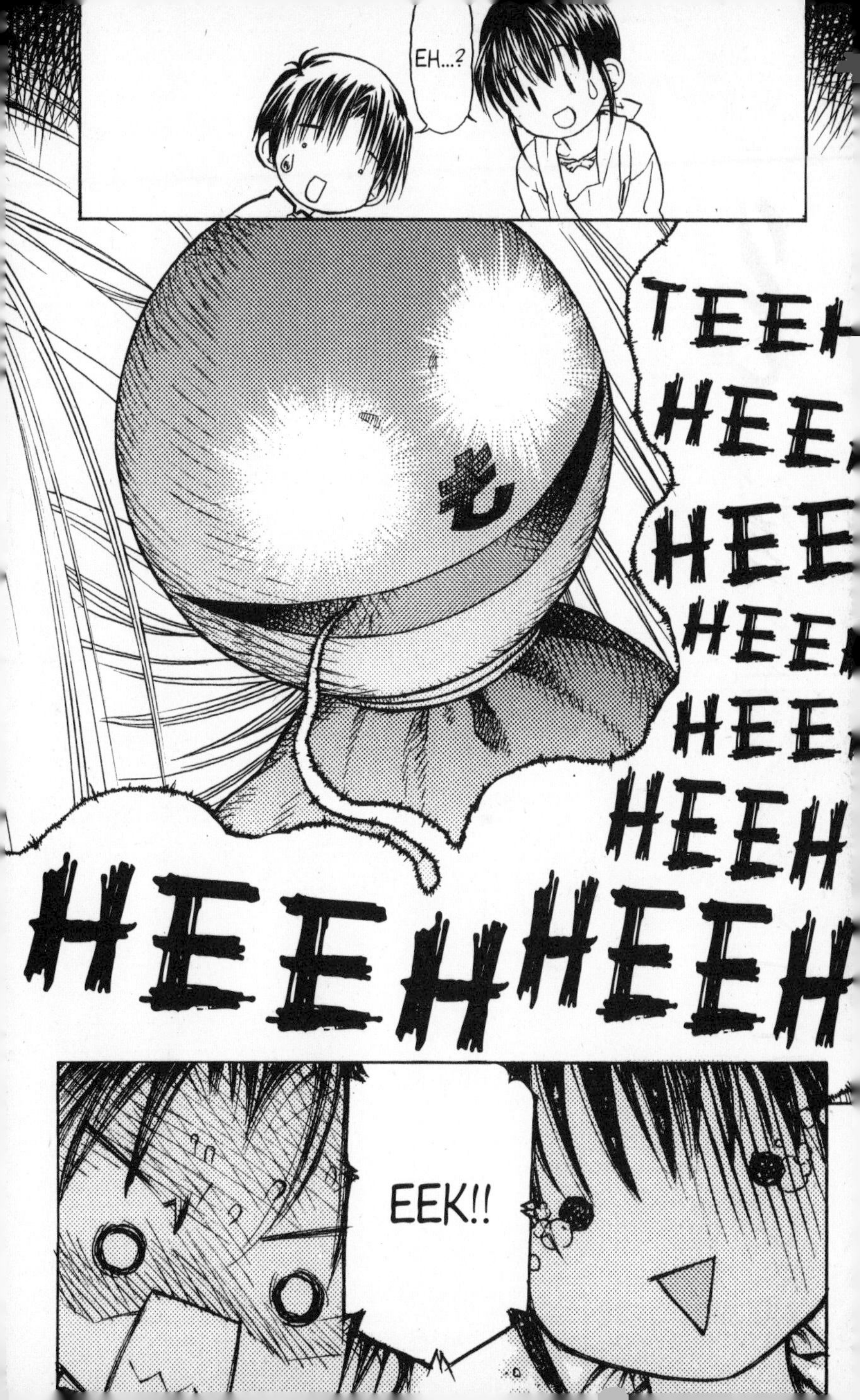
EH...?
TEEHHEEHEEHEEHEEHEEH
HEEHHEEH
EEK!!

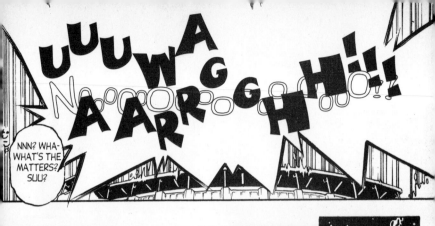

UUUWAAARRGGHH!!!
NOOOOOOOOOOOO!?!?
NNN? WHA-WHAT'S THE MATTERS? SUU?
HOW ON EARTH DID I END UP LOSING ONE OF MY HAIR CHARMS?
D'OH.
I SUPPOSE I SHOULD JUST RECHECK EVERYWHERE I'VE BEEN TODAY.
HEY, MISHA. YOU IN?
EH...?
WHAT'S GOING ON HERE?
AAHHH, SACCHAN! I DON'T KNOWS! THEY...
While I was fast asleepies too!
THEY JUST COLLAPSED ALL A SUDDEN WUDDEN! SUU!!
Tee hee hee hee. Fair Weather Charm. Eh heh heh heh.
CAN'T BELIEVE YOU GOT SCARED BY THAT.
I'M SORRY. IT JUST HAP-PENED.

The End

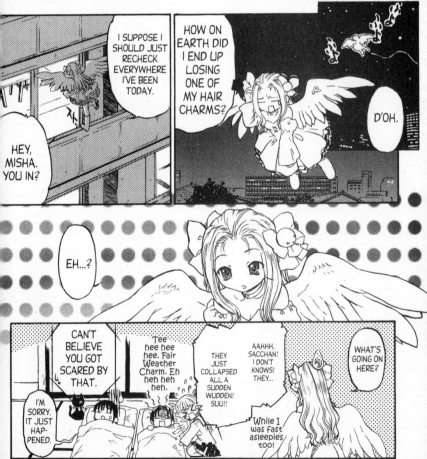

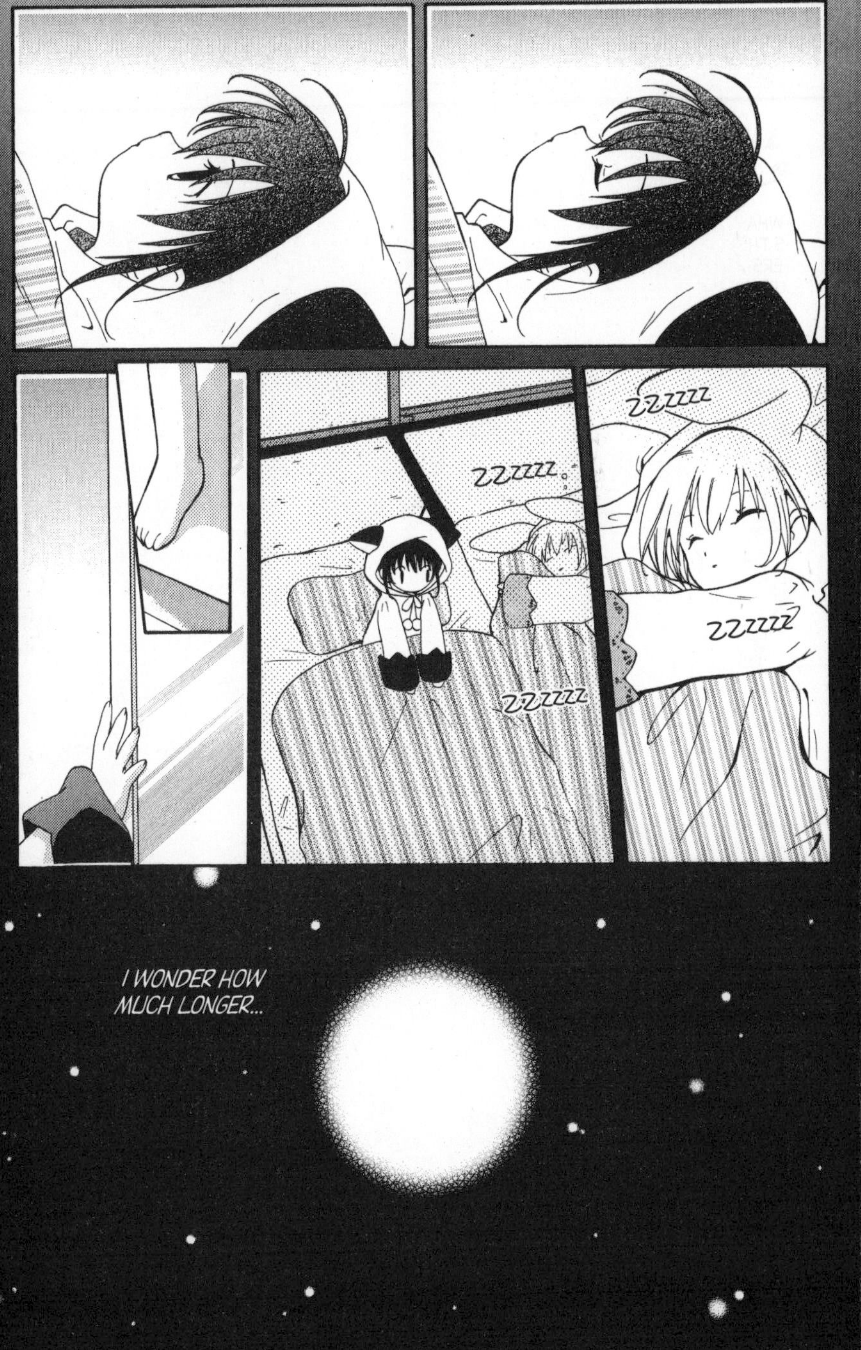
ZZZZZZ
ZZZZZZ
ZZZZZZ.
ZZZZZZ
I WONDER HOW MUCH LONGER...

Where Dreams Are

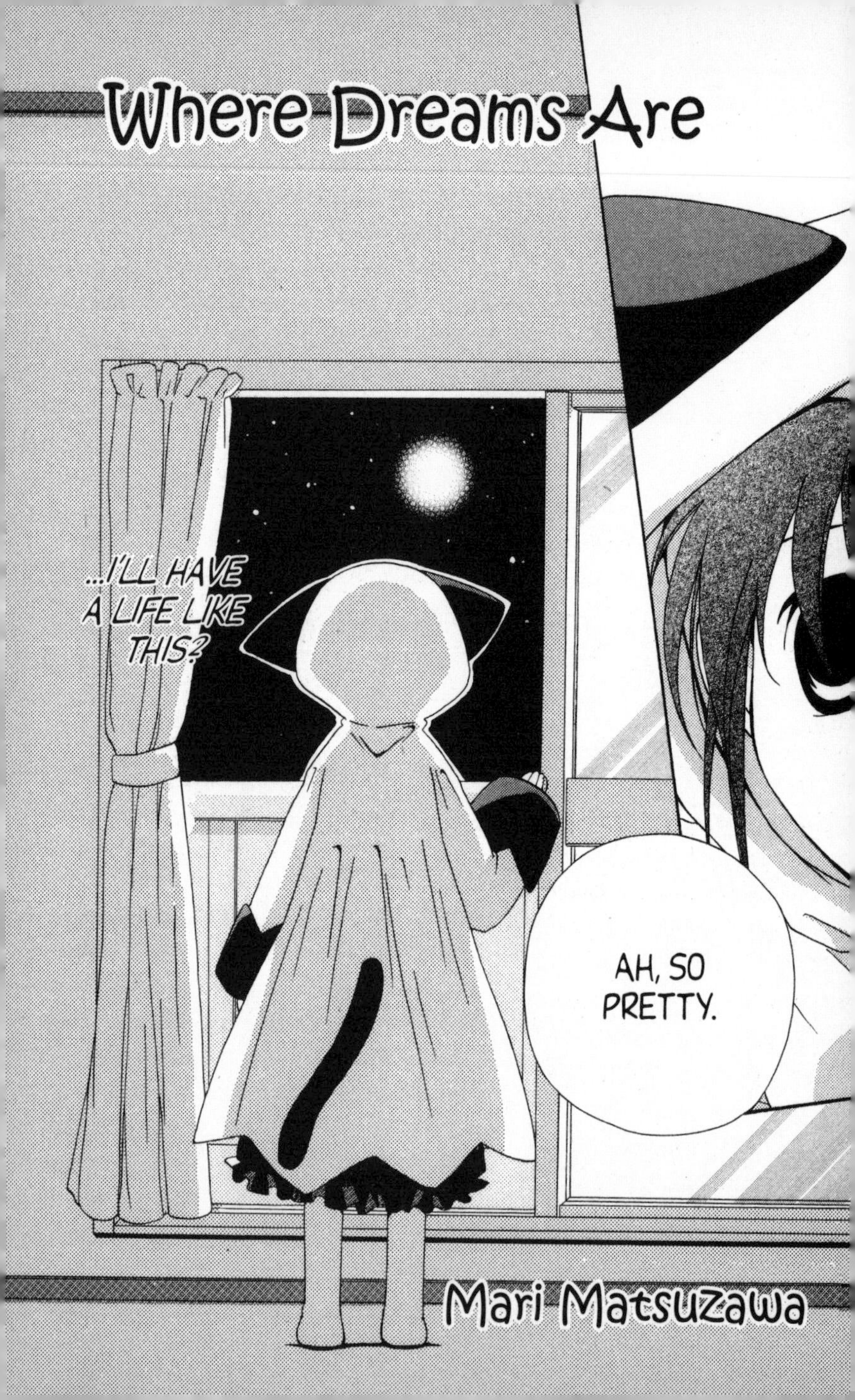
AH, SO PRETTY.
...I'LL HAVE A LIFE LIKE THIS?

Mari Matsuzawa

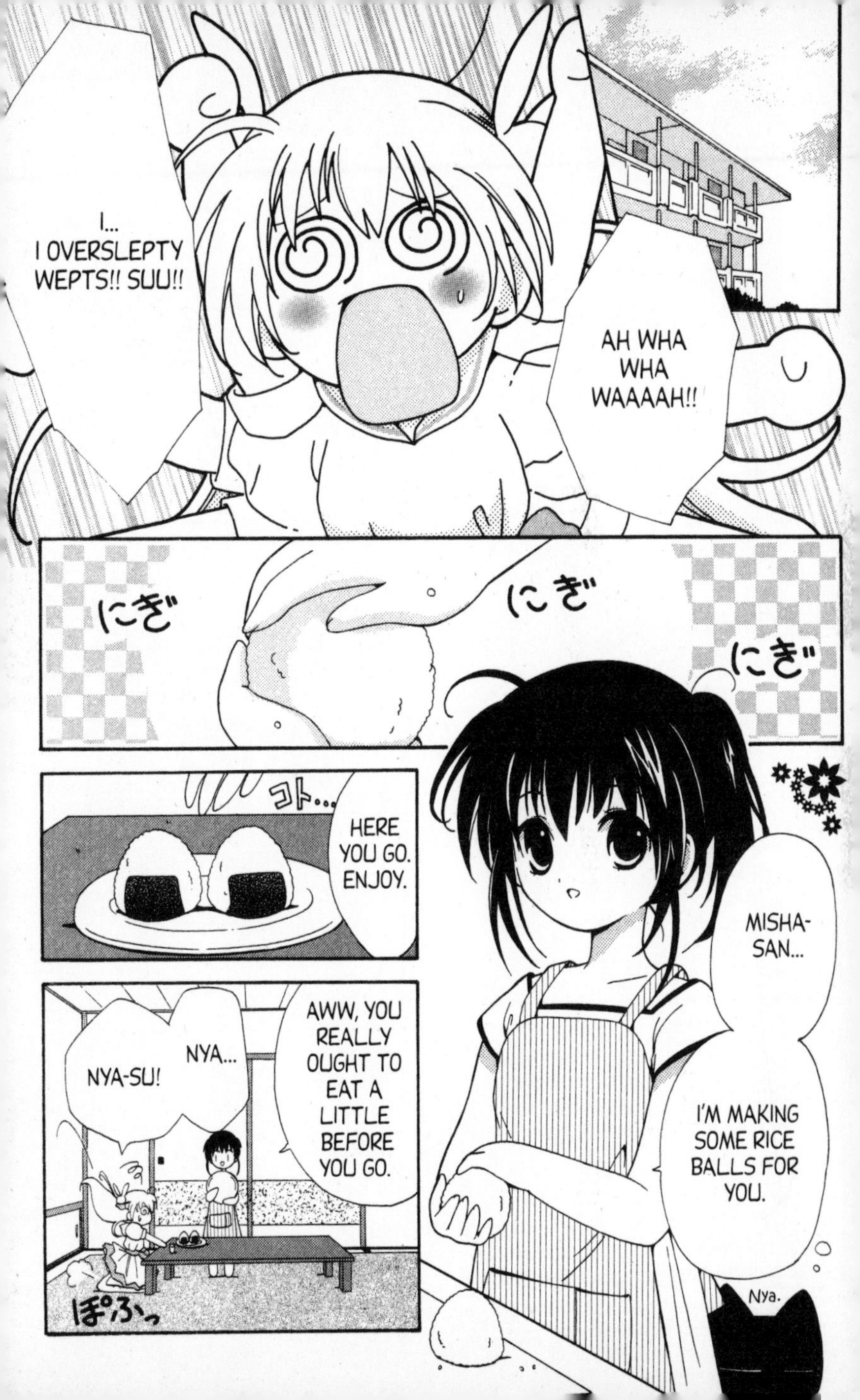
AH WHA WHA WAAAAH!!
I... I OVERSLEPTY WEPTS!! SUU!!
にぎ
にぎ
にぎ
MISHA-SAN...
I'M MAKING SOME RICE BALLS FOR YOU.
Nya.
コト...
HERE YOU GO. ENJOY.
AWW, YOU REALLY OUGHT TO EAT A LITTLE BEFORE YOU GO.
NYA...
NYA-SU!
ぽふっ

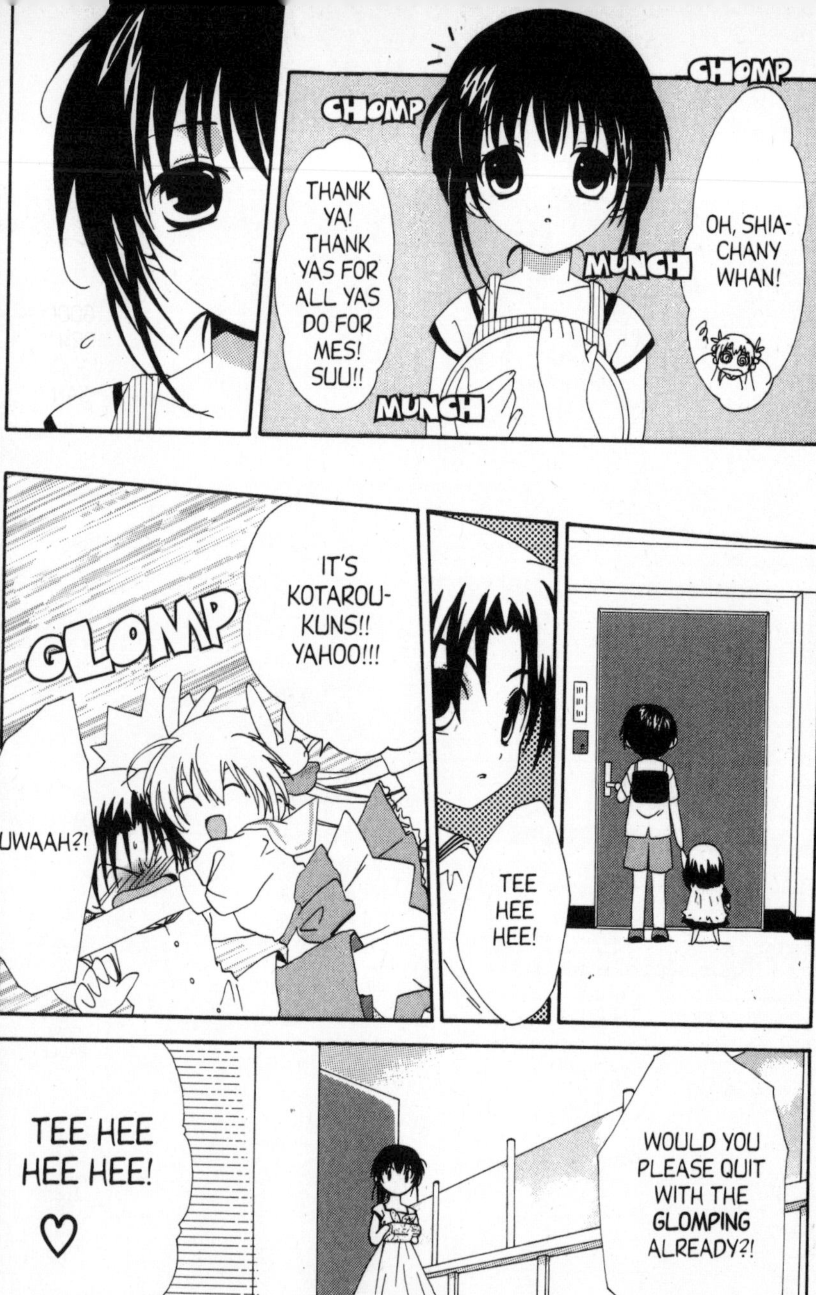
CHOMP
OH, SHIA-CHANY WHAN!
MUNCH
CHOMP
THANK YA! THANK YAS FOR ALL YAS DO FOR MES! SUU!!
MUNCH
TEE HEE HEE!
IT'S KOTAROU-KUNS!! YAHOO!!!
GLOMP
UWAAH?!
WOULD YOU PLEASE QUIT WITH THE **GLOMPING** ALREADY?!
TEE HEE HEE HEE! ♡

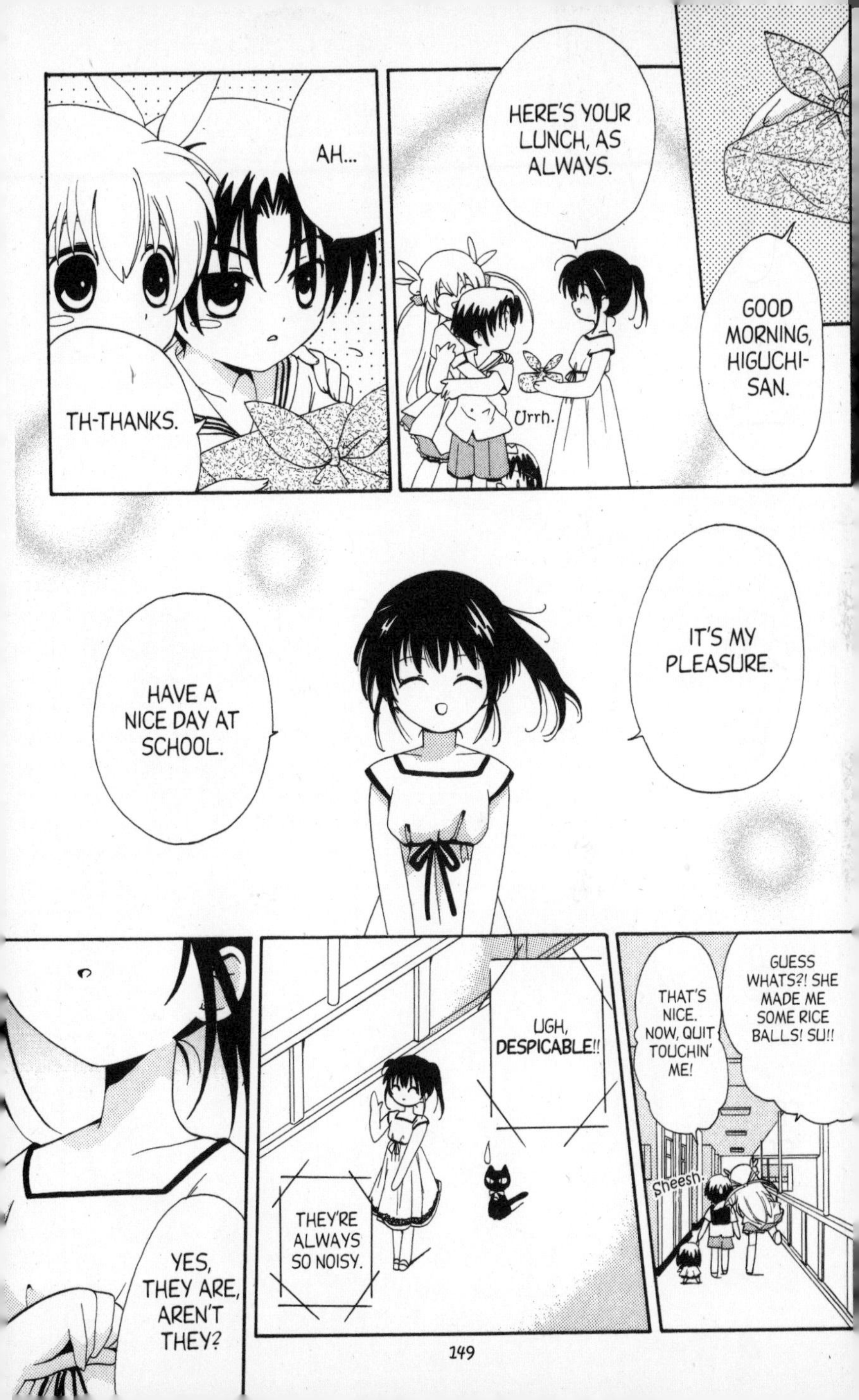
GOOD MORNING, HIGUCHI-SAN.
HERE'S YOUR LUNCH, AS ALWAYS.
Urrh.
AH...
TH-THANKS.
IT'S MY PLEASURE.
HAVE A NICE DAY AT SCHOOL.
GUESS WHATS?! SHE MADE ME SOME RICE BALLS! SU!!
THAT'S NICE. NOW, QUIT TOUCHIN' ME!
Sheesh.
UGH, DESPICABLE!!
THEY'RE ALWAYS SO NOISY.
YES, THEY ARE, AREN'T THEY?

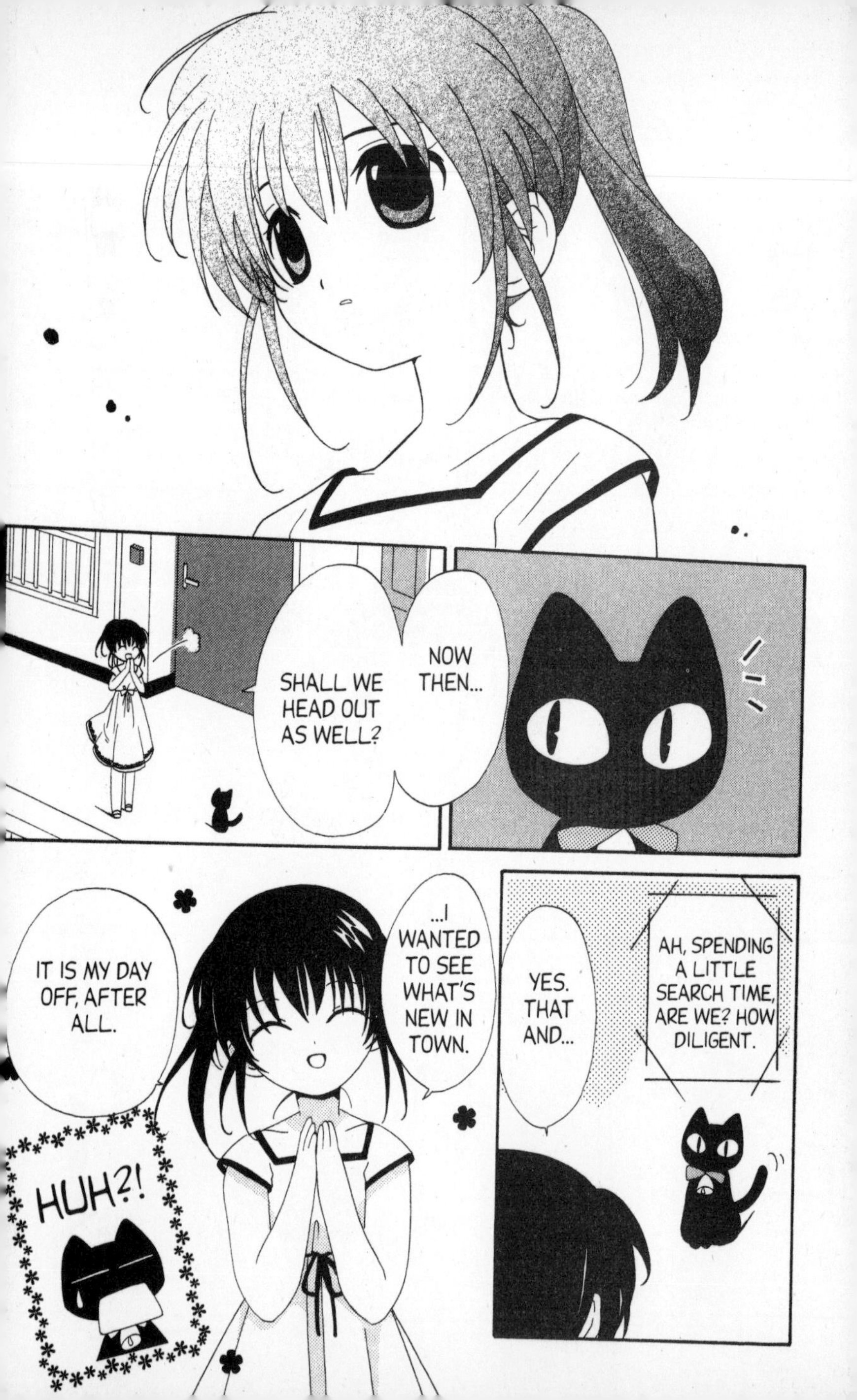
NOW THEN...
SHALL WE HEAD OUT AS WELL?
AH, SPENDING A LITTLE SEARCH TIME, ARE WE? HOW DILIGENT.
YES. THAT AND...
...I WANTED TO SEE WHAT'S NEW IN TOWN.
IT IS MY DAY OFF, AFTER ALL.
HUH?!

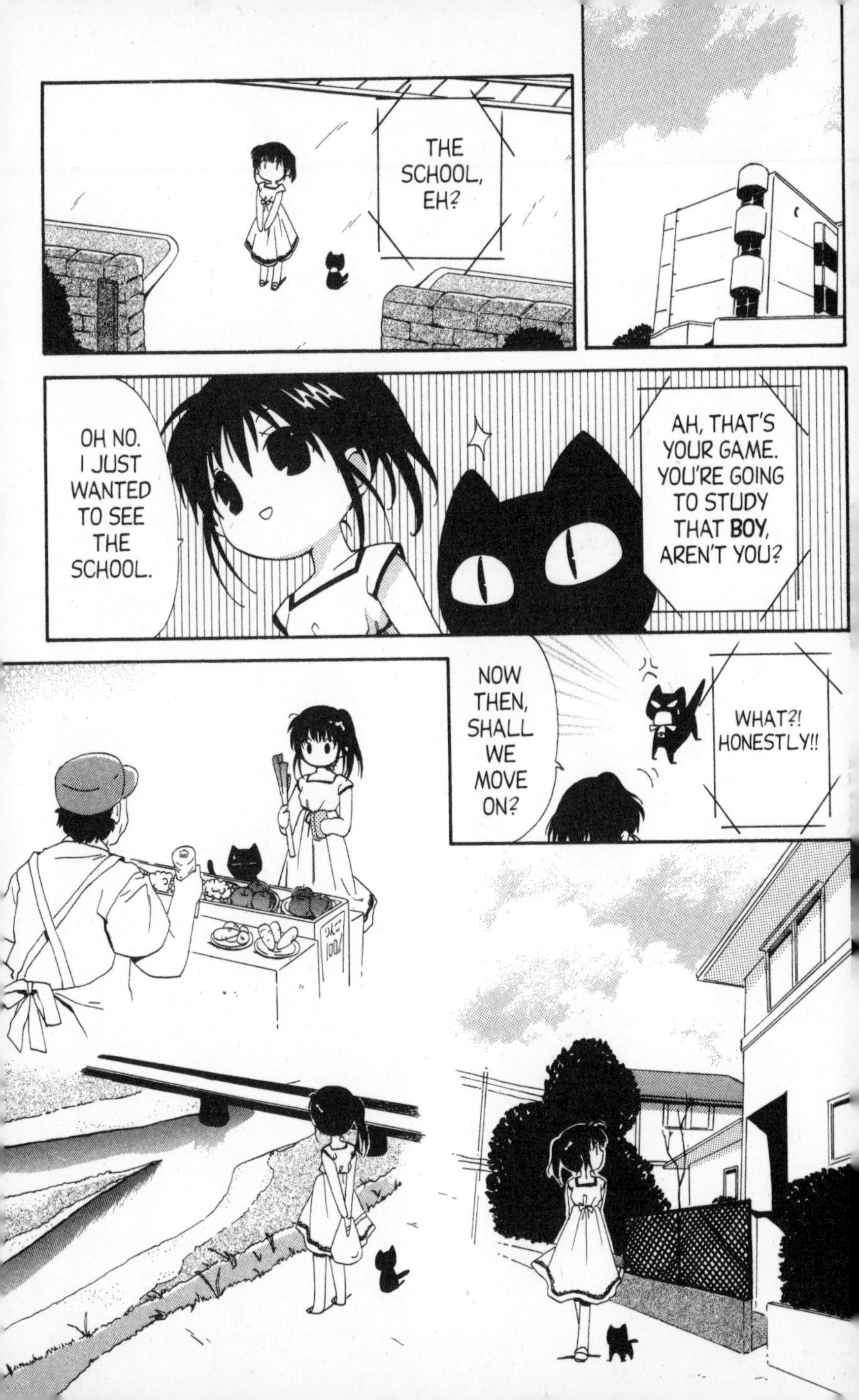
THE SCHOOL, EH?
AH, THAT'S YOUR GAME. YOU'RE GOING TO STUDY THAT **BOY**, AREN'T YOU?
OH NO. I JUST WANTED TO SEE THE SCHOOL.
WHAT?! HONESTLY!!
NOW THEN, SHALL WE MOVE ON?

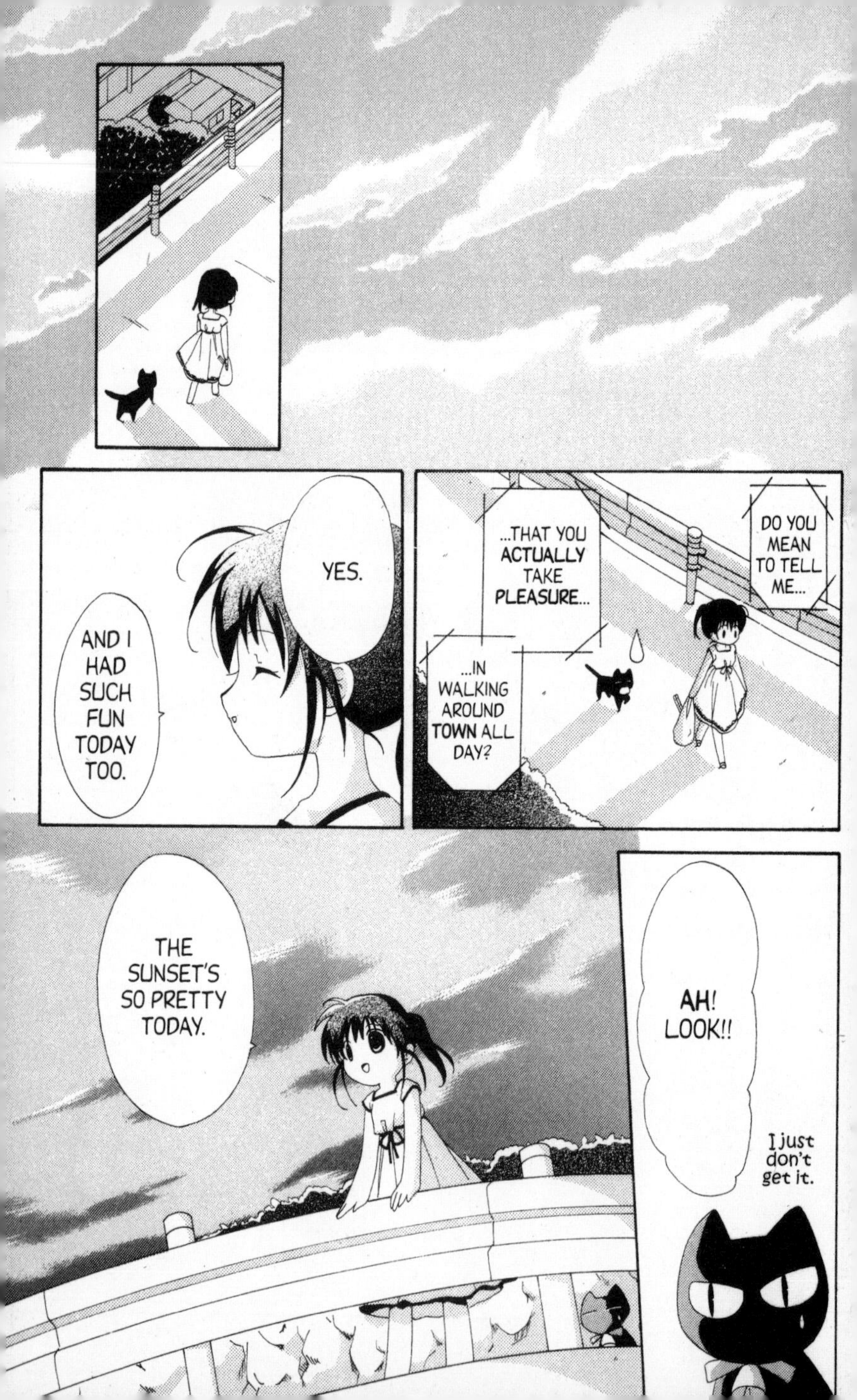
DO YOU MEAN TO TELL ME...
...THAT YOU ACTUALLY TAKE PLEASURE...
...IN WALKING AROUND TOWN ALL DAY?
YES.
AND I HAD SUCH FUN TODAY TOO.
AH! LOOK!!
I just don't get it.
THE SUNSET'S SO PRETTY TODAY.

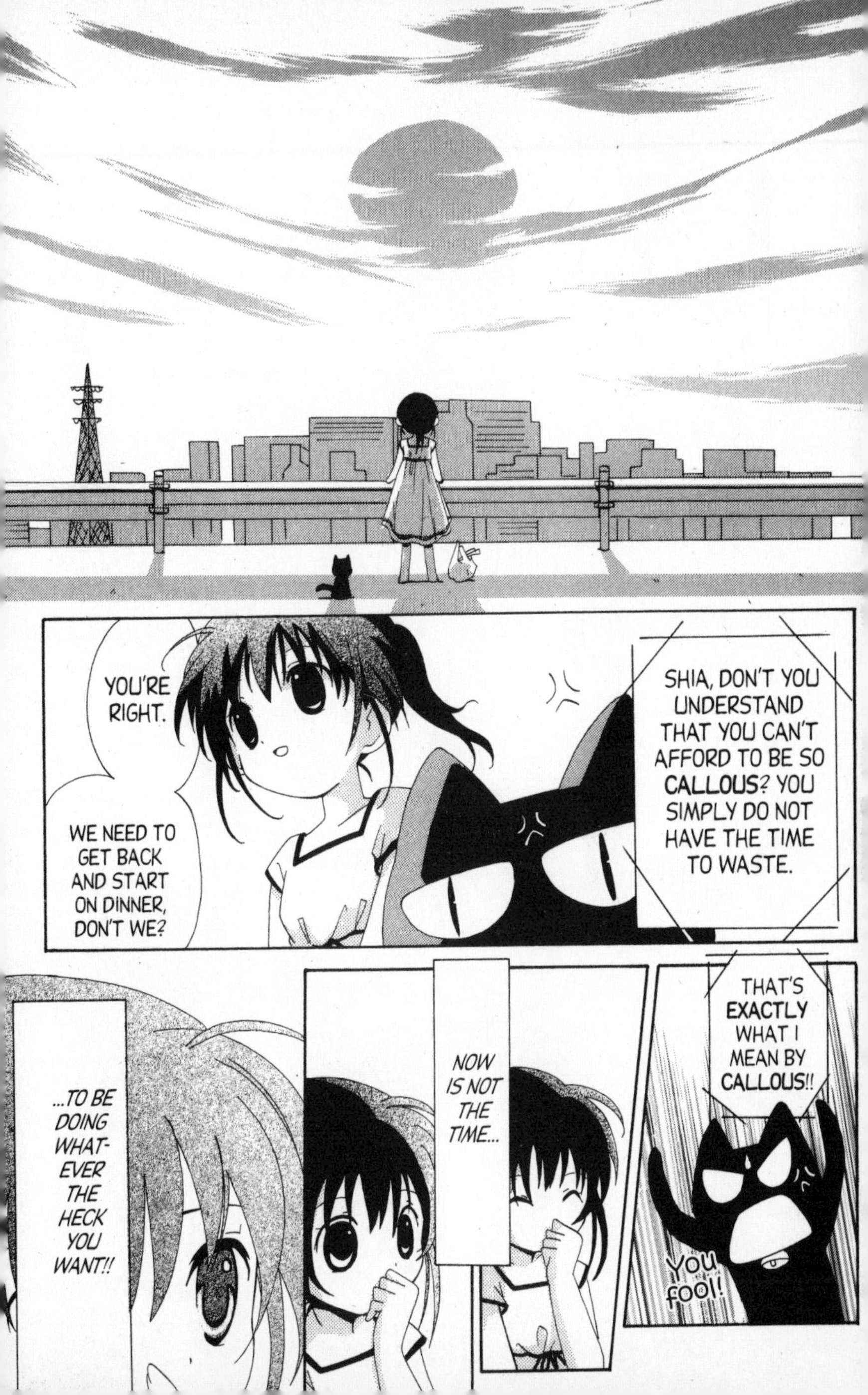
SHIA, DON'T YOU UNDERSTAND THAT YOU CAN'T AFFORD TO BE SO CALLOUS? YOU SIMPLY DO NOT HAVE THE TIME TO WASTE.
YOU'RE RIGHT.
WE NEED TO GET BACK AND START ON DINNER, DON'T WE?
THAT'S EXACTLY WHAT I MEAN BY CALLOUS!!
YOU FOOL!
NOW IS NOT THE TIME...
...TO BE DOING WHAT-EVER THE HECK YOU WANT!!

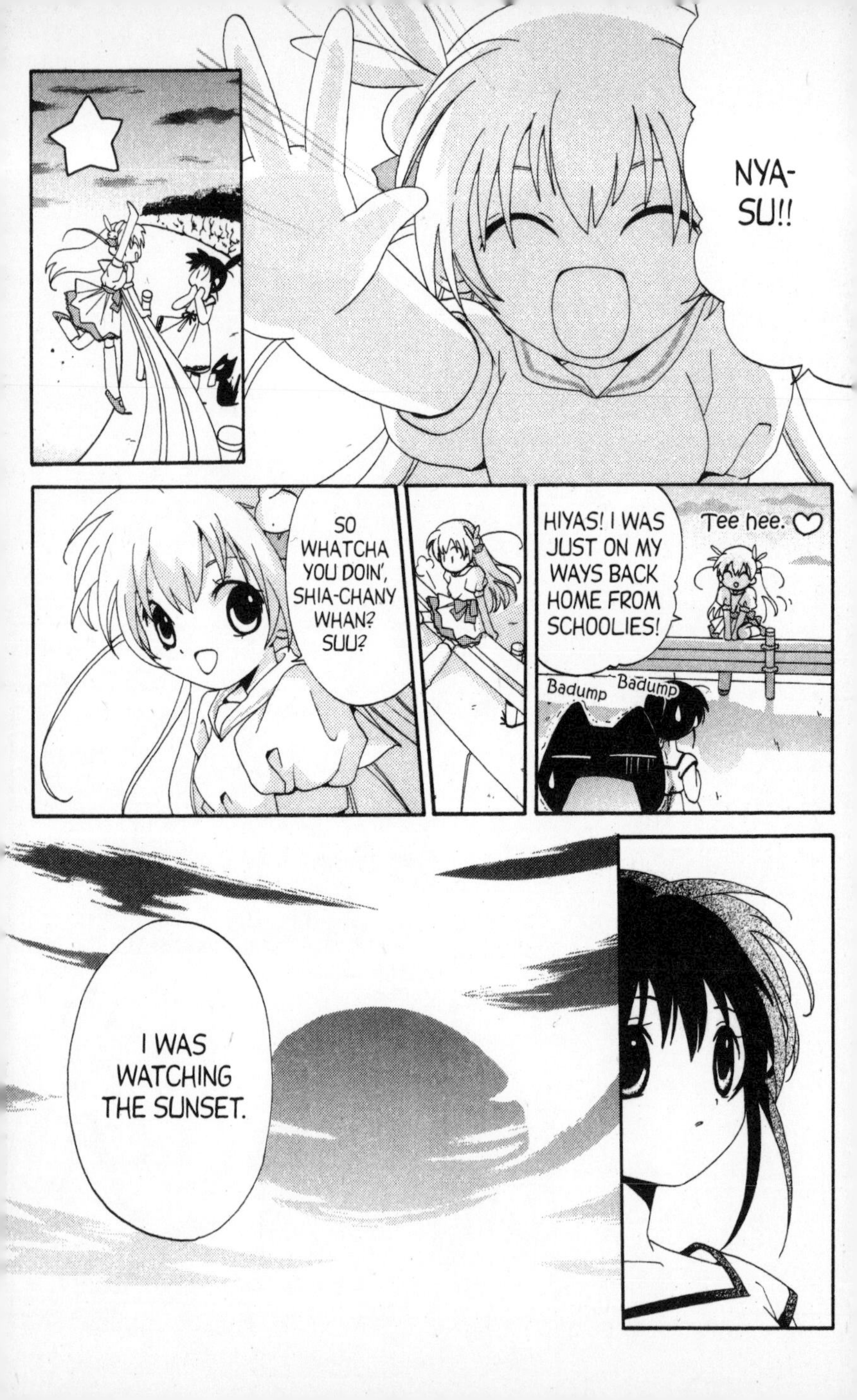
NYA-SU!!
HIYAS! I WAS JUST ON MY WAYS BACK HOME FROM SCHOOLIES!
Tee hee. ♡
Badump
Badump
SO WHATCHA YOU DOIN', SHIA-CHANY WHAN? SUU?
I WAS WATCHING THE SUNSET.

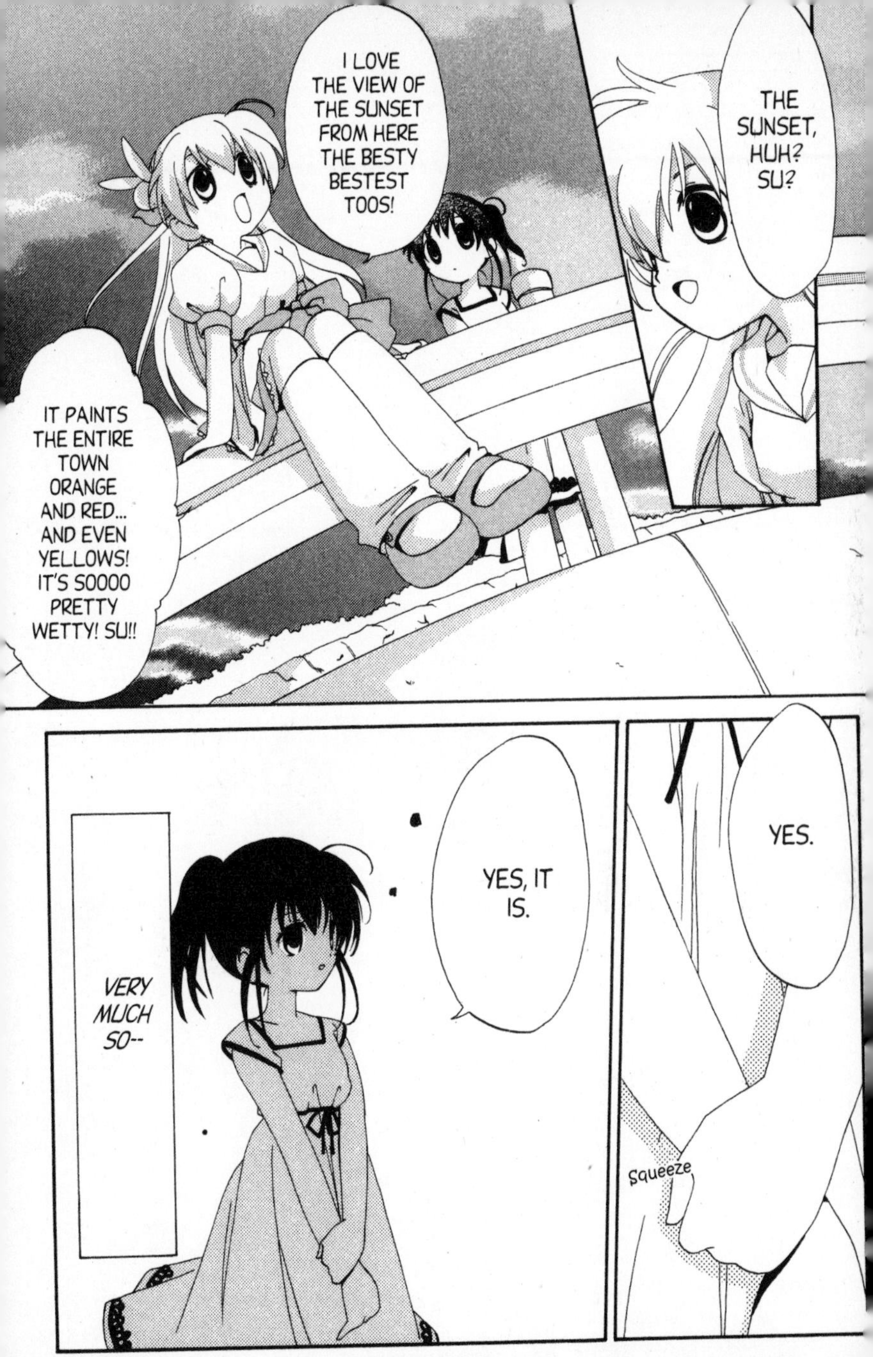
THE SUNSET, HUH? SU?
I LOVE THE VIEW OF THE SUNSET FROM HERE THE BESTY BESTEST TOOS!
IT PAINTS THE ENTIRE TOWN ORANGE AND RED... AND EVEN YELLOWS! IT'S SOOOO PRETTY WETTY! SU!!
YES.
Squeeze
YES, IT IS.
VERY MUCH SO--

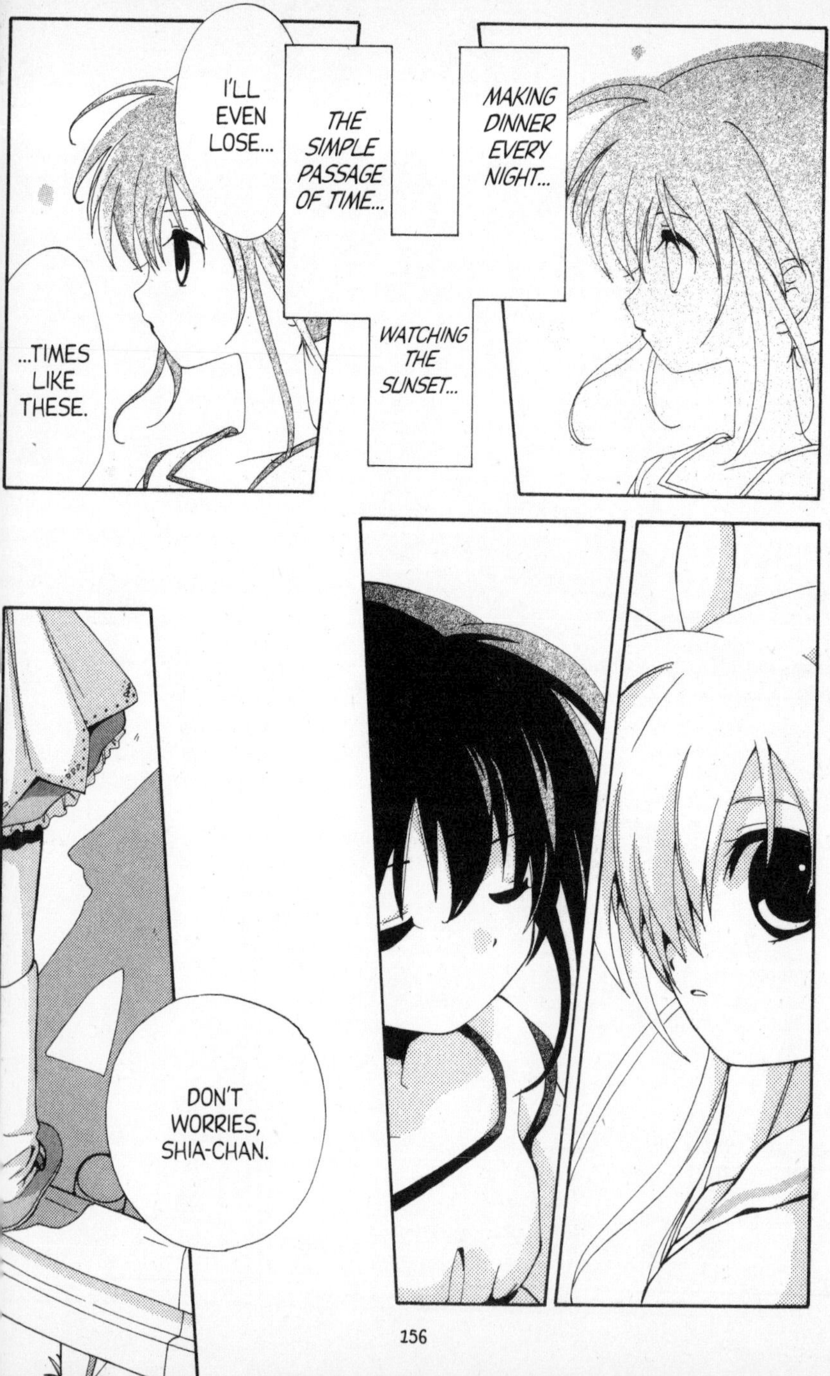
MAKING DINNER EVERY NIGHT...
WATCHING THE SUNSET...
THE SIMPLE PASSAGE OF TIME...
I'LL EVEN LOSE...
...TIMES LIKE THESE.
DON'T WORRIES, SHIA-CHAN.

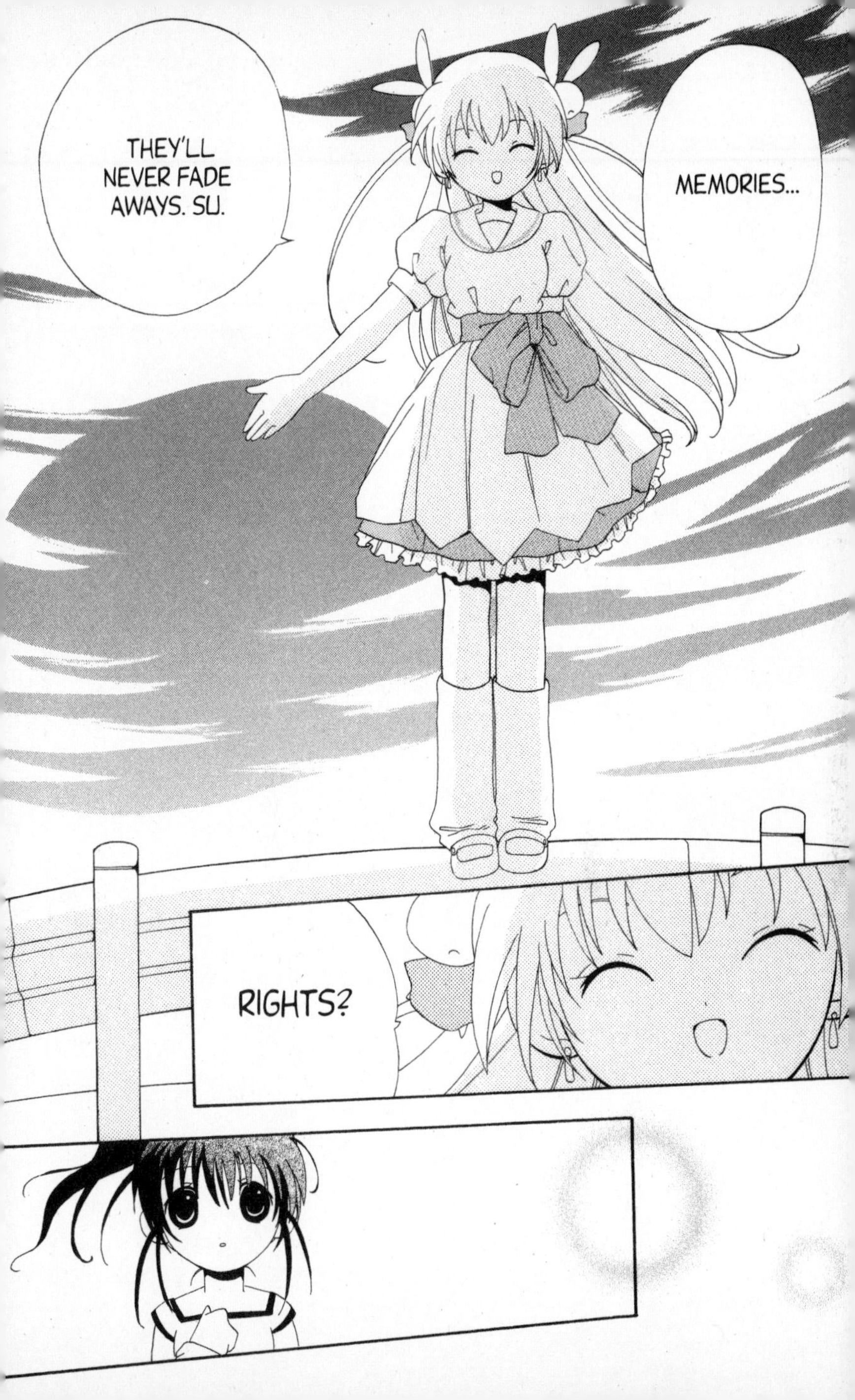
MEMORIES...
THEY'LL NEVER FADE AWAYS. SU.
RIGHTS?

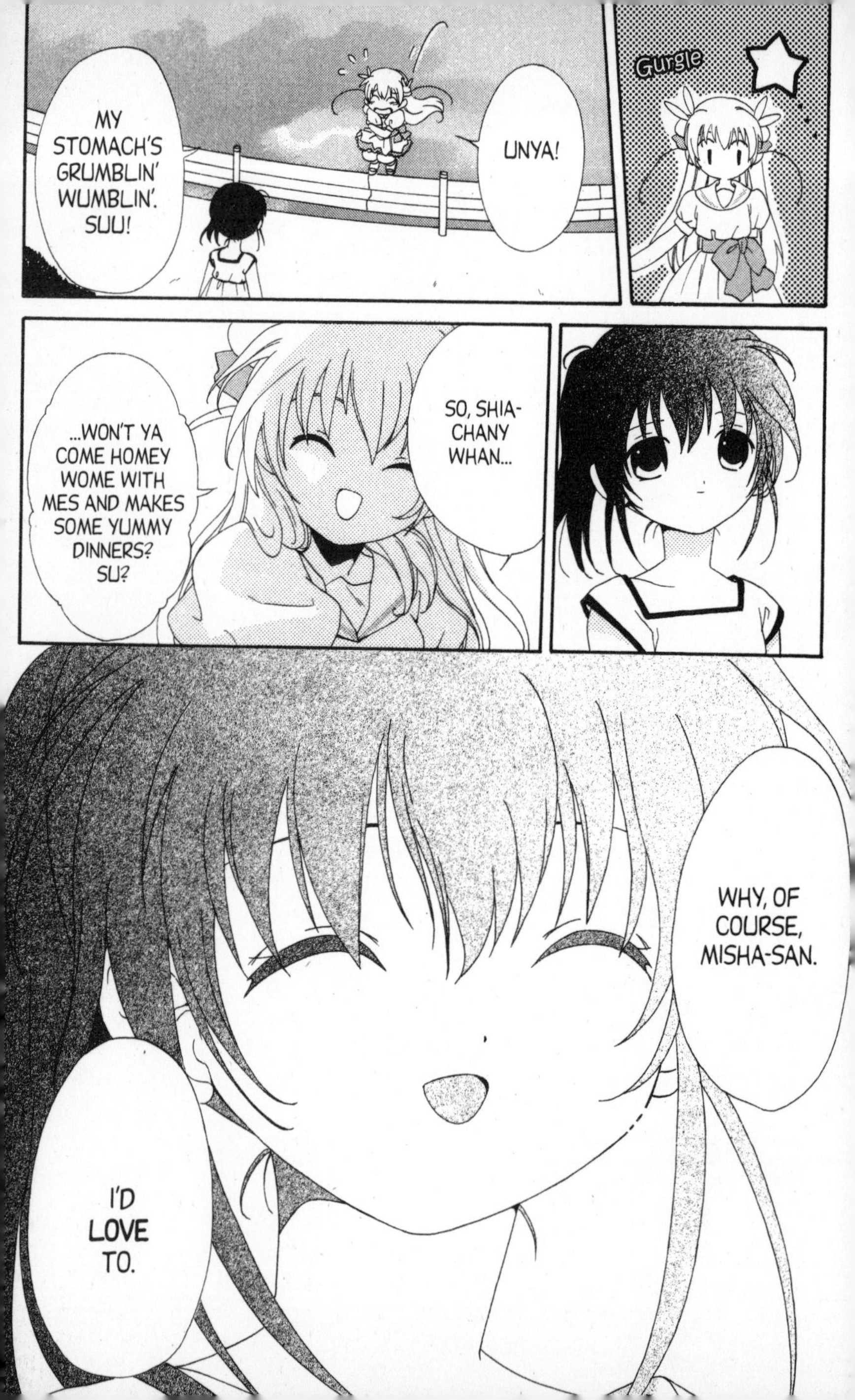
Gurgle
UNYA!
MY STOMACH'S GRUMBLIN' WUMBLIN'. SUU!
SO, SHIA-CHANY WHAN...
...WON'T YA COME HOMEY WOME WITH MES AND MAKES SOME YUMMY DINNERS? SU?
WHY, OF COURSE, MISHA-SAN.
I'D **LOVE** TO.

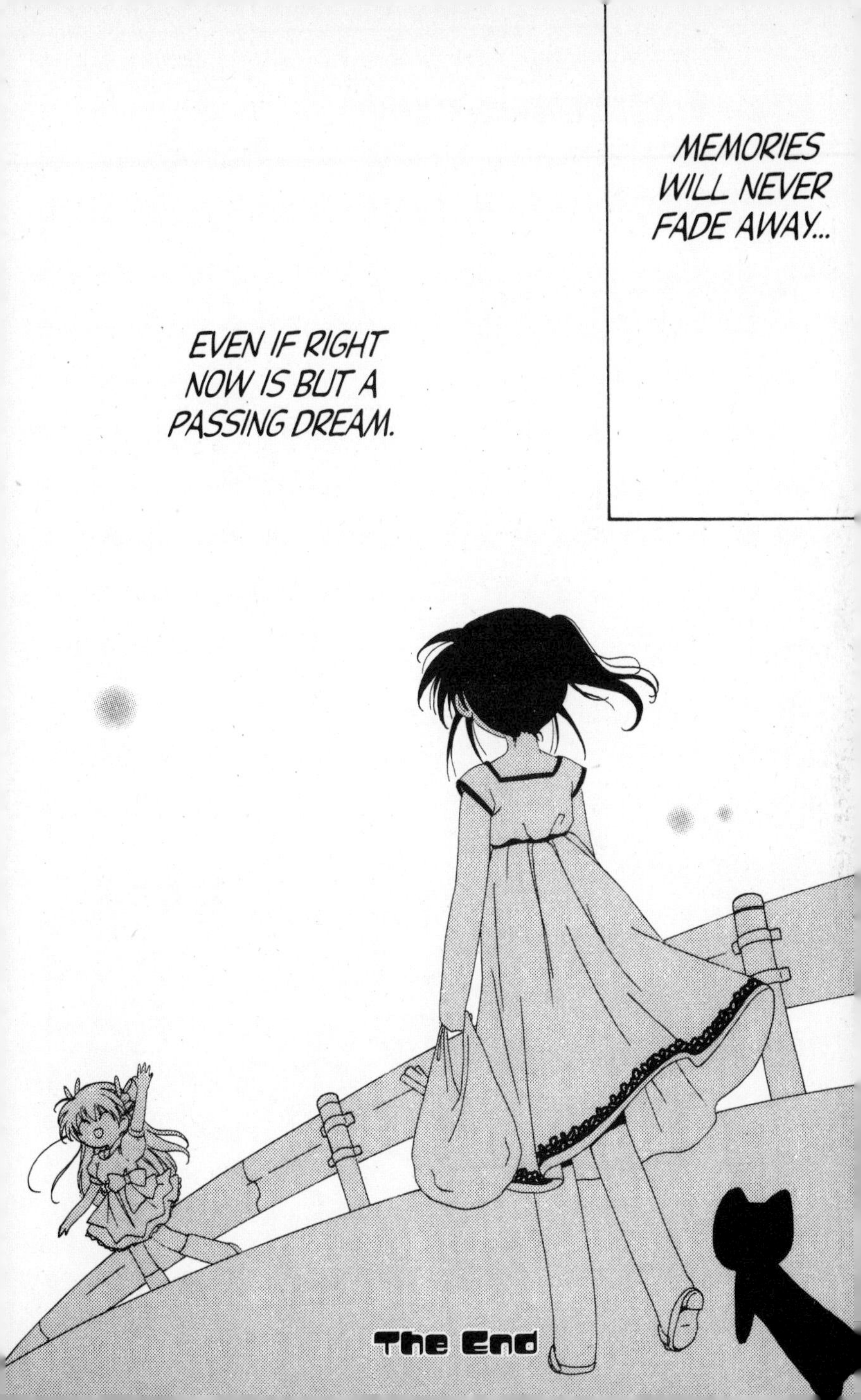
MEMORIES WILL NEVER FADE AWAY...
EVEN IF RIGHT NOW IS BUT A PASSING DREAM.
The End

Mari Matsuzawa

I've learned so much from being allowed to participate in these three volumes. Thank you!

-Mari Matsuzawa

Writer's Talk

Mook

The secret of *Pita-Ten's* success?

Why the hot guys, of course!

Ten and Kota

How to Enjoy Manga: Part 3

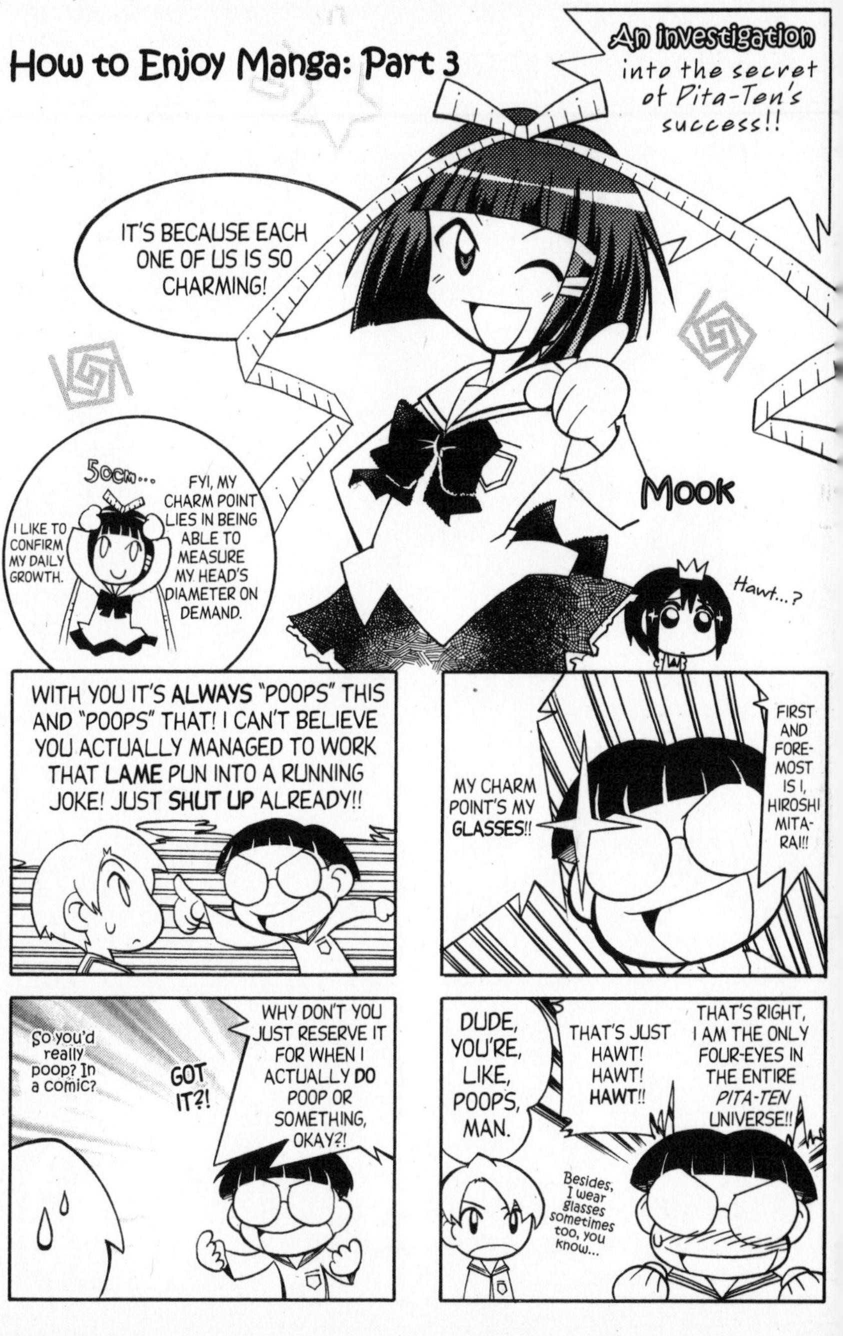
An investigation into the secret of Pita-Ten's success!!
IT'S BECAUSE EACH ONE OF US IS SO CHARMING!
MOOK
Hawt...?
50cm...
FYI, MY CHARM POINT LIES IN BEING ABLE TO MEASURE MY HEAD'S DIAMETER ON DEMAND.
I LIKE TO CONFIRM MY DAILY GROWTH.
FIRST AND FORE-MOST IS I, HIROSHI MITA-RAI!!
MY CHARM POINT'S MY GLASSES!!
WITH YOU IT'S ALWAYS "POOPS" THIS AND "POOPS" THAT! I CAN'T BELIEVE YOU ACTUALLY MANAGED TO WORK THAT LAME PUN INTO A RUNNING JOKE! JUST SHUT UP ALREADY!!
THAT'S RIGHT, I AM THE ONLY FOUR-EYES IN THE ENTIRE PITA-TEN UNIVERSE!!
THAT'S JUST HAWT! HAWT! HAWT!!
DUDE, YOU'RE, LIKE, POOPS, MAN.
Besides, I wear glasses sometimes too, you know...
WHY DON'T YOU JUST RESERVE IT FOR WHEN I ACTUALLY DO POOP OR SOMETHING, OKAY?!
GOT IT?!
So you'd really poop? In a comic?

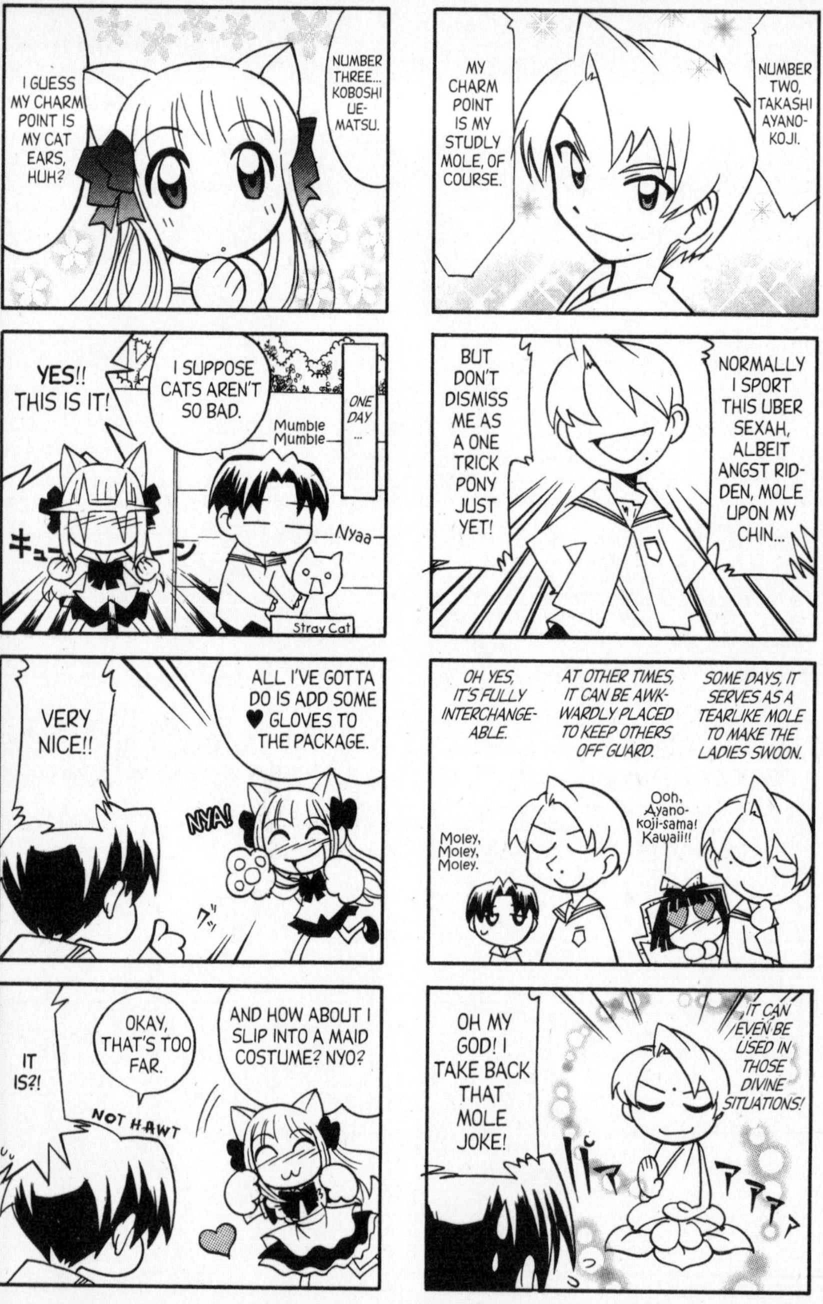
NUMBER TWO, TAKASHI AYANO-KOJI.
MY CHARM POINT IS MY STUDLY MOLE, OF COURSE.
NORMALLY I SPORT THIS UBER SEXAH, ALBEIT ANGST RID-DEN, MOLE UPON MY CHIN...
BUT DON'T DISMISS ME AS A ONE TRICK PONY JUST YET!
SOME DAYS, IT SERVES AS A TEARLIKE MOLE TO MAKE THE LADIES SWOON.
AT OTHER TIMES, IT CAN BE AWK-WARDLY PLACED TO KEEP OTHERS OFF GUARD.
OH YES, IT'S FULLY INTERCHANGE-ABLE.
Ooh, Ayano-koji-sama! Kawaii!!!
Moley, Moley, Moley.
IT CAN EVEN BE USED IN THOSE DIVINE SITUATIONS!
OH MY GOD! I TAKE BACK THAT MOLE JOKE!
NUMBER THREE... KOBOSHI UE-MATSU.
I GUESS MY CHARM POINT IS MY CAT EARS, HUH?
ONE DAY ...
I SUPPOSE CATS AREN'T SO BAD.
Mumble Mumble
Nyaa
Stray Cat
YES!! THIS IS IT!
ALL I'VE GOTTA DO IS ADD SOME ♥ GLOVES TO THE PACKAGE.
NYA!
VERY NICE!!
AND HOW ABOUT I SLIP INTO A MAID COSTUME? NYO?
OKAY, THAT'S TOO FAR.
IT IS?!
NOT HAWT

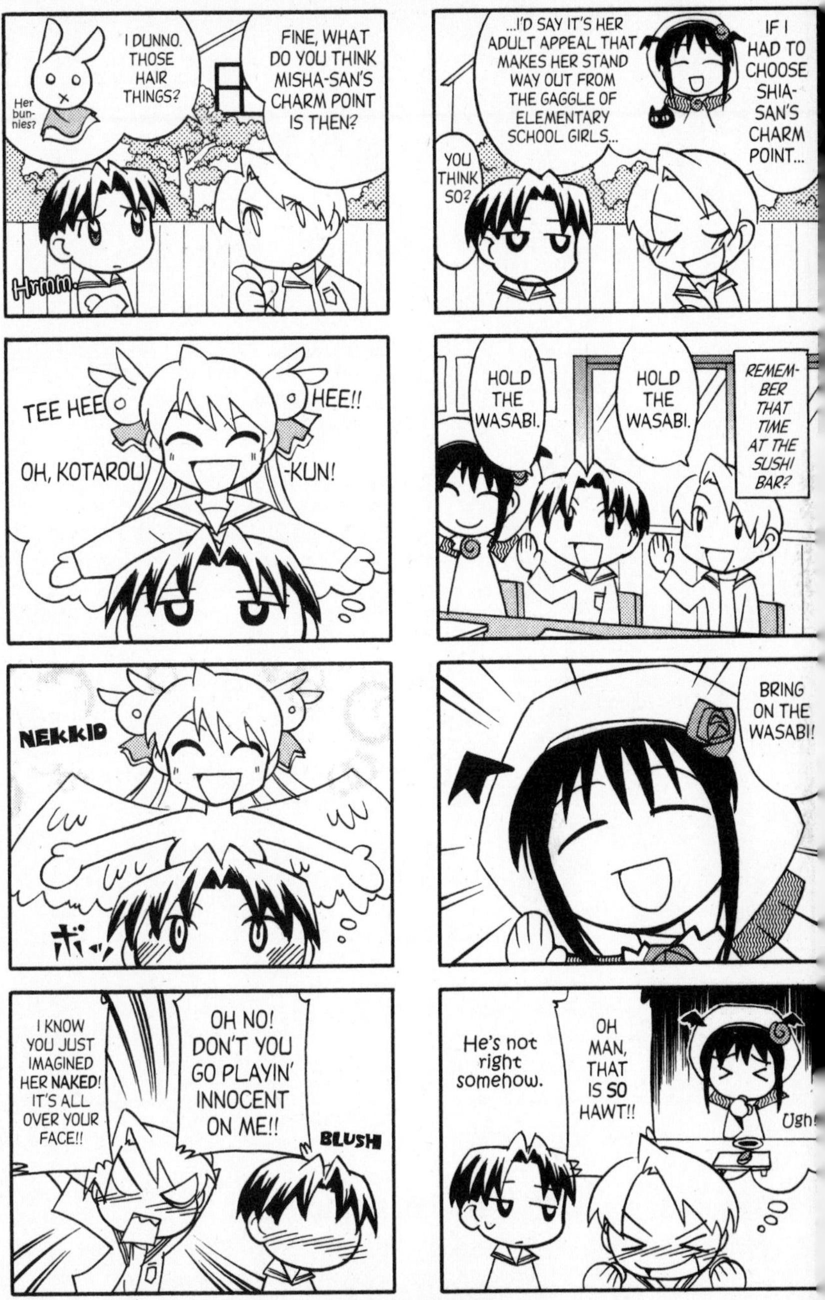
IF I HAD TO CHOOSE SHIA-SAN'S CHARM POINT...
...I'D SAY IT'S HER ADULT APPEAL THAT MAKES HER STAND WAY OUT FROM THE GAGGLE OF ELEMENTARY SCHOOL GIRLS...
YOU THINK SO?
REMEMBER THAT TIME AT THE SUSHI BAR?
HOLD THE WASABI.
HOLD THE WASABI.
BRING ON THE WASABI!
Ugh
OH MAN, THAT IS SO HAWT!!
He's not right somehow.
FINE, WHAT DO YOU THINK MISHA-SAN'S CHARM POINT IS THEN?
I DUNNO. THOSE HAIR THINGS?
Her bunnies?
Hrmm.
TEE HEE HEE!!
OH, KOTAROU-KUN!
NEKKID
ボッ
OH NO! DON'T YOU GO PLAYIN' INNOCENT ON ME!!
BLUSH
I KNOW YOU JUST IMAGINED HER NAKED! IT'S ALL OVER YOUR FACE!!

The End

Writer's Talk

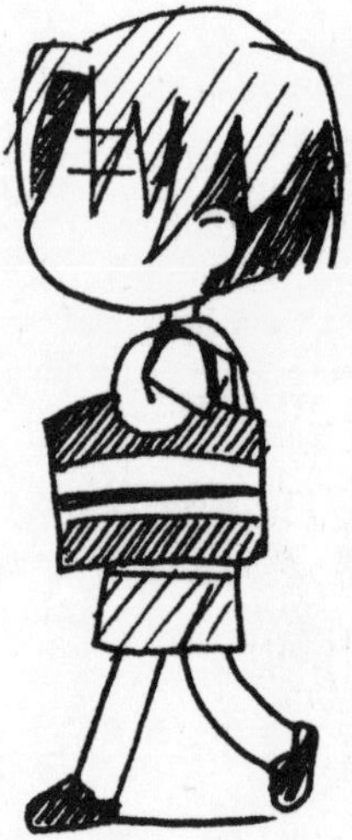

While I was drawing this particular story, all of a sudden, I remembered that I had done this sort of side story before back when I was around the fifth episode.

You remember, the one where Kotarou has a crush on a girl in his study class? It's not that I had any desire to put her in the story. I just hadn't remembered her is all. (I guess you could say that I had just plumb forgotten about it all up until now.)

For me, I rather like it when you suddenly recall something that you had forgotten for quite a while. Like how Shia's waitress outfit was different in the initial run than in the printed version, or how Kotarou's mom's name was really Eriko-san.

Even I'd totally forgotten that!
Well, this is the end for now.

Take care, everyone!

2002 koga.

Koge-Donbo

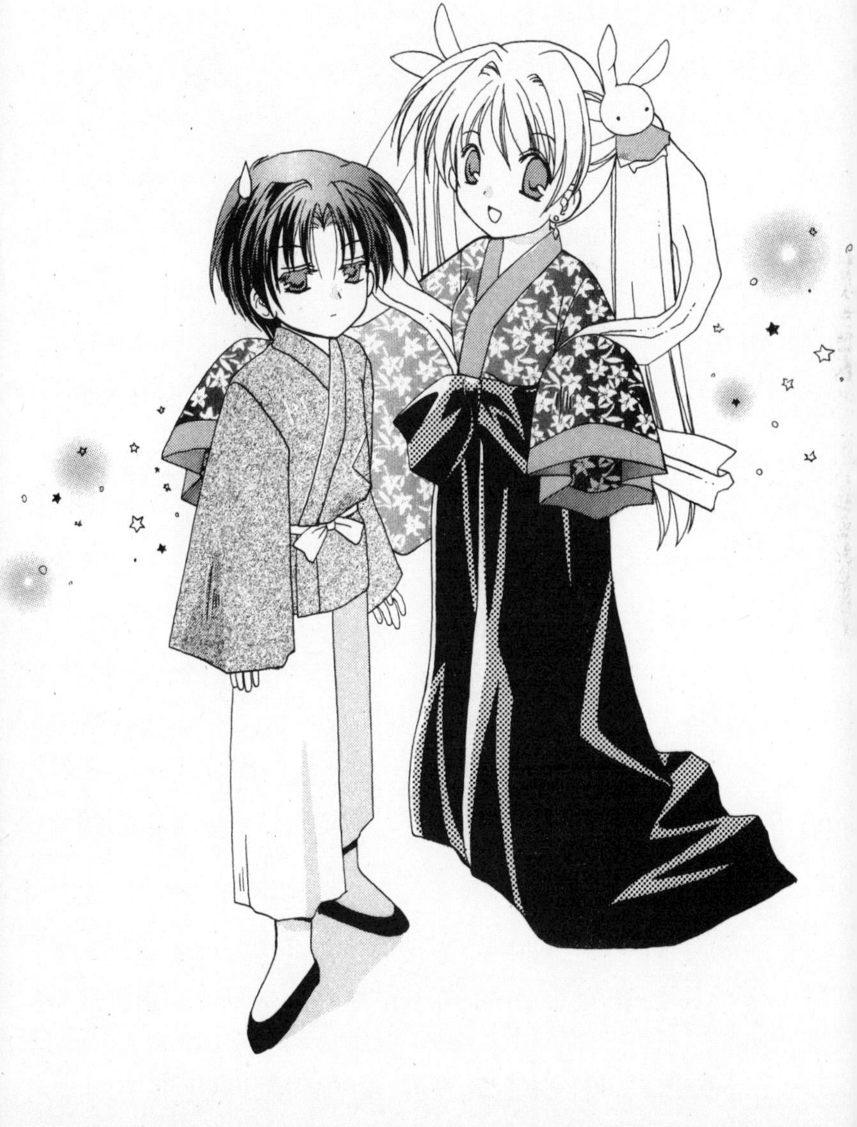

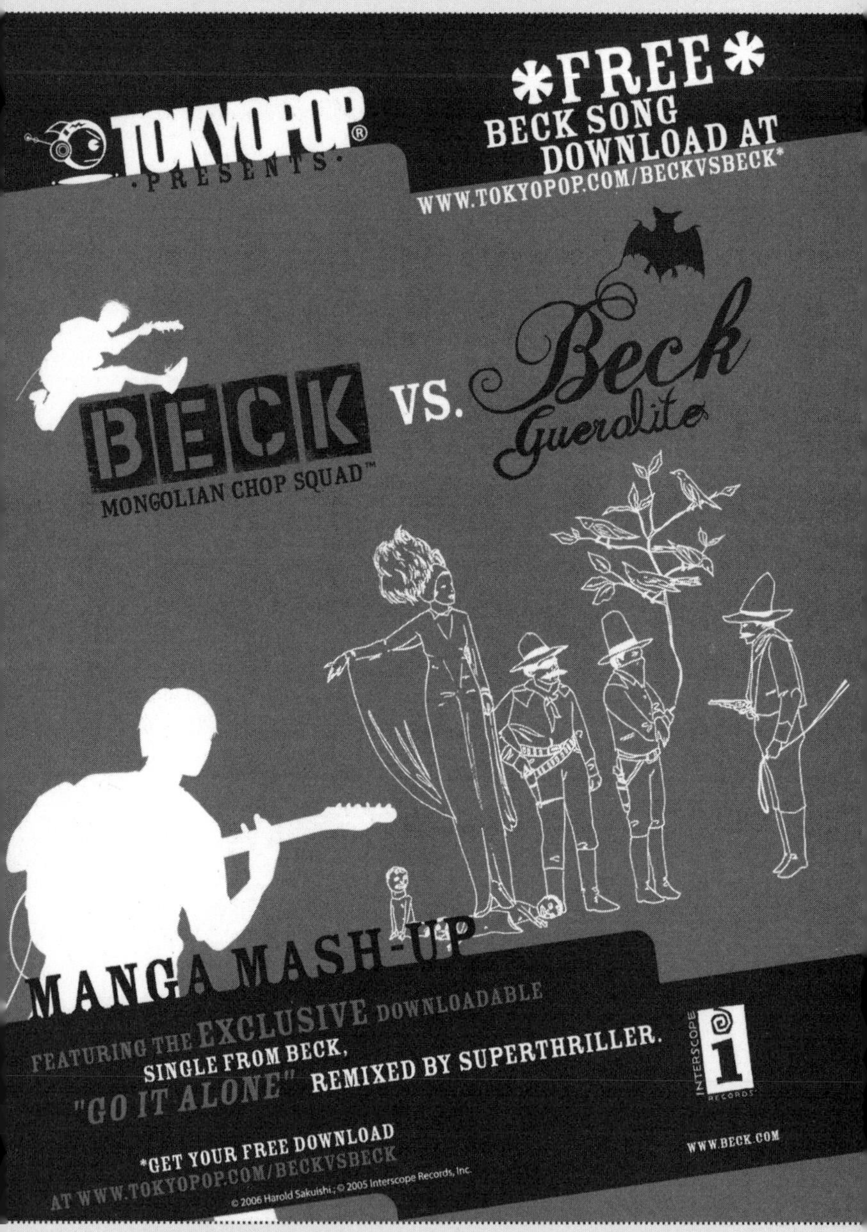
TOKYOPOP® PRESENTS
FREE
BECK SONG
DOWNLOAD AT
WWW.TOKYOPOP.COM/BECKVSBECK*
BECK
MONGOLIAN CHOP SQUAD™
VS.
Beck
Guerolito
MANGA MASH-UP
FEATURING THE EXCLUSIVE DOWNLOADABLE
SINGLE FROM BECK,
"GO IT ALONE" REMIXED BY SUPERTHRILLER.
INTERSCOPE RECORDS
*GET YOUR FREE DOWNLOAD
AT WWW.TOKYOPOP.COM/BECKVSBECK
WWW.BECK.COM
© 2006 Harold Sakuishi; © 2005 Interscope Records, Inc.

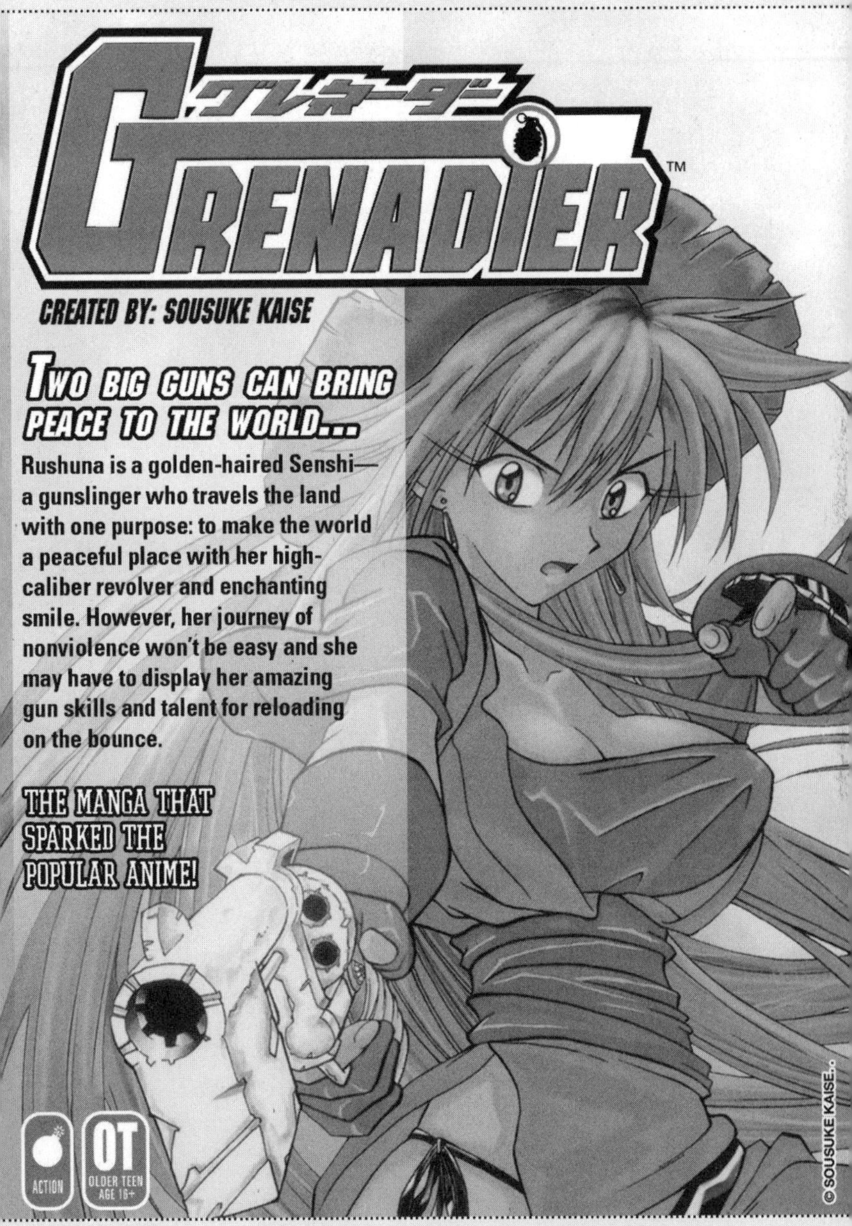
グレネーダー
GRENADIER™
CREATED BY: SOUSUKE KAISE
TWO BIG GUNS CAN BRING PEACE TO THE WORLD...
Rushuna is a golden-haired Senshi—a gunslinger who travels the land with one purpose: to make the world a peaceful place with her high-caliber revolver and enchanting smile. However, her journey of nonviolence won't be easy and she may have to display her amazing gun skills and talent for reloading on the bounce.
THE MANGA THAT SPARKED THE POPULAR ANIME!
ACTION
OT
OLDER TEEN AGE 16+
© SOUSUKE KAISE.

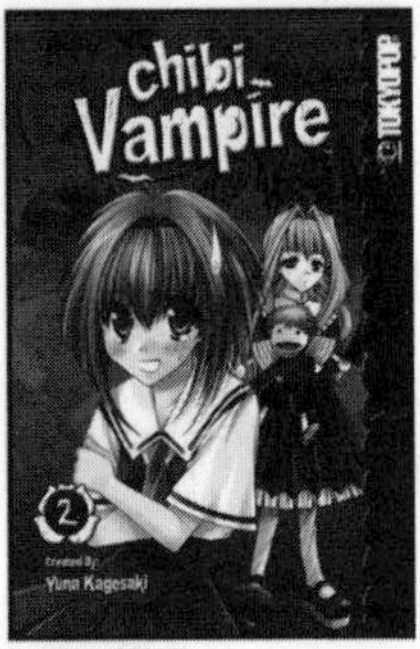
chibi Vampire
TOKYOPOP
2
Yuna Kagesaki

CHIBI VAMPIRE VOLUME 2

BY YUNA KAGESAKI

This bloody-good vampire has a big crush on her prey!

COMEDY | OT OLDER TEEN AGE 16+

Inspired the hit anime!

DEVIL MAY CRY 3 VOLUME 2

BY SUGURO CHAYAMACHI

The secret of the seven seals will release the demon world unto the earth!

It's good against evil... and brother against brother!

ACTION | OT OLDER TEEN AGE 16+

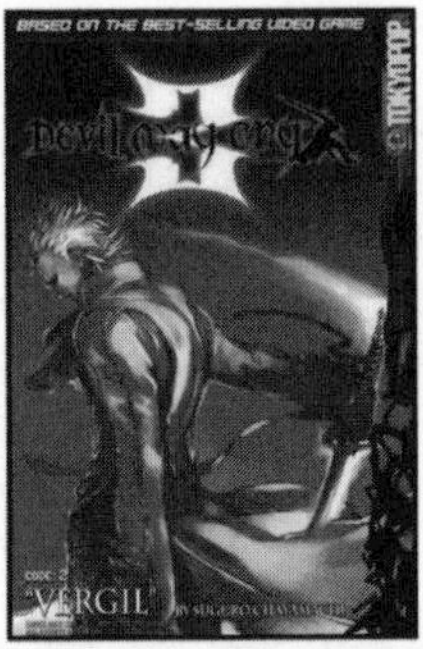
BASED ON THE BEST-SELLING VIDEO GAME
TOKYOPOP
VERGIL

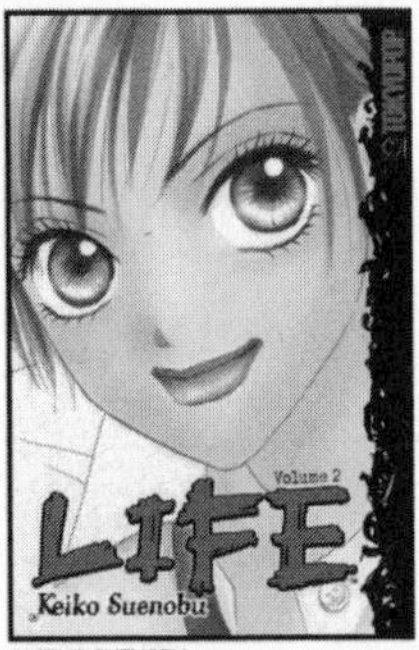
Volume 2
LIFE
Keiko Suenobu
TOKYOPOP

LIFE VOLUME 2

BY KEIKO SUENOBU

It's about real teenagers...
real high school...
real life!

DRAMA | OT OLDER TEEN AGE 16+

Every life has a story...
Every story has a life of its own.

TOKYOPOP SHOP

STOP!

This is the back of the book.
You wouldn't want to spoil a great ending!

This book is printed "manga-style," in the authentic Japanese right-to-left format. Since none of the artwork has been flipped or altered, readers get to experience the story just as the creator intended. You've been asking for it, so TOKYOPOP® delivered: authentic, hot-off-the-press, and far more fun!

DIRECTIONS

If this is your first time reading manga-style, here's a quick guide to help you understand how it works.

It's easy... just start in the top right panel and follow the numbers. Have fun, and look for more 100% authentic manga from TOKYOPOP®!